Marmalade Boy

Other 100% Authentic Manga Available from TOKYOPOP®:

COWBOY BEBOP 1-3 (of 3)
All-new adventures of interstellar bounty hunting, based on the hit anime seen on Cartoon Network.

MARMALADE BOY 1-3 (of 8)
A tangled teen romance for the new millennium.

REAL BOUT HIGH SCHOOL 1-4 (of 4+)
At Daimon High, teachers don't break up fights…they grade them.

MARS 1-4 (of 15)
Biker Rei and artist Kira are as different as night and day, but fate binds them in this angst-filled romance.

GTO 1-6 (of 23+)
Biker gang member Onizuka is going back to school…as a teacher!

CHOBITS 1-3 (of 5+)
In the future, boys will be boys and girls will be…robots? The newest hit series from CLAMP!

SKULL MAN 1-3 (of 7+)
They took his family. They took his face. They took his soul. Now, he's going to take his revenge.

DRAGON KNIGHTS 1-4 (of 17)
Part dragon, part knight, ALL glam. The most inept knights on the block are out to kick some demon butt.

INITIAL D 1-3 (of 23+)
Delivery boy Tak has a gift for driving, but can he compete in the high-stakes world of street racing?

PARADISE KISS 1-3 (of 3+)
High fashion and deep passion collide in this hot new shojo series!

KODOCHA: Sana's Stage 1-3 (of 10)
There's a rumble in the jungle gym when child star Sana Kurata and bully Akito Hayama collide.

ANGELIC LAYER 1-2 (of 5)
In the future, the most popular game is Angelic Layer, where hand-raised robots battle for supremacy.

LOVE HINA 1-6 (of 14)
Can Keitaro handle living in a dorm with five cute girls…and still make it through school?

Also Available from TOKYOPOP®:

PRIEST 1-2 (of 10+)
The quick and the undead in one macabre manga.

RAGNAROK 1-3 (of 9+)
In the final battle between gods and men, only a small band of heroes stand in the way of total annihilation.

Marmalade Boy

Vol. 2

By

Wataru Yoshizumi

Los Angeles • Tokyo

Translator – Jack Niida
English Adaptation – Jake Forbes
Retouch and Lettering – Carol Conception and Jinky DeLeon
Production Specialist – Dolly Chan
Graphic Designer – Anna Kernbaum
Editor – Trisha Kunimoto
Associate Editors – Robert Coyner,
Paul Morrissey and Mark Paniccia

Senior Editor – Jake Forbes
Production Manager – Fred Lui
Art Director – Matthew Alford
Brand Manager – Kimberly J. Bird
VP of Production – Ron Klamert
Publisher – Stuart Levy

Email: editor@tokyopop.com
Come visit us online at www.TOKYOPOP.com

 A **TOKYOPOP**® MANGA

TOKYOPOP® is an imprint of Mixx Entertainment, Inc.
5900 Wilshire Blvd. Ste 2000, Los Angeles, CA 90036

ISBN: 1-931514-55-0

First TOKYOPOP® printing: June 2002

10 9 8 7 6 5 4 3

Printed in Canada

MAIN CHARACTERS

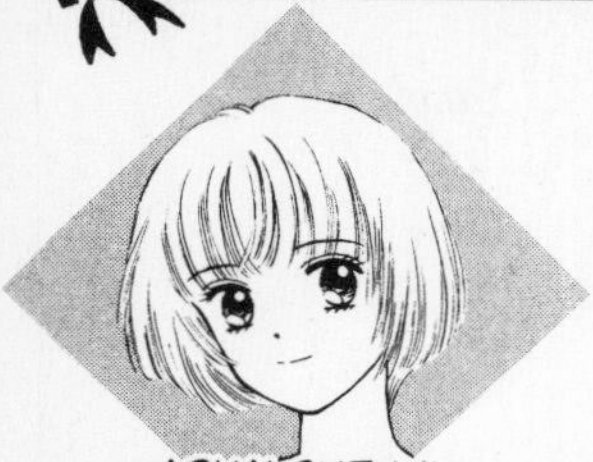

ARIMI SUZUKI
PERSUADED YUU TO GO OUT WITH HER ON A BET. YUU DUMPED HER, BUT SHE STILL LIKES HIM. SHE GOES TO A NEARBY SCHOOL.

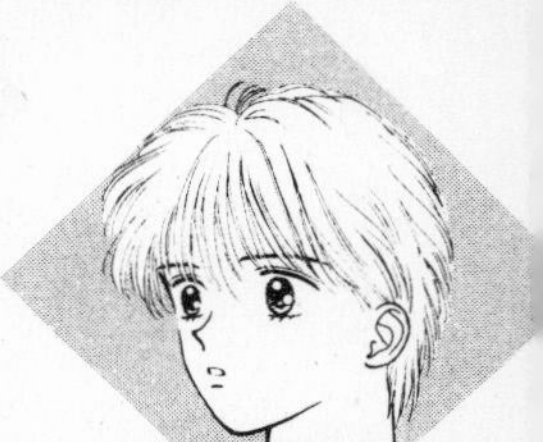

YUU MATSUURA
MIKI'S STEP-BROTHER... KINDA. HE'S GOOD-LOOKING, BUT TEASES MIKI. KISSED MIKI WHEN HE THOUGHT SHE WAS SLEEPING.

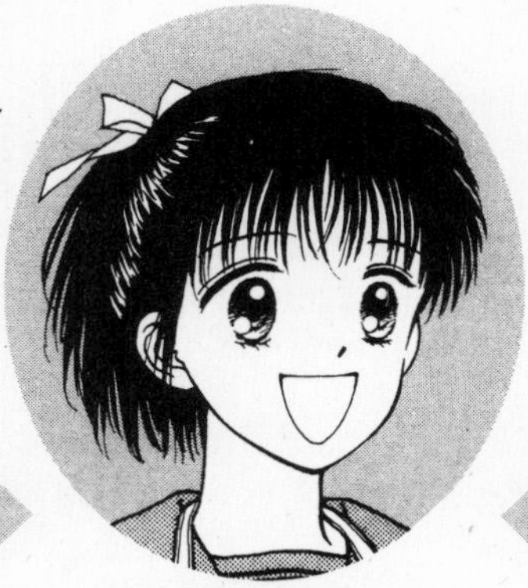

MIKI KOISHIKAWA
ALWAYS CHEERFUL, BUT SLOW ON THE UPTAKE. HAS A HARD TIME ADJUSTING TO HER CRAZY FAMILY.

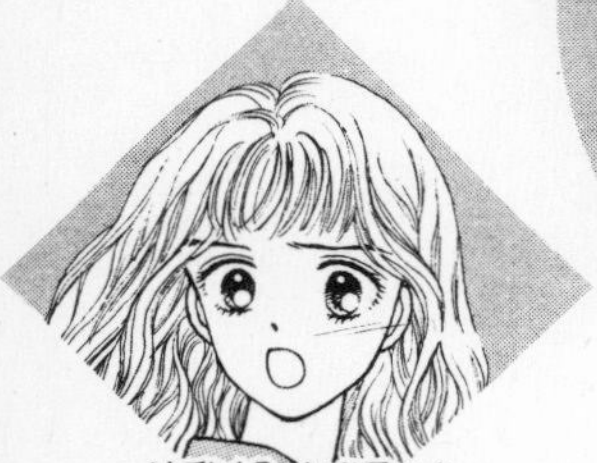

MEIKO AKIZUKI
MIKI'S BEST FRIEND. MEMBER OF THE LITERARY CLUB. HAS AN AIR OF MYSTERY ABOUT HER.

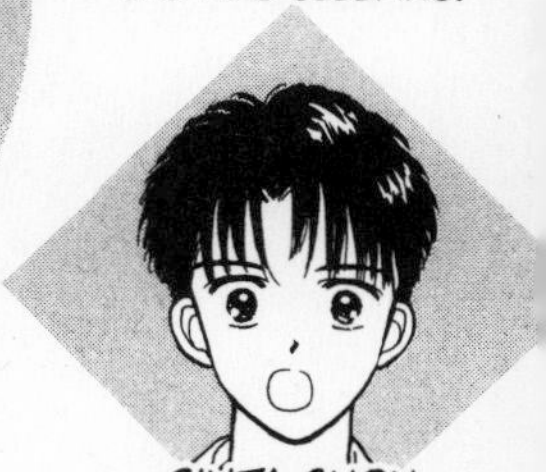

GINTA SUOU
MIKI HAD A CRUSH ON HIM. HE LIKED HER BUT DIDN'T ADMIT IT 'TIL NOW. HE'S ON THE TENNIS TEAM WITH MIKI.

THE STORY SO FAR...

DURING BREAKFAST ONE DAY, MIKI'S PARENTS BREAK IT TO HER THAT THEY'RE GETTING DIVORCED AND SWAPPING PARTNERS WITH ANOTHER COUPLE! NOW MIKI HAS FOUR PARENTS AND A NEW "STEP-BROTHER," YUU, WHO KEEPS TEASING HER. YUU'S SWEET ON THE OUTSIDE, BUT HE'S GOT A BITTER STREAK - A "MARMALADE BOY!" AS MIKI GETS TO KNOW YUU, SHE STARTS TO FORM A CRUSH ON HIM.

THINGS GET COMPLICATED WHEN MIKI'S OLD CRUSH, THE TENNIS CHAMP GINTA, CONFESSES HIS LOVE FOR HER. MIKI WROTE HIM A LOVE LETTER BACK IN JUNIOR HIGH, BUT WHEN HE SHARED IT WITH HIS FRIENDS, SHE WOULDN'T SPEAK TO HIM FOR A WHOLE YEAR. SINCE THEN, THEY'VE JUST BEEN FRIENDS.

AND THEN YUU'S OLD GIRLFRIEND, THE BEAUTIFUL ARIMI, APPEARS AT MIKI'S SCHOOL AND AGGRESSIVELY TRIES TO WIN BACK YUU'S AFFECTIONS! IN JUNIOR HIGH, SHE BET YUU THAT IF HE WENT OUT WITH HER FOR THREE MONTHS, HE'D FALL MADLY IN LOVE WITH HER. AFTER THOSE THREE MONTHS, HE WANTED TO JUST BE FRIENDS. THEY SEEMED SO PERFECT TOGETHER! CAN YUU EVER REALLY FALL IN LOVE?

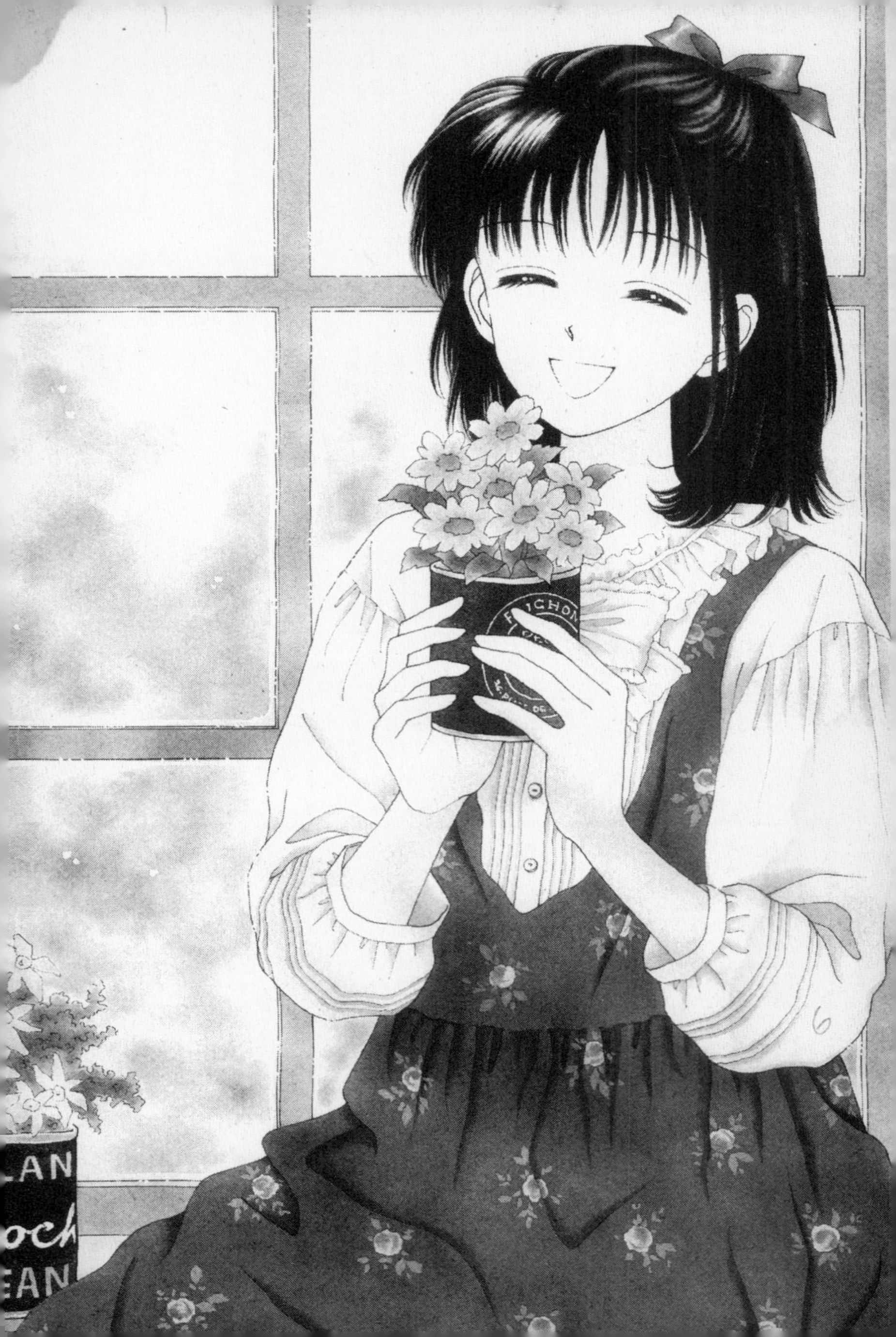

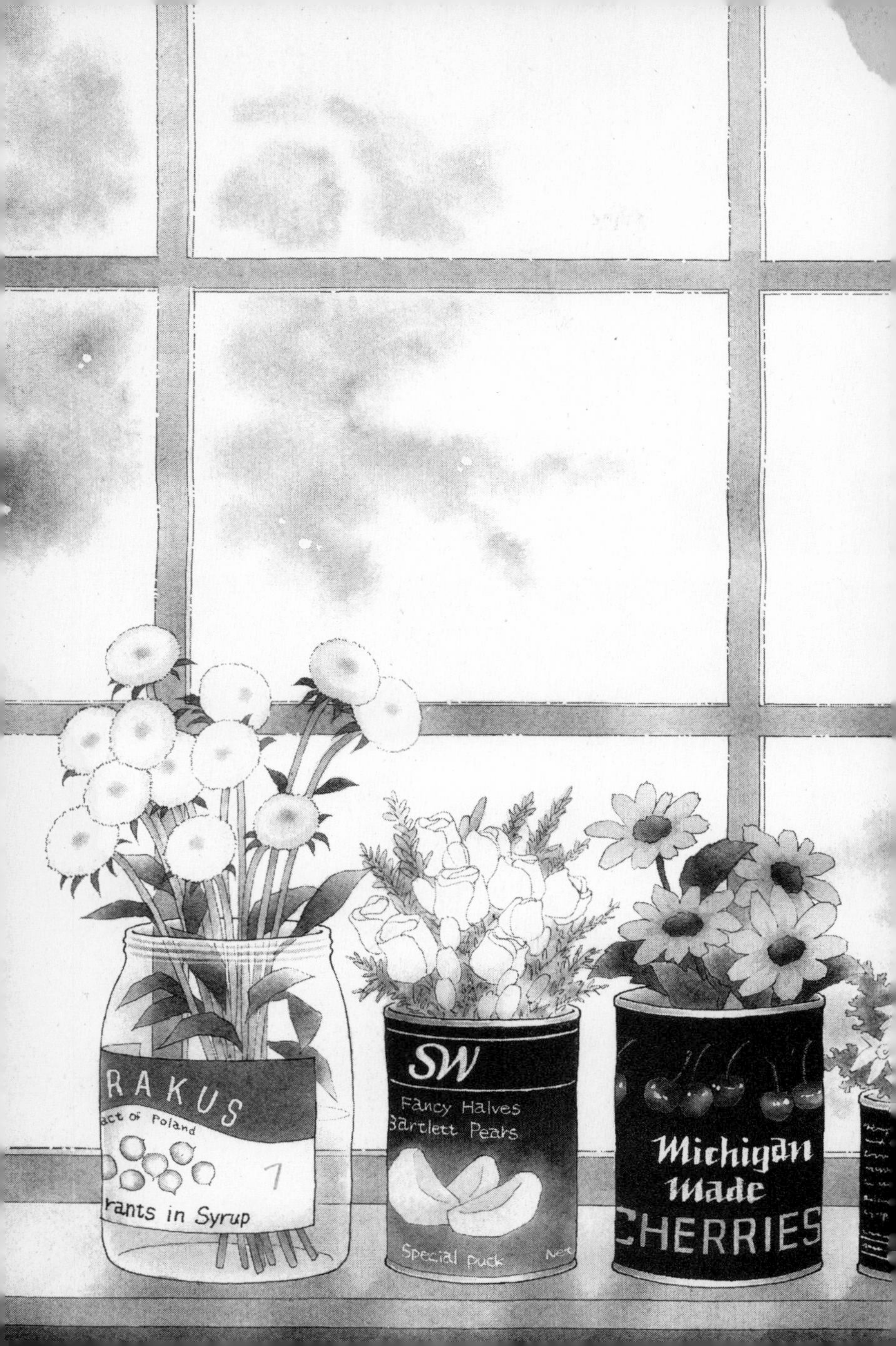
RAKUS
act of Poland
rants in Syrup
SW
Fancy Halves
Bartlett Pears
Special Puck
Net
Michigan
Made
CHERRIES

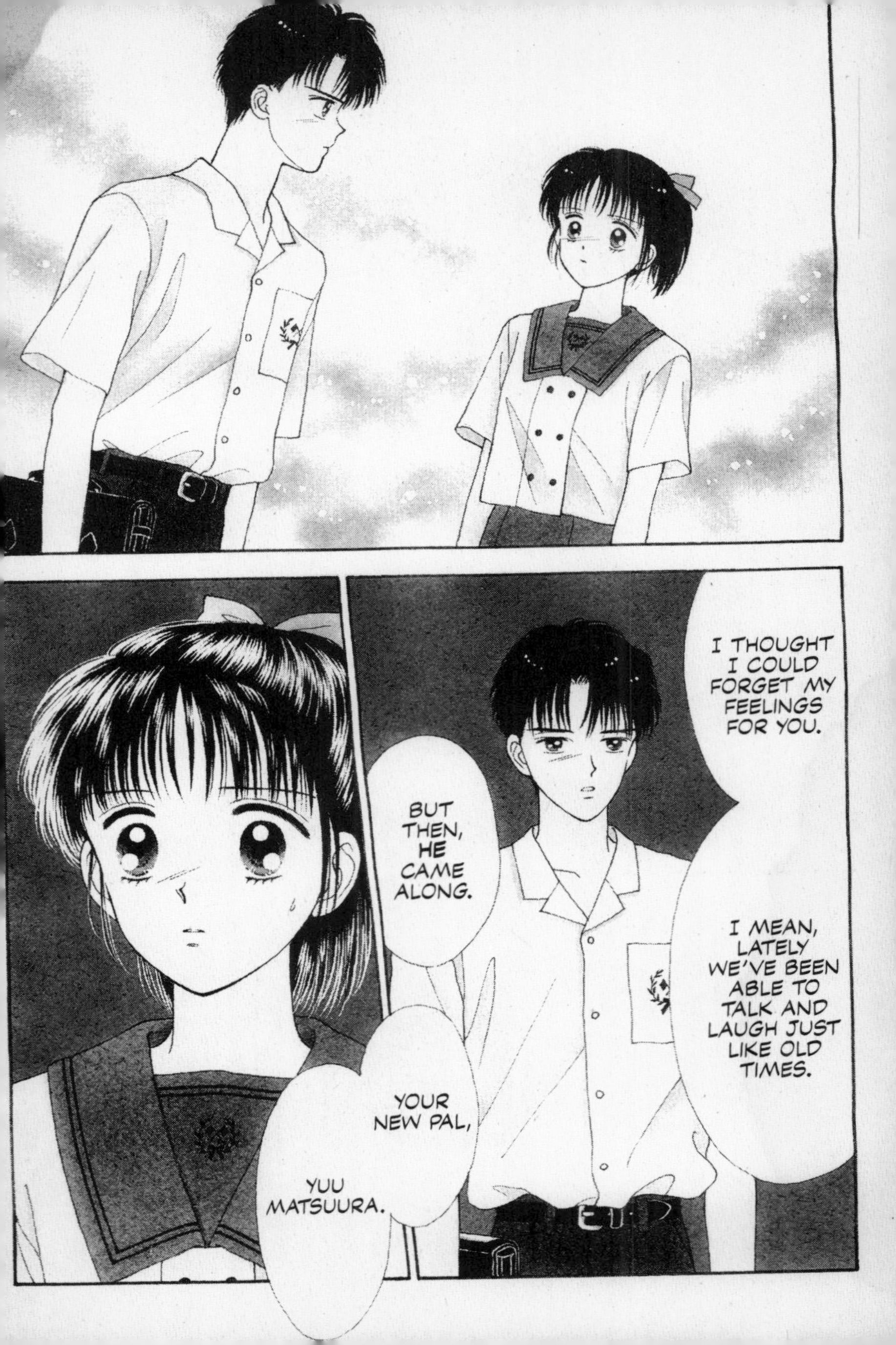
I THOUGHT I COULD FORGET MY FEELINGS FOR YOU.
I MEAN, LATELY WE'VE BEEN ABLE TO TALK AND LAUGH JUST LIKE OLD TIMES.
BUT THEN, HE CAME ALONG.
YOUR NEW PAL,
YUU MATSUURA.

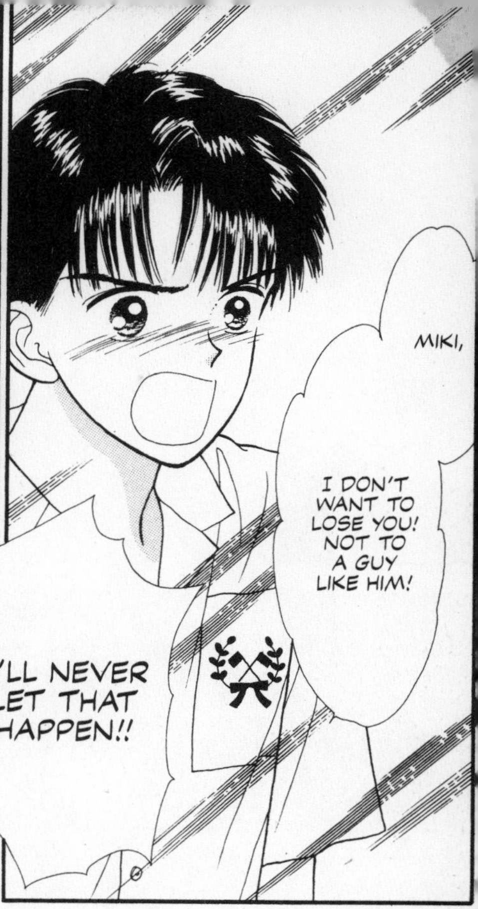
MIKI,
I DON'T WANT TO LOSE YOU! NOT TO A GUY LIKE HIM!
I'LL NEVER LET THAT HAPPEN!!

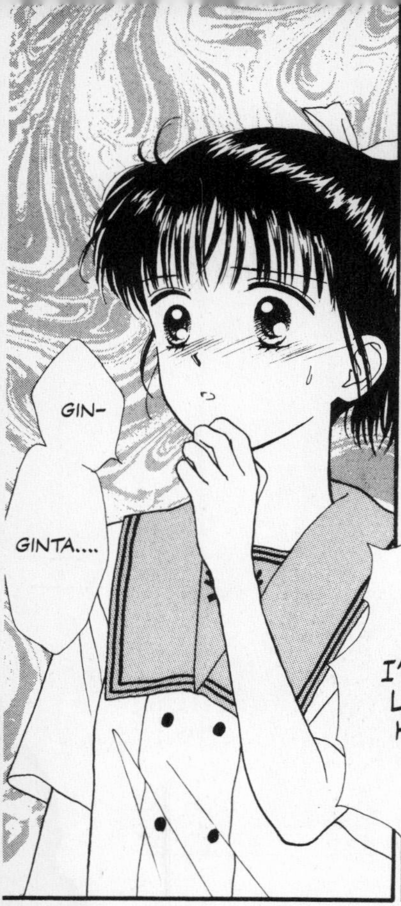
GIN-
GINTA....

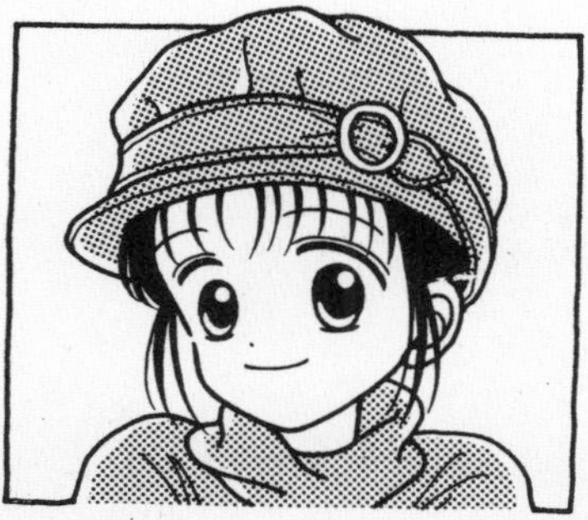

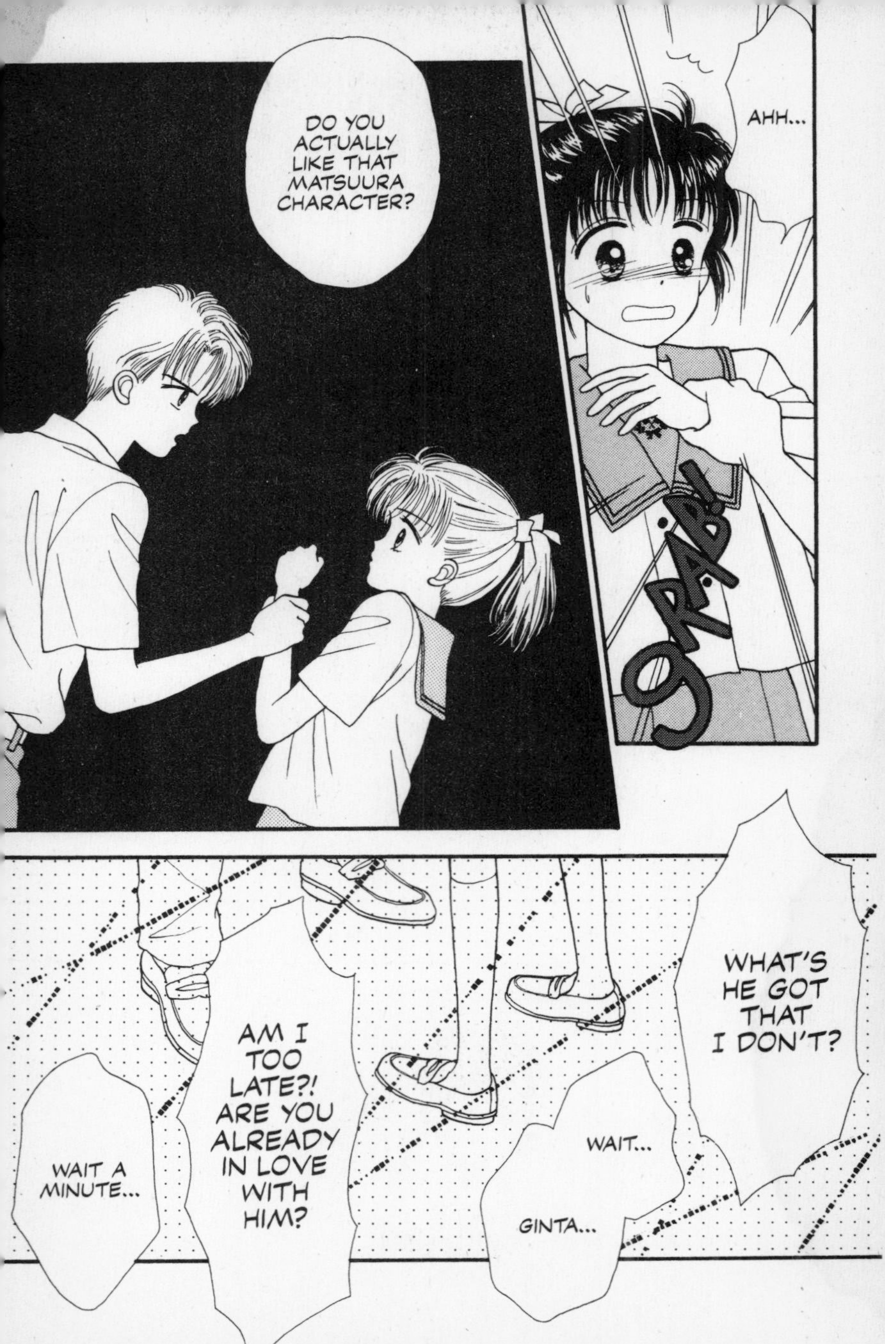
AHH...
GRAB!
DO YOU ACTUALLY LIKE THAT MATSUURA CHARACTER?
WHAT'S HE GOT THAT I DON'T?
WAIT... GINTA...
AM I TOO LATE?! ARE YOU ALREADY IN LOVE WITH HIM?
WAIT A MINUTE...

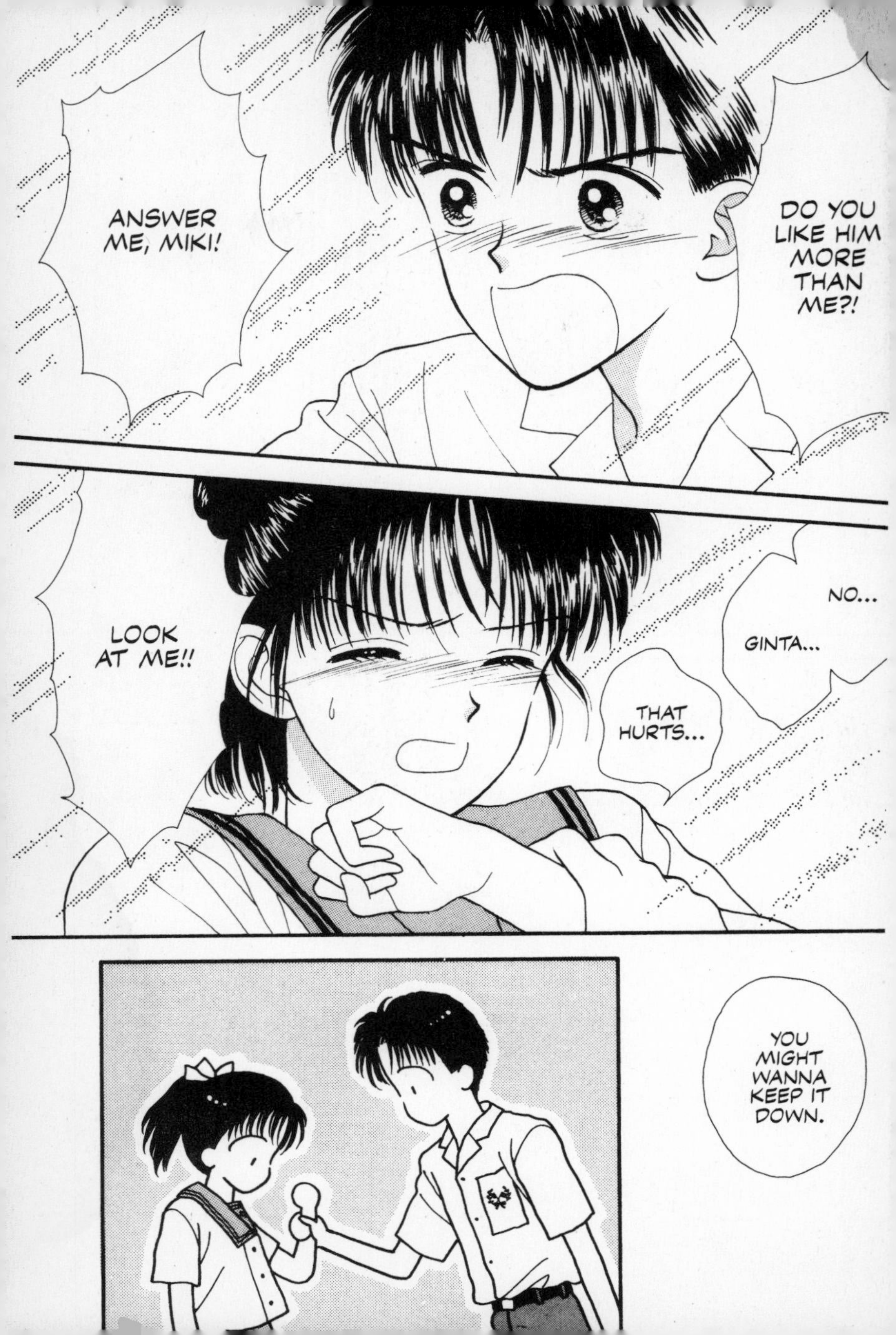
DO YOU LIKE HIM MORE THAN ME?!
ANSWER ME, MIKI!
NO...
GINTA...
THAT HURTS...
LOOK AT ME!!
YOU MIGHT WANNA KEEP IT DOWN.

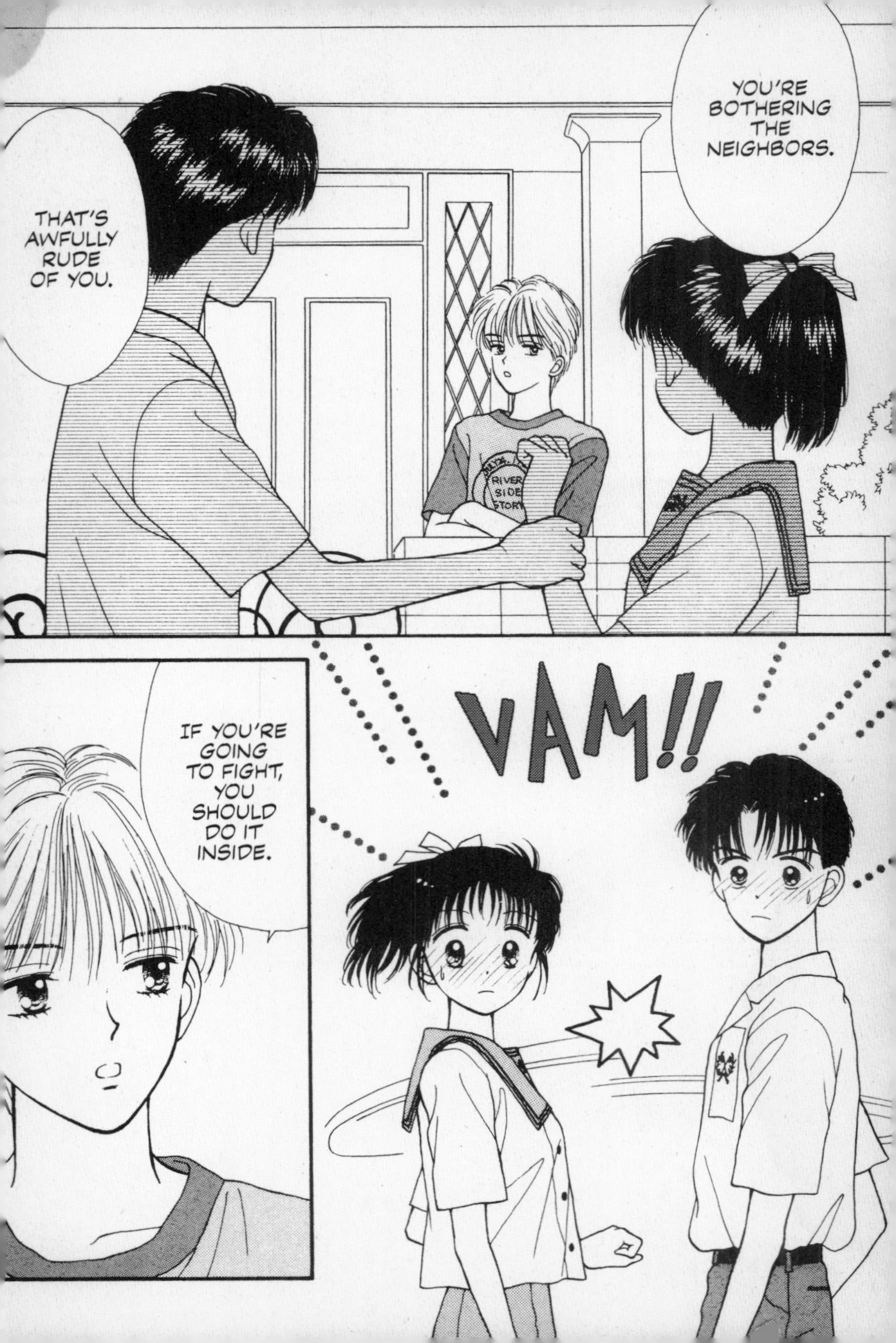
YOU'RE BOTHERING THE NEIGHBORS.
RIVER SIDE STORY
THAT'S AWFULLY RUDE OF YOU.
VAM!!
IF YOU'RE GOING TO FIGHT, YOU SHOULD DO IT INSIDE.

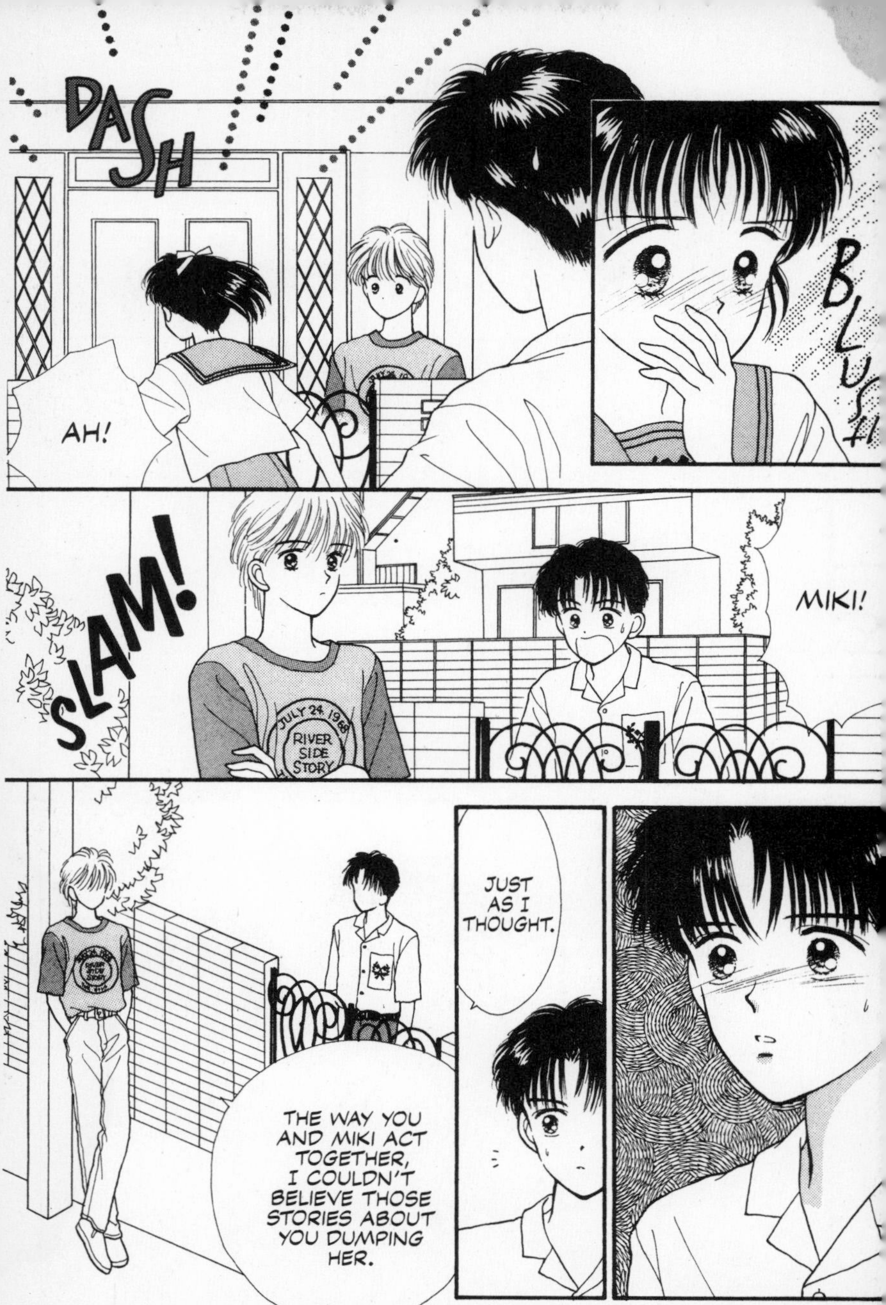
BLUSH!!
DASH
AH!
MIKI!
SLAM!
JULY 24 1968 RIVER SIDE STORY
JUST AS I THOUGHT.
THE WAY YOU AND MIKI ACT TOGETHER, I COULDN'T BELIEVE THOSE STORIES ABOUT YOU DUMPING HER.

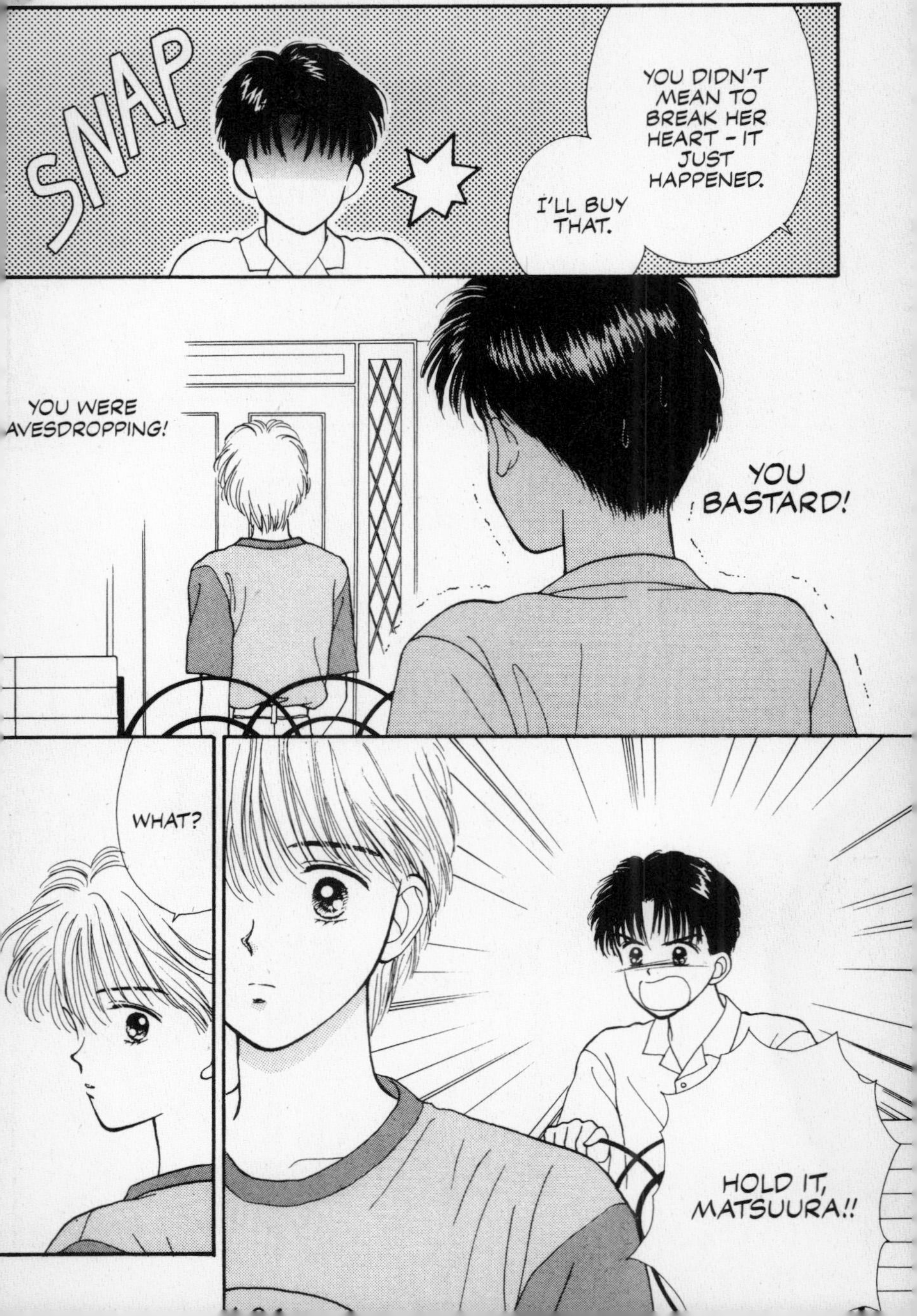
YOU DIDN'T MEAN TO BREAK HER HEART - IT JUST HAPPENED.
I'LL BUY THAT.
SNAP
YOU BASTARD!
AVESDROPPING!
YOU WERE
HOLD IT, MATSUURA!!
WHAT?

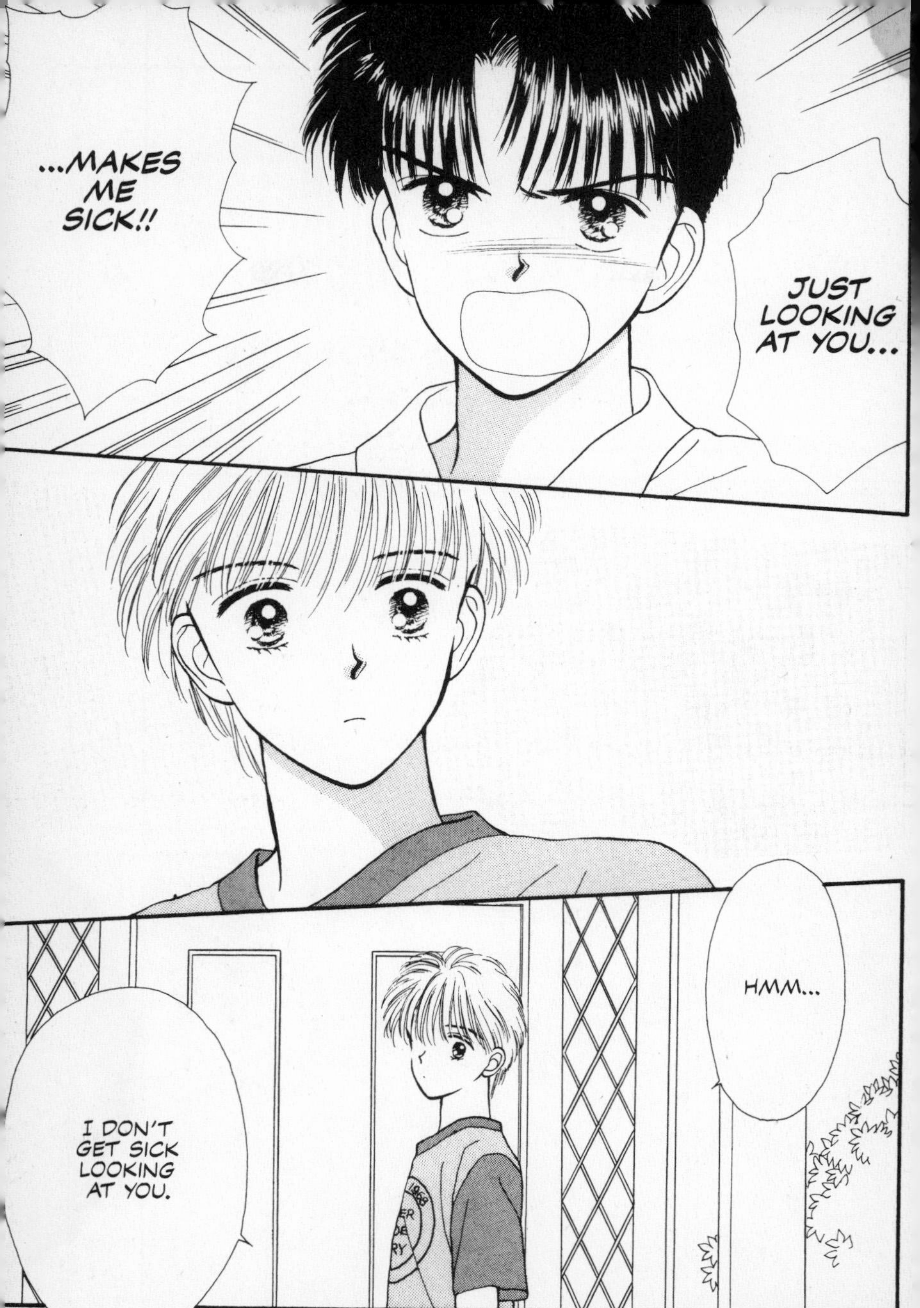
JUST LOOKING AT YOU...
...MAKES ME SICK!!
HMM...
I DON'T GET SICK LOOKING AT YOU.

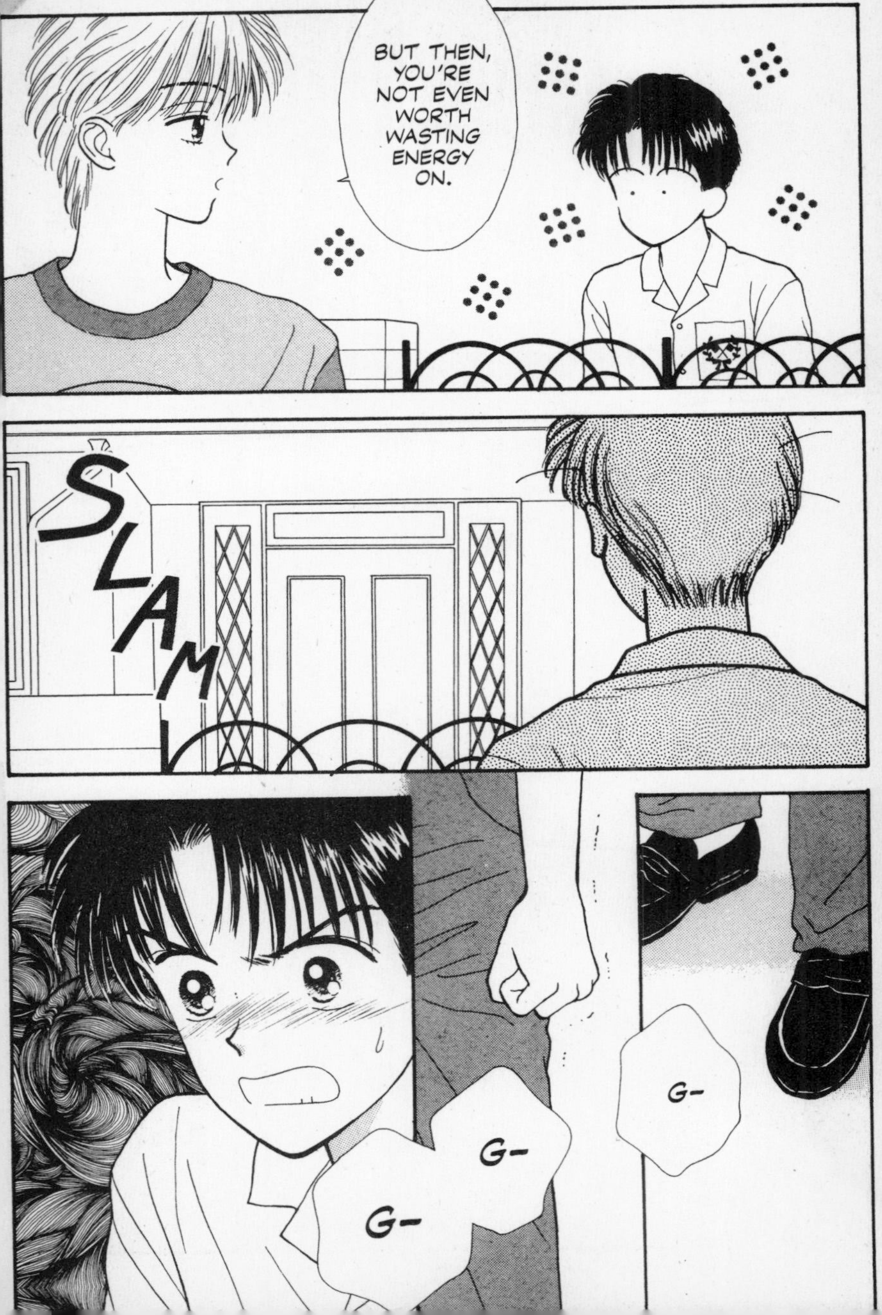
BUT THEN, YOU'RE NOT EVEN WORTH WASTING ENERGY ON.
SLAM
G-
G-
G-

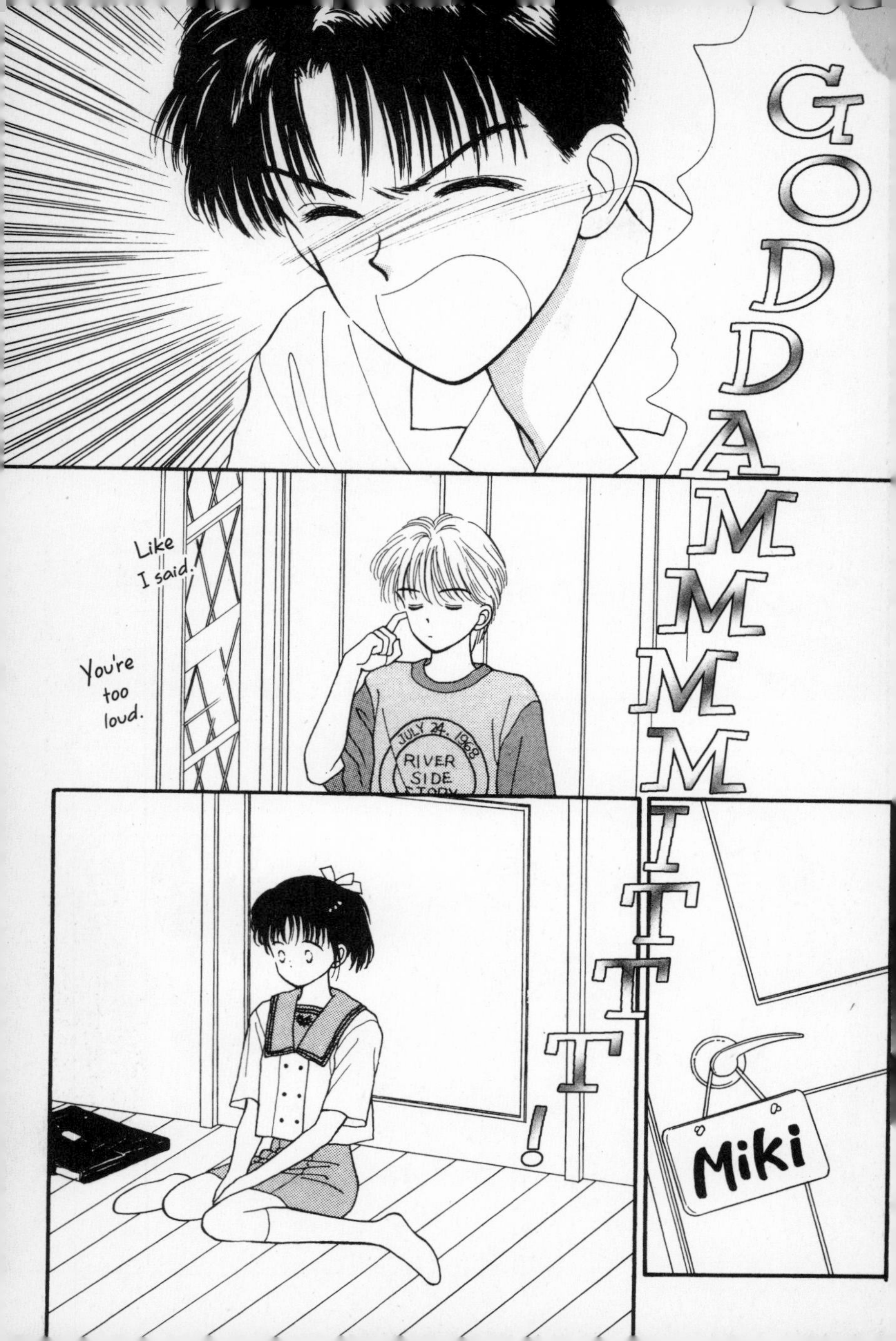
GODDAMMMMITTTT!
Like I said.
You're too loud.
JULY 24, 1968
RIVER SIDE
Miki

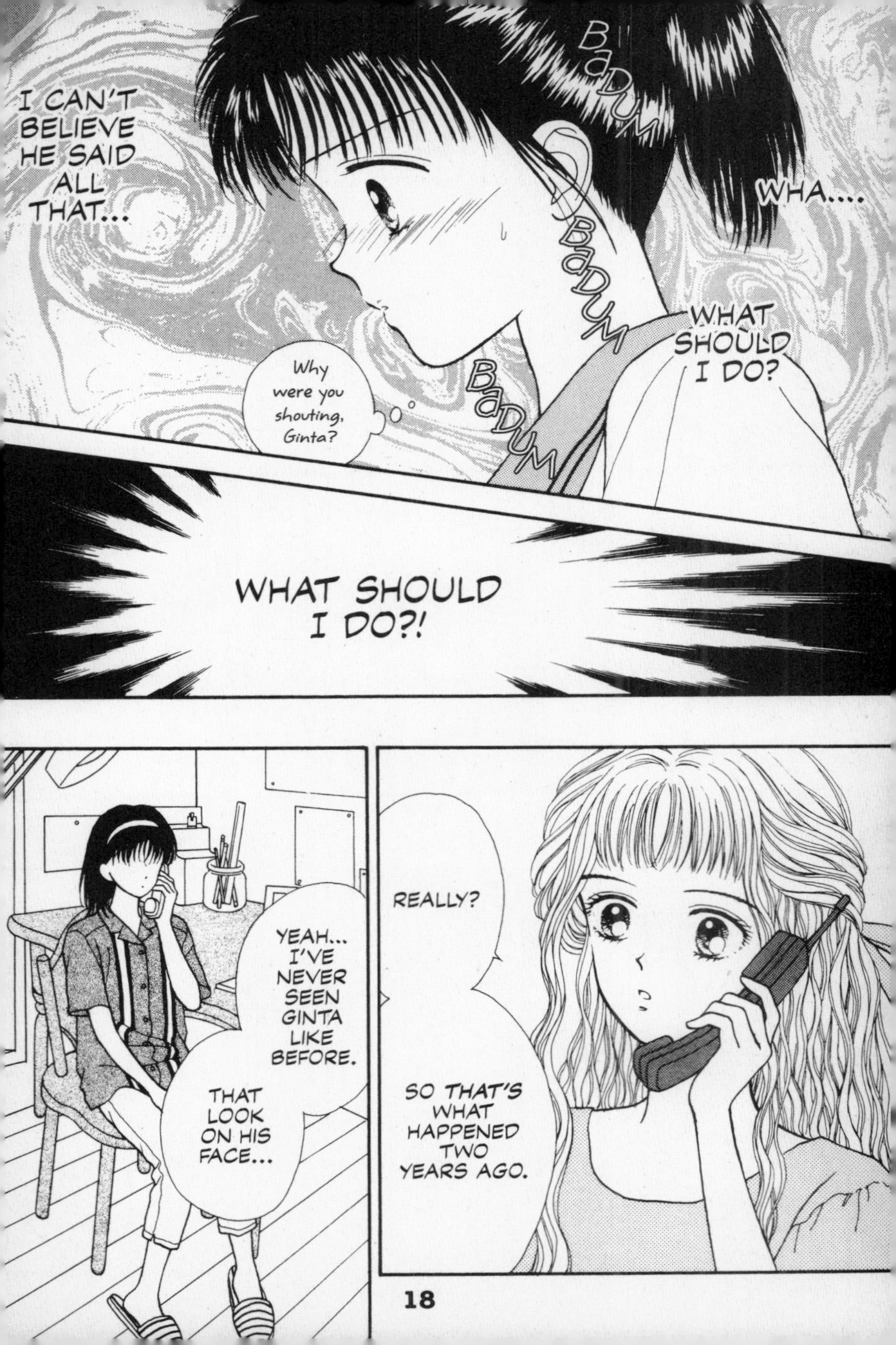

BADUM
WHA....
BADUM
BADUM
WHAT SHOULD I DO?
I CAN'T BELIEVE HE SAID ALL THAT...
BADUM
Why were you shouting, Ginta?
WHAT SHOULD I DO?!
REALLY?
SO THAT'S WHAT HAPPENED TWO YEARS AGO.
YEAH... I'VE NEVER SEEN GINTA LIKE BEFORE.
THAT LOOK ON HIS FACE...

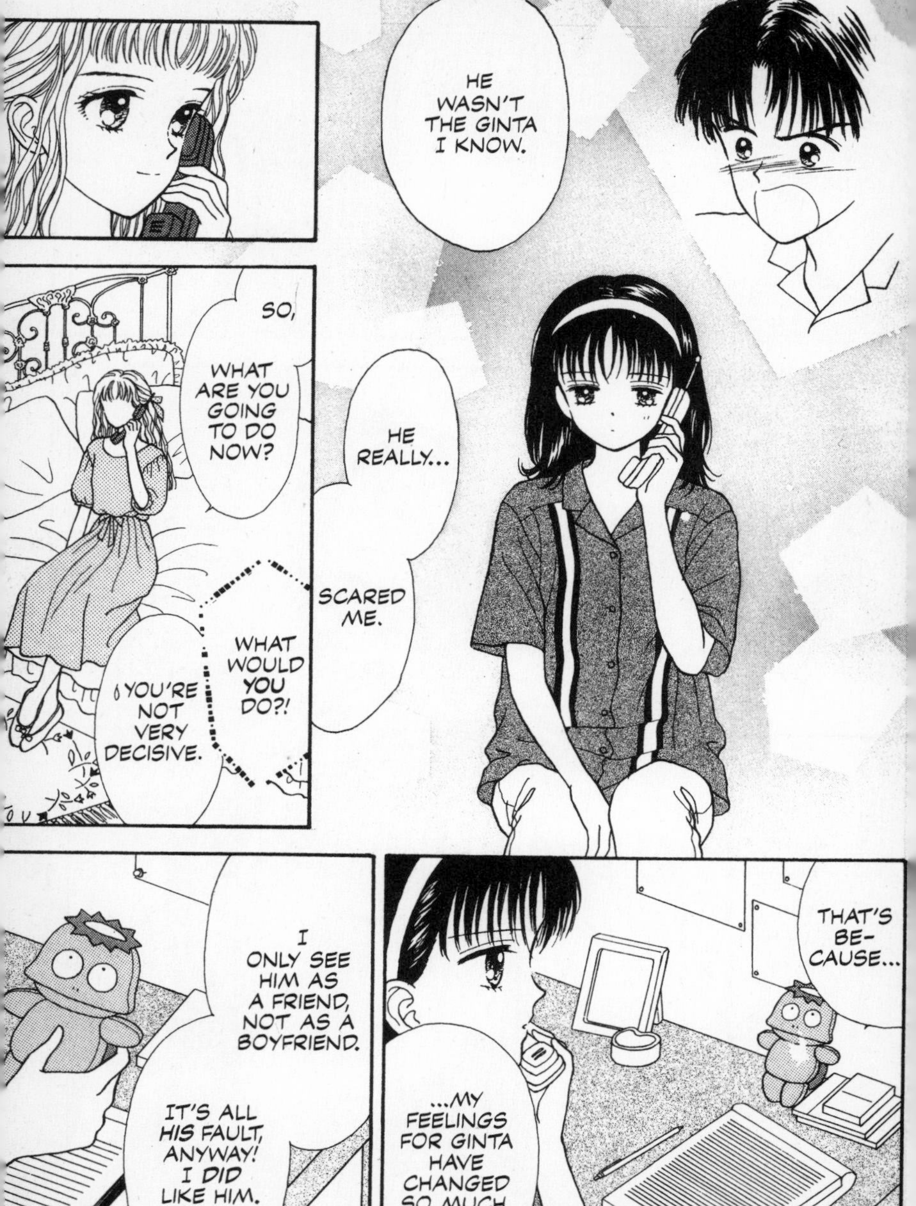
HE WASN'T THE GINTA I KNOW.
HE REALLY...
SCARED ME.
SO, WHAT ARE YOU GOING TO DO NOW?
WHAT WOULD YOU DO?!
YOU'RE NOT VERY DECISIVE.
THAT'S BE-CAUSE...
...MY FEELINGS FOR GINTA HAVE CHANGED SO MUCH.
I ONLY SEE HIM AS A FRIEND, NOT AS A BOYFRIEND.
IT'S ALL HIS FAULT, ANYWAY! I DID LIKE HIM.

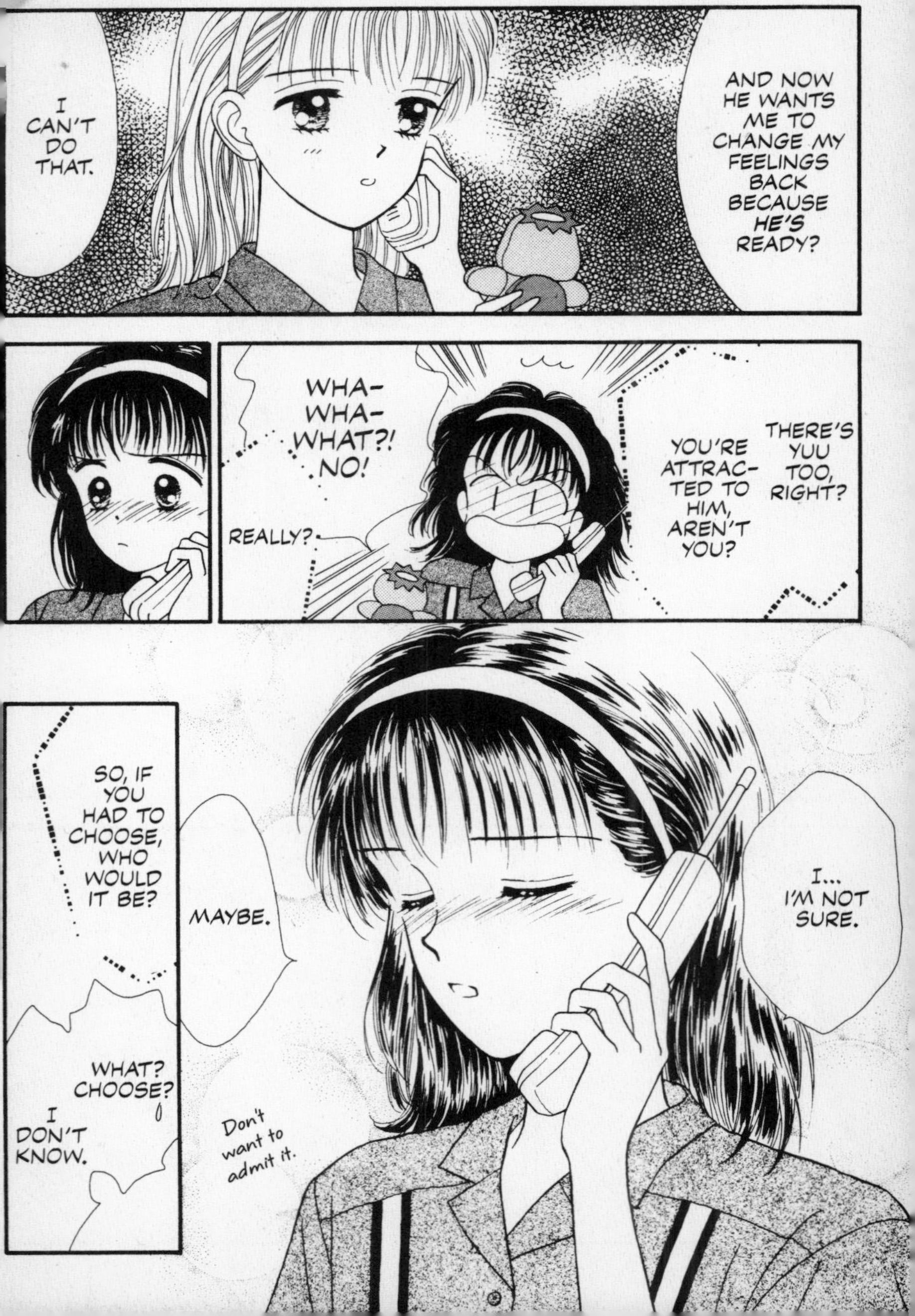
AND NOW HE WANTS ME TO CHANGE MY FEELINGS BACK BECAUSE HE'S READY?
I CAN'T DO THAT.
THERE'S YUU TOO, RIGHT?
YOU'RE ATTRACTED TO HIM, AREN'T YOU?
WHA-WHA-WHAT?! NO!
REALLY?
I... I'M NOT SURE.
MAYBE.
Don't want to admit it.
SO, IF YOU HAD TO CHOOSE, WHO WOULD IT BE?
WHAT? CHOOSE?
I DON'T KNOW.

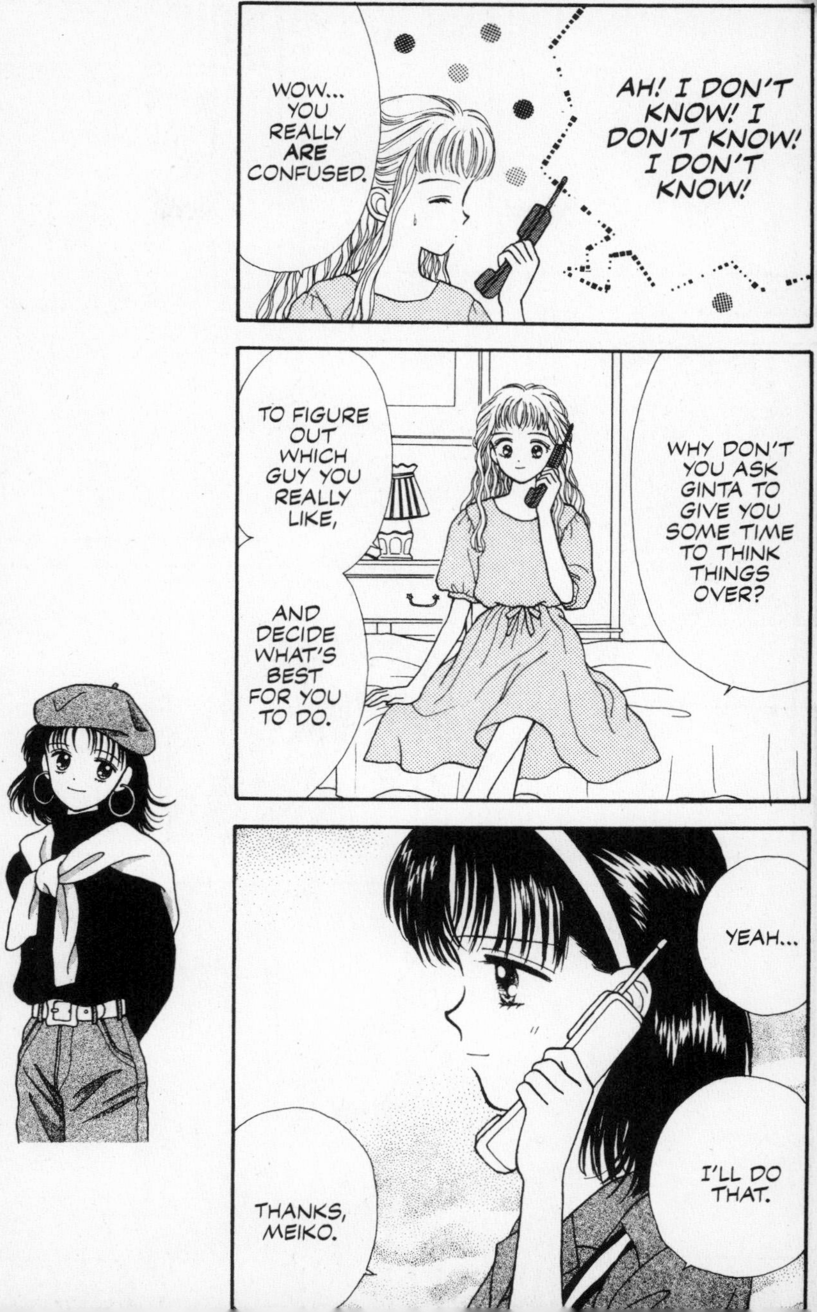
AH! I DON'T KNOW! I DON'T KNOW! I DON'T KNOW!
WOW... YOU REALLY ARE CONFUSED.
WHY DON'T YOU ASK GINTA TO GIVE YOU SOME TIME TO THINK THINGS OVER?
TO FIGURE OUT WHICH GUY YOU REALLY LIKE,
AND DECIDE WHAT'S BEST FOR YOU TO DO.
YEAH...
I'LL DO THAT.
THANKS, MEIKO.

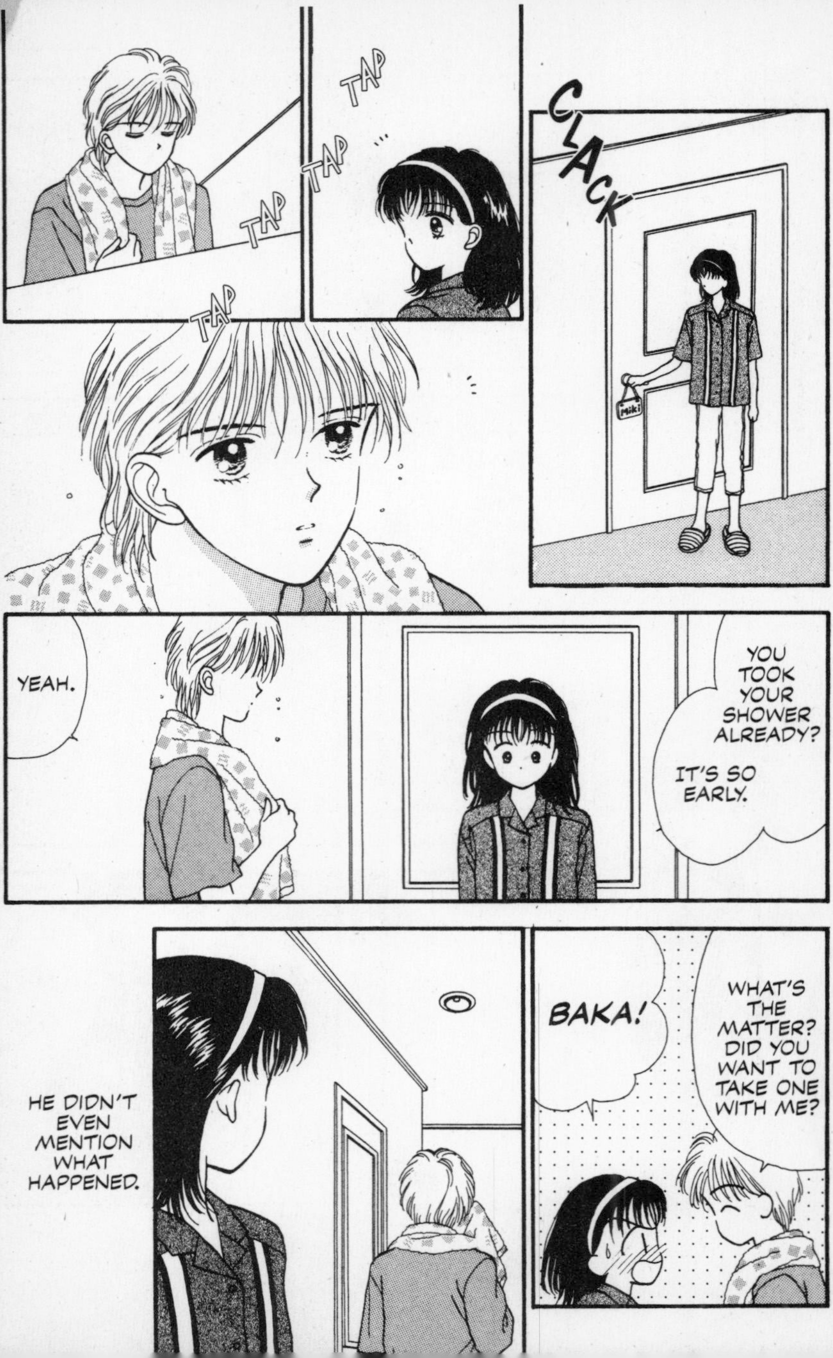
CLACK
TAP TAP TAP TAP
TAP
YOU TOOK YOUR SHOWER ALREADY?
IT'S SO EARLY.
YEAH.
WHAT'S THE MATTER? DID YOU WANT TO TAKE ONE WITH ME?
BAKA!
HE DIDN'T EVEN MENTION WHAT HAPPENED.

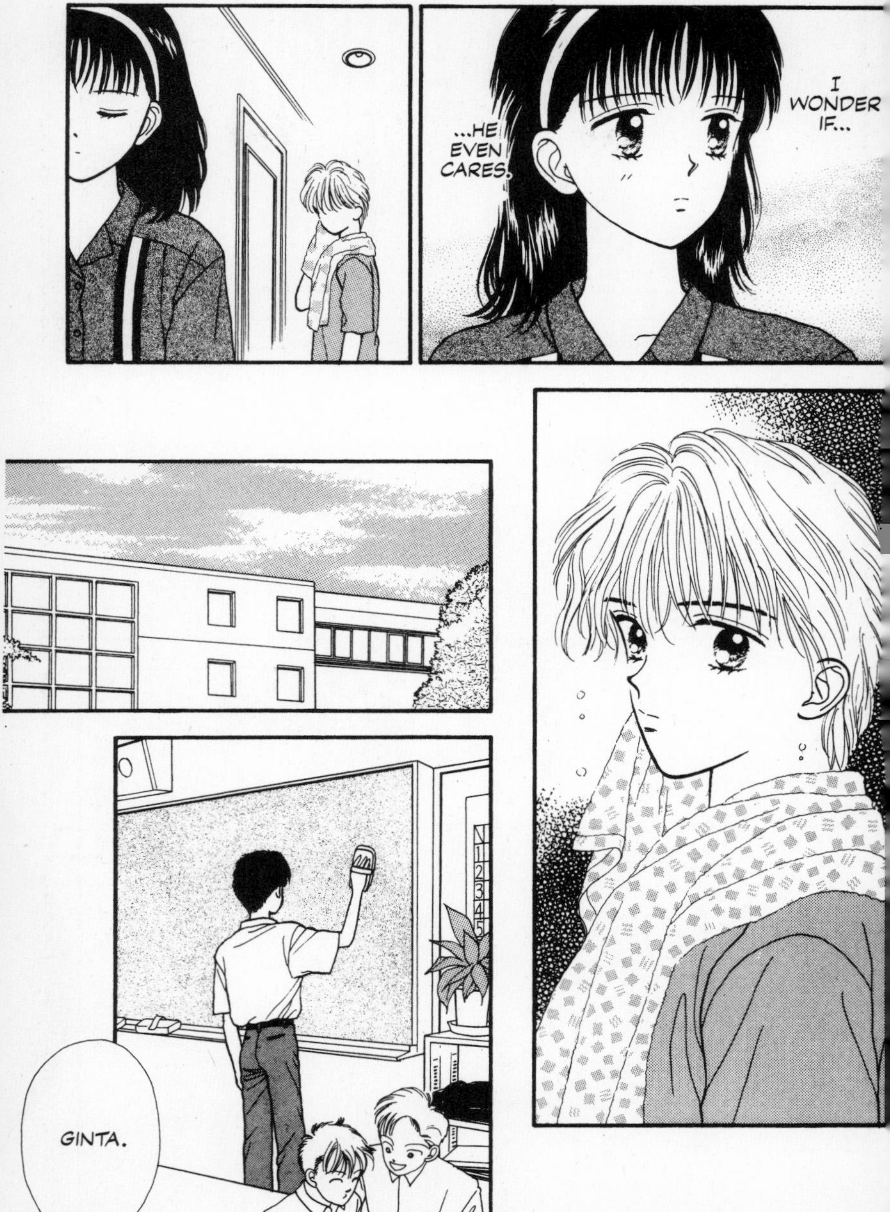
I WONDER IF...
...HE EVEN CARES.
GINTA.

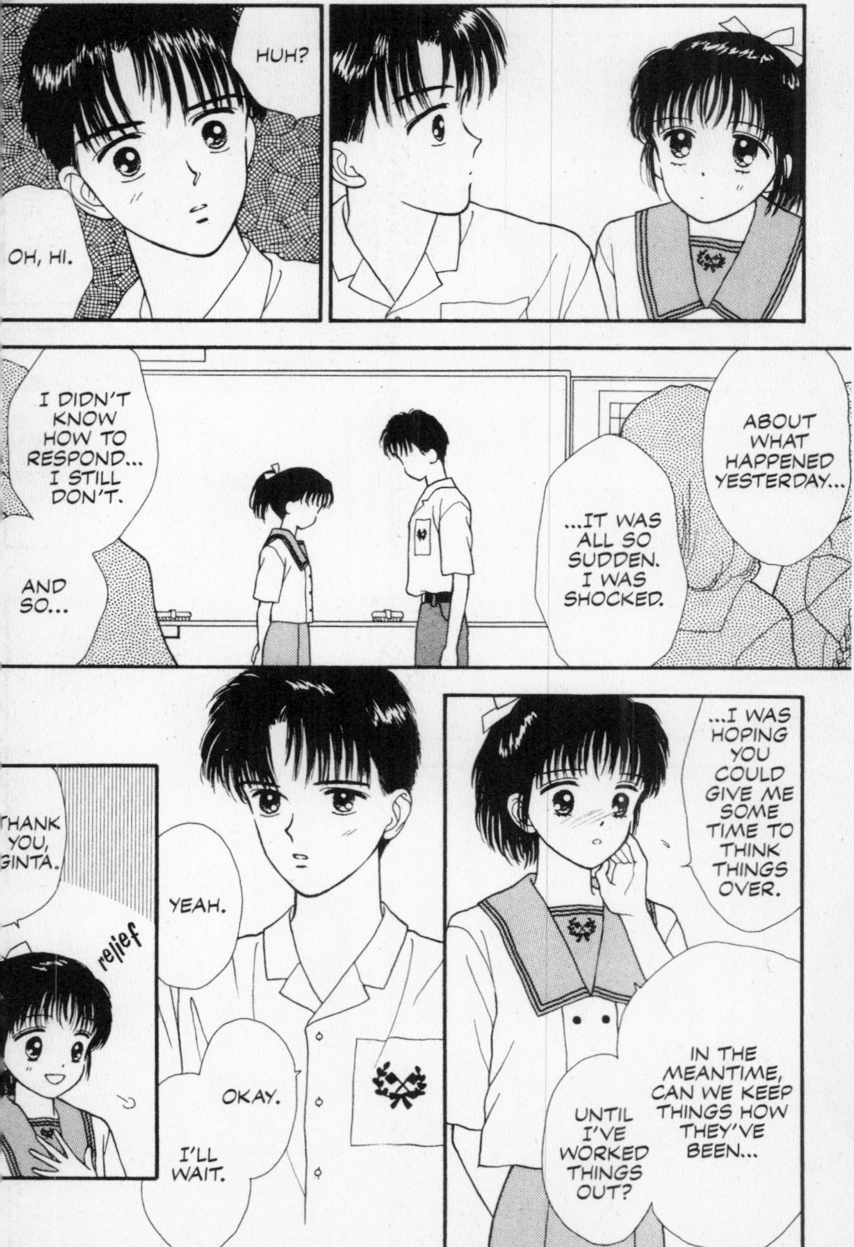

HUH?
OH, HI.
ABOUT WHAT HAPPENED YESTERDAY...
...IT WAS ALL SO SUDDEN. I WAS SHOCKED.
I DIDN'T KNOW HOW TO RESPOND... I STILL DON'T.
AND SO...
...I WAS HOPING YOU COULD GIVE ME SOME TIME TO THINK THINGS OVER.
IN THE MEANTIME, CAN WE KEEP THINGS HOW THEY'VE BEEN...
UNTIL I'VE WORKED THINGS OUT?
YEAH.
OKAY.
I'LL WAIT.
THANK YOU, GINTA.
relief

FREE TALK①

Welcome to book 2 of Marmalade Boy! I hope you're enjoying things so far. You might notice that every so often, we leave in a few words of Japanese, like "baka!" (on page 22). In Japan, their text is sprinkled with English words like "cool" and "love," so we thought it would be fun to sprinkle a few Japanese slang words in this comic. It should be pretty clear from Miki's face what she's saying. In the case of "baka," this means, "You idiot!" We hope you enjoy this Japanese language surprise.

-Editor

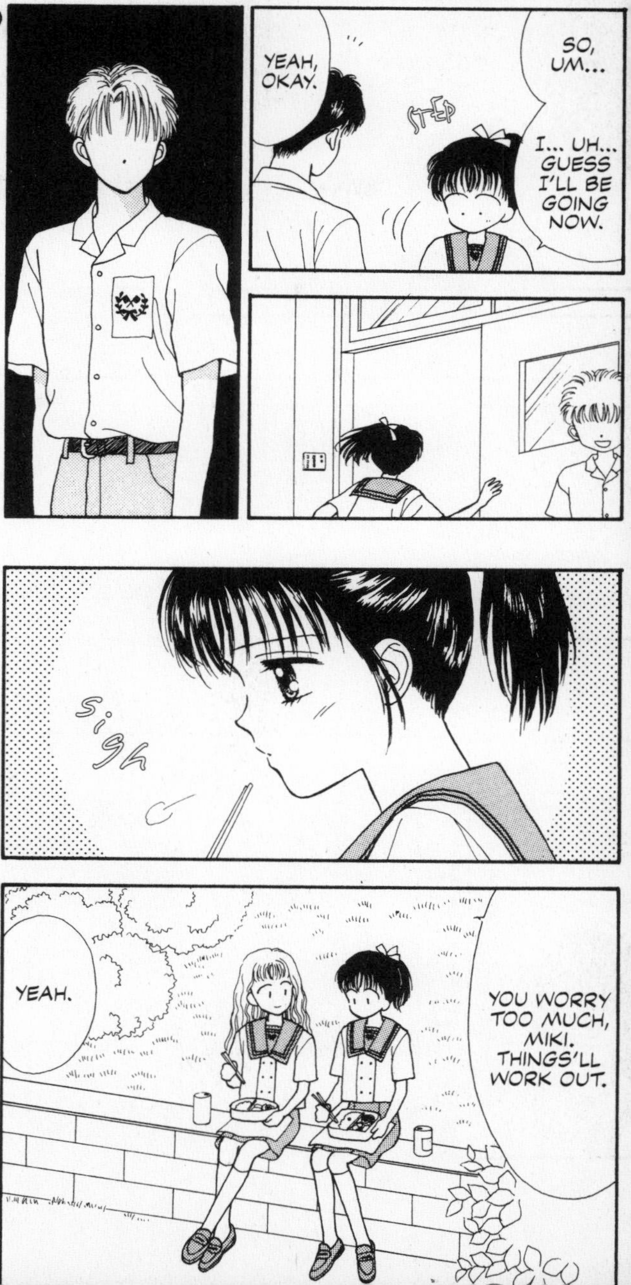

SO, UM...
I... UH... GUESS I'LL BE GOING NOW.
STEP
YEAH, OKAY.
SIGH
YOU WORRY TOO MUCH, MIKI. THINGS'LL WORK OUT.
YEAH.

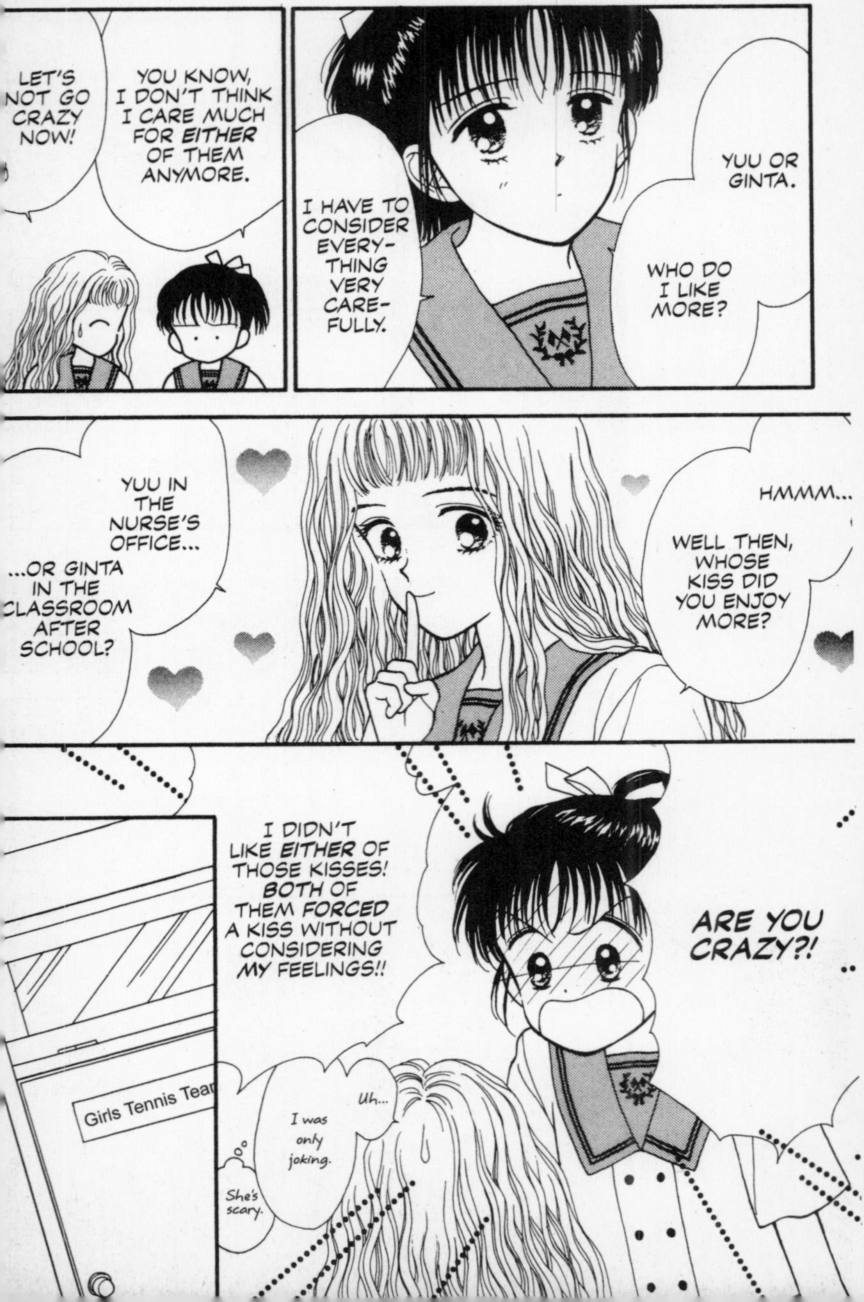
YUU OR GINTA.
WHO DO I LIKE MORE?
I HAVE TO CONSIDER EVERY-THING VERY CARE-FULLY.
YOU KNOW, I DON'T THINK I CARE MUCH FOR *EITHER* OF THEM ANYMORE.
LET'S NOT GO CRAZY NOW!
HMMM...
WELL THEN, WHOSE KISS DID YOU ENJOY MORE?
YUU IN THE NURSE'S OFFICE...
...OR GINTA IN THE CLASSROOM AFTER SCHOOL?
ARE YOU CRAZY?!
I DIDN'T LIKE *EITHER* OF THOSE KISSES! *BOTH* OF THEM *FORCED* A KISS WITHOUT CONSIDERING *MY* FEELINGS!!
Uh...
I was only joking.
She's scary.
Girls Tennis

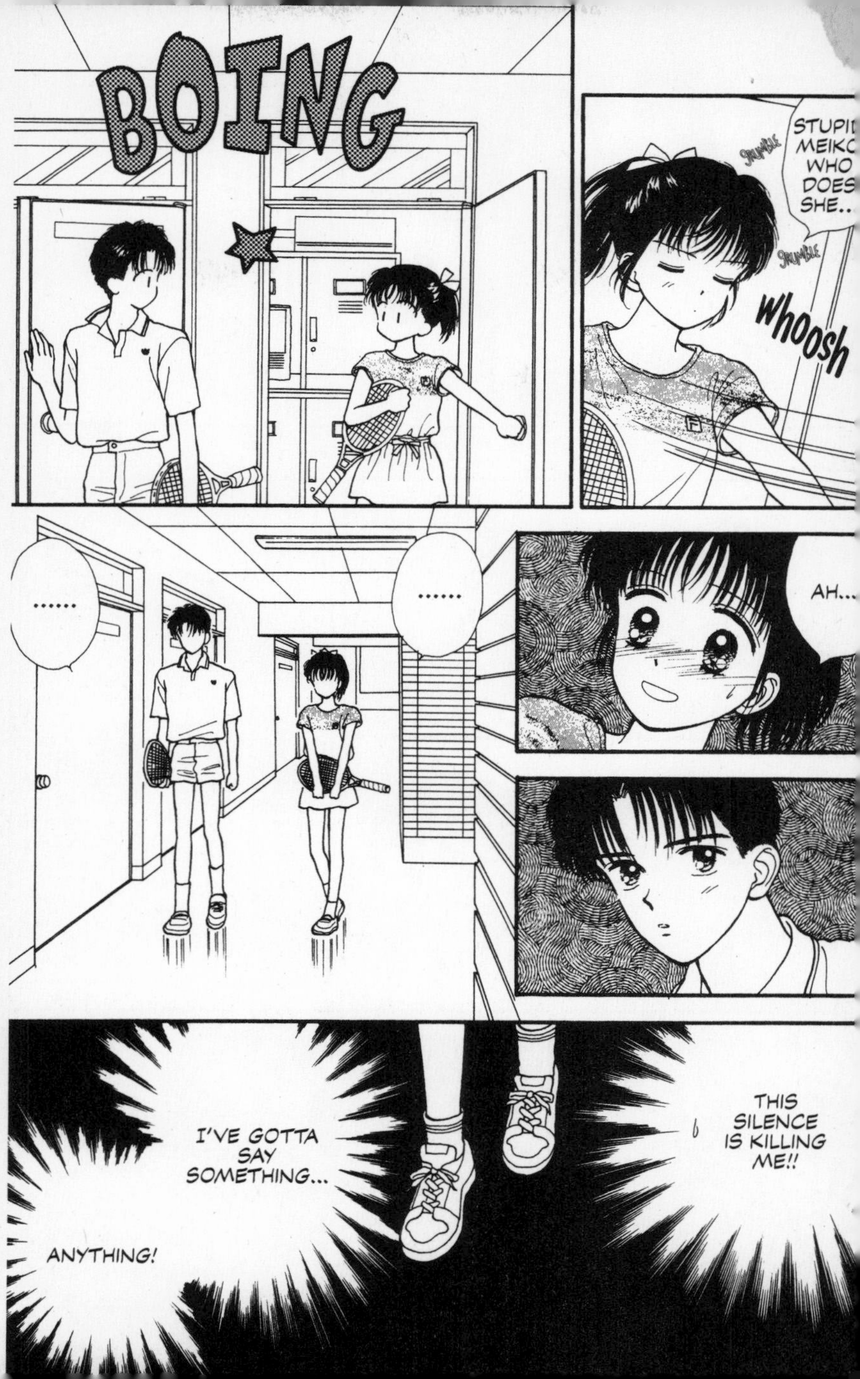
STUPID MEIKO WHO DOES SHE...
GRUMBLE
GRUMBLE
whoosh
BOING
AH...
......
......
THIS SILENCE IS KILLING ME!!
I'VE GOTTA SAY SOMETHING...
ANYTHING!

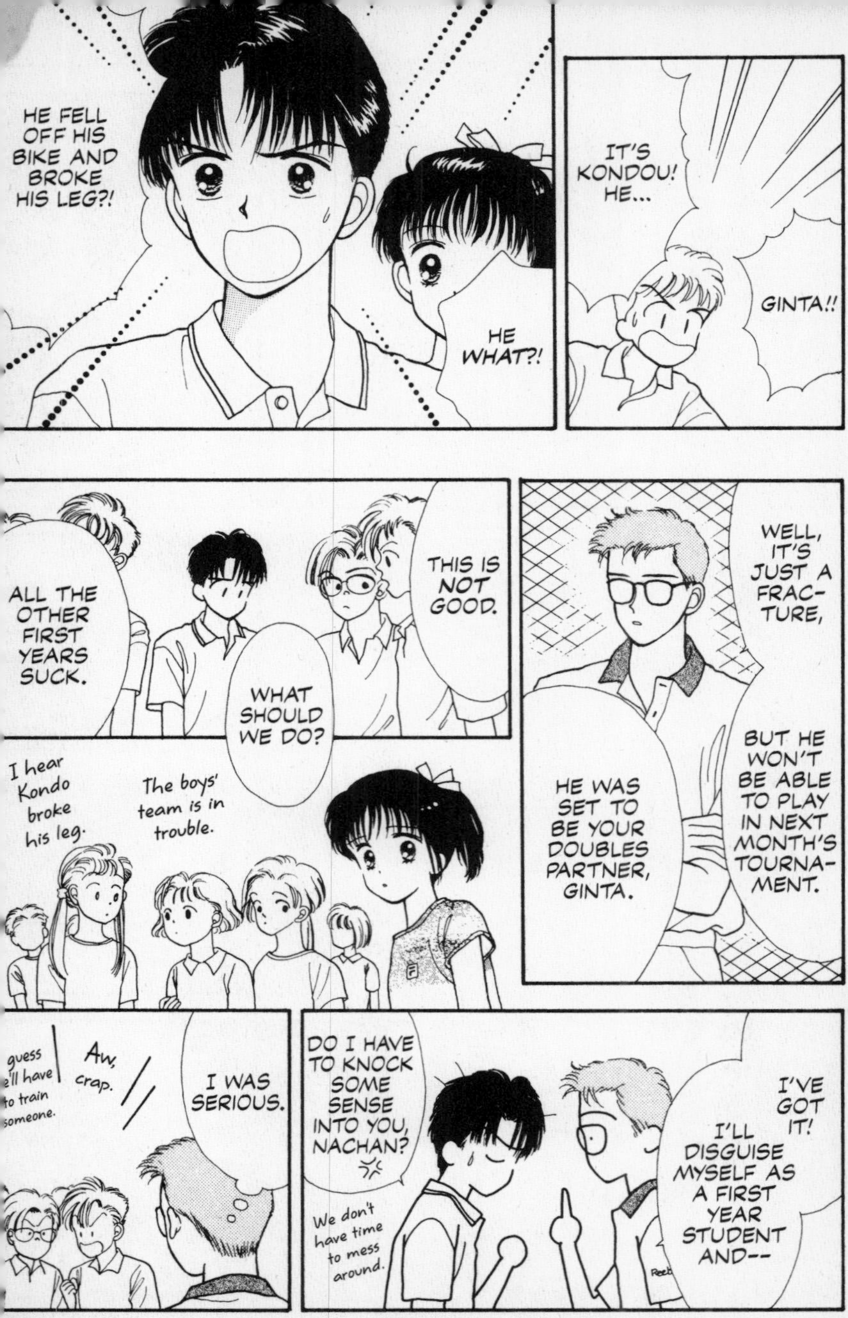

IT'S KONDOU! HE...
GINTA!!
HE FELL OFF HIS BIKE AND BROKE HIS LEG?!
HE WHAT?!
WELL, IT'S JUST A FRACTURE,
BUT HE WON'T BE ABLE TO PLAY IN NEXT MONTH'S TOURNAMENT.
HE WAS SET TO BE YOUR DOUBLES PARTNER, GINTA.
THIS IS NOT GOOD.
WHAT SHOULD WE DO?
ALL THE OTHER FIRST YEARS SUCK.
The boys' team is in trouble.
I hear Kondo broke his leg.
I'VE GOT IT!
I'LL DISGUISE MYSELF AS A FIRST YEAR STUDENT AND--
DO I HAVE TO KNOCK SOME SENSE INTO YOU, NACHAN?
We don't have time to mess around.
I WAS SERIOUS.
Aw, crap.
guess e'll have to train someone.

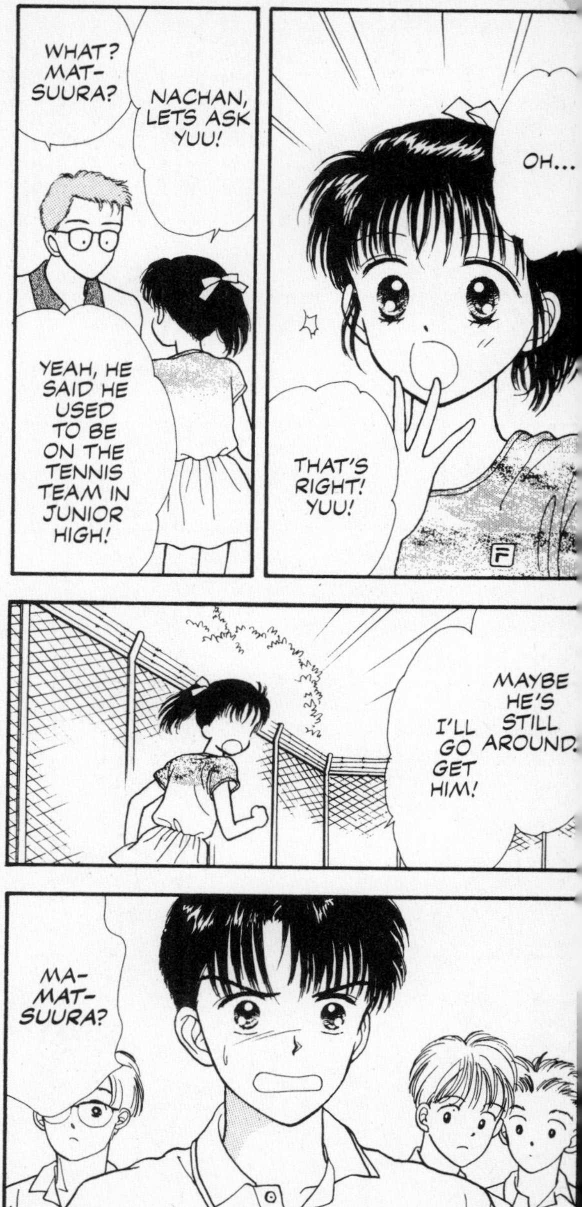
OH...
THAT'S RIGHT! YUU!
NACHAN, LETS ASK YUU!
WHAT? MAT-SUURA?
YEAH, HE SAID HE USED TO BE ON THE TENNIS TEAM IN JUNIOR HIGH!
MAYBE HE'S STILL AROUND.
I'LL GO GET HIM!
MA-MAT-SUURA?

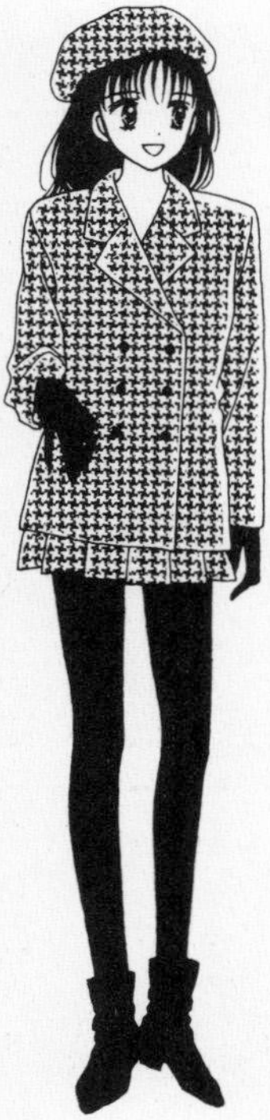

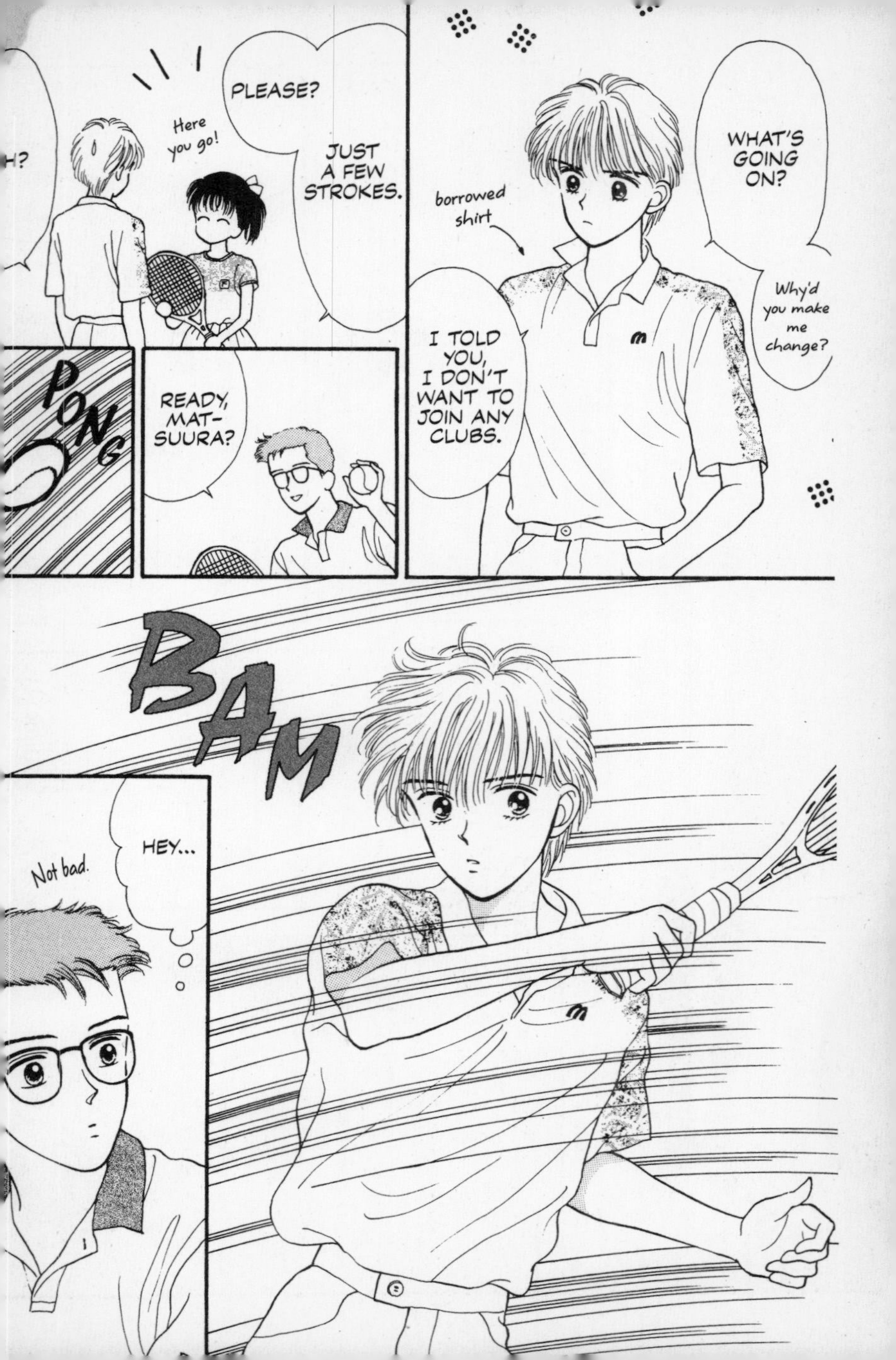
WHAT'S GOING ON?
Why'd you make me change?
borrowed shirt
I TOLD YOU, I DON'T WANT TO JOIN ANY CLUBS.
PLEASE?
JUST A FEW STROKES.
Here you go!
H?
READY, MAT-SUURA?
PONG
BAM
HEY...
Not bad.

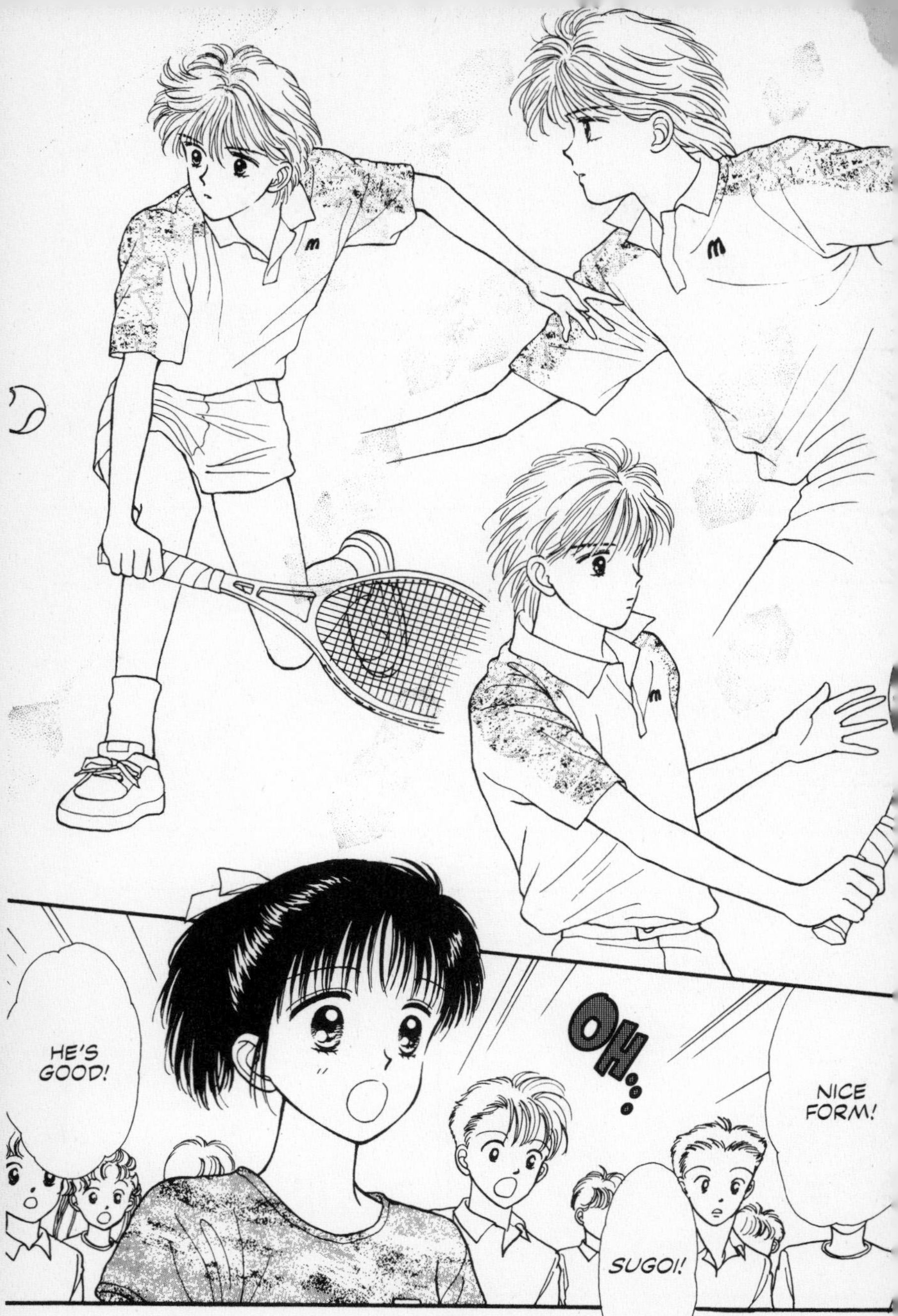

NICE FORM!
OH...
SUGOI!
HE'S GOOD!

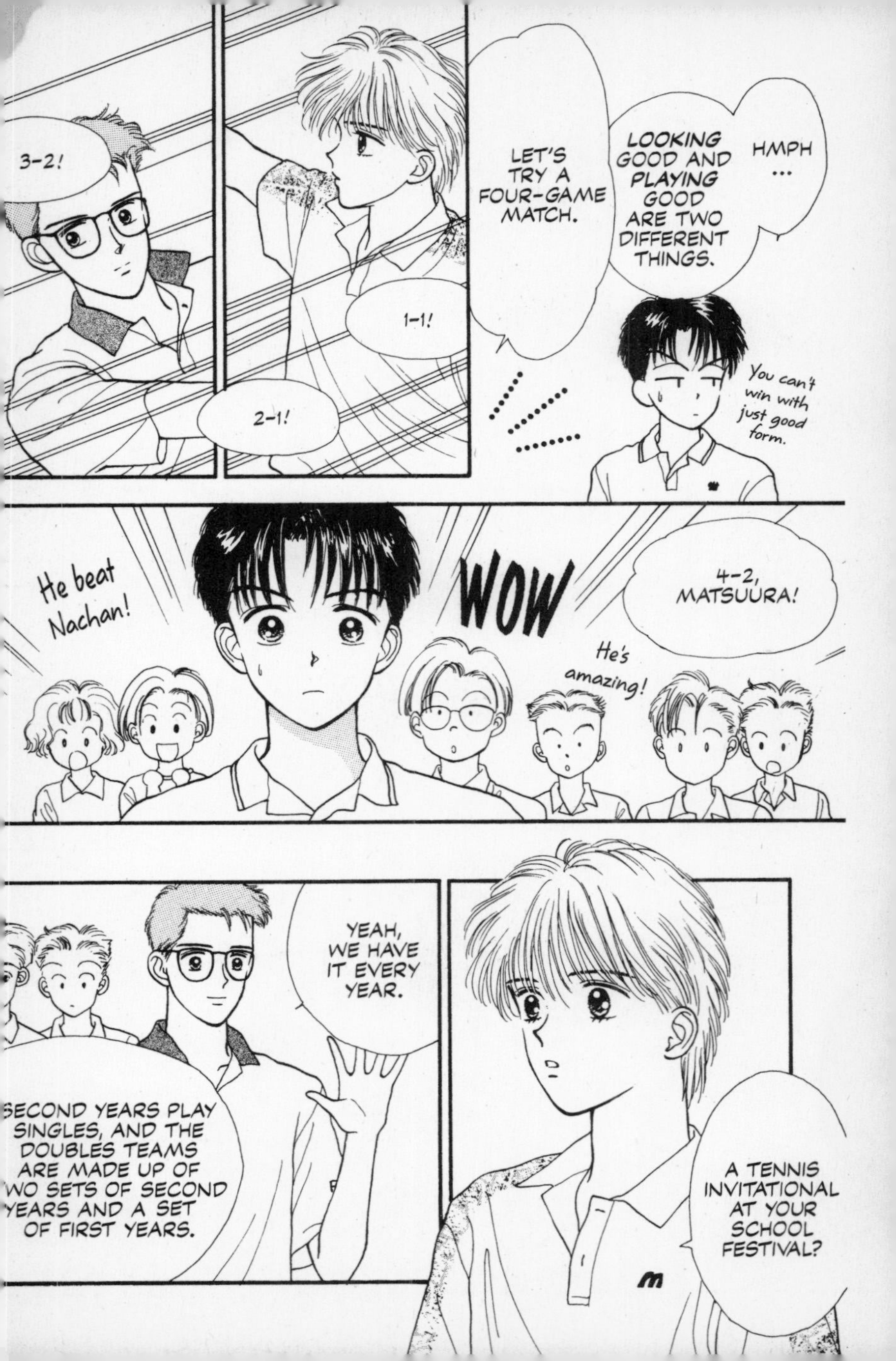
HMPH ...
LOOKING GOOD AND PLAYING GOOD ARE TWO DIFFERENT THINGS.
LET'S TRY A FOUR-GAME MATCH.
You can't win with just good form.
......
1-1!
2-1!
3-2!
4-2, MATSUURA!
He's amazing!
WOW
He beat Nachan!
A TENNIS INVITATIONAL AT YOUR SCHOOL FESTIVAL?
YEAH, WE HAVE IT EVERY YEAR.
SECOND YEARS PLAY SINGLES, AND THE DOUBLES TEAMS ARE MADE UP OF TWO SETS OF SECOND YEARS AND A SET OF FIRST YEARS.

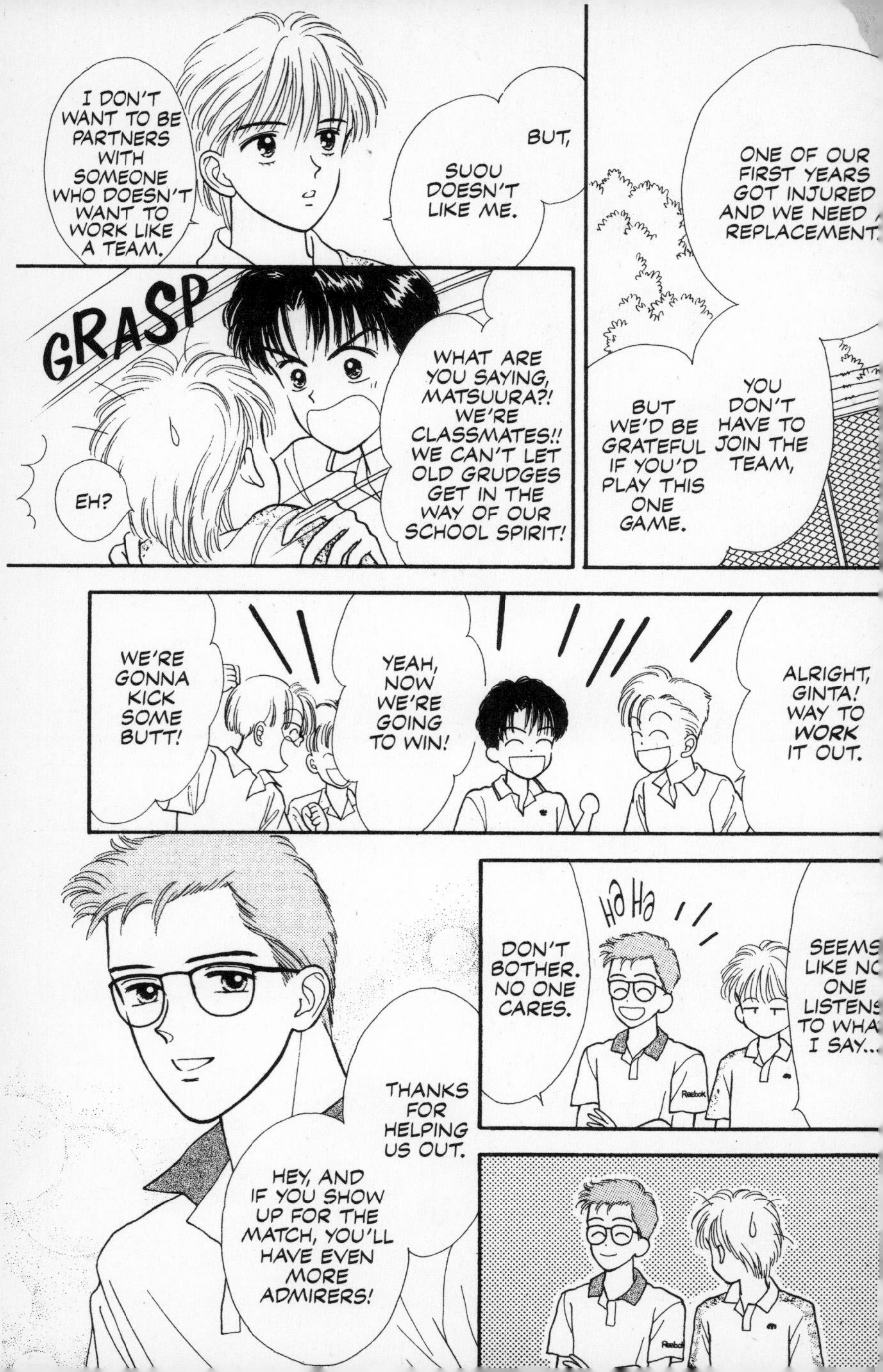
ONE OF OUR FIRST YEARS GOT INJURED AND WE NEED A REPLACEMENT.
YOU DON'T HAVE TO JOIN THE TEAM,
BUT WE'D BE GRATEFUL IF YOU'D PLAY THIS ONE GAME.
BUT,
SUOU DOESN'T LIKE ME.
I DON'T WANT TO BE PARTNERS WITH SOMEONE WHO DOESN'T WANT TO WORK LIKE A TEAM.
GRASP
WHAT ARE YOU SAYING, MATSUURA?! WE'RE CLASSMATES!! WE CAN'T LET OLD GRUDGES GET IN THE WAY OF OUR SCHOOL SPIRIT!
EH?
ALRIGHT, GINTA! WAY TO WORK IT OUT.
YEAH, NOW WE'RE GOING TO WIN!
WE'RE GONNA KICK SOME BUTT!
SEEMS LIKE NO ONE LISTENS TO WHAT I SAY...
HA HA
DON'T BOTHER. NO ONE CARES.
THANKS FOR HELPING US OUT.
HEY, AND IF YOU SHOW UP FOR THE MATCH, YOU'LL HAVE EVEN MORE ADMIRERS!

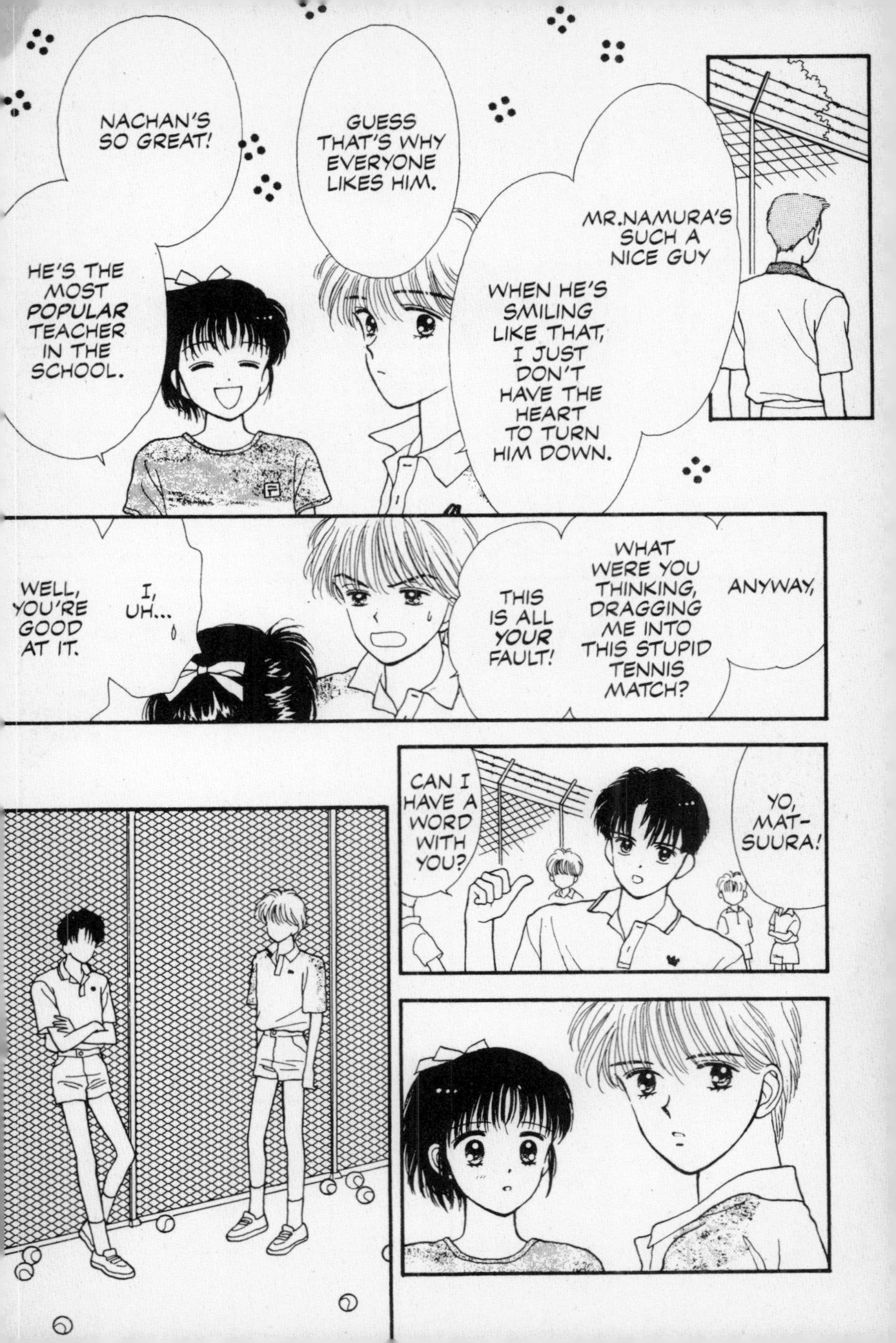
MR.NAMURA'S SUCH A NICE GUY
WHEN HE'S SMILING LIKE THAT, I JUST DON'T HAVE THE HEART TO TURN HIM DOWN.
GUESS THAT'S WHY EVERYONE LIKES HIM.
NACHAN'S SO GREAT!
HE'S THE MOST POPULAR TEACHER IN THE SCHOOL.
ANYWAY,
WHAT WERE YOU THINKING, DRAGGING ME INTO THIS STUPID TENNIS MATCH?
THIS IS ALL YOUR FAULT!
I, UH...
WELL, YOU'RE GOOD AT IT.
YO, MAT-SUURA!
CAN I HAVE A WORD WITH YOU?

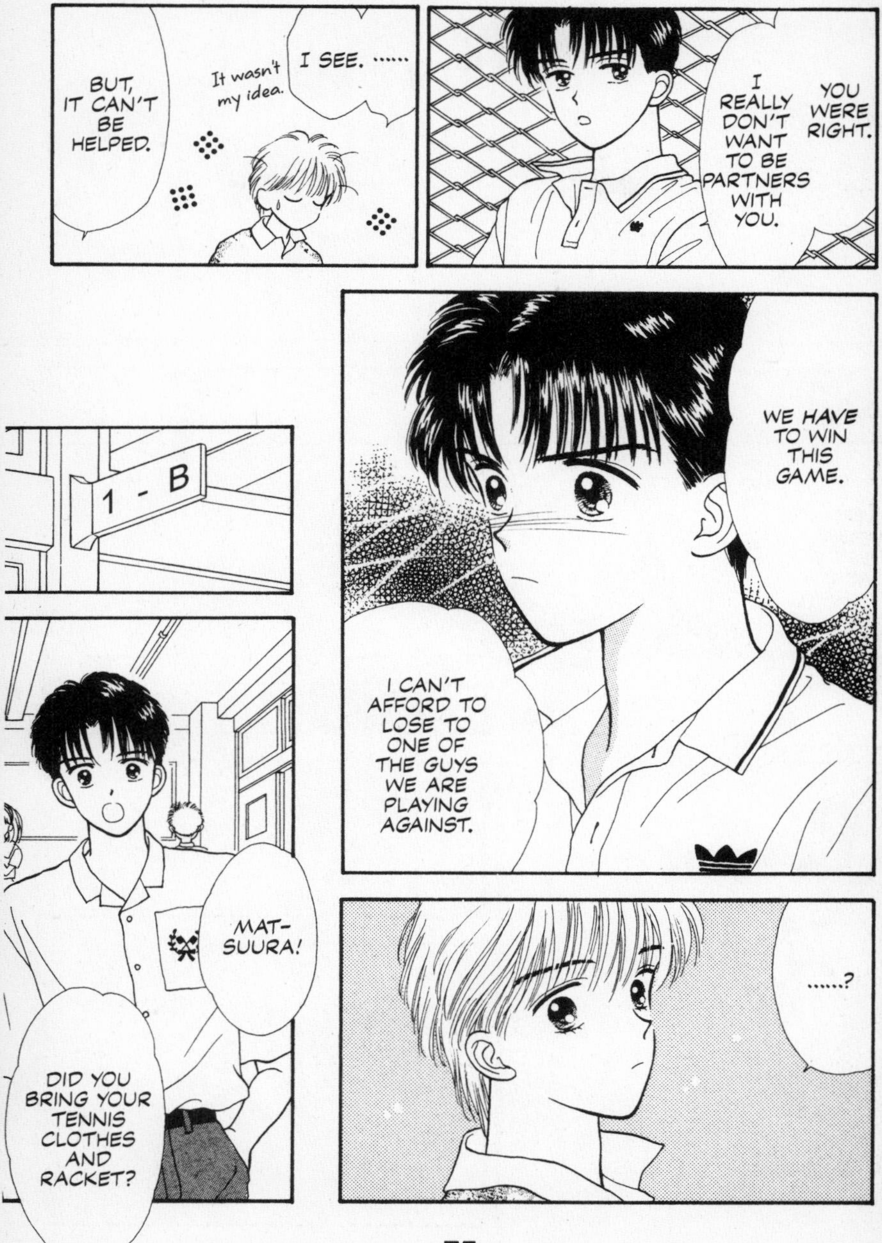
YOU WERE RIGHT.
I REALLY DON'T WANT TO BE PARTNERS WITH YOU.
I SEE. ......
It wasn't my idea.
BUT, IT CAN'T BE HELPED.
WE *HAVE* TO WIN THIS GAME.
I CAN'T AFFORD TO LOSE TO ONE OF THE GUYS WE ARE PLAYING AGAINST.
......?
1 - B
MAT-SUURA!
DID YOU BRING YOUR TENNIS CLOTHES AND RACKET?

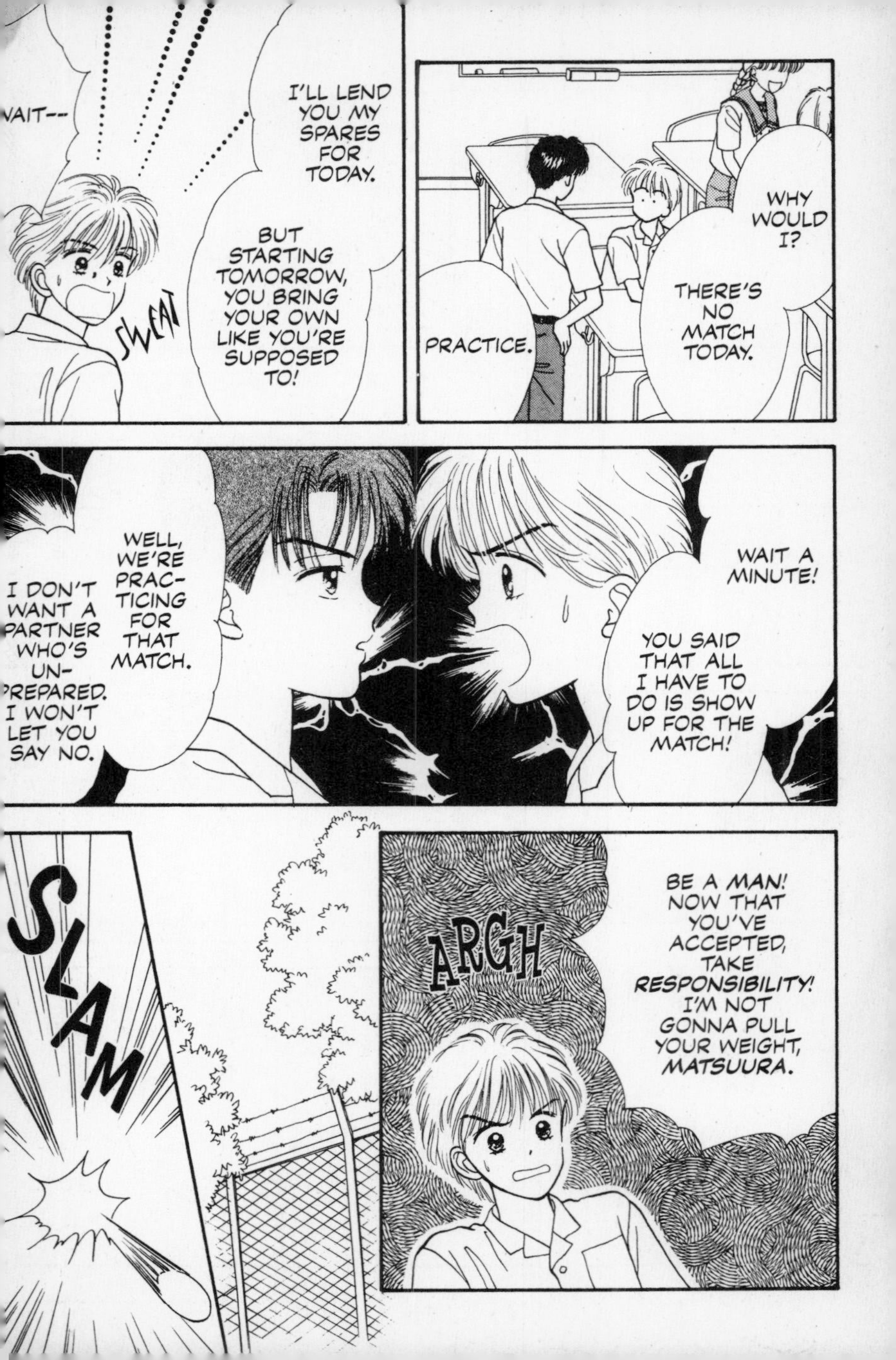
WHY WOULD I?
THERE'S NO MATCH TODAY.
PRACTICE.
I'LL LEND YOU MY SPARES FOR TODAY.
BUT STARTING TOMORROW, YOU BRING YOUR OWN LIKE YOU'RE SUPPOSED TO!
VAIT--
SWEAT
WAIT A MINUTE!
YOU SAID THAT ALL I HAVE TO DO IS SHOW UP FOR THE MATCH!
WELL, WE'RE PRACTICING FOR THAT MATCH.
I DON'T WANT A PARTNER WHO'S UNPREPARED. I WON'T LET YOU SAY NO.
BE A MAN! NOW THAT YOU'VE ACCEPTED, TAKE RESPONSIBILITY! I'M NOT GONNA PULL YOUR WEIGHT, MATSUURA.
ARGH
SLAM

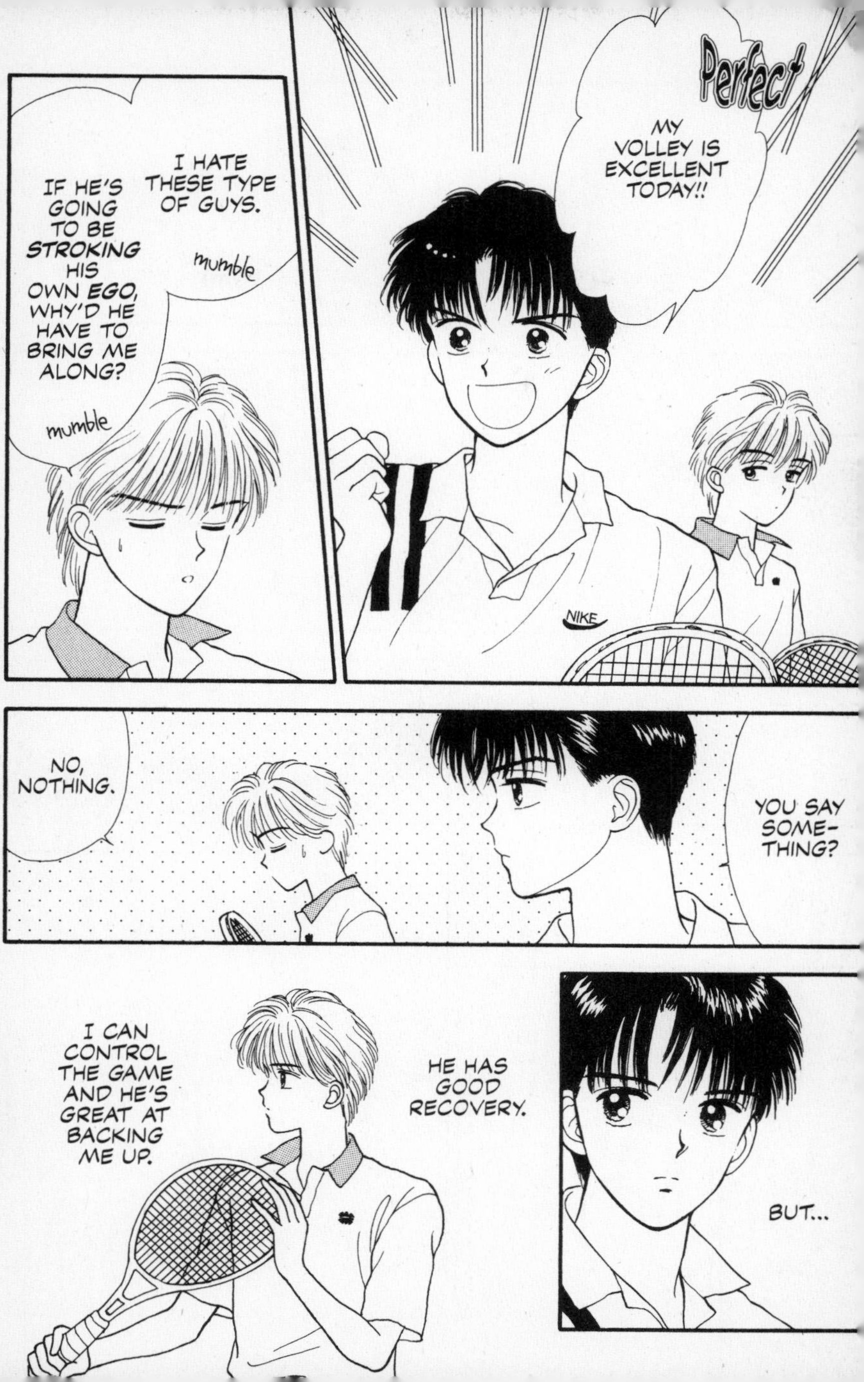
Perfect
MY VOLLEY IS EXCELLENT TODAY!!
NIKE
I HATE THESE TYPE OF GUYS.
mumble
IF HE'S GOING TO BE STROKING HIS OWN EGO, WHY'D HE HAVE TO BRING ME ALONG?
mumble
YOU SAY SOME-THING?
NO, NOTHING.
BUT...
HE HAS GOOD RECOVERY.
I CAN CONTROL THE GAME AND HE'S GREAT AT BACKING ME UP.

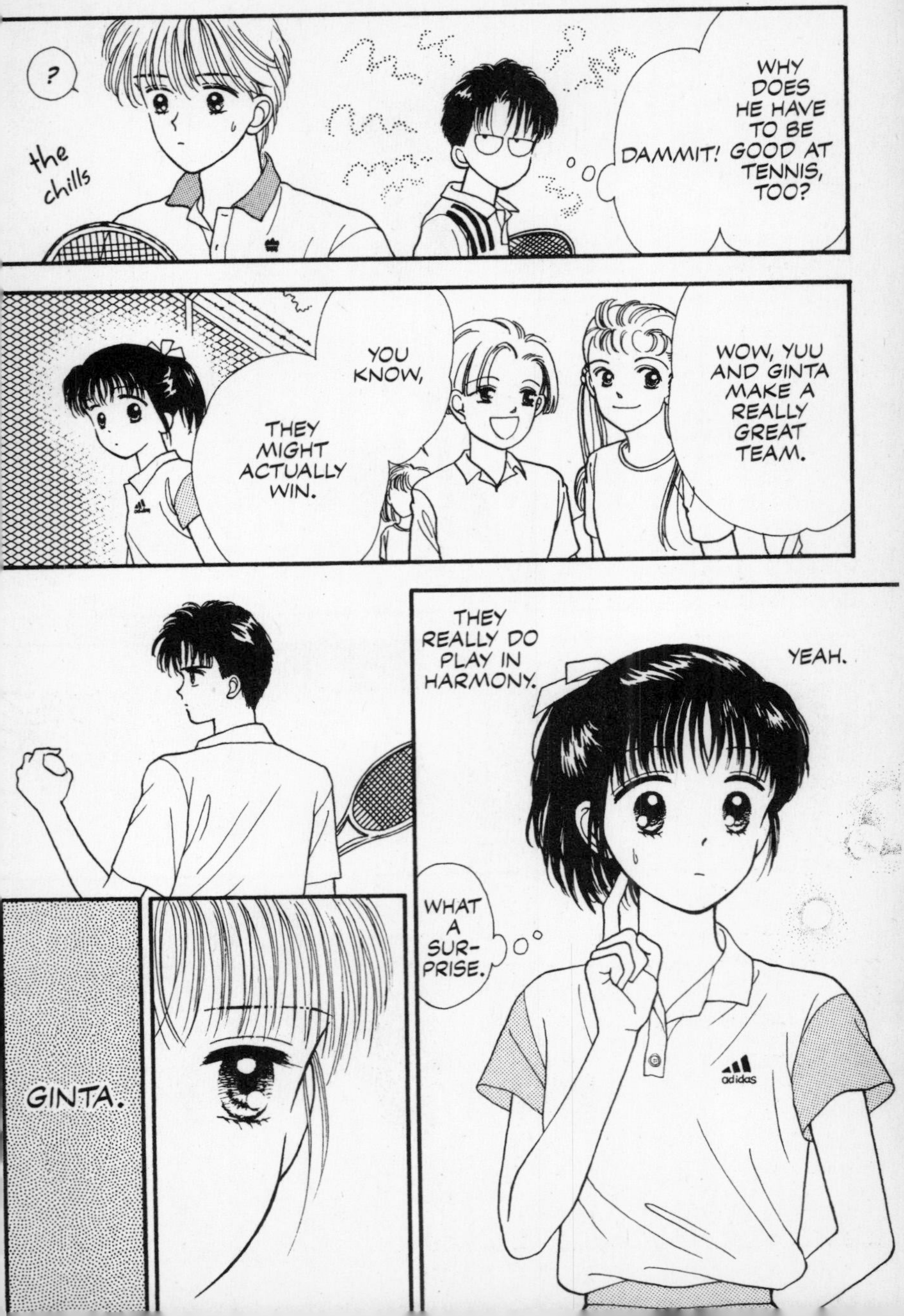
WHY DOES HE HAVE TO BE GOOD AT TENNIS, TOO?
DAMMIT!
?
the chills
WOW, YUU AND GINTA MAKE A REALLY GREAT TEAM.
YOU KNOW,
THEY MIGHT ACTUALLY WIN.
YEAH.
THEY REALLY DO PLAY IN HARMONY.
WHAT A SUR-PRISE.
GINTA.

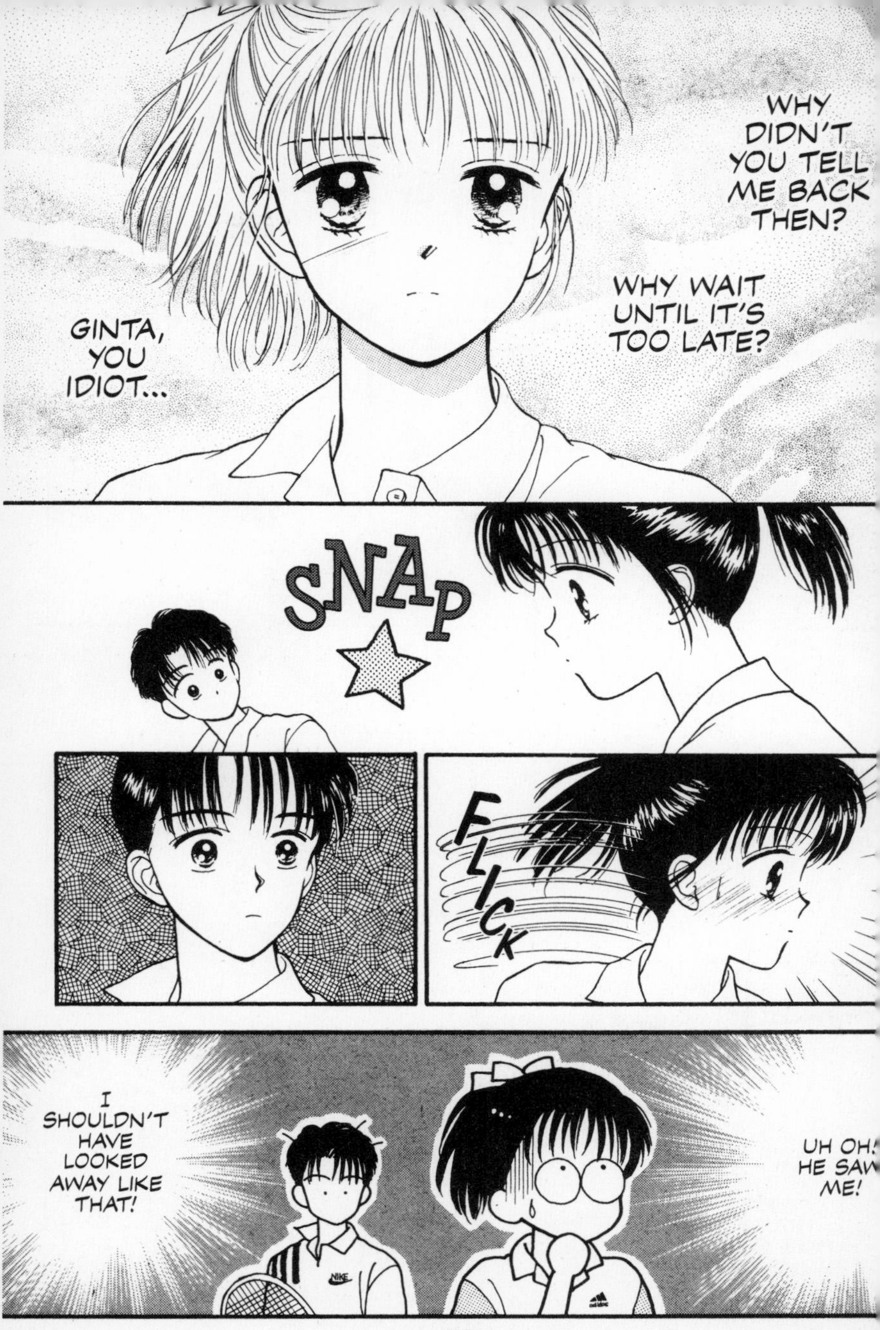
WHY DIDN'T YOU TELL ME BACK THEN?
WHY WAIT UNTIL IT'S TOO LATE?
GINTA, YOU IDIOT...
SNAP
FLICK
UH OH! HE SAW ME!
I SHOULDN'T HAVE LOOKED AWAY LIKE THAT!

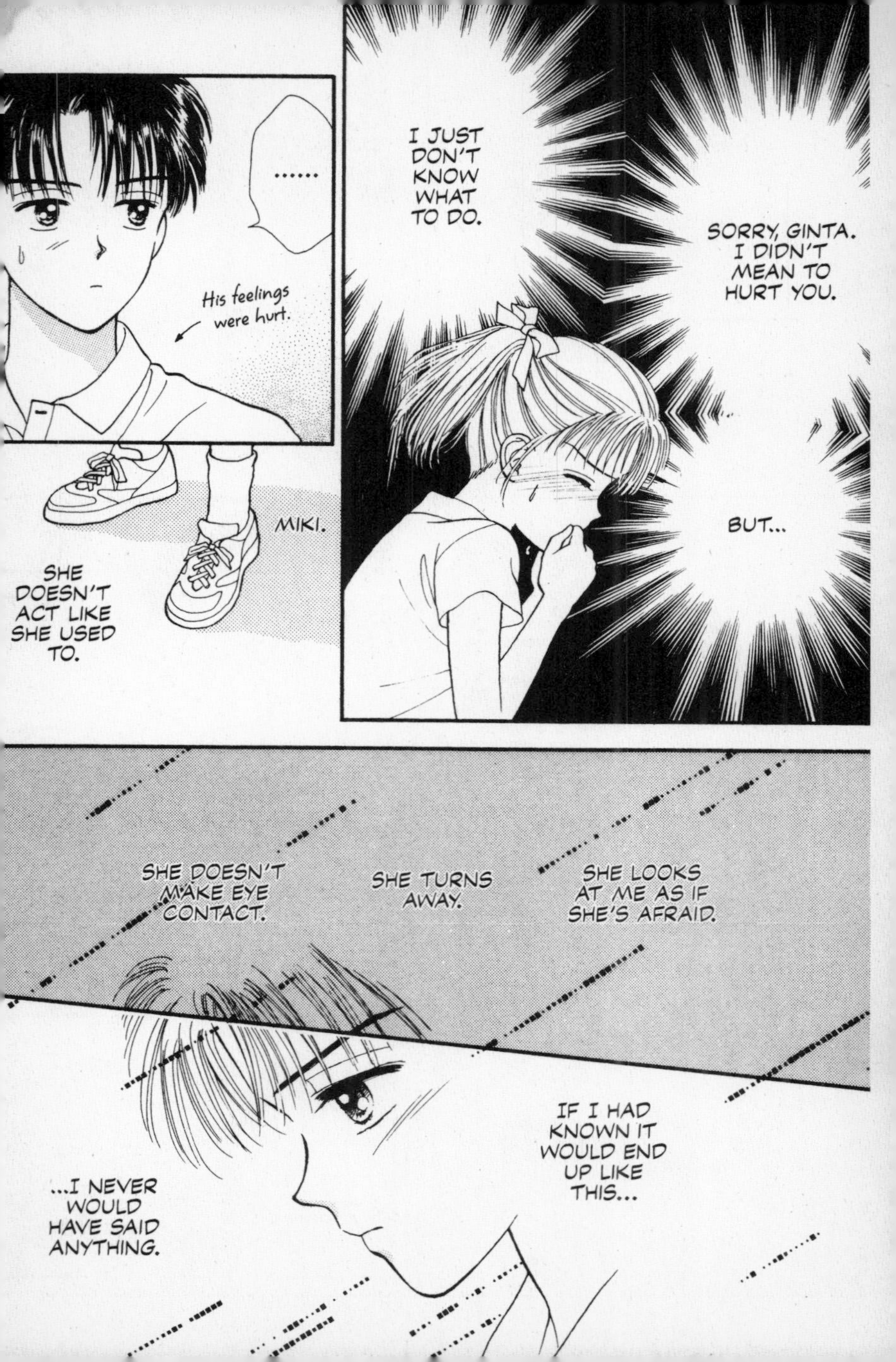
SORRY, GINTA. I DIDN'T MEAN TO HURT YOU.
BUT...
I JUST DON'T KNOW WHAT TO DO.
......
His feelings were hurt.
MIKI.
SHE DOESN'T ACT LIKE SHE USED TO.
SHE LOOKS AT ME AS IF SHE'S AFRAID.
SHE TURNS AWAY.
SHE DOESN'T MAKE EYE CONTACT.
IF I HAD KNOWN IT WOULD END UP LIKE THIS...
...I NEVER WOULD HAVE SAID ANYTHING.

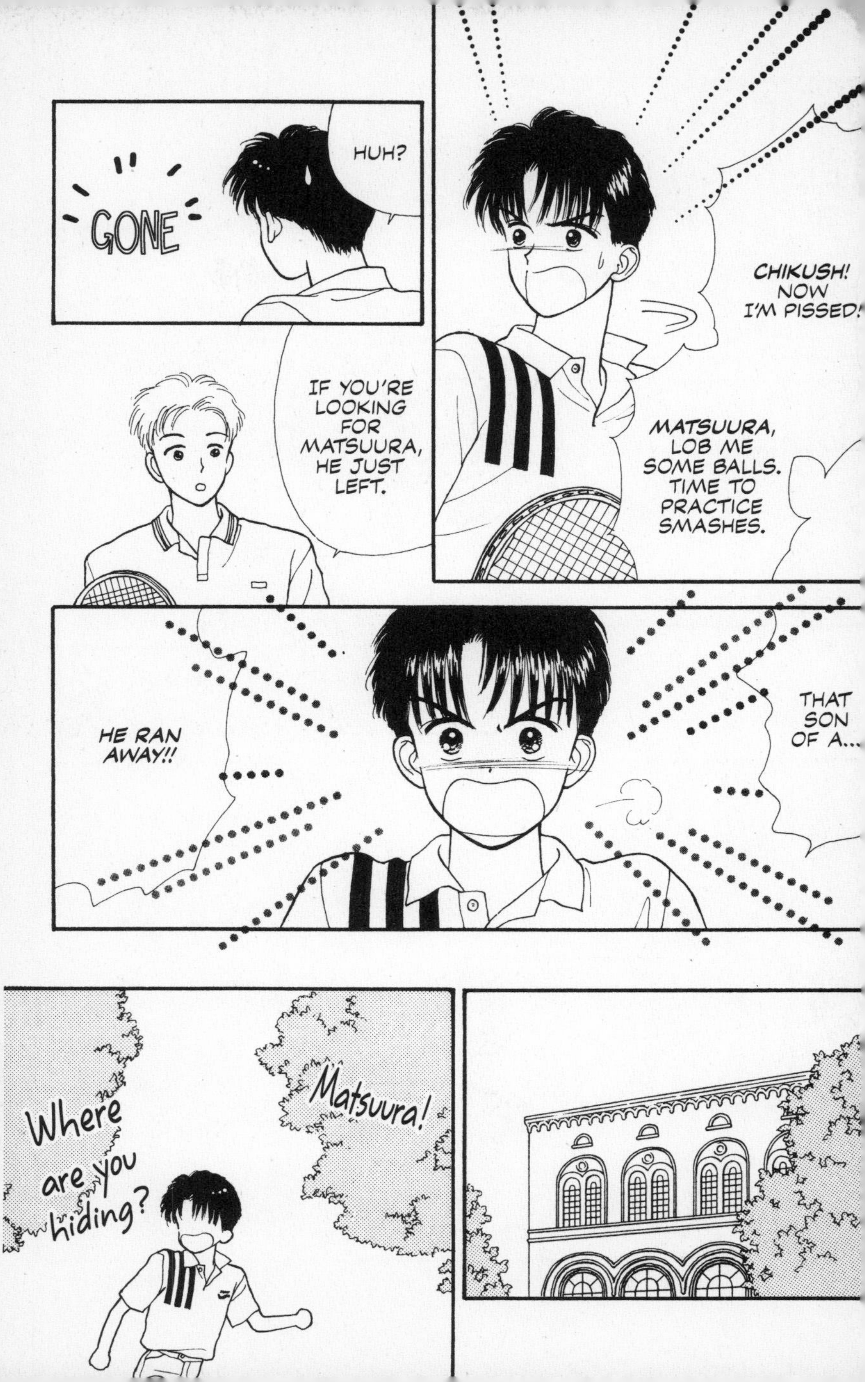
CHIKUSH! NOW I'M PISSED!
MATSUURA, LOB ME SOME BALLS. TIME TO PRACTICE SMASHES.
HUH?
GONE
IF YOU'RE LOOKING FOR MATSUURA, HE JUST LEFT.
THAT SON OF A...
HE RAN AWAY!!
Matsuura!
Where are you hiding?

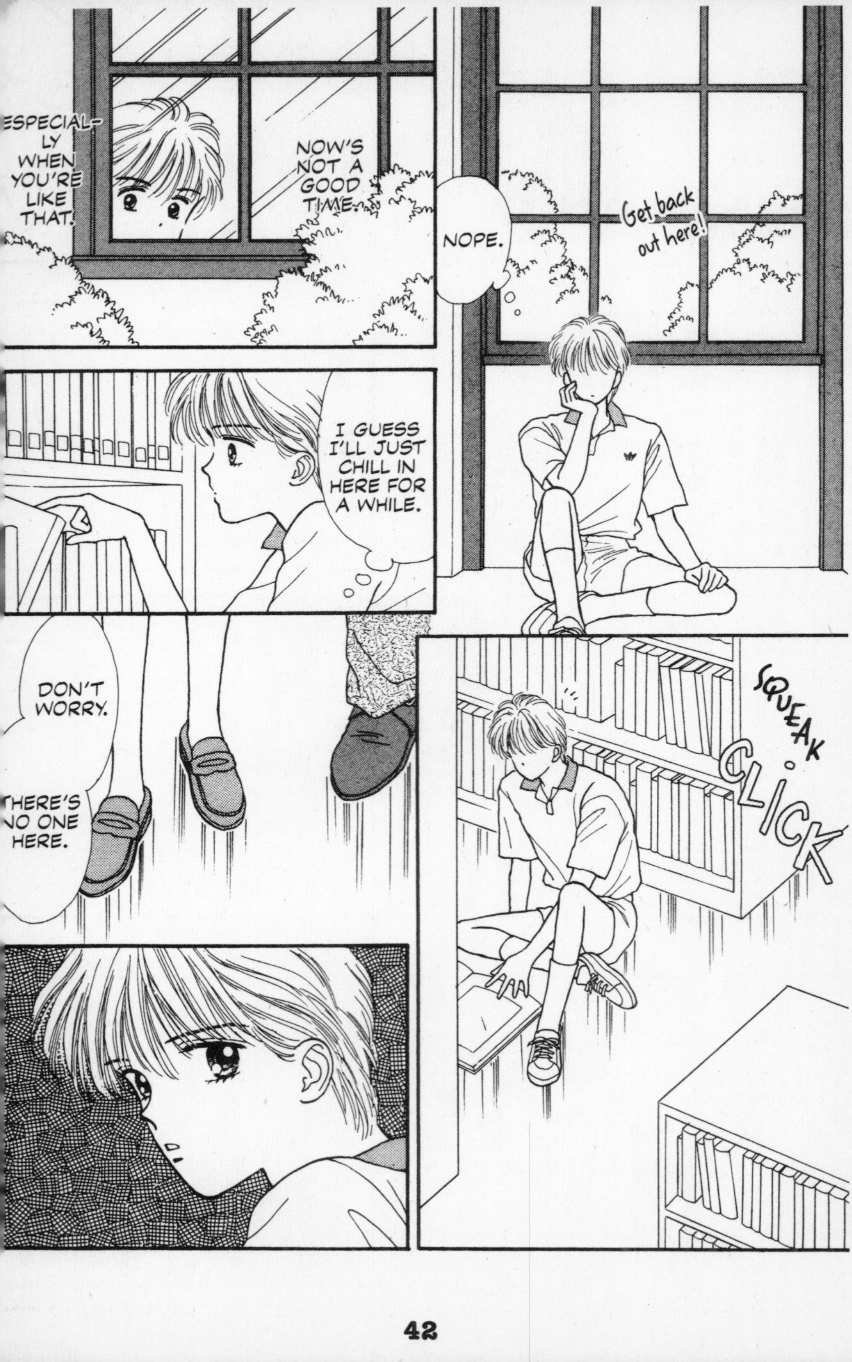

Get back out here!
NOPE.
NOW'S NOT A GOOD TIME.
ESPECIAL-LY WHEN YOU'RE LIKE THAT!
I GUESS I'LL JUST CHILL IN HERE FOR A WHILE.
SQUEAK
CLICK
DON'T WORRY.
THERE'S NO ONE HERE.

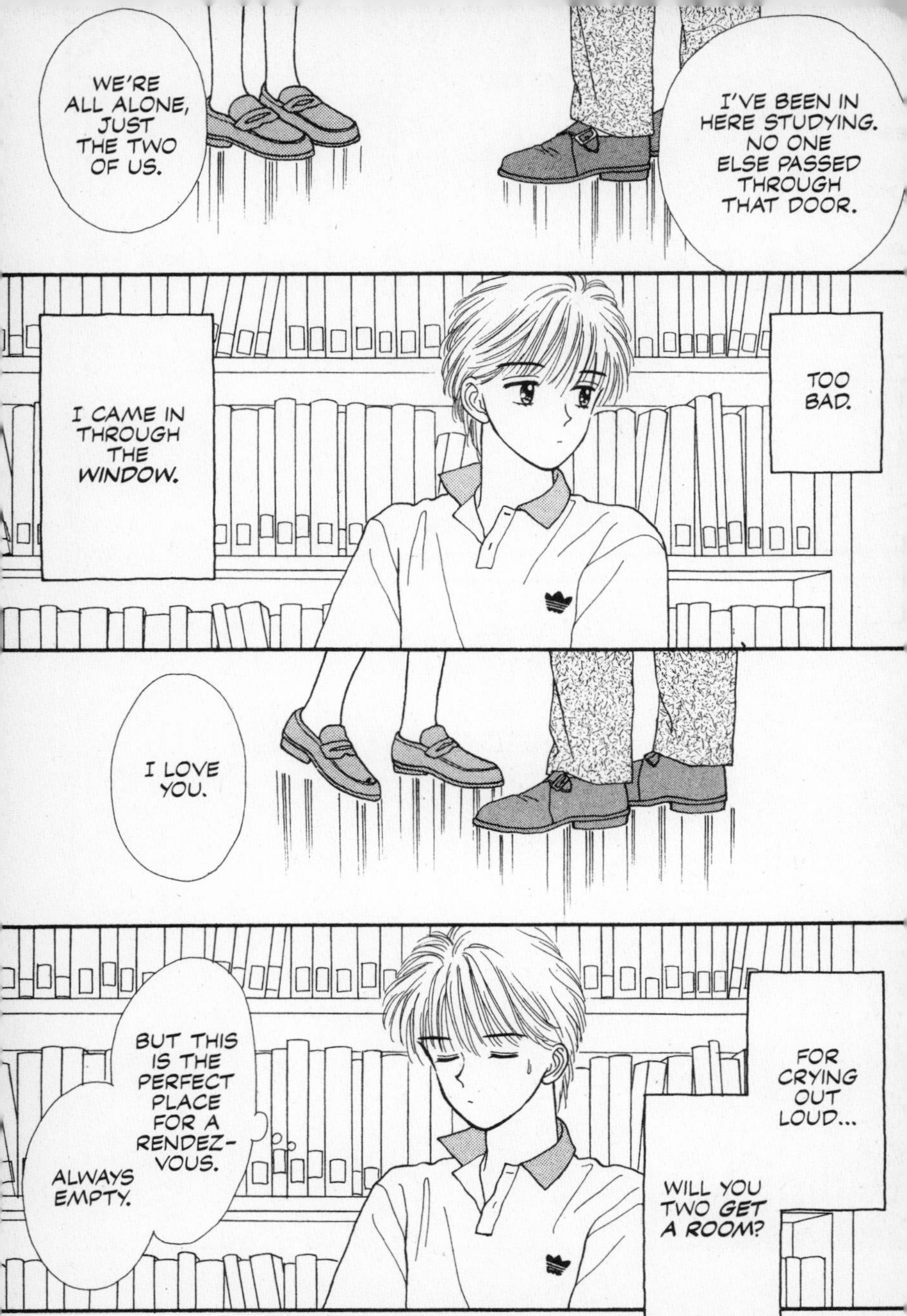
I'VE BEEN IN HERE STUDYING. NO ONE ELSE PASSED THROUGH THAT DOOR.
WE'RE ALL ALONE, JUST THE TWO OF US.
TOO BAD.
I CAME IN THROUGH THE WINDOW.
I LOVE YOU.
FOR CRYING OUT LOUD...
WILL YOU TWO GET A ROOM?
BUT THIS IS THE PERFECT PLACE FOR A RENDEZ-VOUS.
ALWAYS EMPTY.

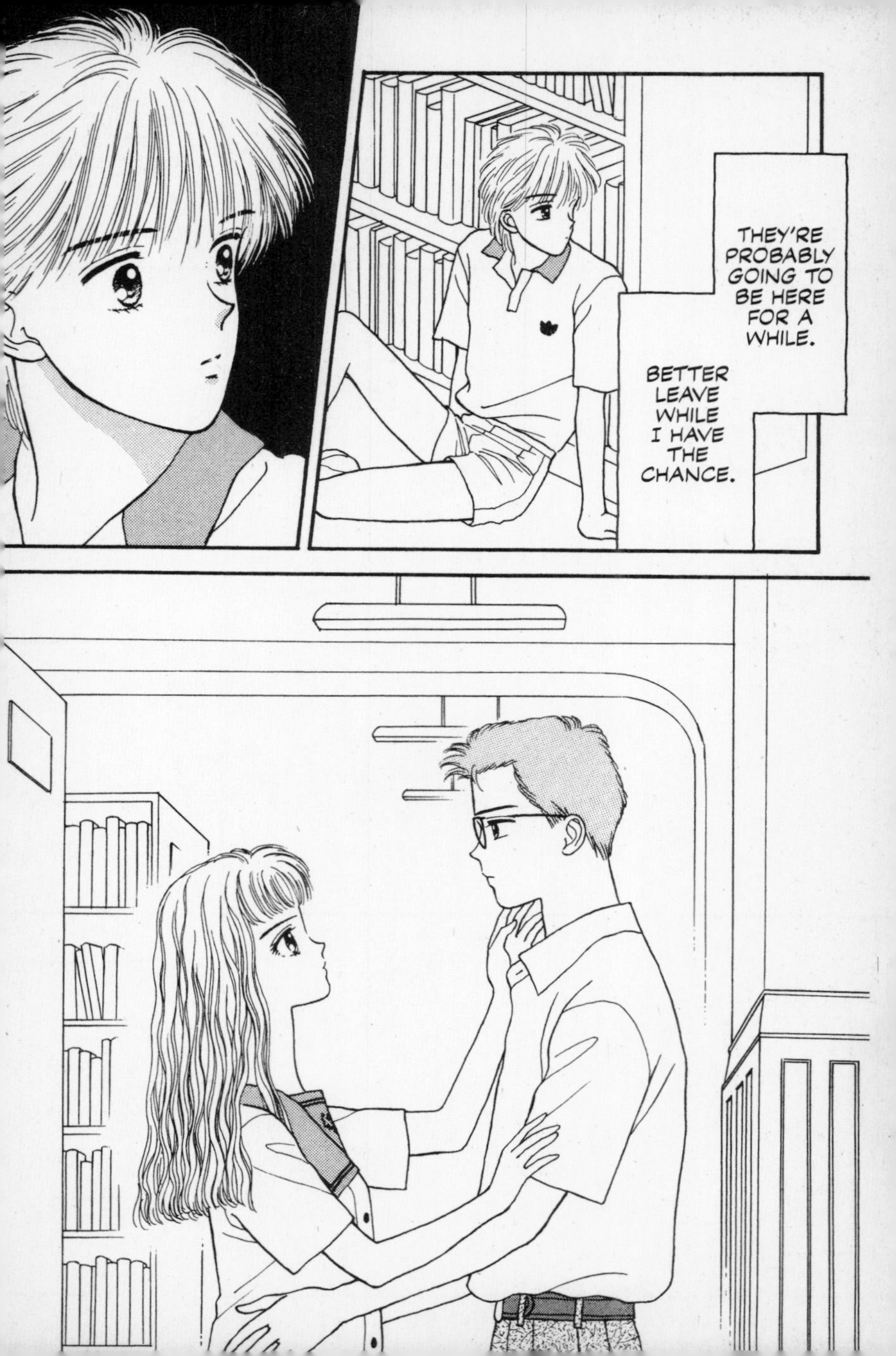
THEY'RE PROBABLY GOING TO BE HERE FOR A WHILE.
BETTER LEAVE WHILE I HAVE THE CHANCE.

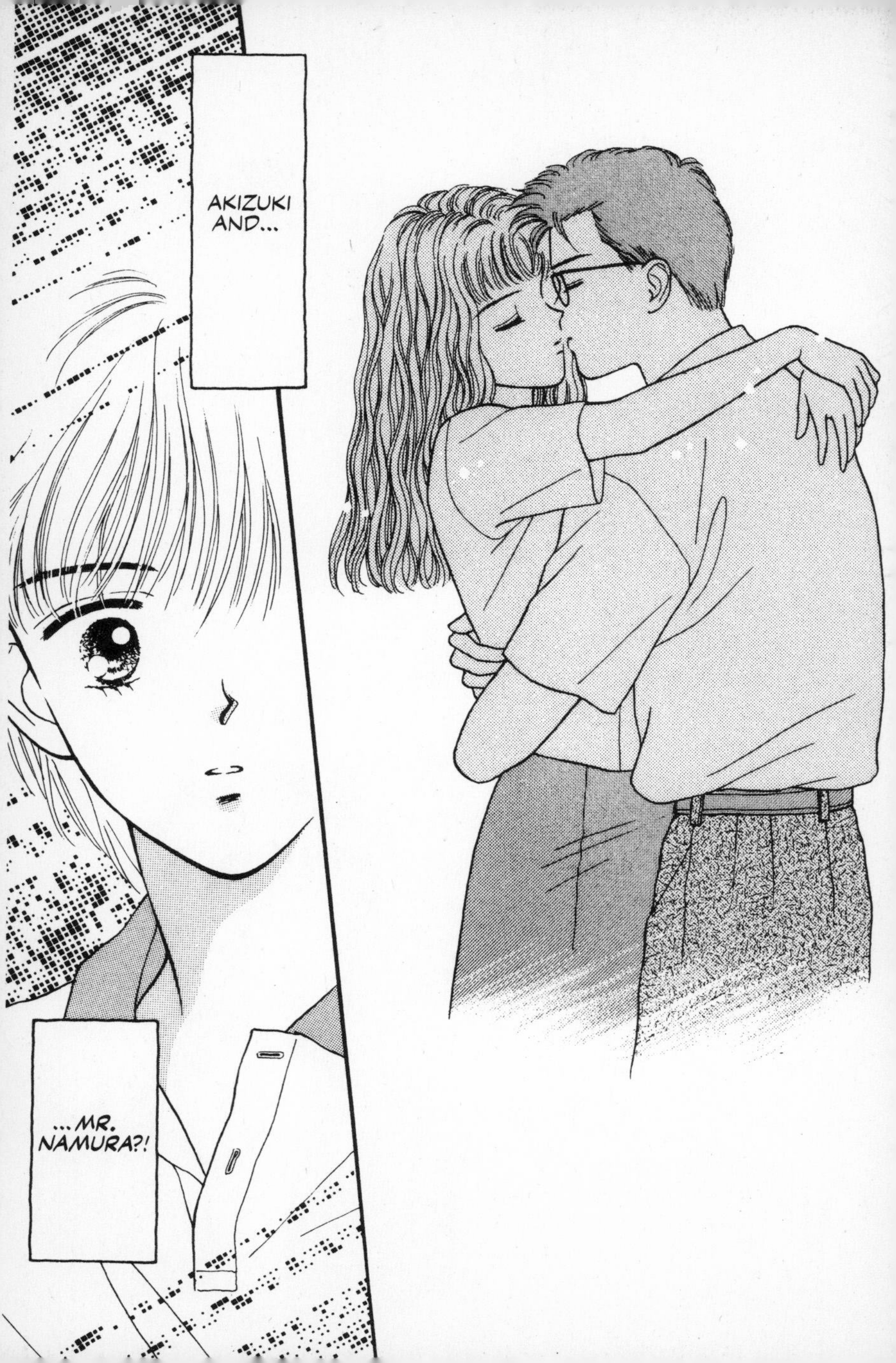
AKIZUKI AND...
...MR. NAMURA?!

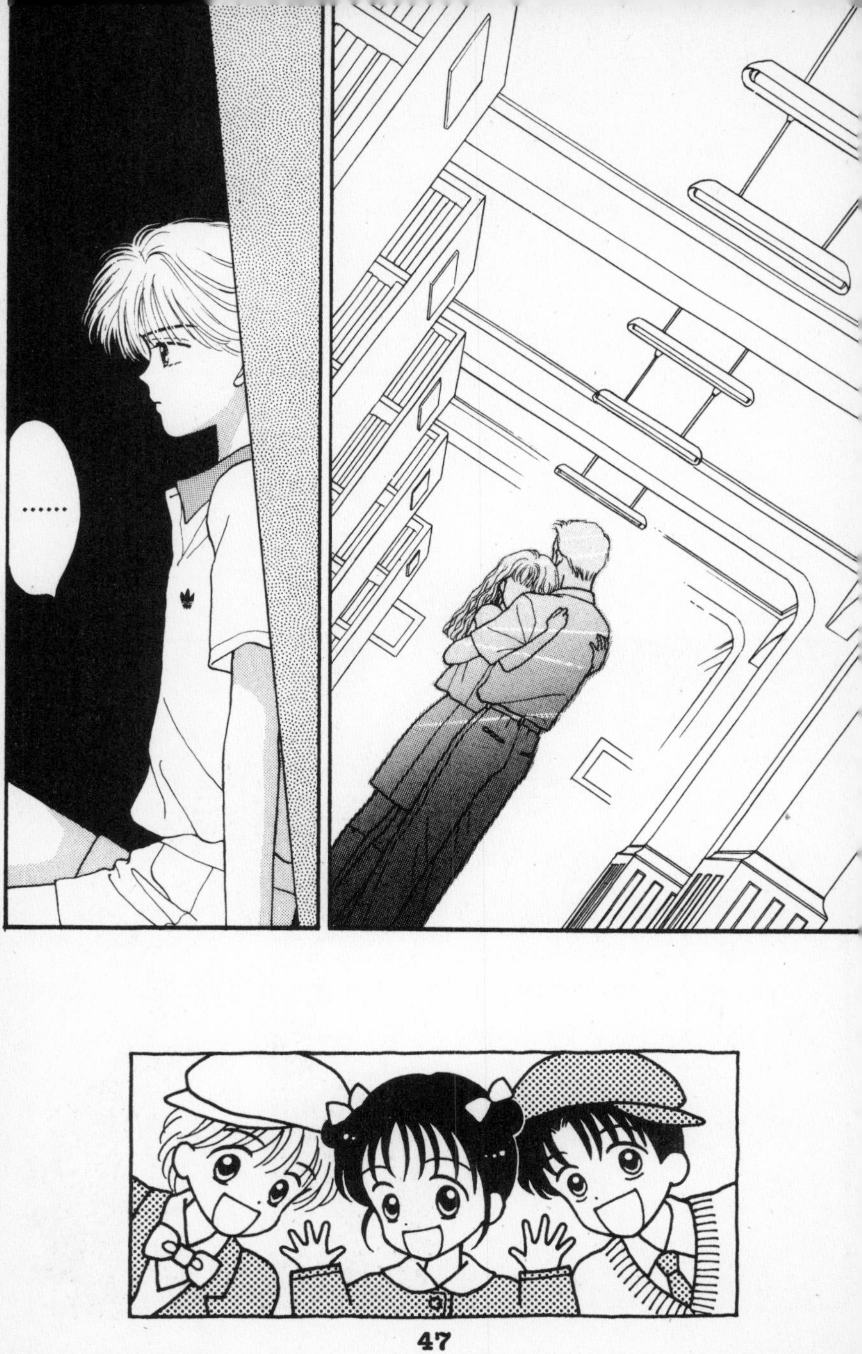
......

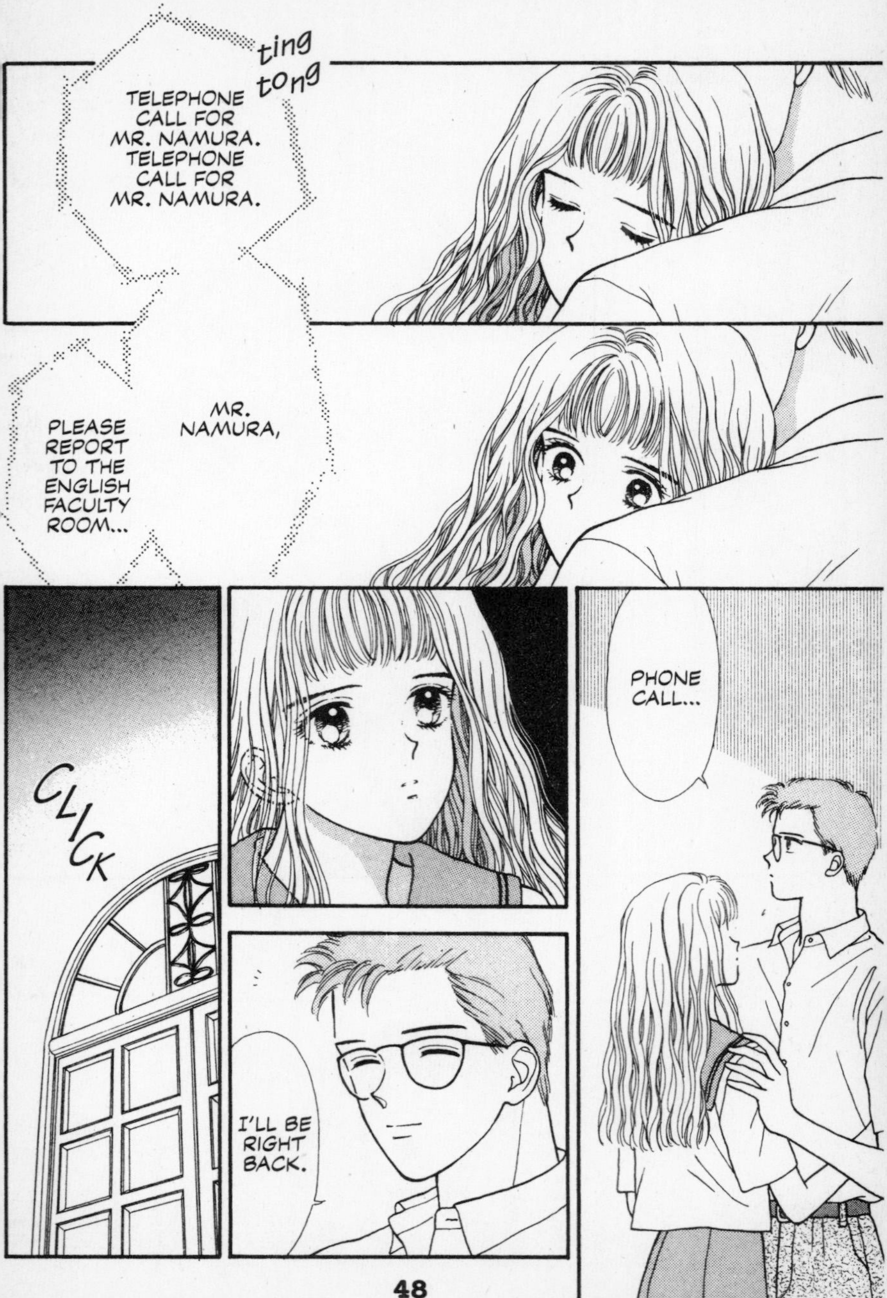
ting tong
TELEPHONE CALL FOR MR. NAMURA. TELEPHONE CALL FOR MR. NAMURA.
MR. NAMURA,
PLEASE REPORT TO THE ENGLISH FACULTY ROOM...
PHONE CALL...
I'LL BE RIGHT BACK.
CLICK

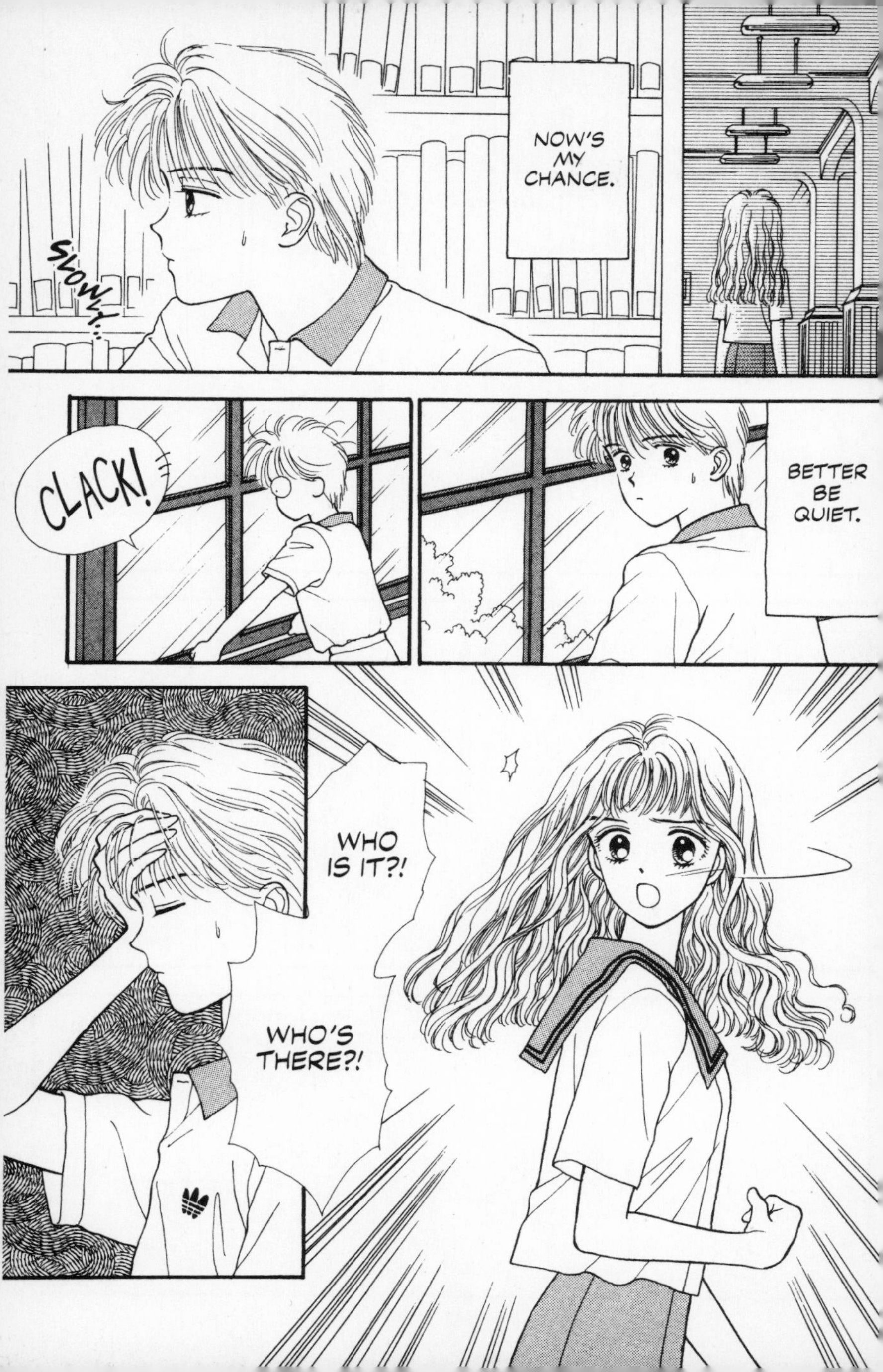
NOW'S MY CHANCE.
SLOWLY...
BETTER BE QUIET.
CLACK!
WHO IS IT?!
WHO'S THERE?!

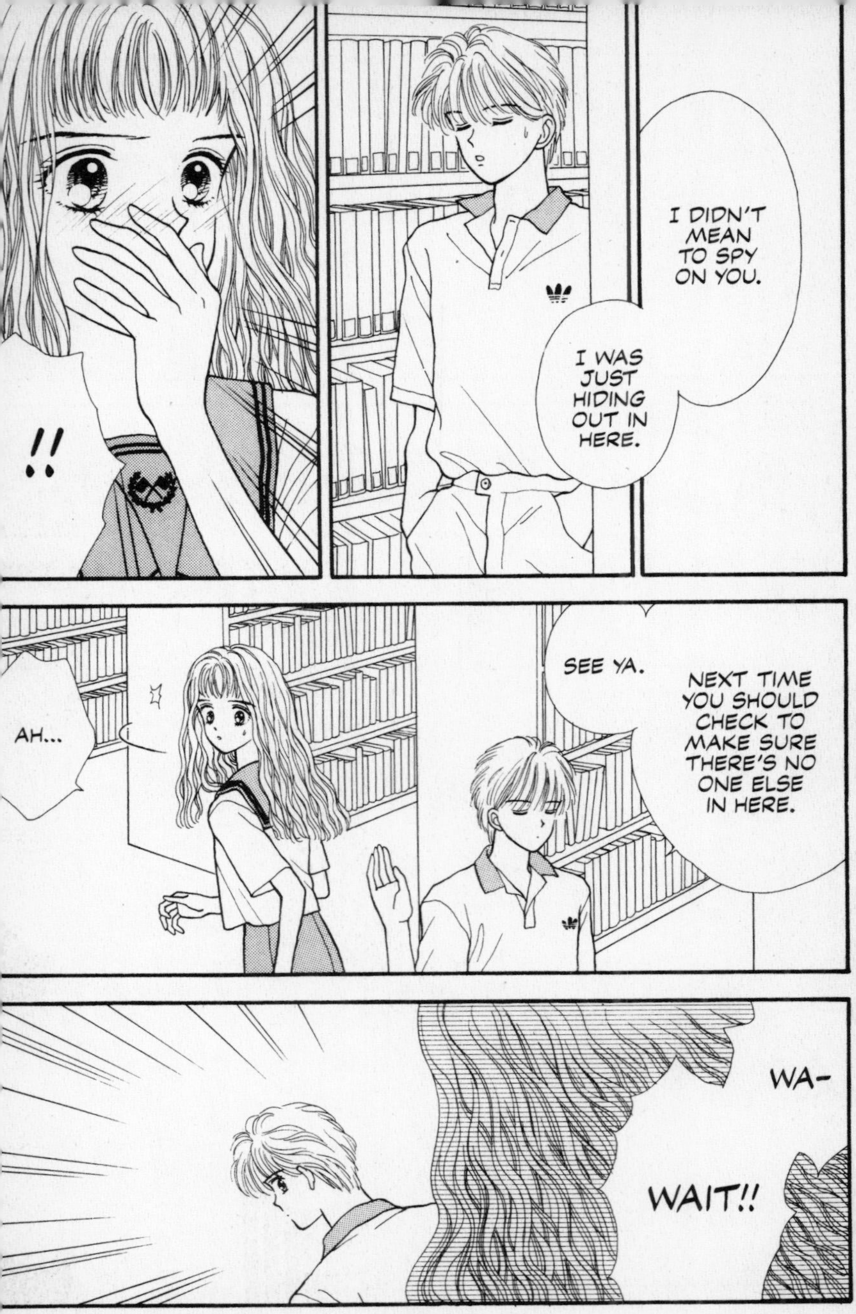
I DIDN'T MEAN TO SPY ON YOU.
I WAS JUST HIDING OUT IN HERE.
!!
NEXT TIME YOU SHOULD CHECK TO MAKE SURE THERE'S NO ONE ELSE IN HERE.
SEE YA.
AH...
WA-
WAIT!!

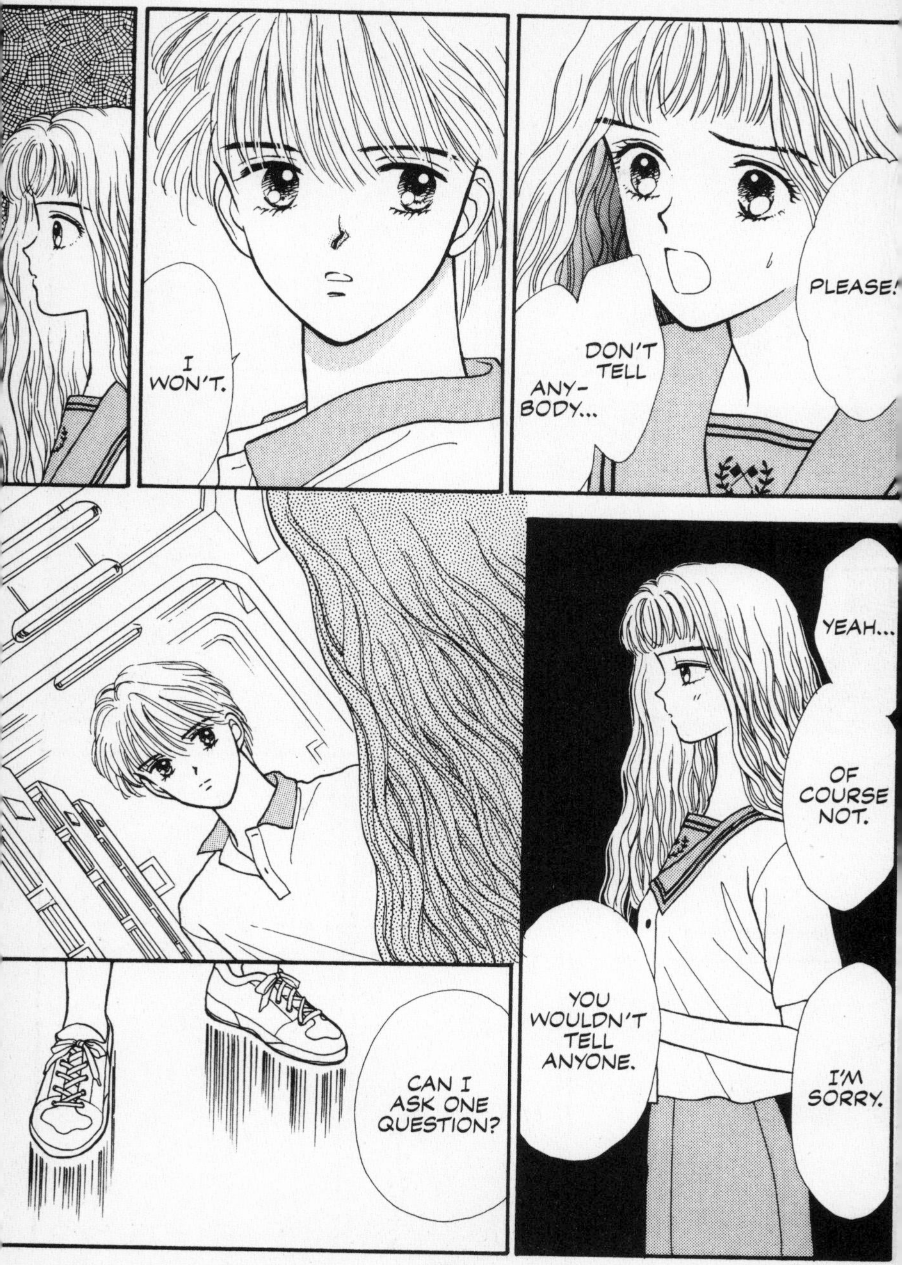
PLEASE!
DON'T TELL ANY-BODY...
I WON'T.
YEAH...
OF COURSE NOT.
YOU WOULDN'T TELL ANYONE.
I'M SORRY.
CAN I ASK ONE QUESTION?

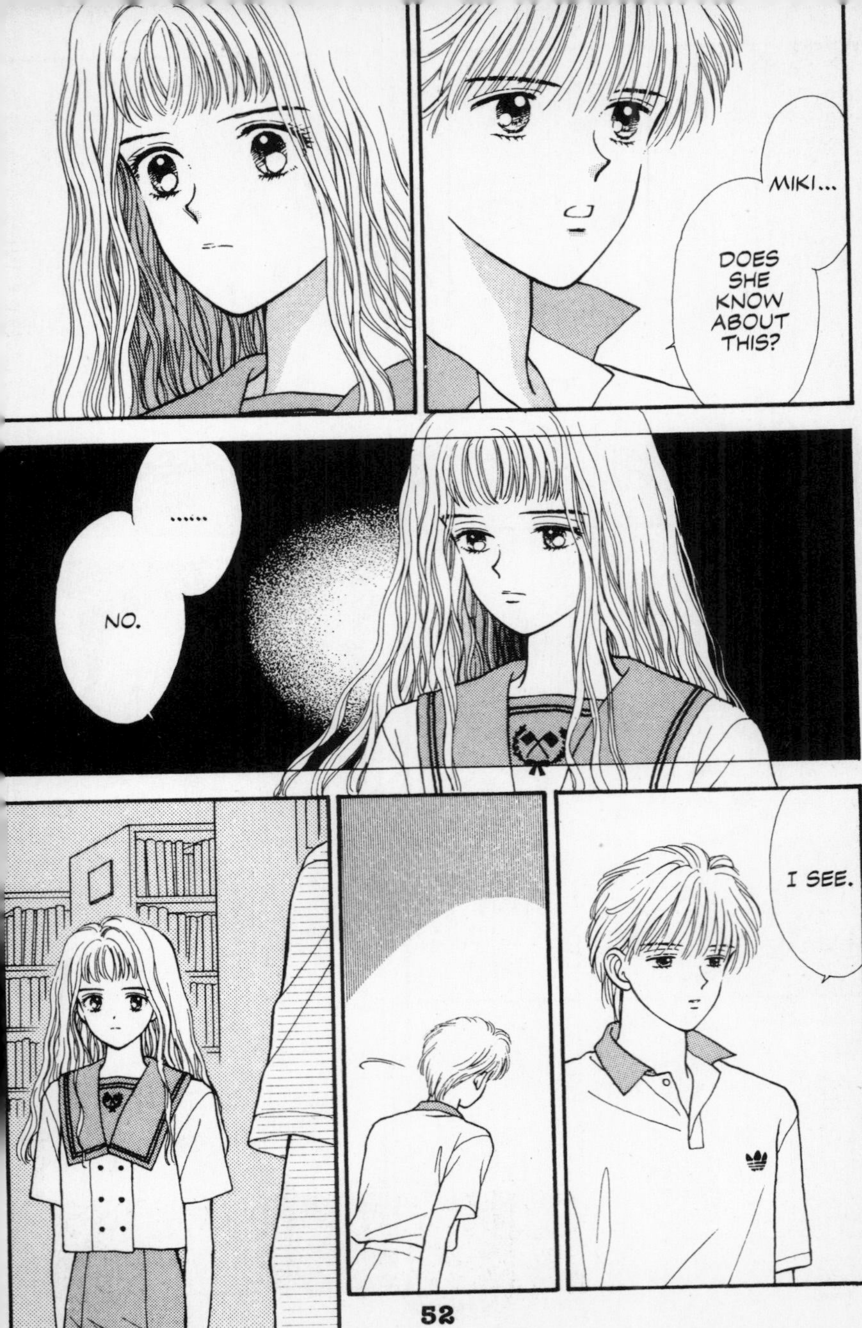
MIKI...
DOES SHE KNOW ABOUT THIS?
......
NO.
I SEE.

FREE TALK ②

This may seem a bit random, but I'm going to talk about gardening for a bit. (Being from Tokyo, I'm drawn to whatever nature I can get!) The other day I bought some flower seeds in a package labeled "Paint With Flowers." It had seeds for at least a dozen different colors of flowers inside. They must be so pretty when they're grown! I liked the idea so much that I got a set for my friend, Ai Yazawa (the manga-ka who does *Paradise Kiss*), since she likes flowers too. The package was an import and I couldn't read the label on how to grow them! I hope that Ai can figure it out and show me how! I also bought some seeds for Forget-Me-Not flowers. But since those are fall flowers, I can't plant them yet. I want to make sure I do it right and I'll take great care of them so they'll bloom into beautiful flowers.

The seeds of the Balloon Flower have a heart on them. Aren't they pretty? A fan gave them to me. I wonder when I'm supposed to plant them...

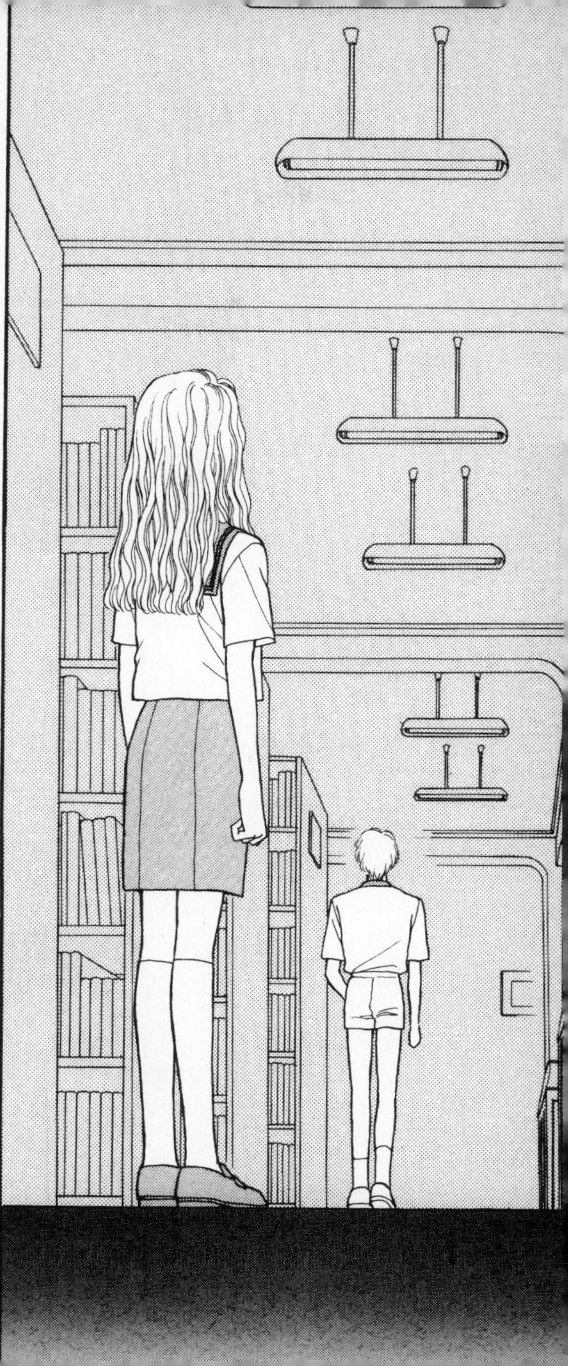

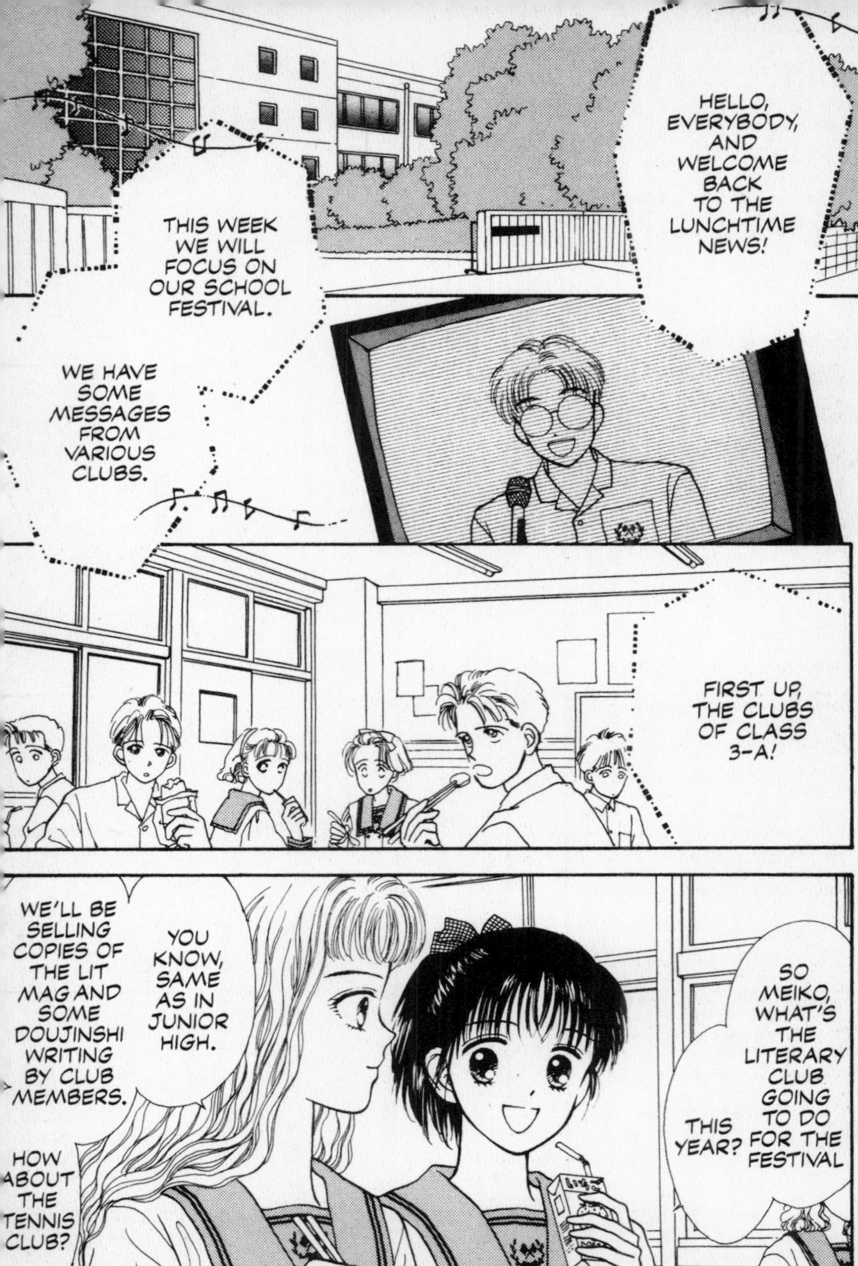
HELLO, EVERYBODY, AND WELCOME BACK TO THE LUNCHTIME NEWS!
THIS WEEK WE WILL FOCUS ON OUR SCHOOL FESTIVAL.
WE HAVE SOME MESSAGES FROM VARIOUS CLUBS.
FIRST UP, THE CLUBS OF CLASS 3-A!
SO MEIKO, WHAT'S THE LITERARY CLUB GOING TO DO FOR THE FESTIVAL THIS YEAR?
YOU KNOW, SAME AS IN JUNIOR HIGH.
WE'LL BE SELLING COPIES OF THE LIT MAG AND SOME DOUJINSHI WRITING BY CLUB MEMBERS.
HOW ABOUT THE TENNIS CLUB?

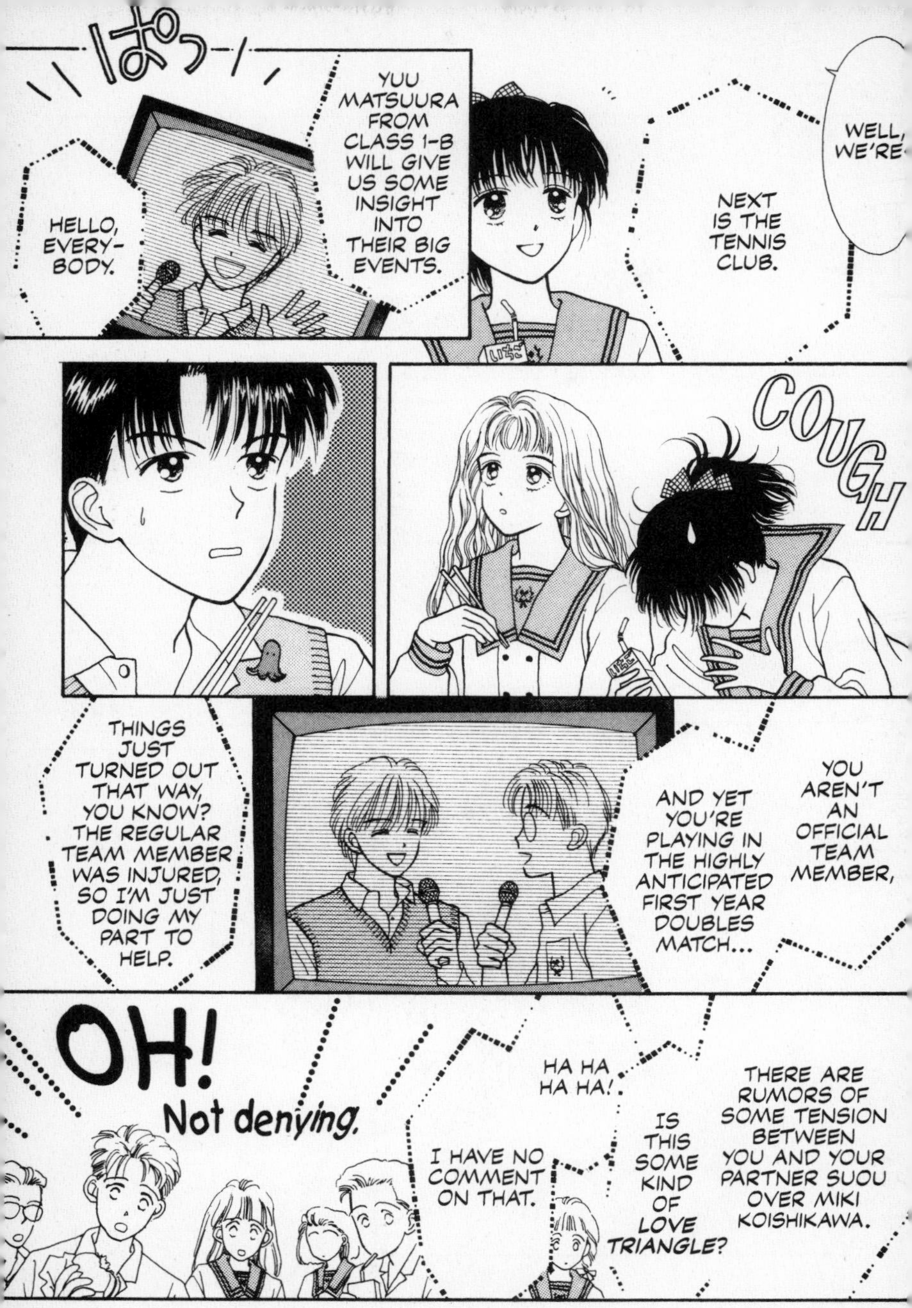
WELL, WE'RE
NEXT IS THE TENNIS CLUB.
YUU MATSUURA FROM CLASS 1-B WILL GIVE US SOME INSIGHT INTO THEIR BIG EVENTS.
ぱっ
HELLO, EVERY-BODY.
COUGH
YOU AREN'T AN OFFICIAL TEAM MEMBER,
AND YET YOU'RE PLAYING IN THE HIGHLY ANTICIPATED FIRST YEAR DOUBLES MATCH...
THINGS JUST TURNED OUT THAT WAY, YOU KNOW? THE REGULAR TEAM MEMBER WAS INJURED, SO I'M JUST DOING MY PART TO HELP.
THERE ARE RUMORS OF SOME TENSION BETWEEN YOU AND YOUR PARTNER SUOU OVER MIKI KOISHIKAWA.
IS THIS SOME KIND OF LOVE TRIANGLE?
HA HA HA HA!
I HAVE NO COMMENT ON THAT.
OH!
Not denying.

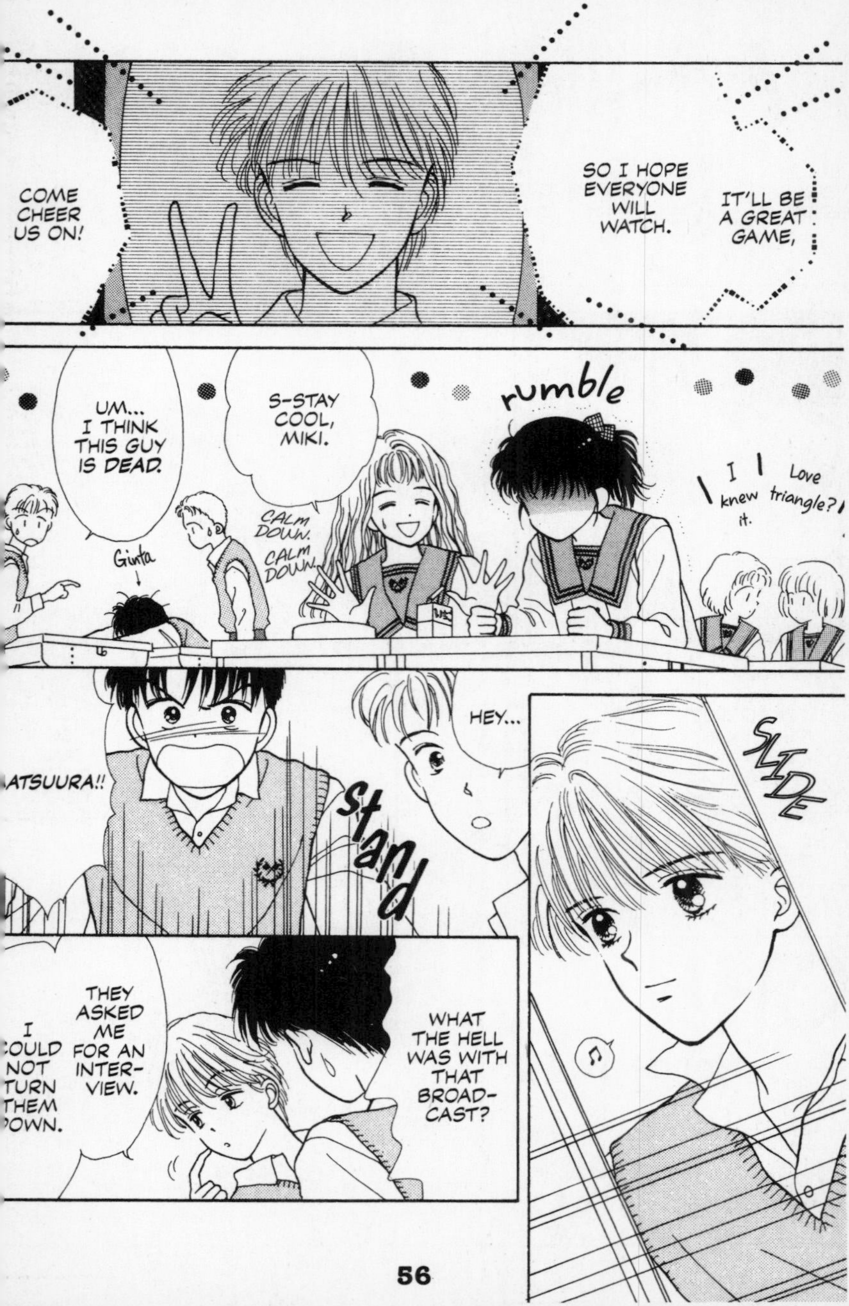

IT'LL BE A GREAT GAME,
SO I HOPE EVERYONE WILL WATCH.
COME CHEER US ON!
I knew it.
Love triangle?
rumble
S-STAY COOL, MIKI.
CALM DOWN. CALM DOWN.
UM... I THINK THIS GUY IS DEAD.
Ginta
SLIDE
HEY...
stand
ATSUURA!!
WHAT THE HELL WAS WITH THAT BROADCAST?
THEY ASKED ME FOR AN INTER-VIEW.
I COULD NOT TURN THEM DOWN.

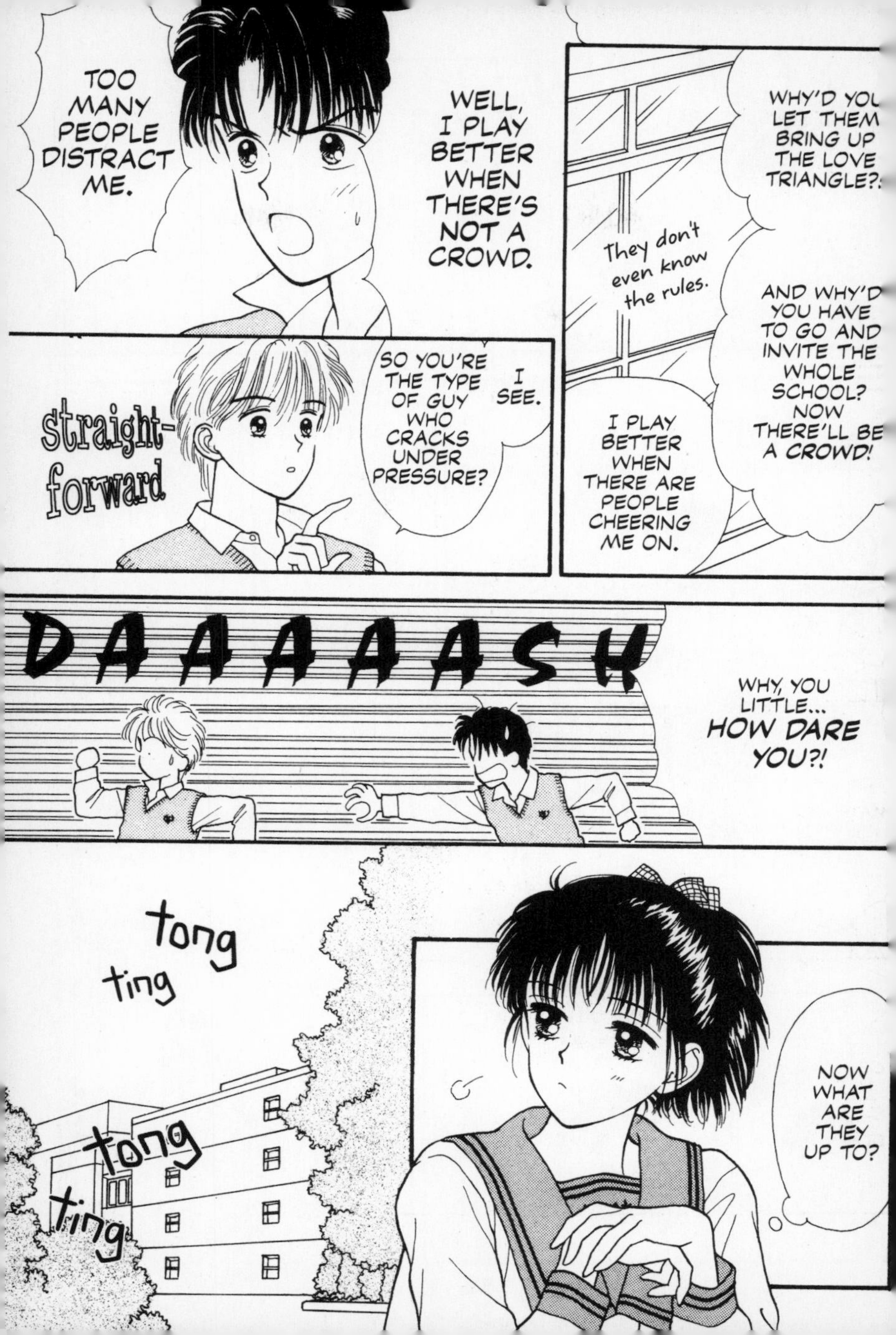
WHY'D YOU LET THEM BRING UP THE LOVE TRIANGLE?!
AND WHY'D YOU HAVE TO GO AND INVITE THE WHOLE SCHOOL? NOW THERE'LL BE A CROWD!
They don't even know the rules.
I PLAY BETTER WHEN THERE ARE PEOPLE CHEERING ME ON.
WELL, I PLAY BETTER WHEN THERE'S NOT A CROWD.
TOO MANY PEOPLE DISTRACT ME.
I SEE.
SO YOU'RE THE TYPE OF GUY WHO CRACKS UNDER PRESSURE?
straight-forward
WHY, YOU LITTLE... HOW DARE YOU?!
DAAAAASH
NOW WHAT ARE THEY UP TO?
tong
ting
tong
ting

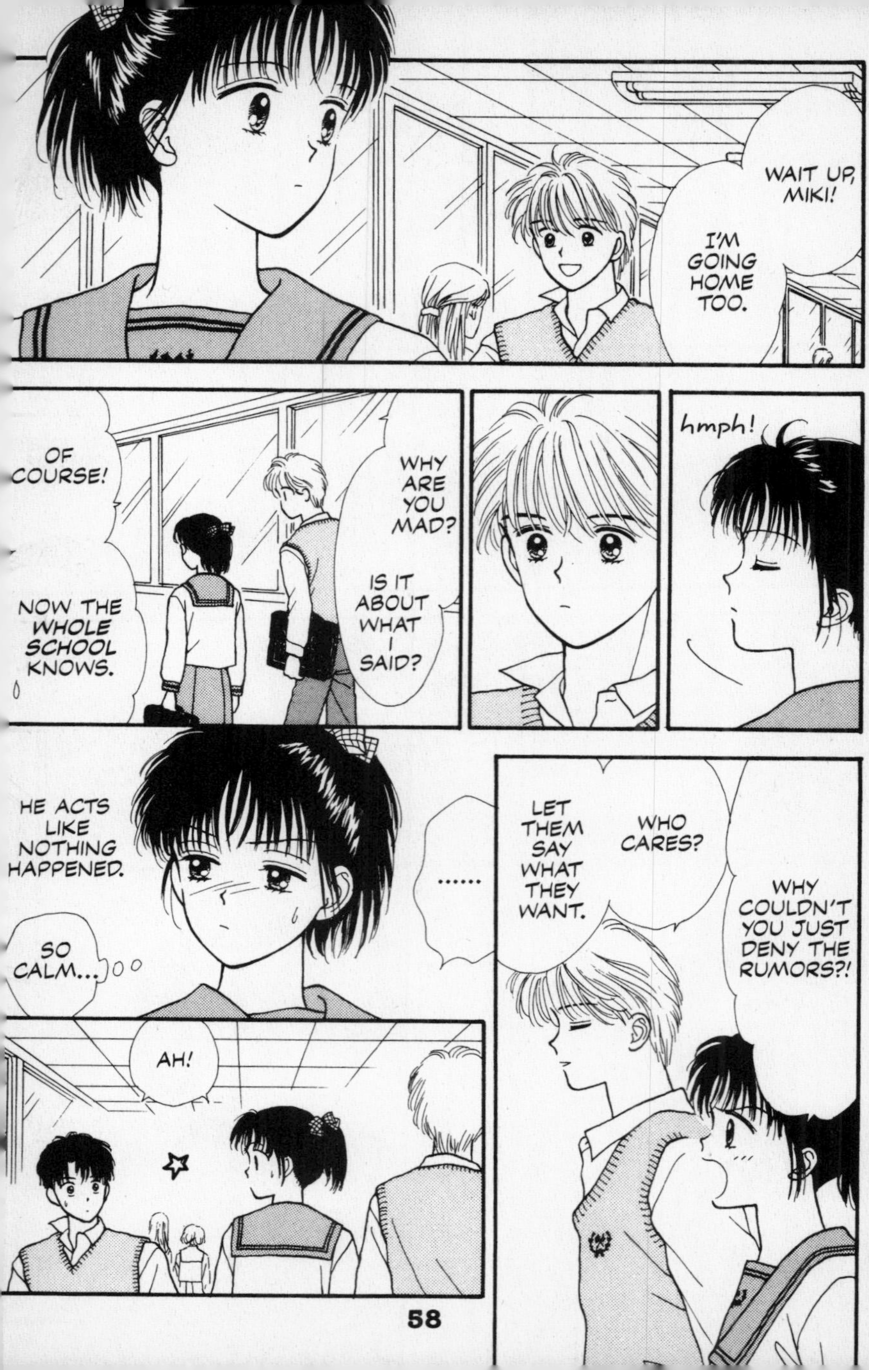
WAIT UP, MIKI!
I'M GOING HOME TOO.
hmph!
WHY ARE YOU MAD?
IS IT ABOUT WHAT I SAID?
OF COURSE!
NOW THE WHOLE SCHOOL KNOWS.
WHY COULDN'T YOU JUST DENY THE RUMORS?!
WHO CARES?
LET THEM SAY WHAT THEY WANT.
......
HE ACTS LIKE NOTHING HAPPENED.
SO CALM...
AH!

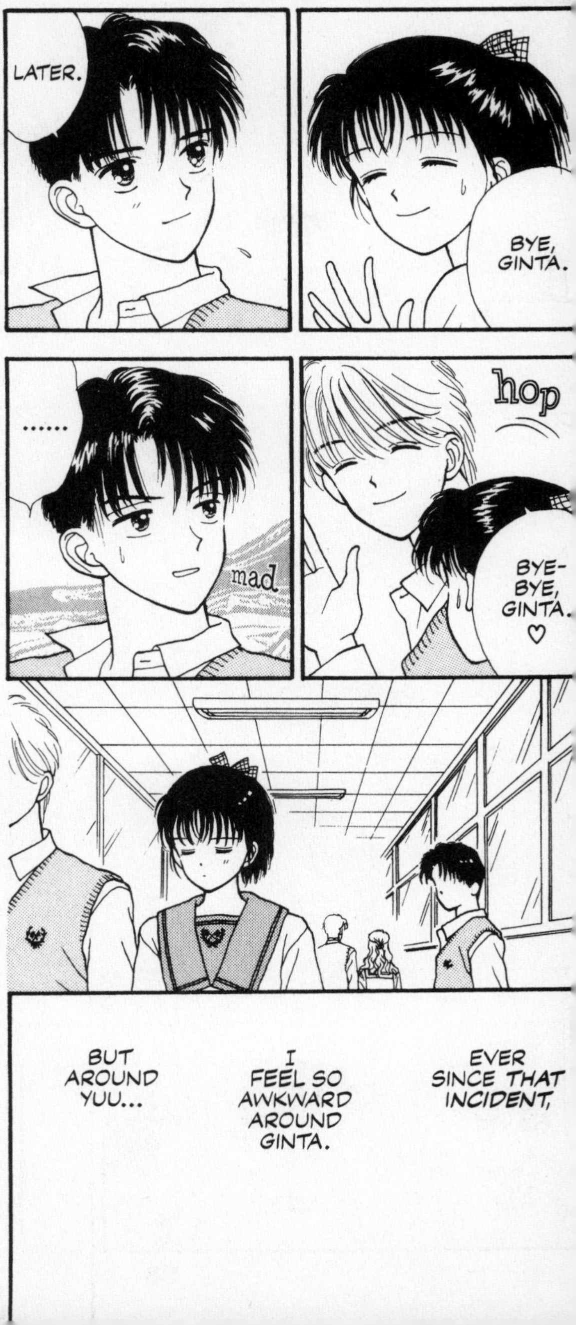
BYE, GINTA.
LATER.
hop
BYE-BYE, GINTA. ♡
......
mad
EVER SINCE THAT INCIDENT,
I FEEL SO AWKWARD AROUND GINTA.
BUT AROUND YUU...
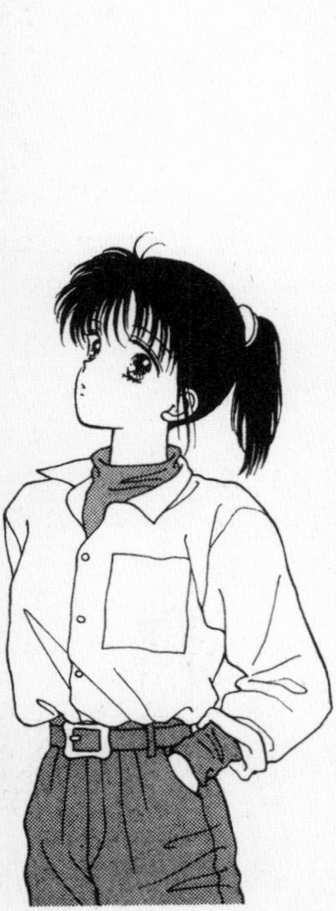

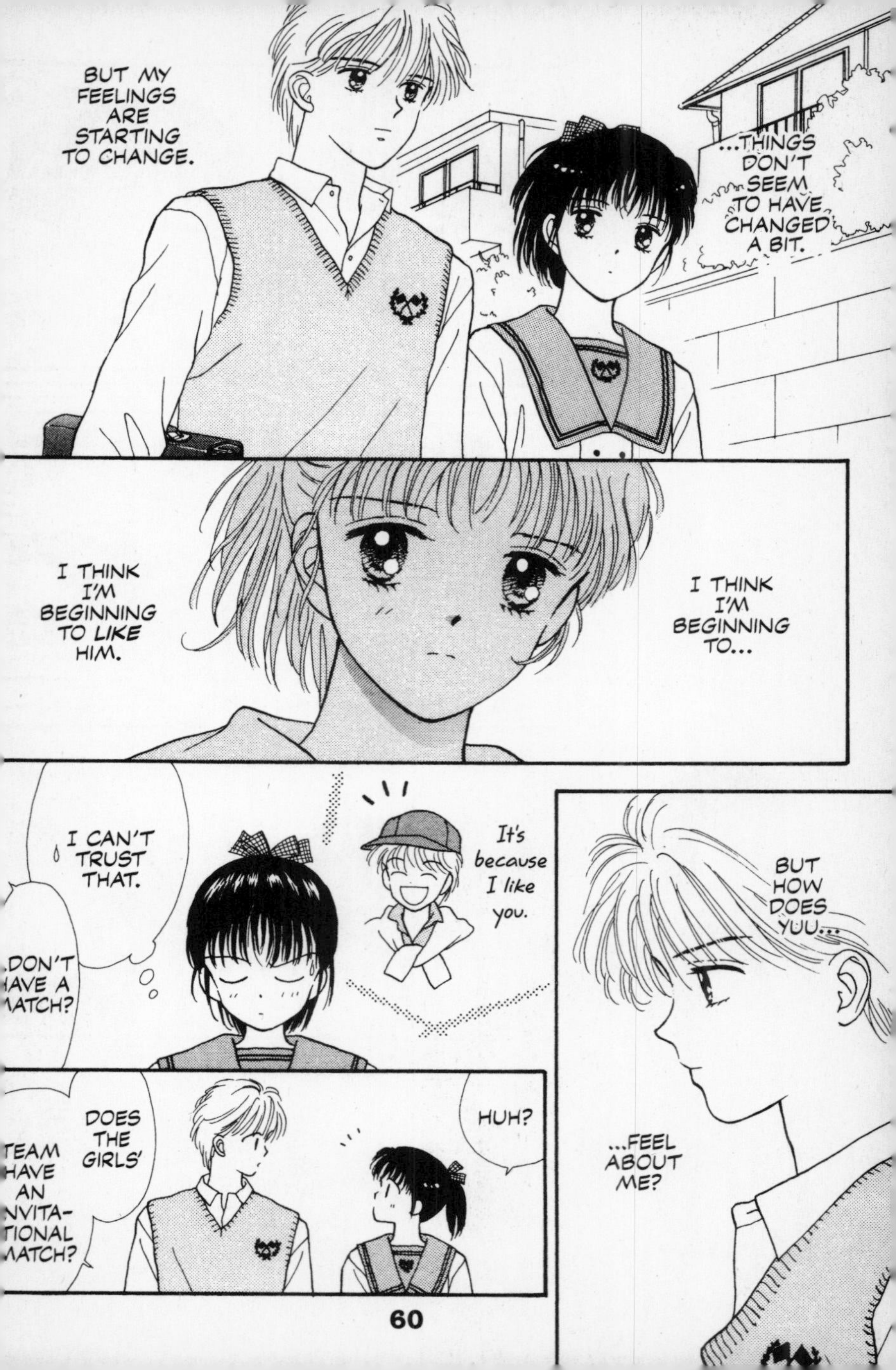
...THINGS DON'T SEEM TO HAVE CHANGED A BIT.
BUT MY FEELINGS ARE STARTING TO CHANGE.
I THINK I'M BEGINNING TO...
I THINK I'M BEGINNING TO LIKE HIM.
BUT HOW DOES YUU...
...FEEL ABOUT ME?
It's because I like you.
I CAN'T TRUST THAT.
.DON'T HAVE A MATCH?
HUH?
DOES THE GIRLS' TEAM HAVE AN NVITA-TIONAL MATCH?

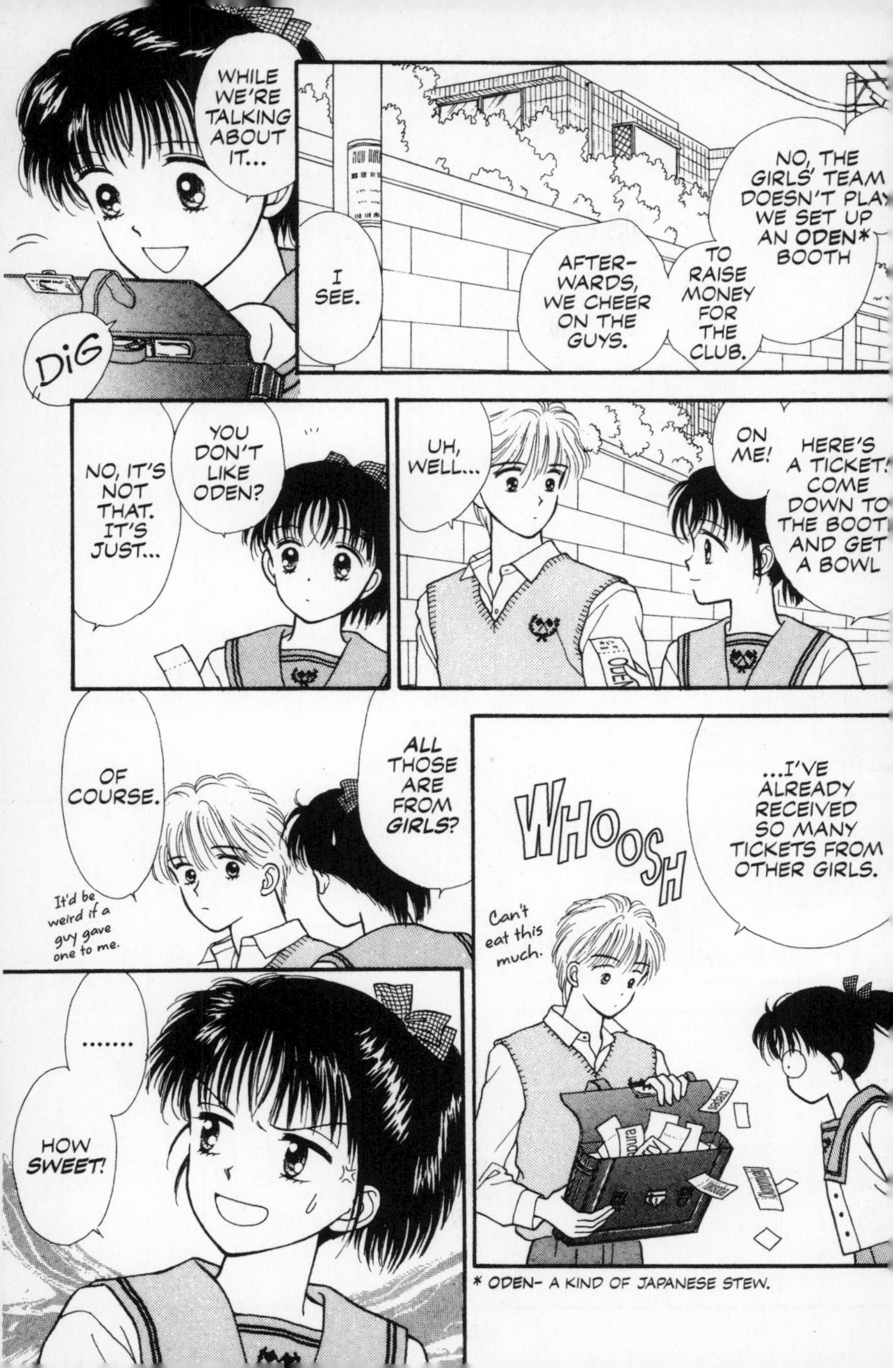
NO, THE GIRLS' TEAM DOESN'T PLA WE SET UP AN ODEN* BOOTH
TO RAISE MONEY FOR THE CLUB.
AFTER-WARDS, WE CHEER ON THE GUYS.
I SEE.
WHILE WE'RE TALKING ABOUT IT...
DiG
HERE'S A TICKET COME DOWN TO THE BOOT AND GET A BOWL
ON ME!
UH, WELL...
YOU DON'T LIKE ODEN?
NO, IT'S NOT THAT. IT'S JUST...
...I'VE ALREADY RECEIVED SO MANY TICKETS FROM OTHER GIRLS.
WHOOSH
Can't eat this much.
ALL THOSE ARE FROM GIRLS?
OF COURSE.
It'd be weird if a guy gave one to me.
....
HOW SWEET!

* ODEN- A KIND OF JAPANESE STEW.

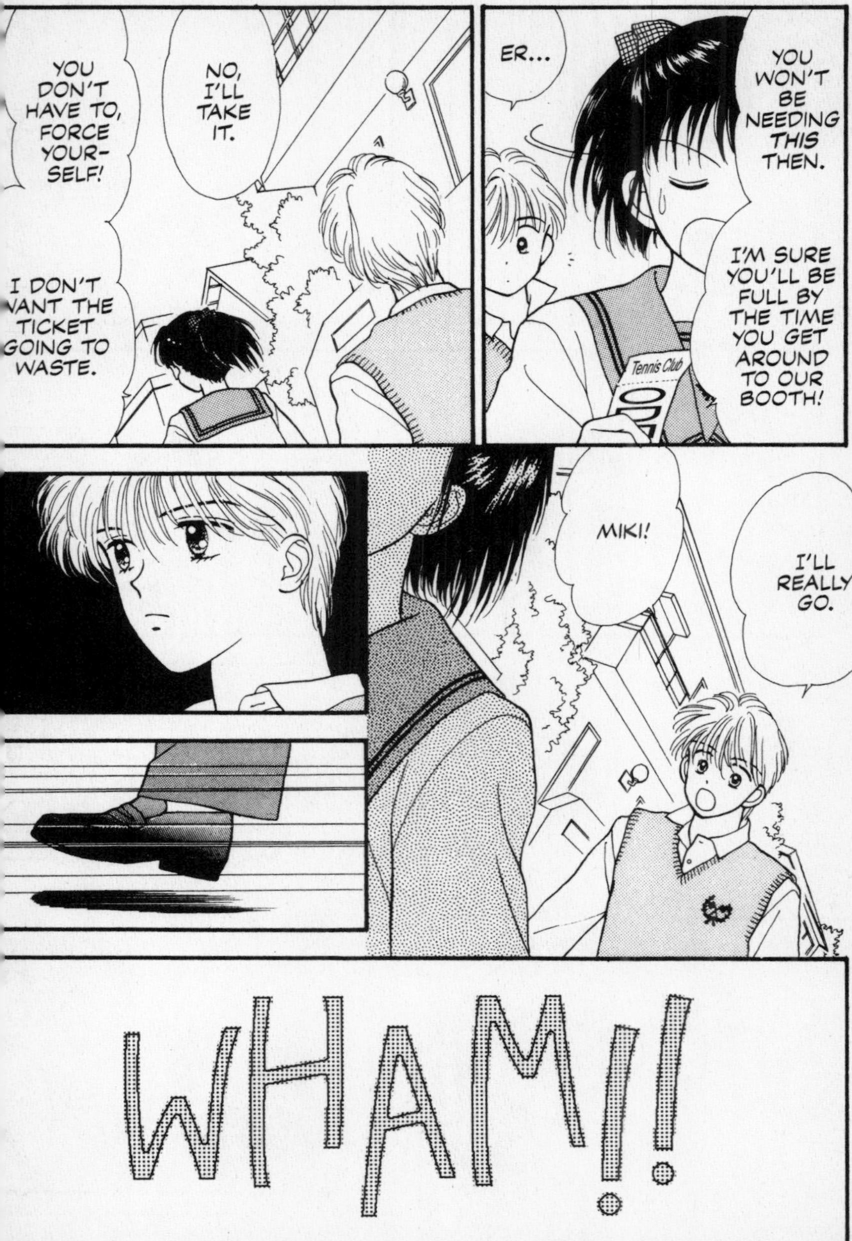
YOU WON'T BE NEEDING THIS THEN.
I'M SURE YOU'LL BE FULL BY THE TIME YOU GET AROUND TO OUR BOOTH!
Tennis Club
ER...
NO, I'LL TAKE IT.
YOU DON'T HAVE TO, FORCE YOURSELF!
I DON'T WANT THE TICKET GOING TO WASTE.
I'LL REALLY GO.
MIKI!
WHAM!

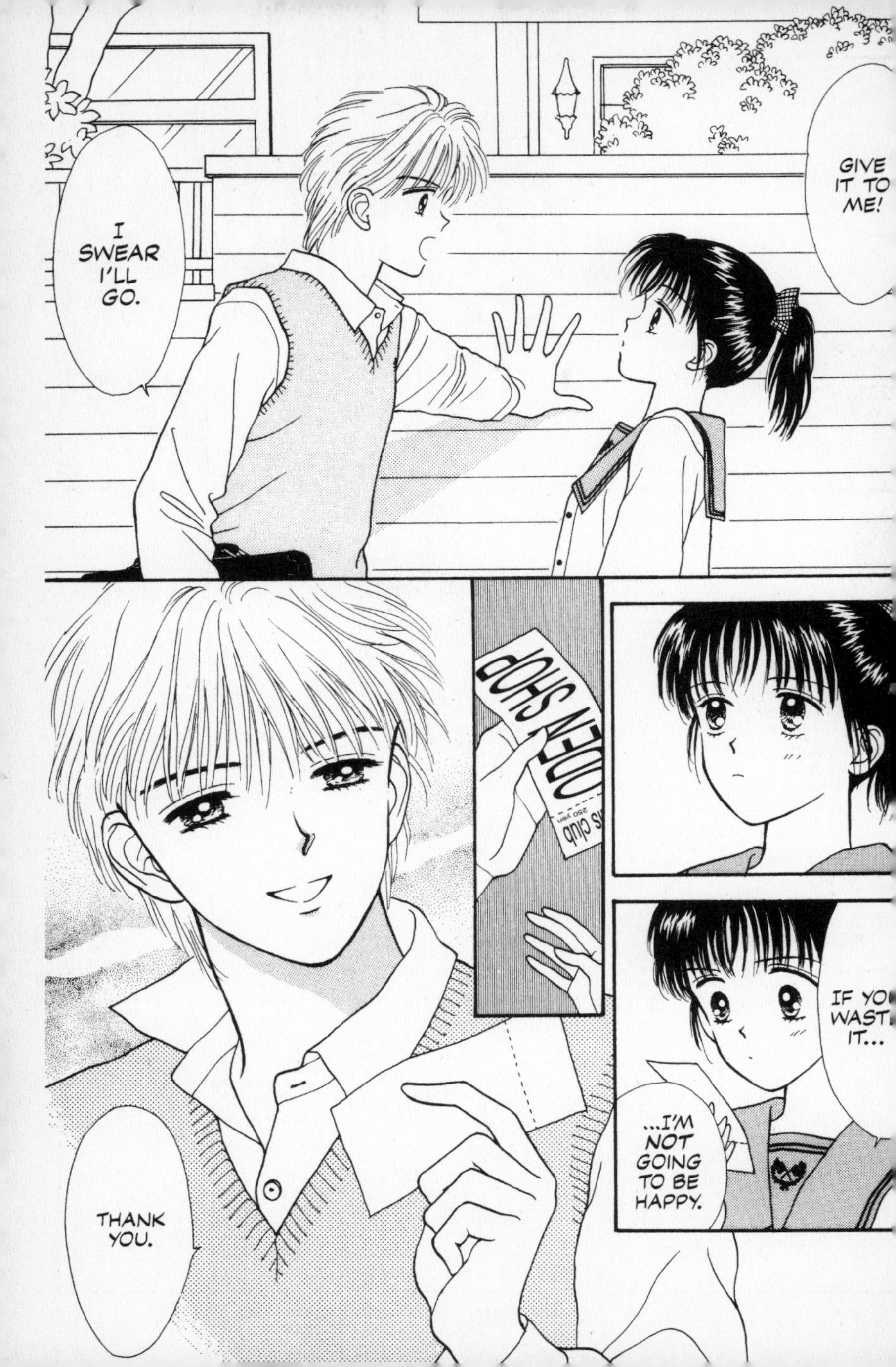
GIVE IT TO ME!
I SWEAR I'LL GO.
IF YO WAST IT...
...I'M NOT GOING TO BE HAPPY.
THANK YOU.

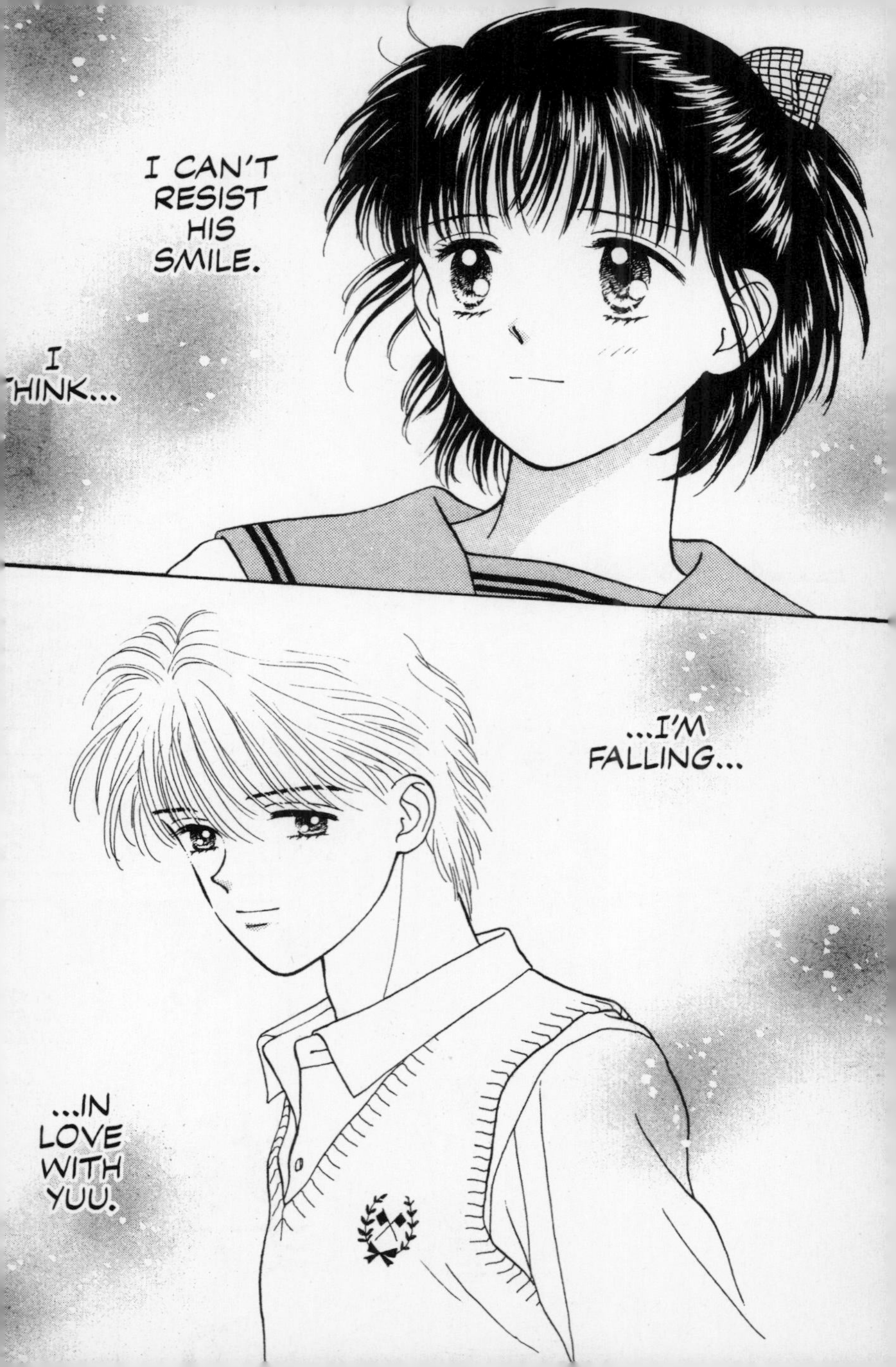
I CAN'T RESIST HIS SMILE.
I THINK...
...I'M FALLING...
...IN LOVE WITH YUU.

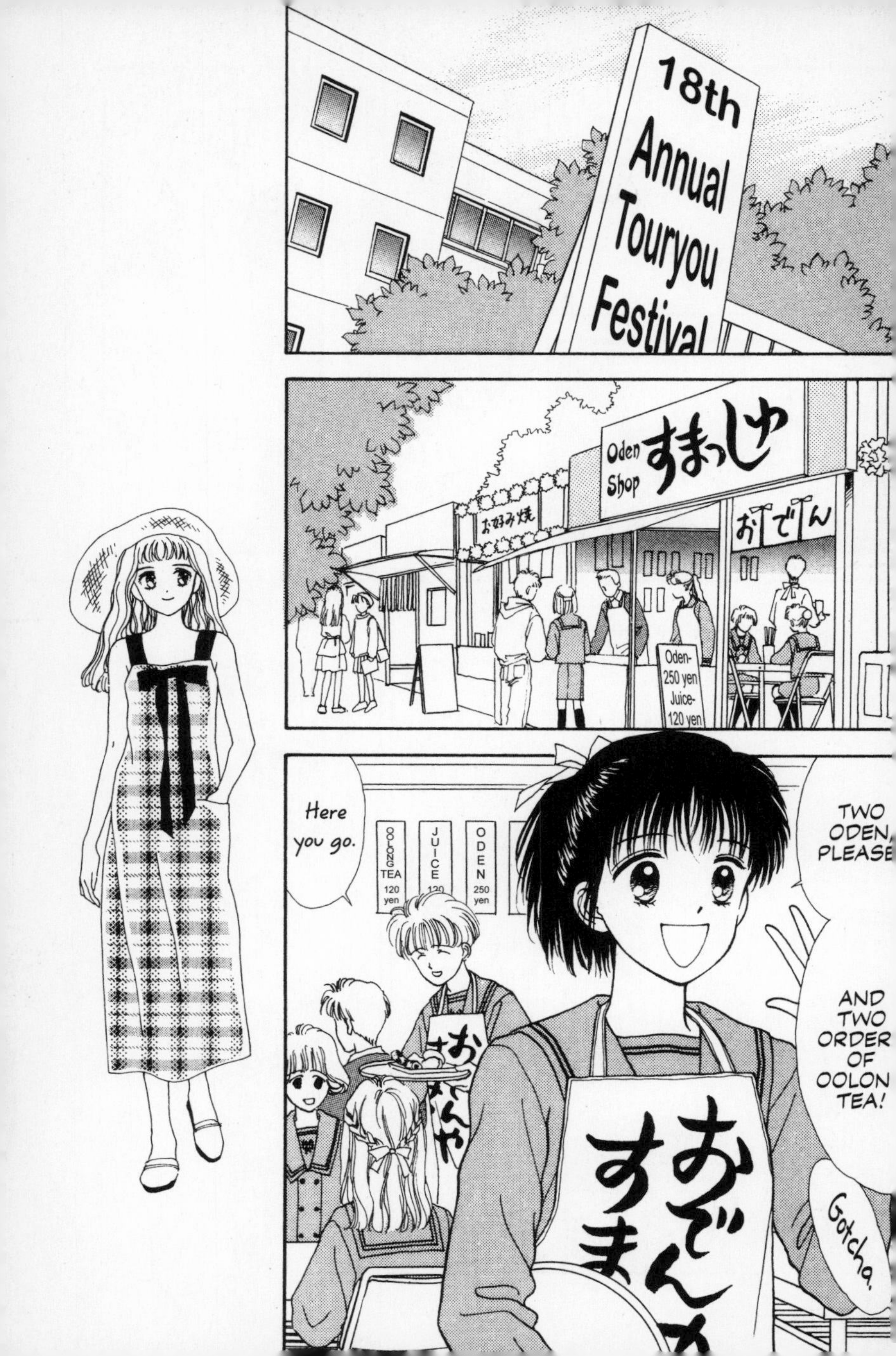
18th Annual Touryou Festival
Oden Shop すまっしゃ
お好み焼
おでん
Oden- 250 yen Juice- 120 yen
TWO ODEN, PLEASE
AND TWO ORDER OF OOLON TEA!
Gotcha.
Here you go.
ODEN 250 yen
JUICE 120
OOLONG TEA 120 yen

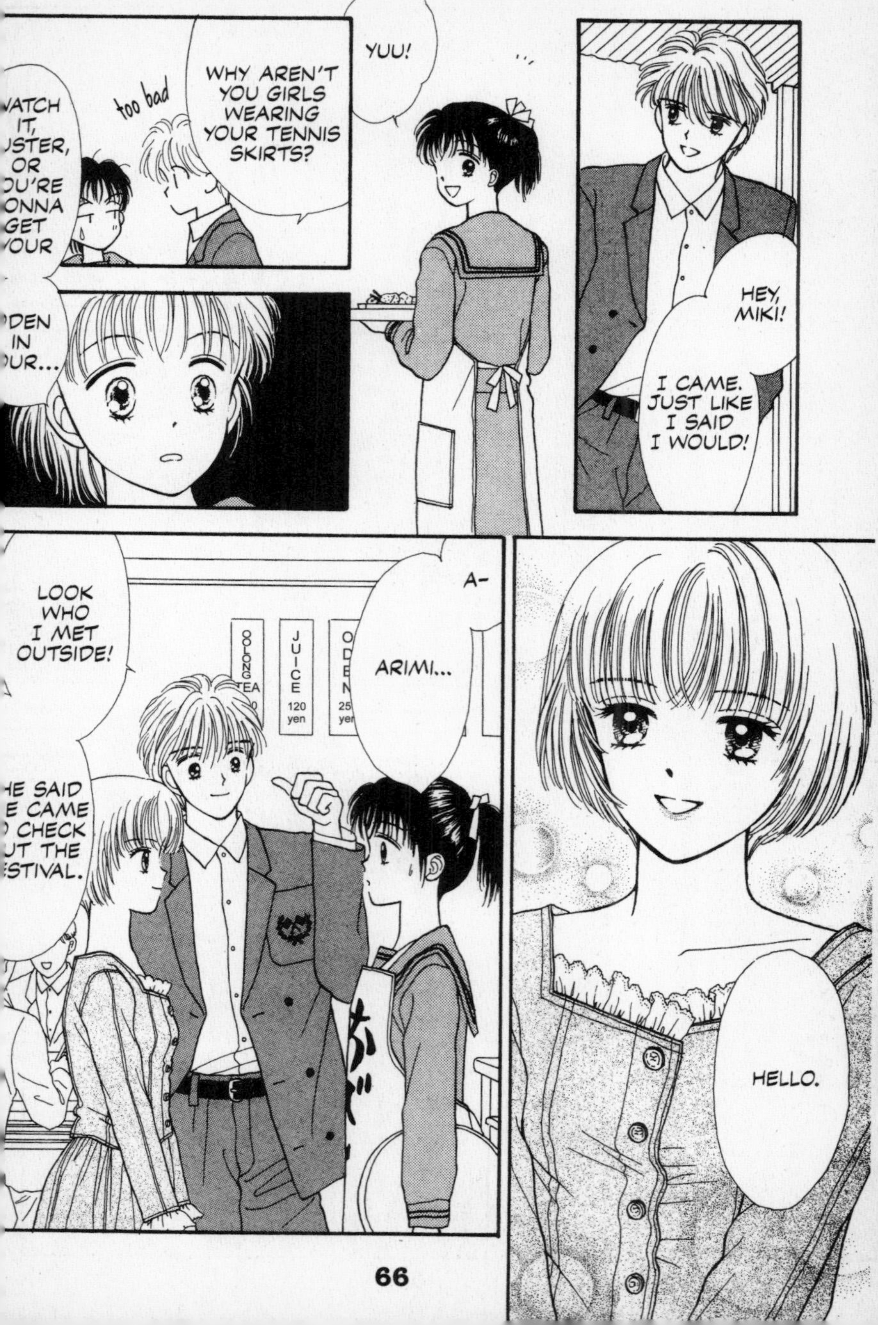
HEY, MIKI!
I CAME. JUST LIKE I SAID I WOULD!
YUU!
WHY AREN'T YOU GIRLS WEARING YOUR TENNIS SKIRTS?
too bad
ATCH IT, USTER, OR OU'RE ONNA GET OUR
DEN IN UR...
HELLO.
A-
ARIMI...
LOOK WHO I MET OUTSIDE!
OOLONG TEA
JUICE 120 yen
HE SAID E CAME CHECK UT THE ESTIVAL.

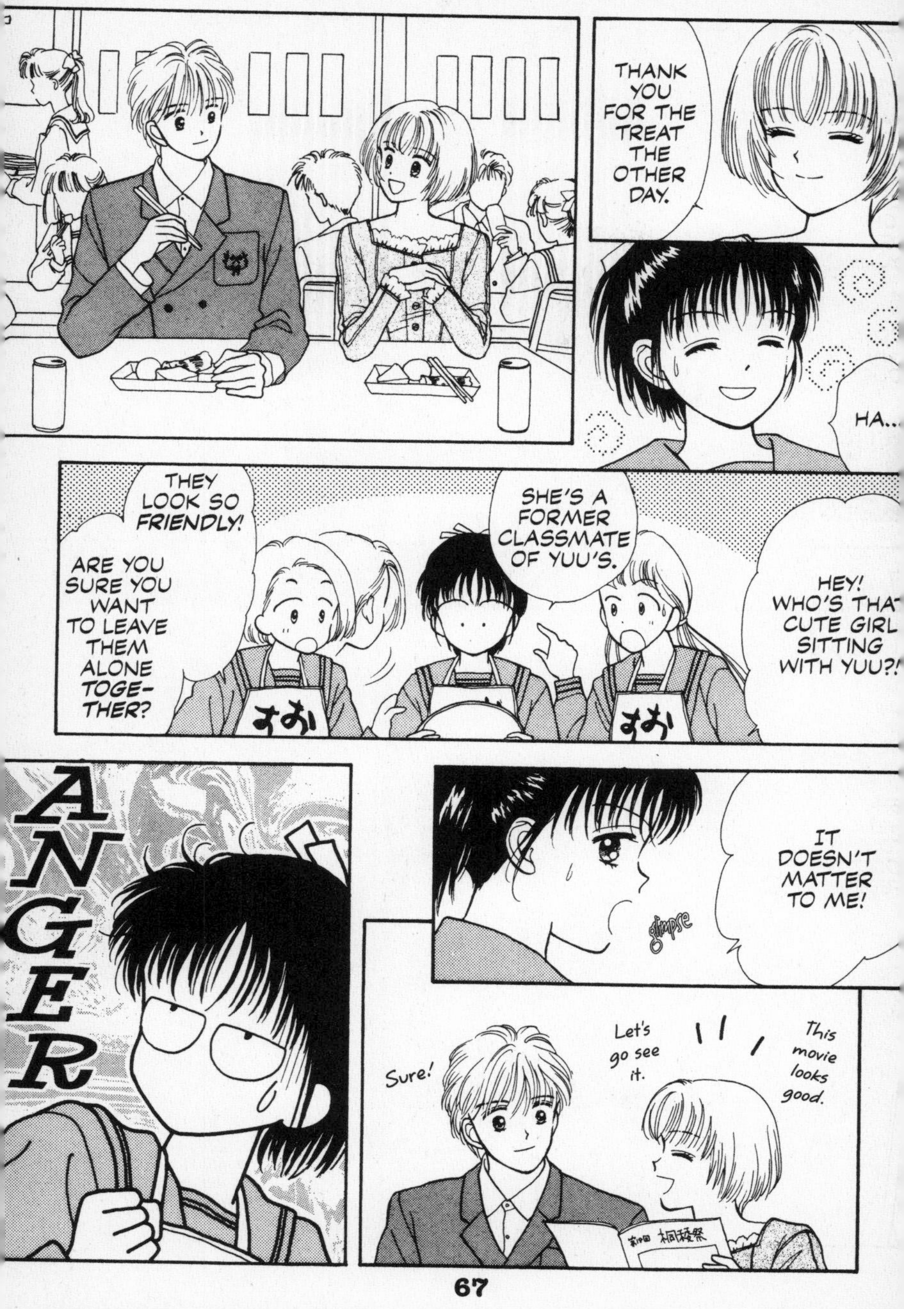
THANK YOU FOR THE TREAT THE OTHER DAY.
HA...
HEY! WHO'S THAT CUTE GIRL SITTING WITH YUU?!
SHE'S A FORMER CLASSMATE OF YUU'S.
THEY LOOK SO FRIENDLY!
ARE YOU SURE YOU WANT TO LEAVE THEM ALONE TOGETHER?
IT DOESN'T MATTER TO ME!
glimpse
This movie looks good.
Let's go see it.
Sure!
ANGER

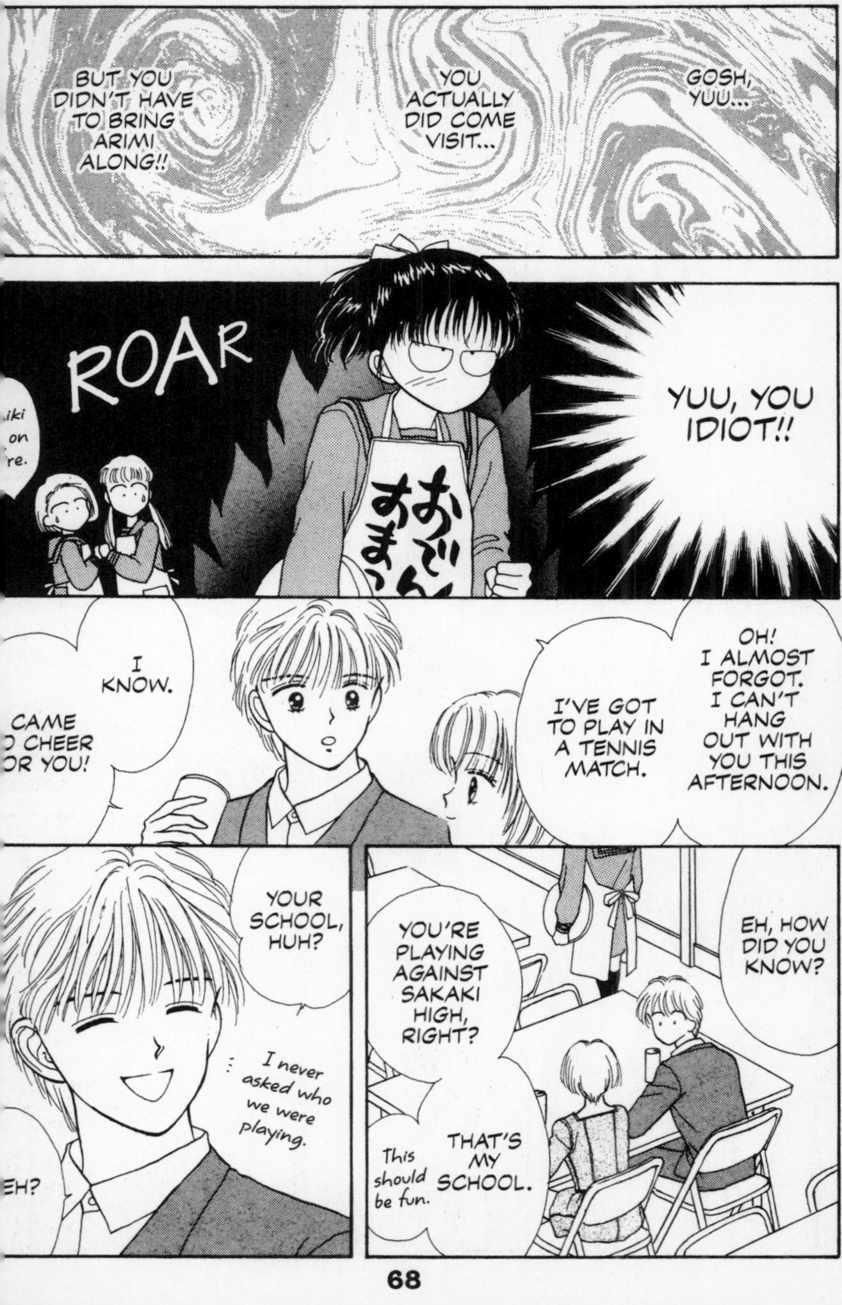
GOSH, YUU...
YOU ACTUALLY DID COME VISIT...
BUT YOU DIDN'T HAVE TO BRING ARIMI ALONG!!
YUU, YOU IDIOT!!
ROAR
OH! I ALMOST FORGOT. I CAN'T HANG OUT WITH YOU THIS AFTERNOON.
I'VE GOT TO PLAY IN A TENNIS MATCH.
I KNOW.
EH, HOW DID YOU KNOW?
YOU'RE PLAYING AGAINST SAKAKI HIGH, RIGHT?
THAT'S MY SCHOOL.
This should be fun.
YOUR SCHOOL, HUH?
I never asked who we were playing.

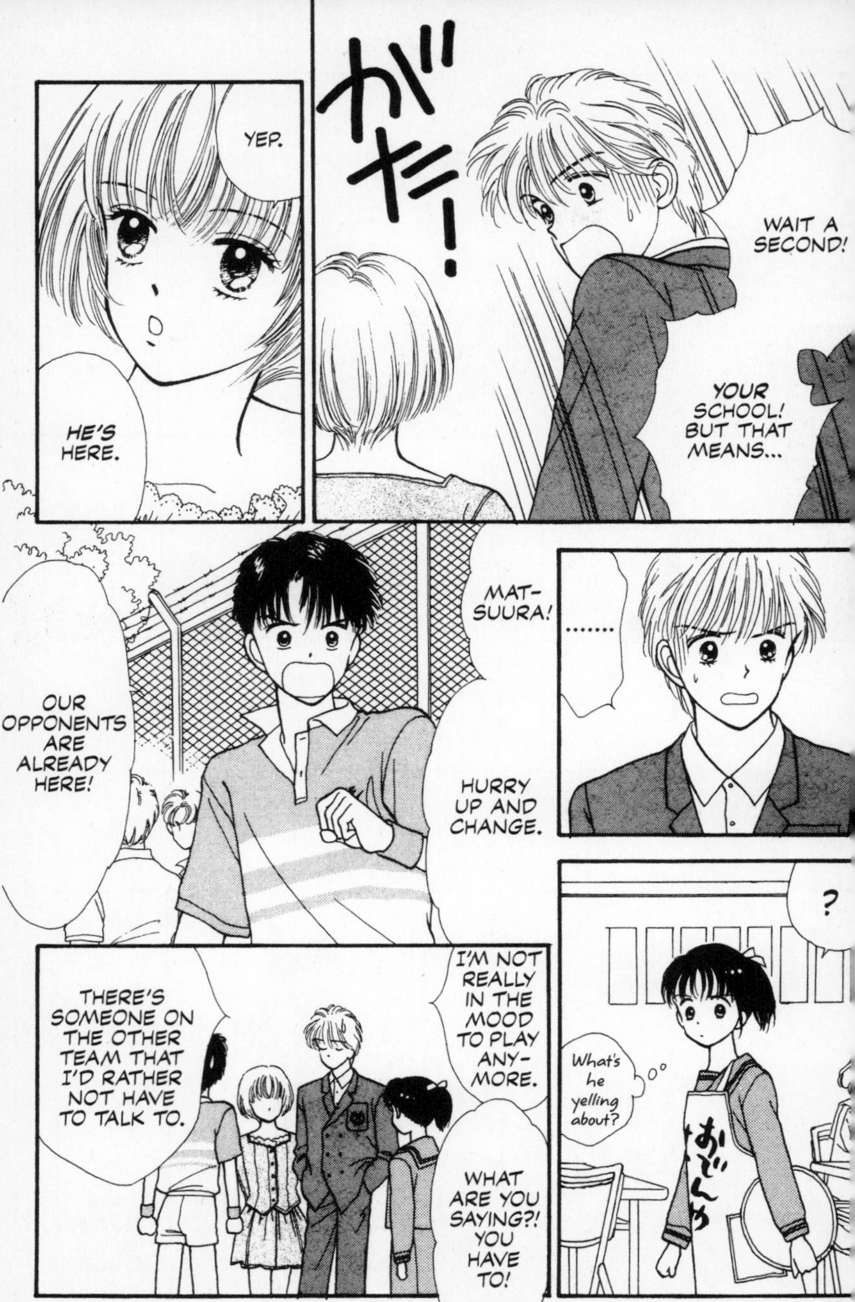
がたー!
WAIT A SECOND!
YOUR SCHOOL! BUT THAT MEANS...
YEP.
HE'S HERE.
....
MAT-SUURA!
HURRY UP AND CHANGE.
OUR OPPONENTS ARE ALREADY HERE!
?
What's he yelling about?
I'M NOT REALLY IN THE MOOD TO PLAY ANY-MORE.
WHAT ARE YOU SAYING?! YOU HAVE TO!
THERE'S SOMEONE ON THE OTHER TEAM THAT I'D RATHER NOT HAVE TO TALK TO.

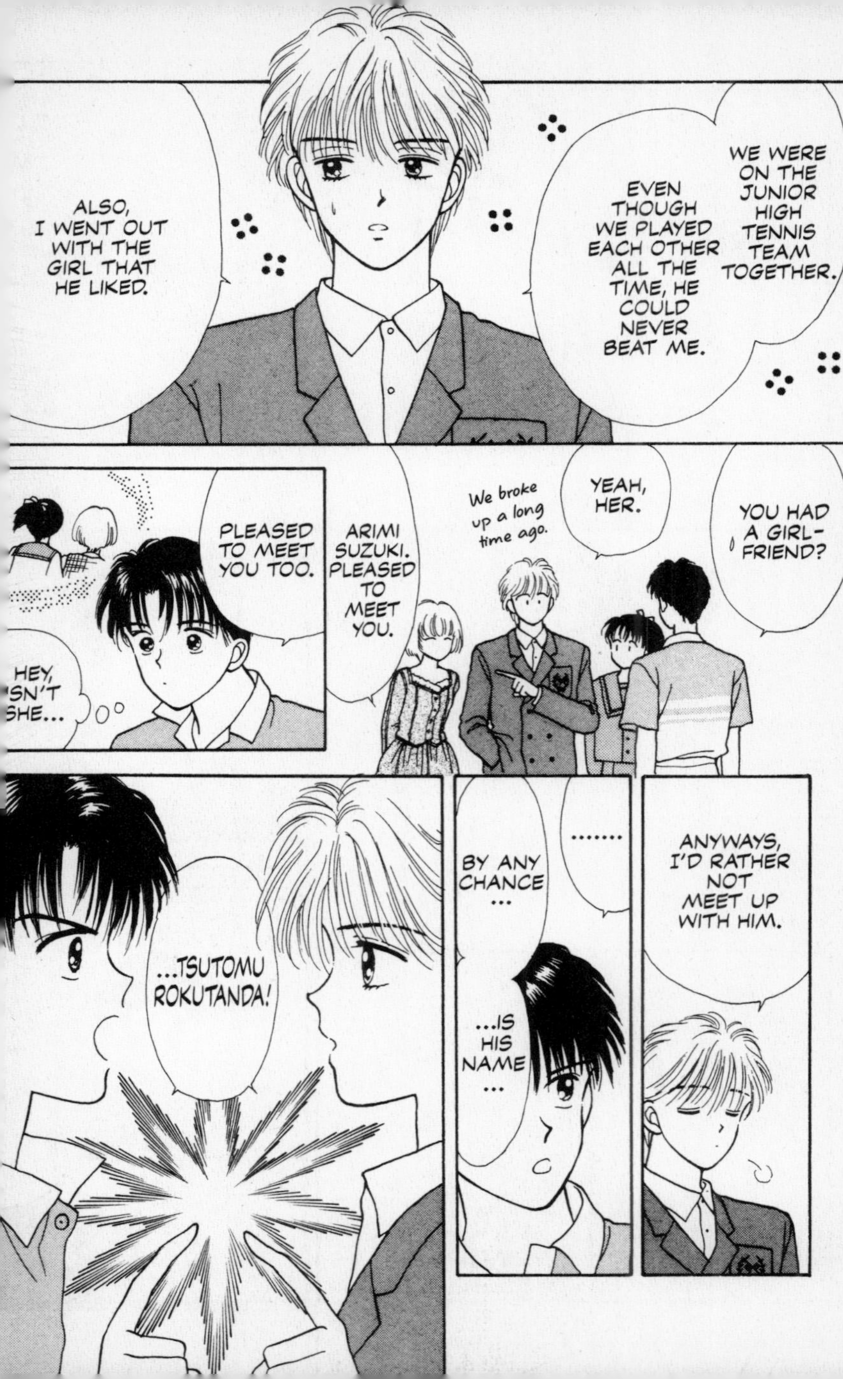
WE WERE ON THE JUNIOR HIGH TENNIS TEAM TOGETHER.
EVEN THOUGH WE PLAYED EACH OTHER ALL THE TIME, HE COULD NEVER BEAT ME.
ALSO, I WENT OUT WITH THE GIRL THAT HE LIKED.
YOU HAD A GIRL-FRIEND?
YEAH, HER.
We broke up a long time ago.
ARIMI SUZUKI. PLEASED TO MEET YOU.
PLEASED TO MEET YOU TOO.
HEY, ISN'T SHE...
ANYWAYS, I'D RATHER NOT MEET UP WITH HIM.
....
BY ANY CHANCE...
...IS HIS NAME...
...TSUTOMU ROKUTANDA!

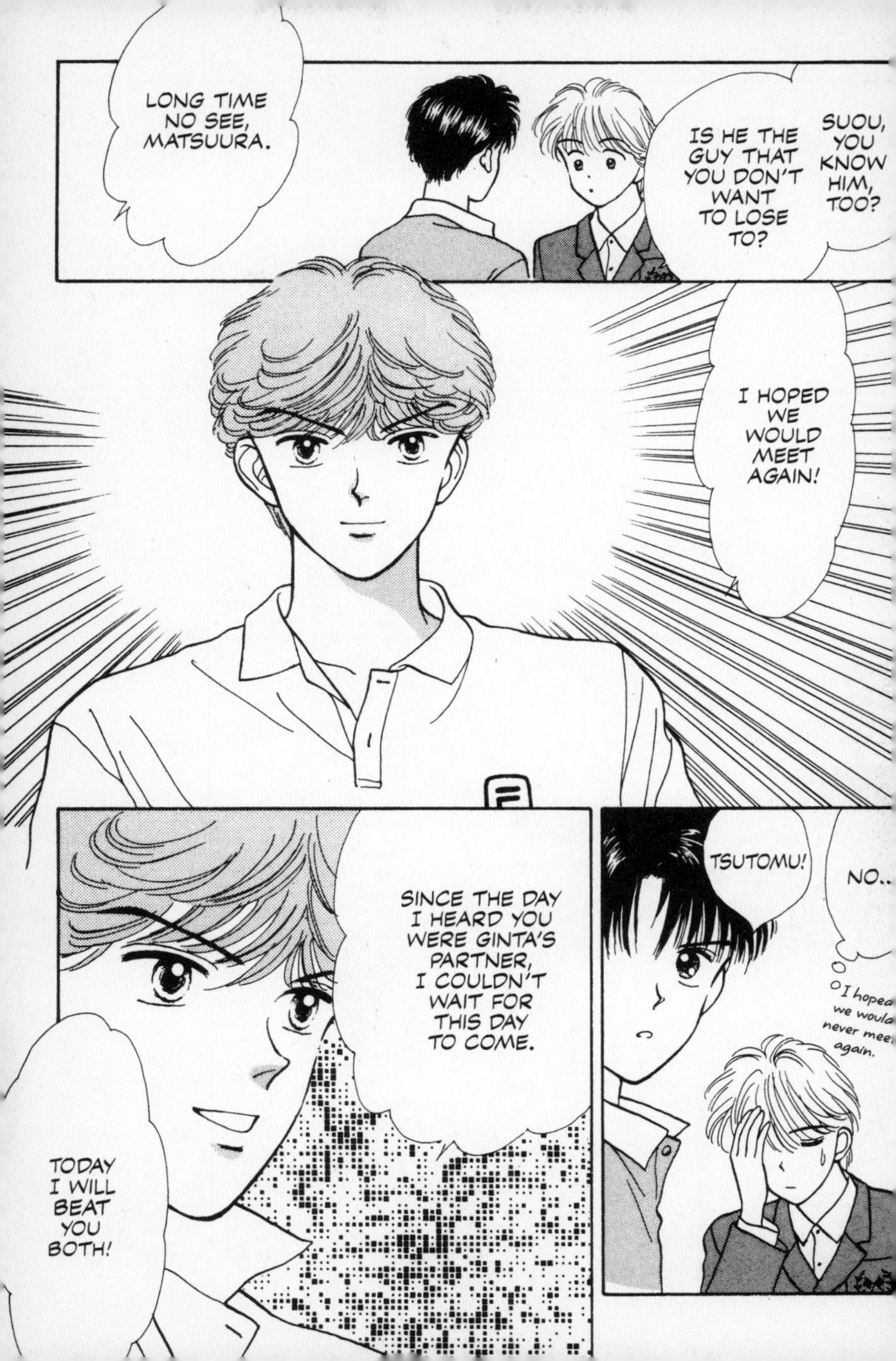
SUOU, YOU KNOW HIM, TOO?
IS HE THE GUY THAT YOU DON'T WANT TO LOSE TO?
LONG TIME NO SEE, MATSUURA.
I HOPED WE WOULD MEET AGAIN!
NO...
TSUTOMU!
I hoped we would never meet again.
SINCE THE DAY I HEARD YOU WERE GINTA'S PARTNER, I COULDN'T WAIT FOR THIS DAY TO COME.
TODAY I WILL BEAT YOU BOTH!

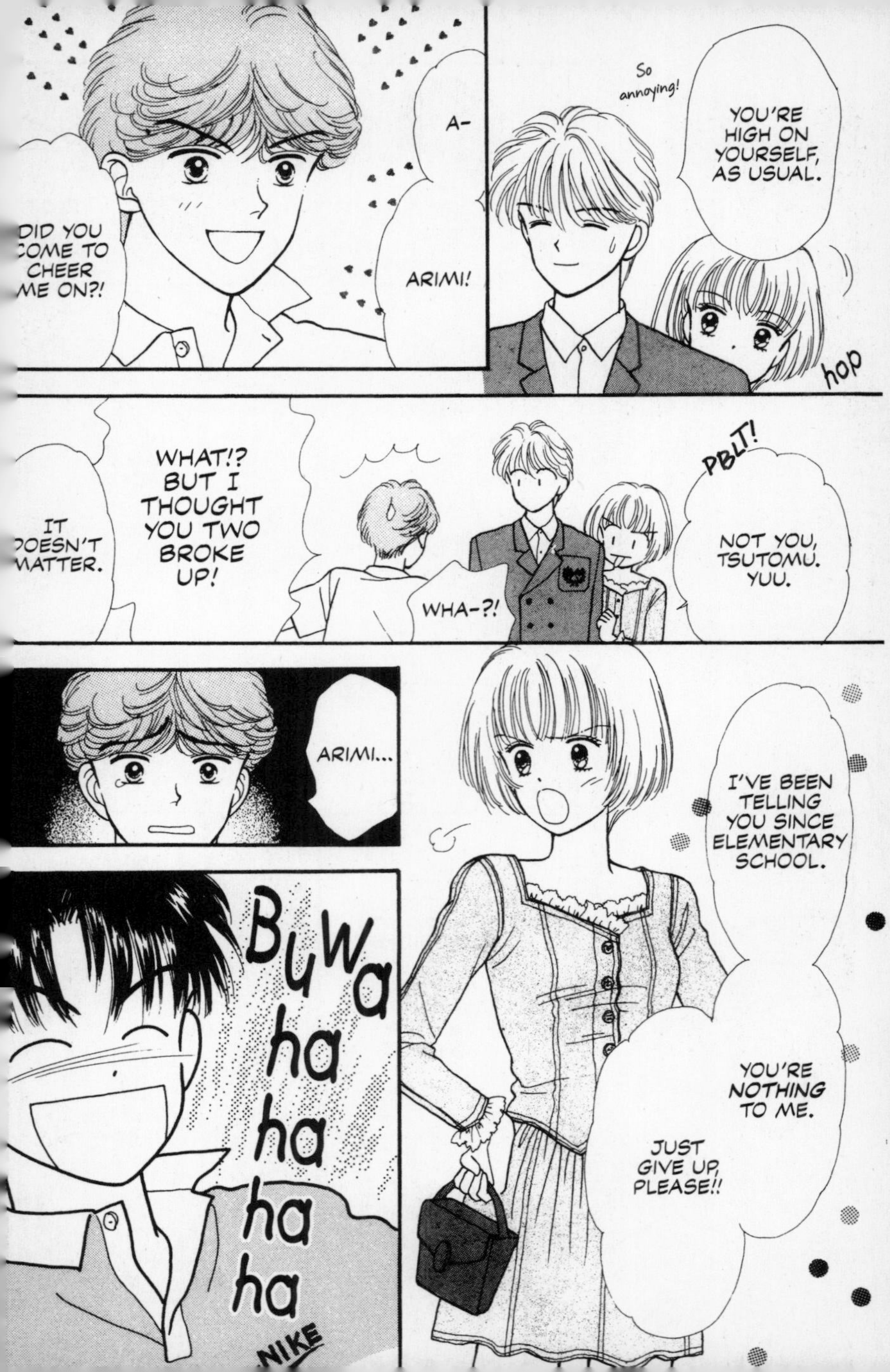
YOU'RE HIGH ON YOURSELF, AS USUAL.
So annoying!
hop
A- ARIMI!
DID YOU COME TO CHEER ME ON?!
PBLT!
NOT YOU, TSUTOMU. YUU.
WHA-?!
WHAT!? BUT I THOUGHT YOU TWO BROKE UP!
IT DOESN'T MATTER.
I'VE BEEN TELLING YOU SINCE ELEMENTARY SCHOOL.
YOU'RE NOTHING TO ME.
JUST GIVE UP, PLEASE!!
ARIMI...
Buwa ha ha ha ha ha
NIKE

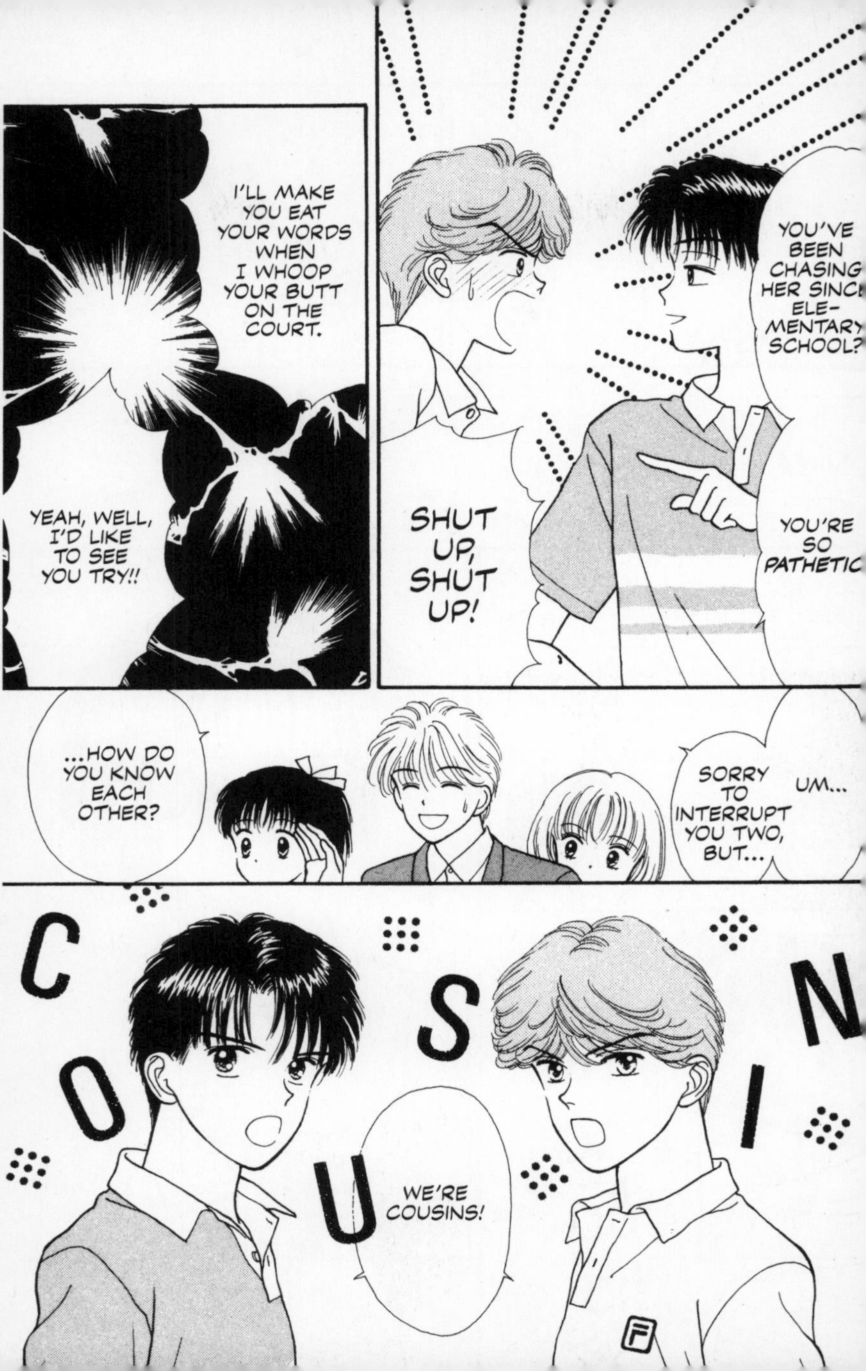
YOU'VE BEEN CHASING HER SINC ELE-MENTARY SCHOOL?
YOU'RE SO PATHETIC
SHUT UP, SHUT UP!
I'LL MAKE YOU EAT YOUR WORDS WHEN I WHOOP YOUR BUTT ON THE COURT.
YEAH, WELL, I'D LIKE TO SEE YOU TRY!!
UM...
SORRY TO INTERRUPT YOU TWO, BUT...
...HOW DO YOU KNOW EACH OTHER?
COUSIN
WE'RE COUSINS!

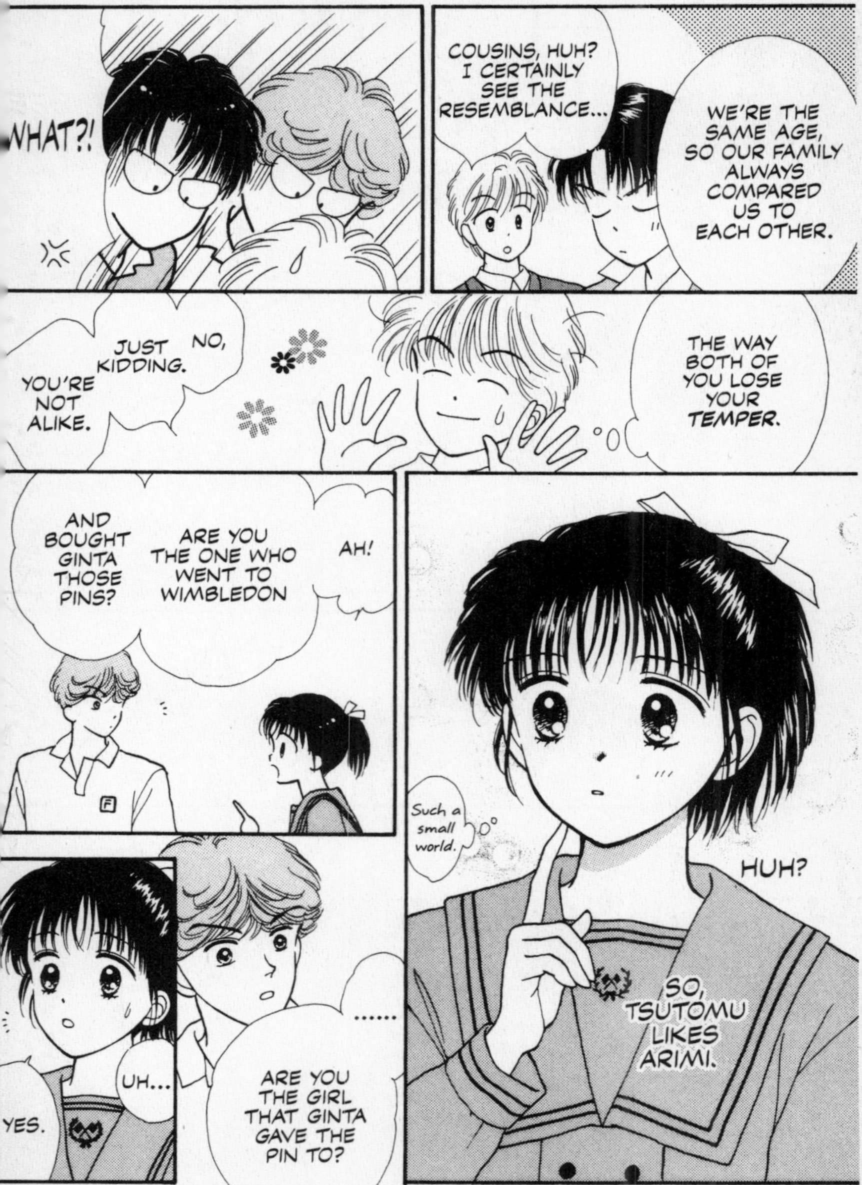
WE'RE THE SAME AGE, SO OUR FAMILY ALWAYS COMPARED US TO EACH OTHER.
COUSINS, HUH? I CERTAINLY SEE THE RESEMBLANCE...
WHAT?!
THE WAY BOTH OF YOU LOSE YOUR TEMPER.
NO, JUST KIDDING. YOU'RE NOT ALIKE.
HUH?
Such a small world.
SO, TSUTOMU LIKES ARIMI.
AH!
ARE YOU THE ONE WHO WENT TO WIMBLEDON
AND BOUGHT GINTA THOSE PINS?
......
ARE YOU THE GIRL THAT GINTA GAVE THE PIN TO?
UH...
YES.

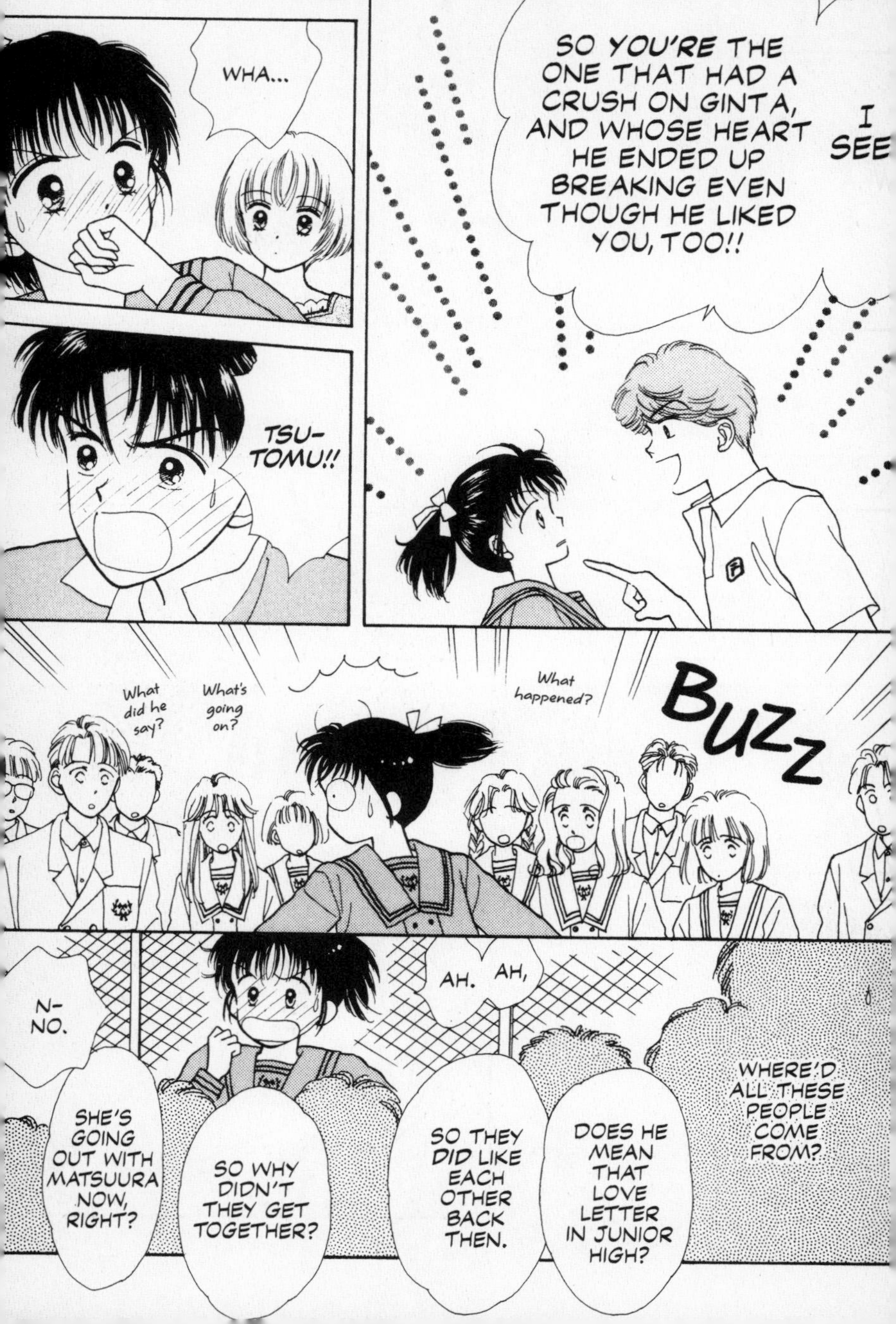

I SEE
SO YOU'RE THE ONE THAT HAD A CRUSH ON GINTA, AND WHOSE HEART HE ENDED UP BREAKING EVEN THOUGH HE LIKED YOU, TOO!!
WHA...
TSU-TOMU!!
BUZZ
What happened?
What's going on?
What did he say?
WHERE'D ALL THESE PEOPLE COME FROM?
DOES HE MEAN THAT LOVE LETTER IN JUNIOR HIGH?
SO THEY DID LIKE EACH OTHER BACK THEN.
AH, AH.
SO WHY DIDN'T THEY GET TOGETHER?
SHE'S GOING OUT WITH MATSUURA NOW, RIGHT?
N-NO.

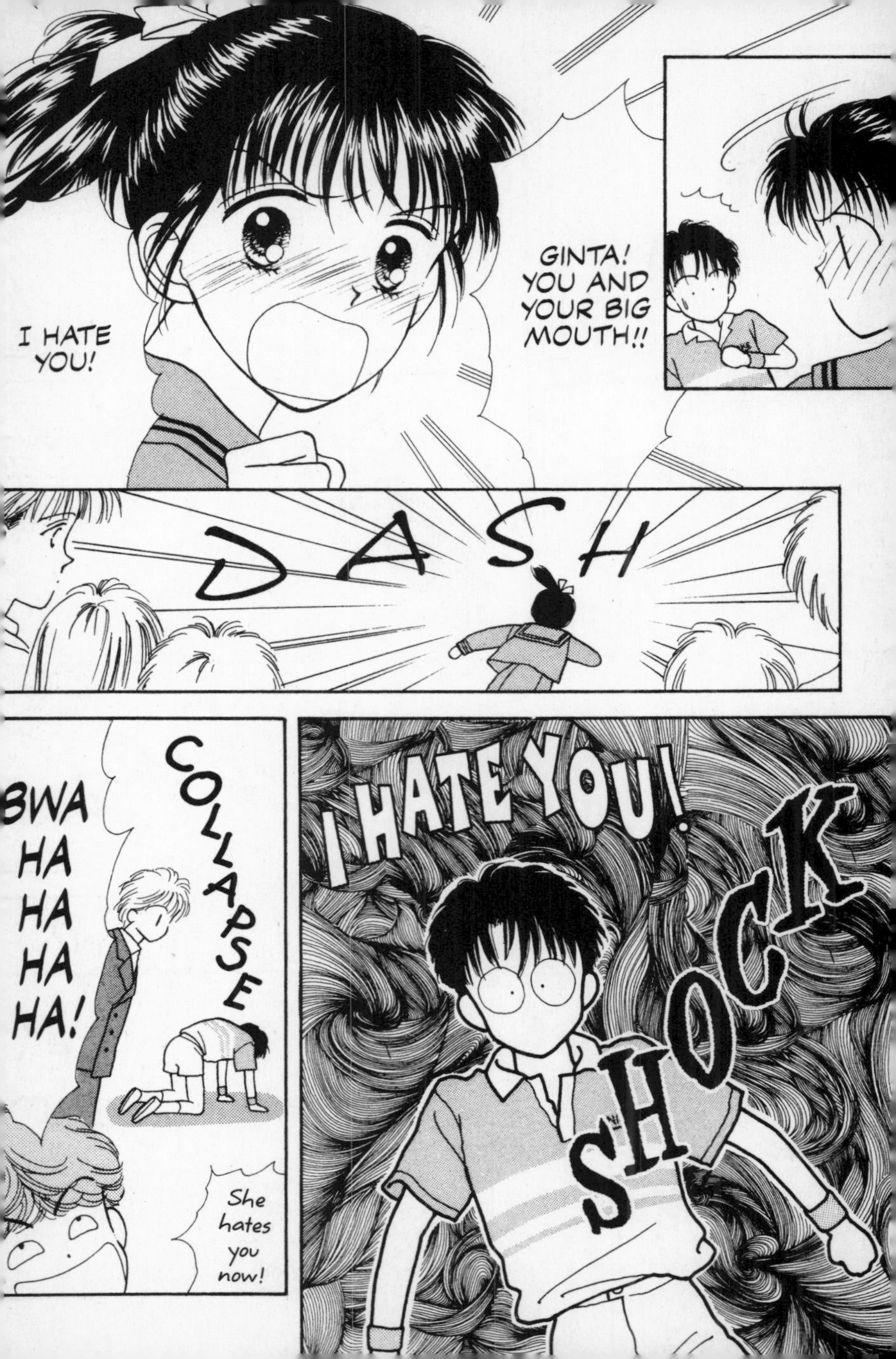
GINTA! YOU AND YOUR BIG MOUTH!!
I HATE YOU!
DASH
I HATE YOU!
SHOCK
COLLAPSE
BWA HA HA HA HA HA!
She hates you now!

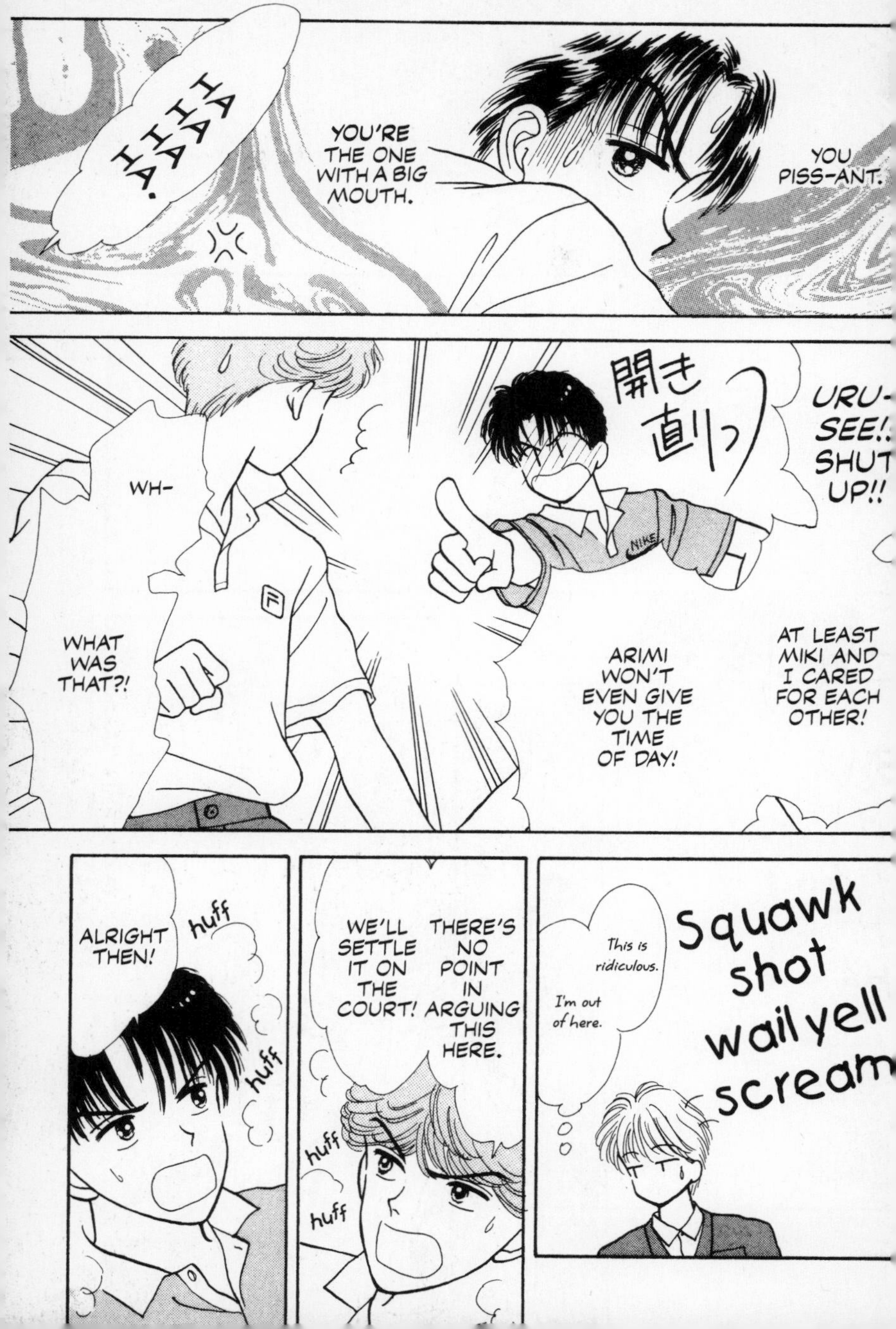
YOU PISS-ANT.
YOU'RE THE ONE WITH A BIG MOUTH.
HA HA HA HA.
URU-SEE!! SHUT UP!!
開き直りっ
AT LEAST MIKI AND I CARED FOR EACH OTHER!
ARIMI WON'T EVEN GIVE YOU THE TIME OF DAY!
WH-
WHAT WAS THAT?!
Squawk shot wail yell scream
This is ridiculous.
I'm out of here.
THERE'S NO POINT IN ARGUING THIS HERE.
WE'LL SETTLE IT ON THE COURT!
huff
huff
huff
ALRIGHT THEN!
huff

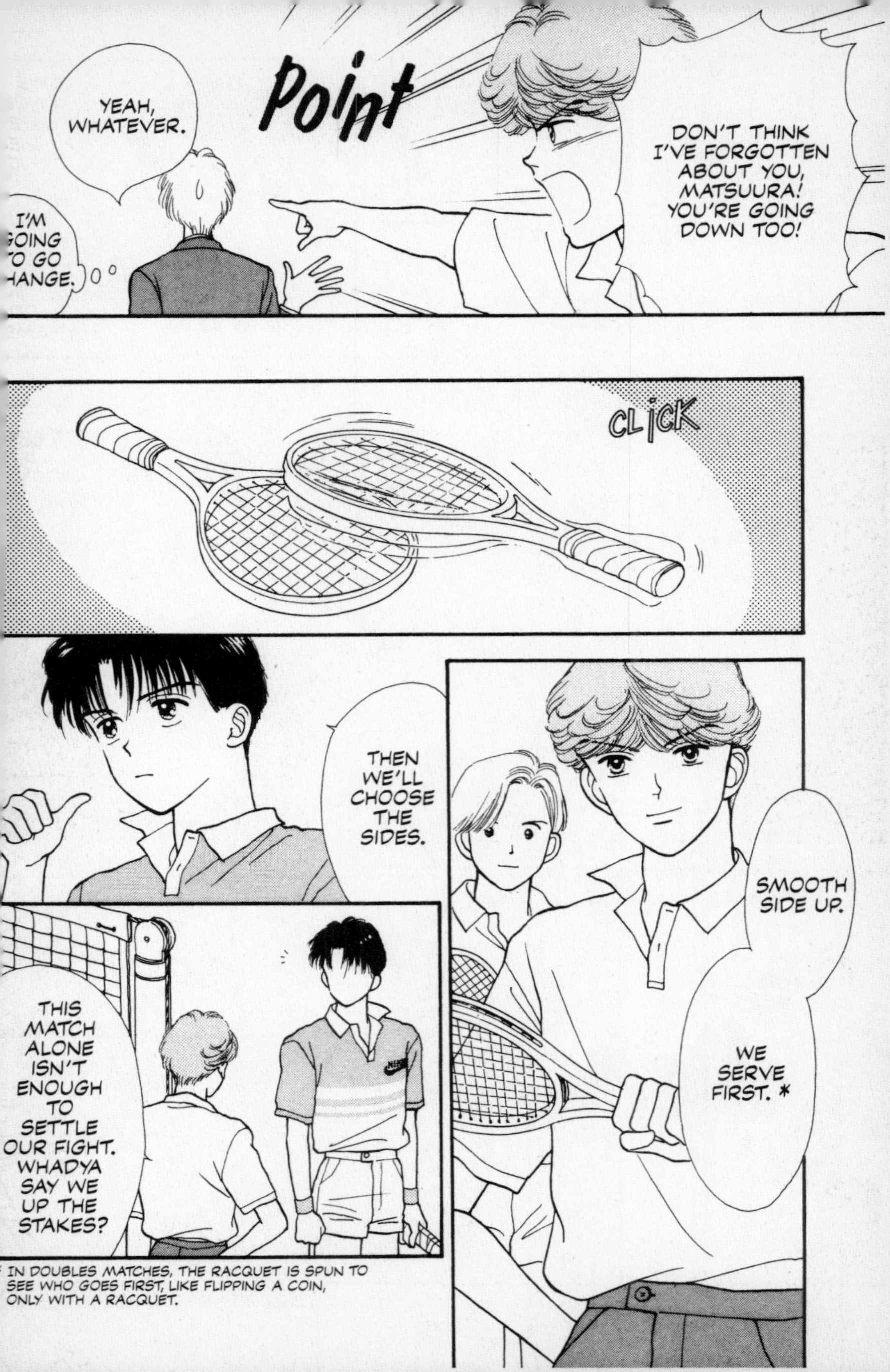
DON'T THINK I'VE FORGOTTEN ABOUT YOU, MATSUURA! YOU'RE GOING DOWN TOO!
Point
YEAH, WHATEVER.
I'M GOING TO GO CHANGE.
CLICK
SMOOTH SIDE UP.
WE SERVE FIRST. *
THEN WE'LL CHOOSE THE SIDES.
THIS MATCH ALONE ISN'T ENOUGH TO SETTLE OUR FIGHT. WHADYA SAY WE UP THE STAKES?

* IN DOUBLES MATCHES, THE RACQUET IS SPUN TO SEE WHO GOES FIRST, LIKE FLIPPING A COIN, ONLY WITH A RACQUET.

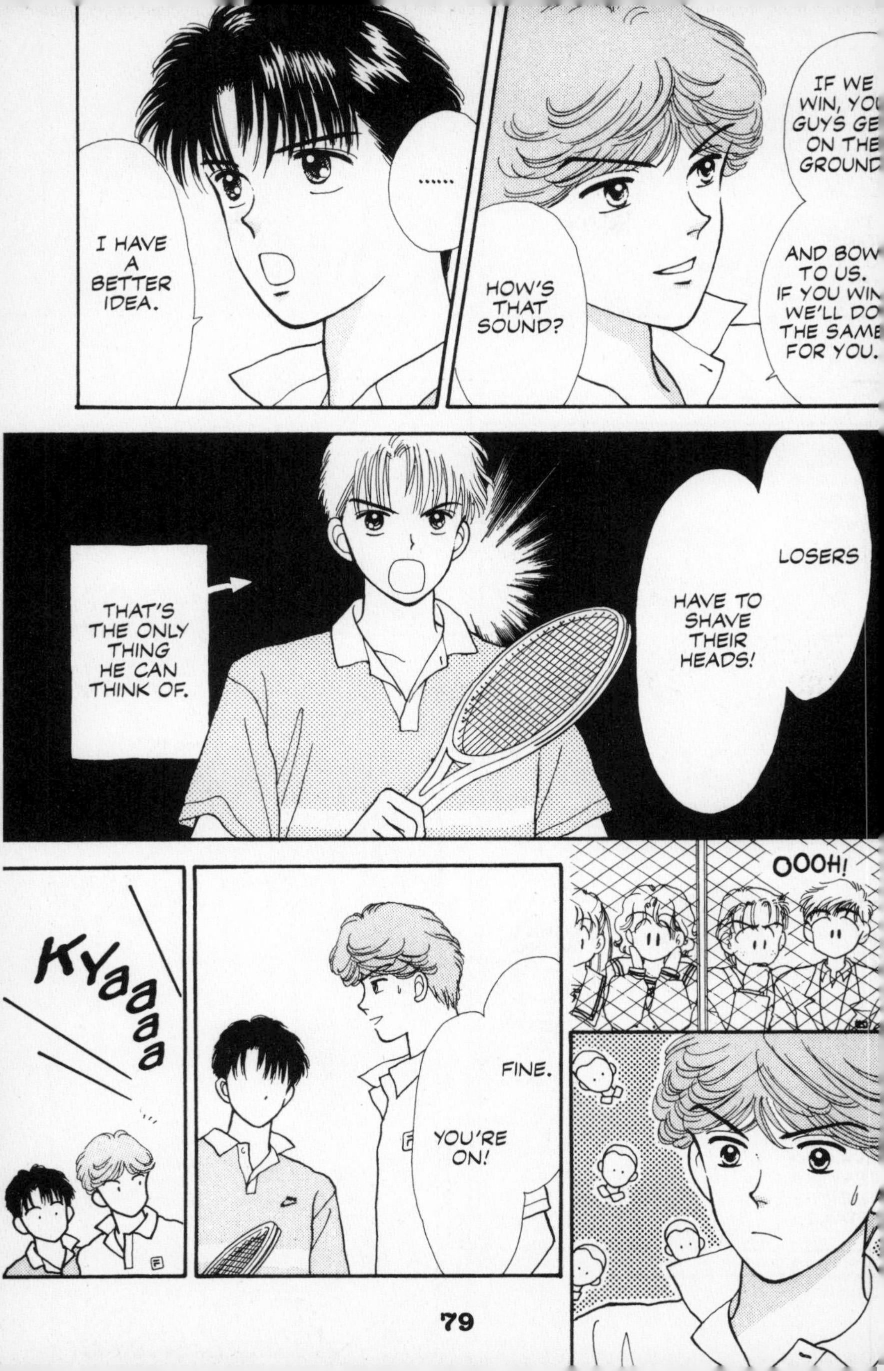
IF WE WIN, YOU GUYS GE ON THE GROUND
AND BOW TO US. IF YOU WIN WE'LL DO THE SAME FOR YOU.
HOW'S THAT SOUND?
......
I HAVE A BETTER IDEA.
LOSERS HAVE TO SHAVE THEIR HEADS!
THAT'S THE ONLY THING HE CAN THINK OF.
OOOH!
FINE. YOU'RE ON!
Kyaaaa

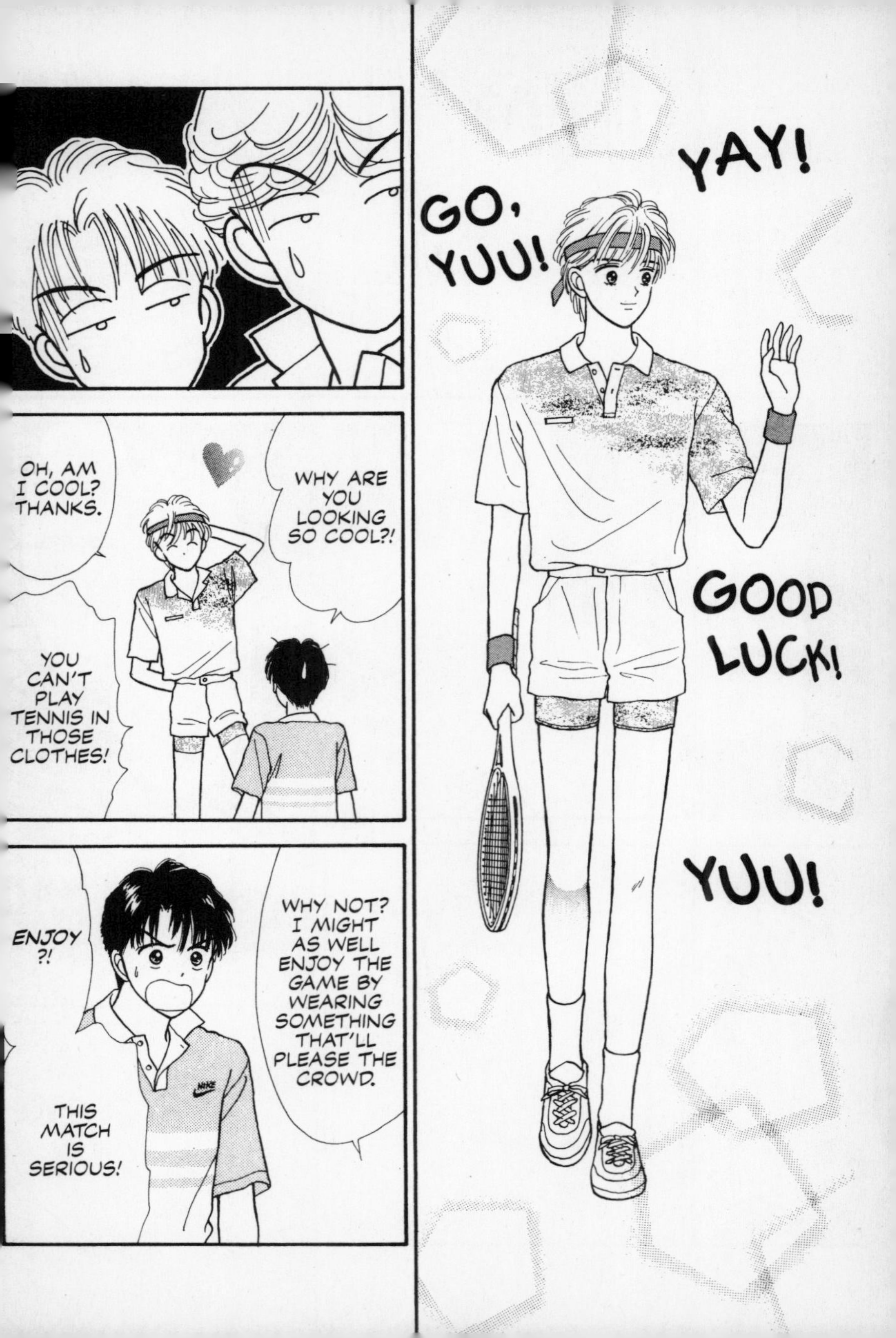
YAY!
GO, YUU!
GOOD LUCK!
YUU!
WHY ARE YOU LOOKING SO COOL?!
OH, AM I COOL? THANKS.
YOU CAN'T PLAY TENNIS IN THOSE CLOTHES!
WHY NOT? I MIGHT AS WELL ENJOY THE GAME BY WEARING SOMETHING THAT'LL PLEASE THE CROWD.
ENJOY?!
THIS MATCH IS SERIOUS!

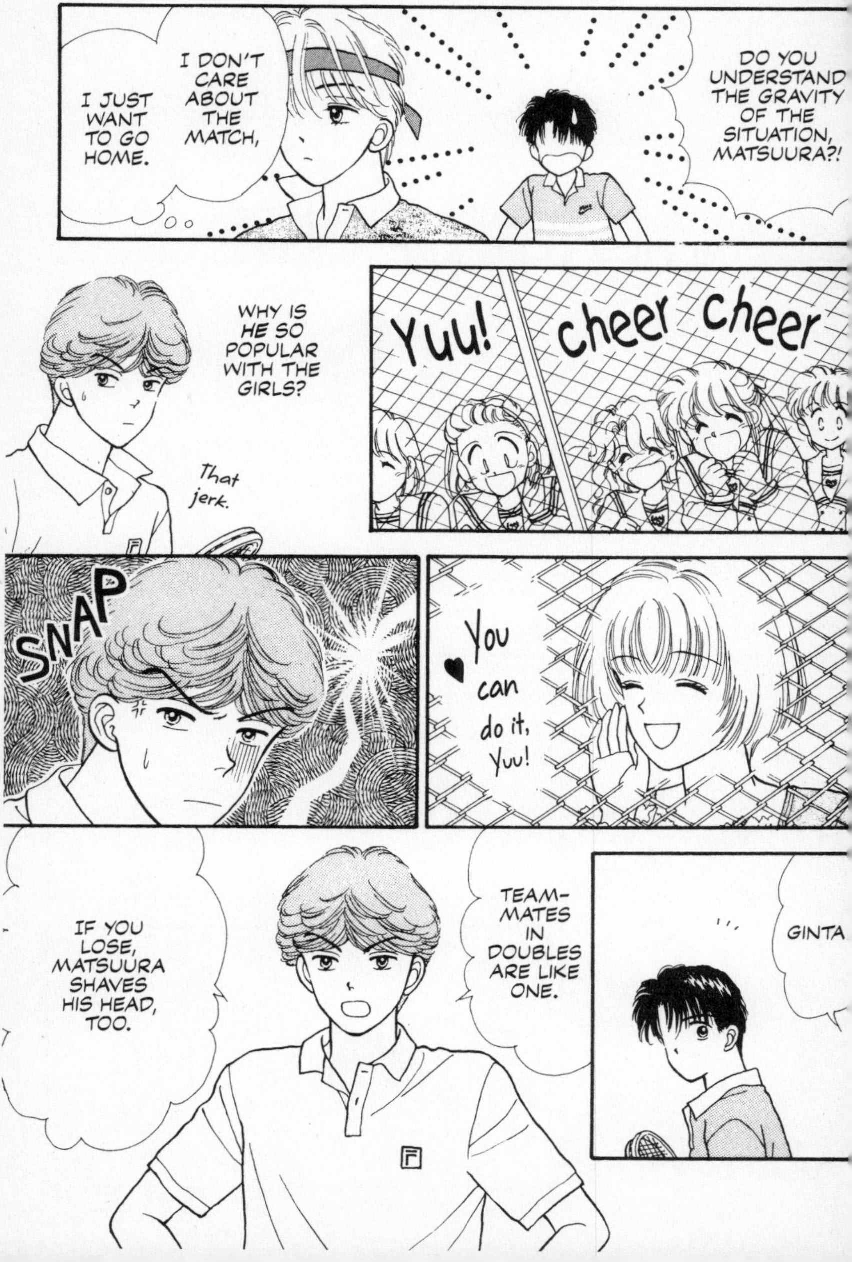
DO YOU UNDERSTAND THE GRAVITY OF THE SITUATION, MATSUURA?!
I DON'T CARE ABOUT THE MATCH,
I JUST WANT TO GO HOME.
Yuu! cheer cheer
WHY IS HE SO POPULAR WITH THE GIRLS?
That jerk.
You can do it, Yuu!
SNAP
GINTA.
TEAM-MATES IN DOUBLES ARE LIKE ONE.
IF YOU LOSE, MATSUURA SHAVES HIS HEAD, TOO.

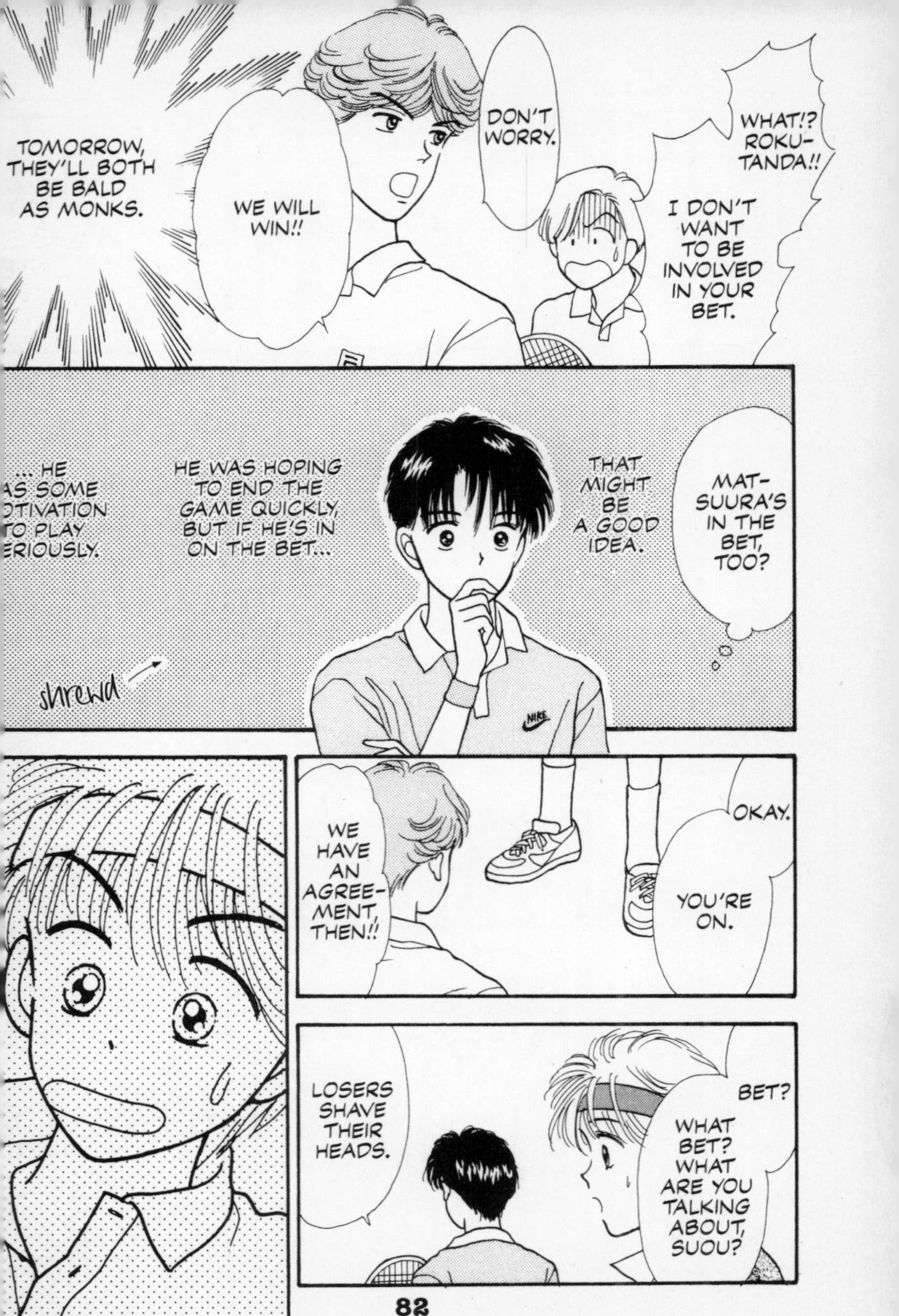
WHAT!? ROKU-TANDA!!
I DON'T WANT TO BE INVOLVED IN YOUR BET.
DON'T WORRY.
WE WILL WIN!!
TOMORROW, THEY'LL BOTH BE BALD AS MONKS.
MAT-SUURA'S IN THE BET, TOO?
THAT MIGHT BE A GOOD IDEA.
HE WAS HOPING TO END THE GAME QUICKLY, BUT IF HE'S IN ON THE BET...
... HE AS SOME OTIVATION TO PLAY ERIOUSLY.
shrewd
OKAY.
YOU'RE ON.
WE HAVE AN AGREEMENT, THEN!!
BET?
WHAT BET? WHAT ARE YOU TALKING ABOUT, SUOU?
LOSERS SHAVE THEIR HEADS.

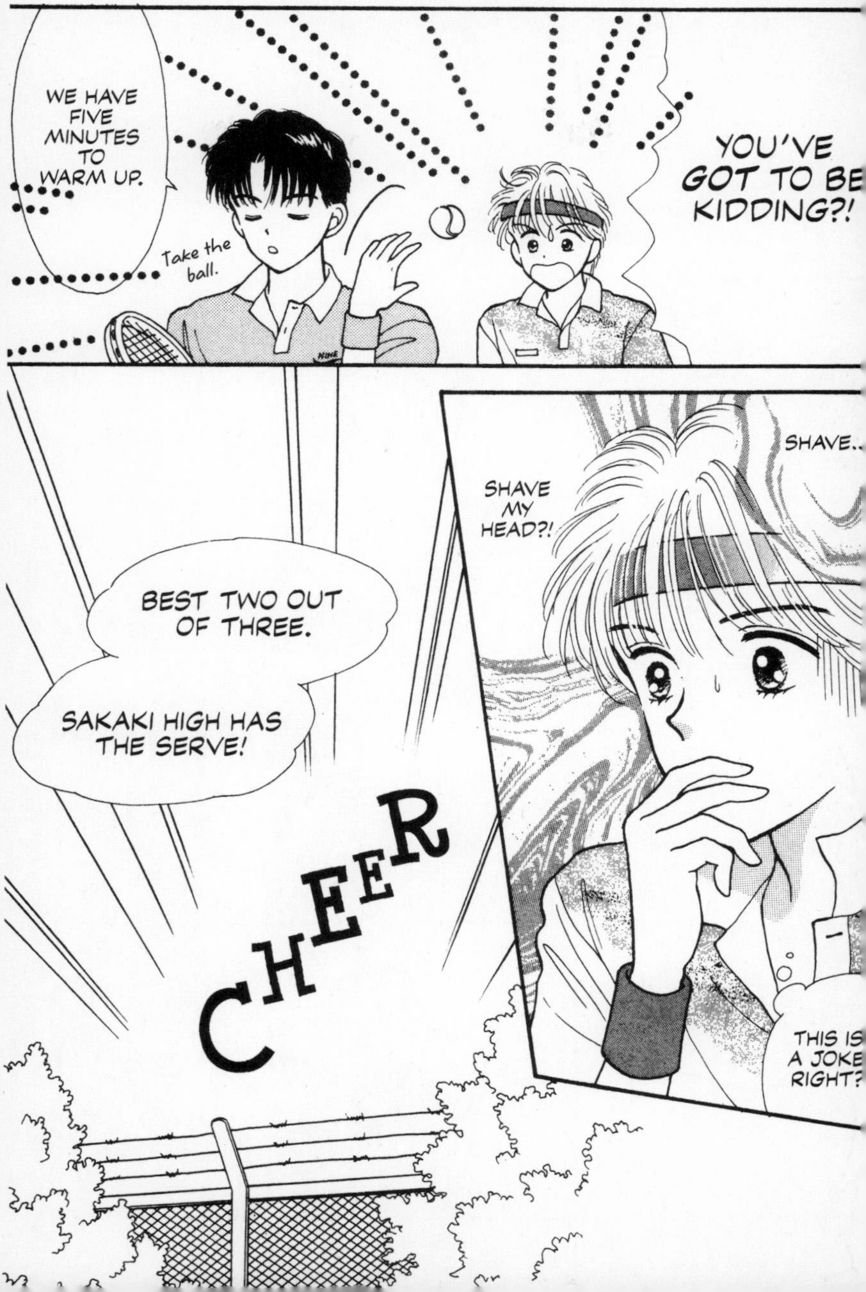
YOU'VE GOT TO BE KIDDING?!
WE HAVE FIVE MINUTES TO WARM UP.
Take the ball.
SHAVE...
SHAVE MY HEAD?!
THIS IS A JOKE RIGHT?
BEST TWO OUT OF THREE.
SAKAKI HIGH HAS THE SERVE!
CHEER

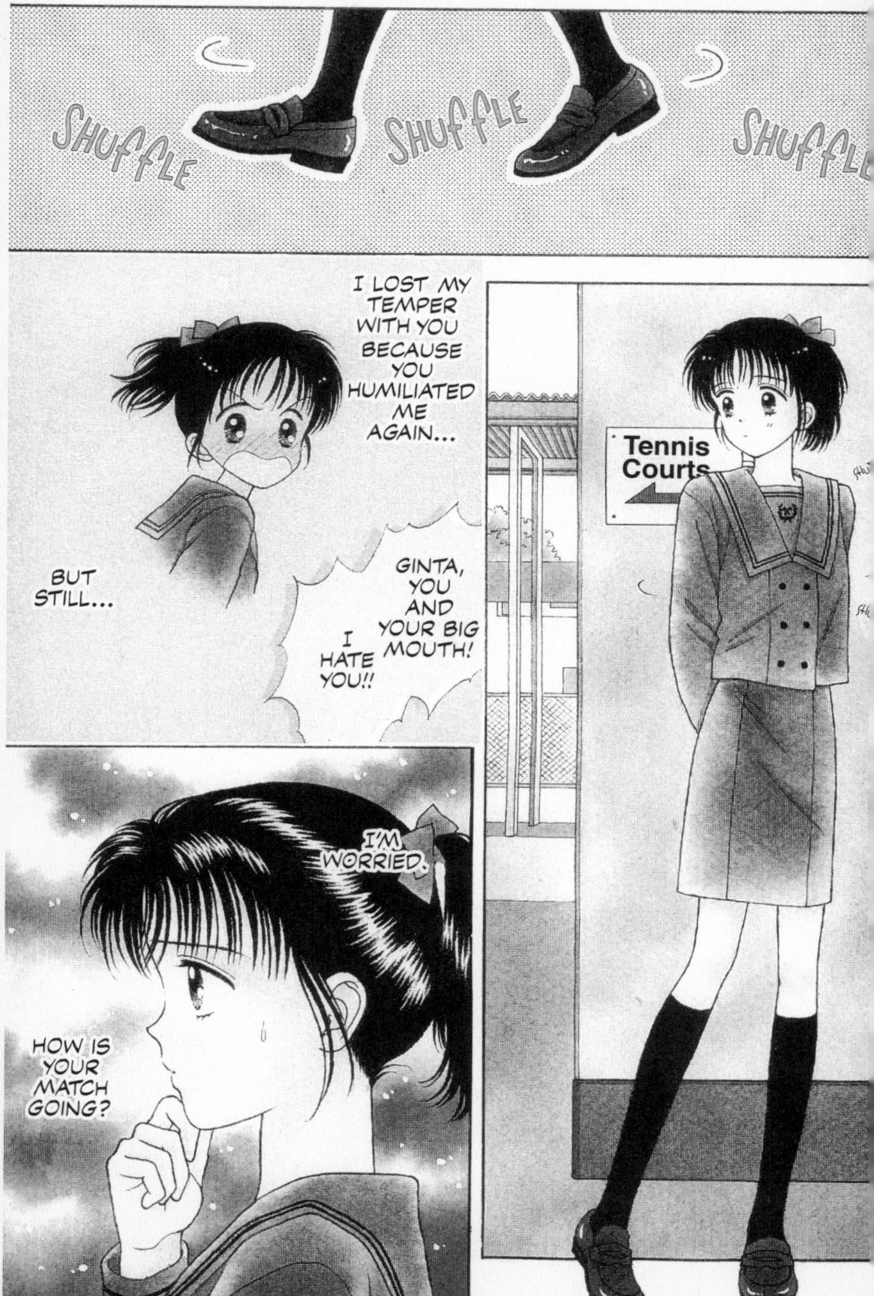
SHUFFLE
SHUFFLE
SHUFFLE
Tennis Courts
I LOST MY TEMPER WITH YOU BECAUSE YOU HUMILIATED ME AGAIN...
GINTA, YOU AND YOUR BIG MOUTH!
I HATE YOU!!
BUT STILL...
I'M WORRIED.
HOW IS YOUR MATCH GOING?

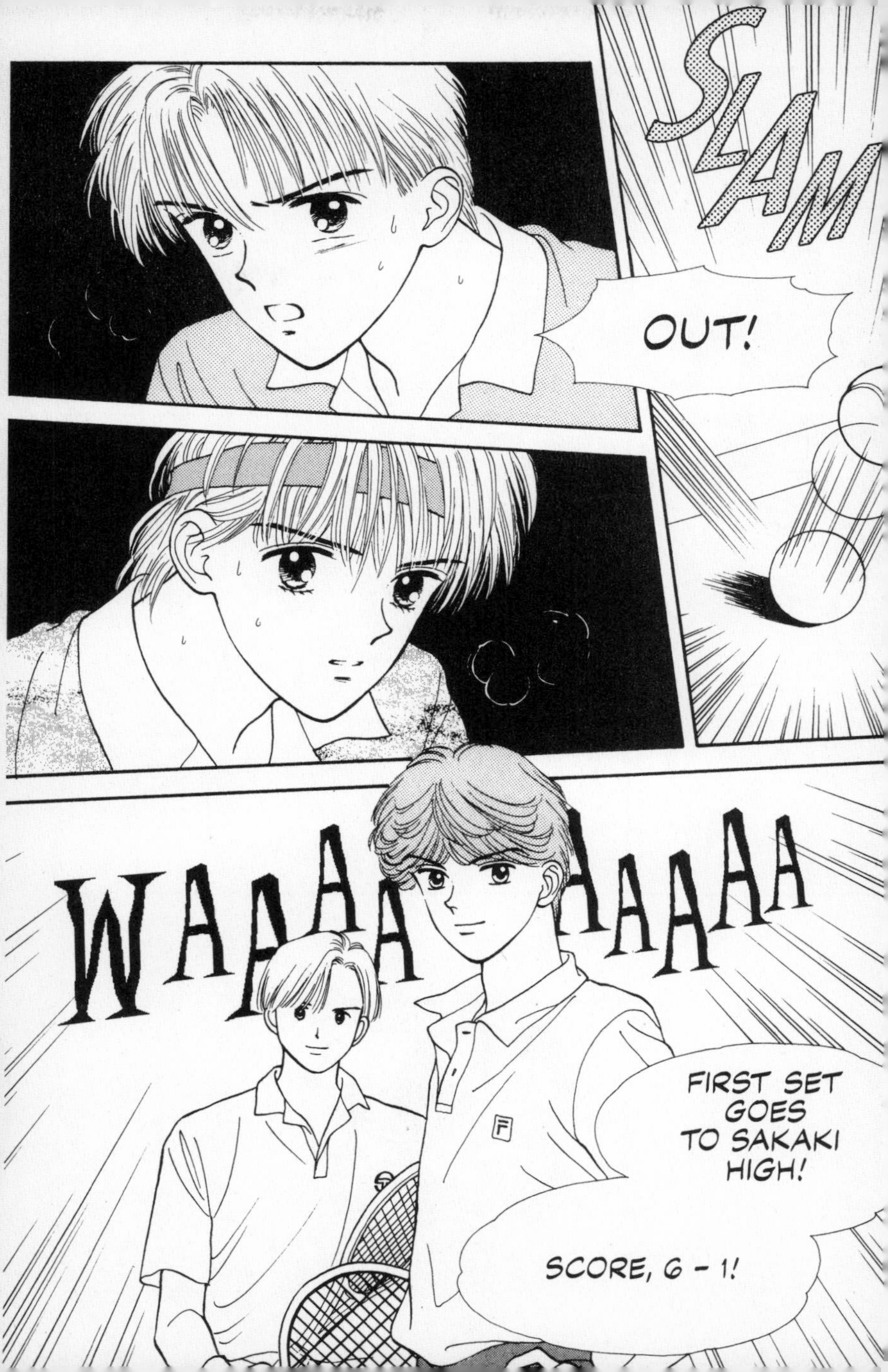
SLAM
OUT!
WAAAAAAAAA
FIRST SET GOES TO SAKAKI HIGH!
SCORE, 6 - 1!

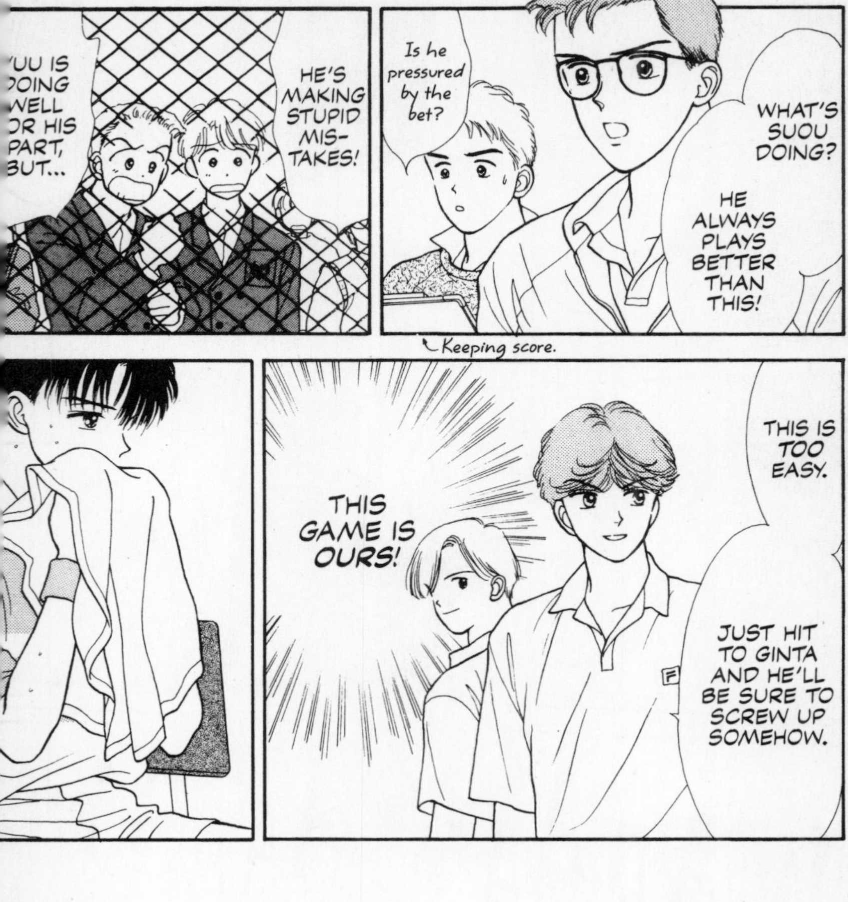
WHAT'S SUOU DOING?
HE ALWAYS PLAYS BETTER THAN THIS!
Is he pressured by the bet?
Keeping score.
HE'S MAKING STUPID MIS- TAKES!
YUU IS DOING WELL OR HIS PART, BUT...
THIS IS TOO EASY.
JUST HIT TO GINTA AND HE'LL BE SURE TO SCREW UP SOMEHOW.
THIS GAME IS OURS!

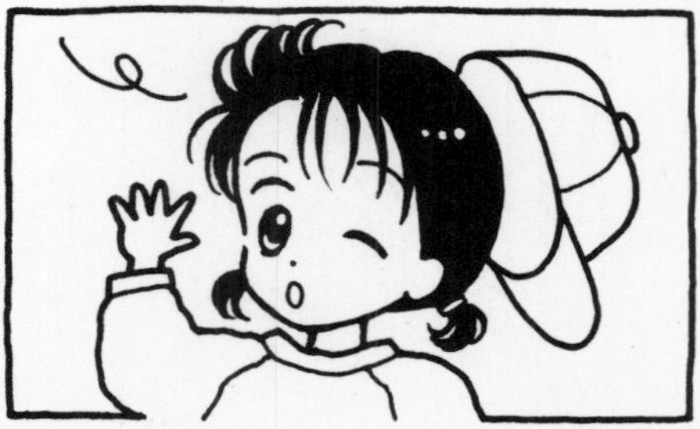

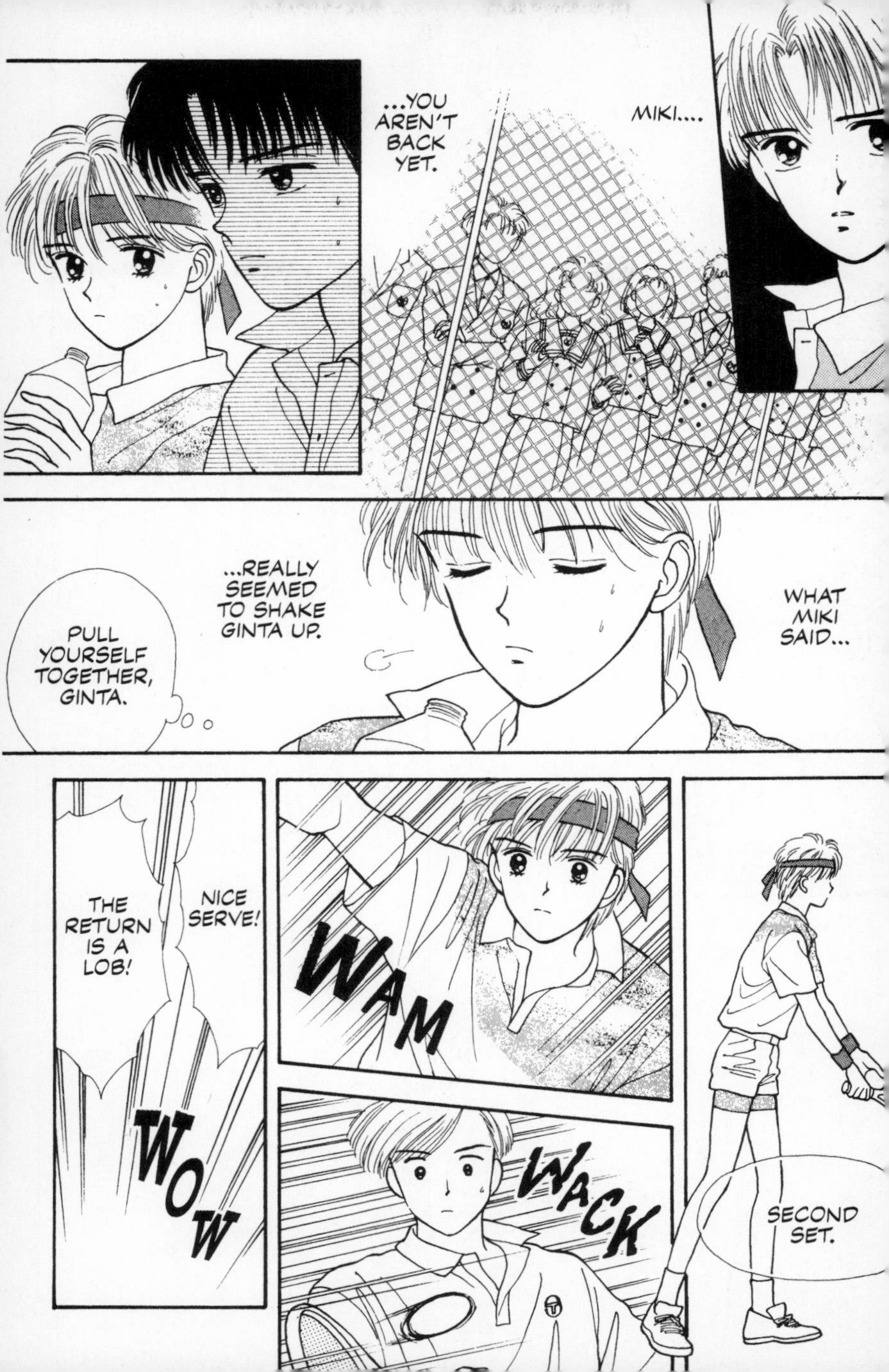
MIKI....
...YOU AREN'T BACK YET.
WHAT MIKI SAID...
...REALLY SEEMED TO SHAKE GINTA UP.
PULL YOURSELF TOGETHER, GINTA.
SECOND SET.
WAM
WACK
NICE SERVE!
THE RETURN IS A LOB!
WOW

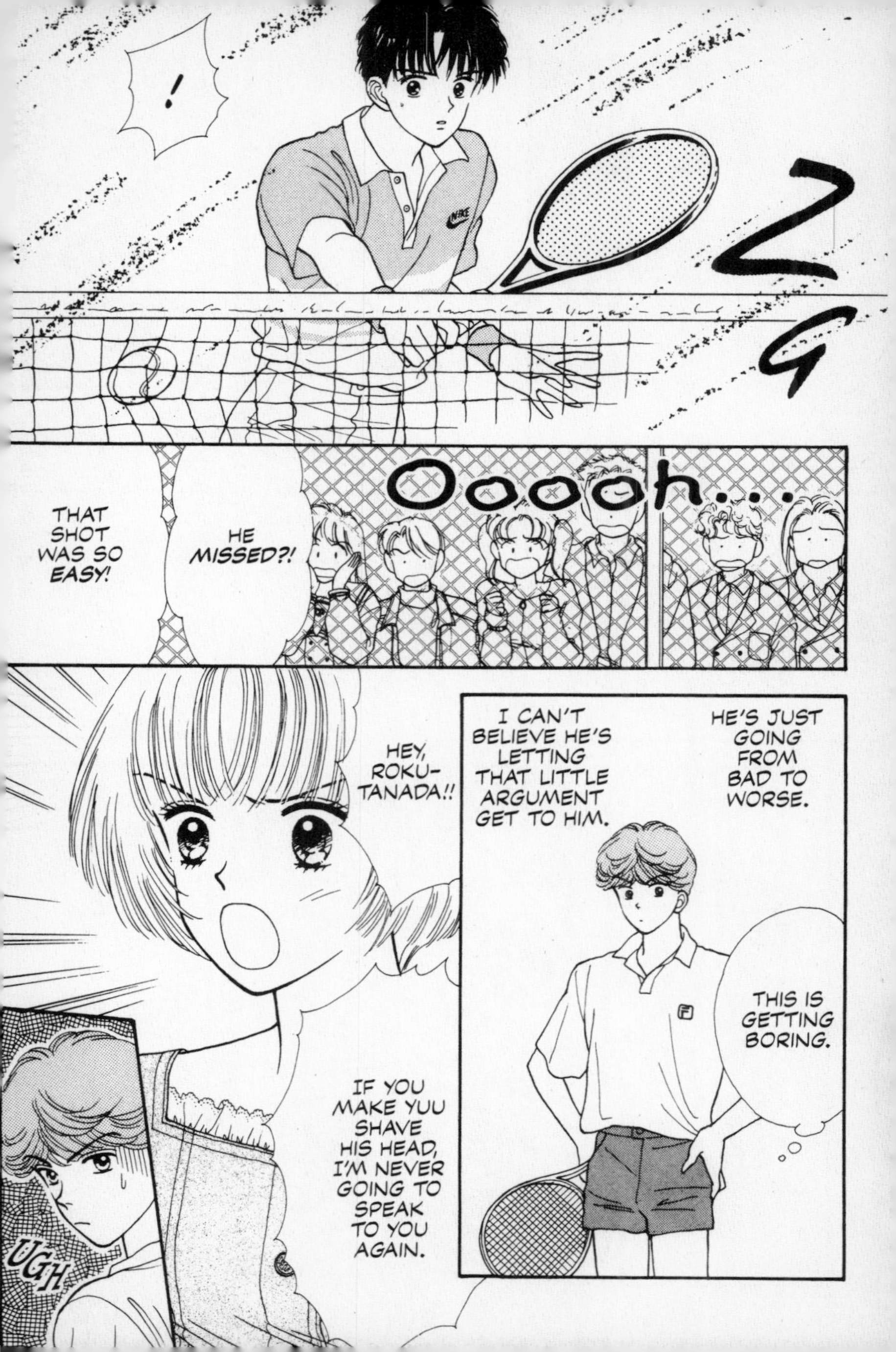
!
Ooooh...
HE MISSED?!
THAT SHOT WAS SO EASY!
HE'S JUST GOING FROM BAD TO WORSE.
I CAN'T BELIEVE HE'S LETTING THAT LITTLE ARGUMENT GET TO HIM.
THIS IS GETTING BORING.
HEY, ROKU-TANADA!!
IF YOU MAKE YUU SHAVE HIS HEAD, I'M NEVER GOING TO SPEAK TO YOU AGAIN.
UGH

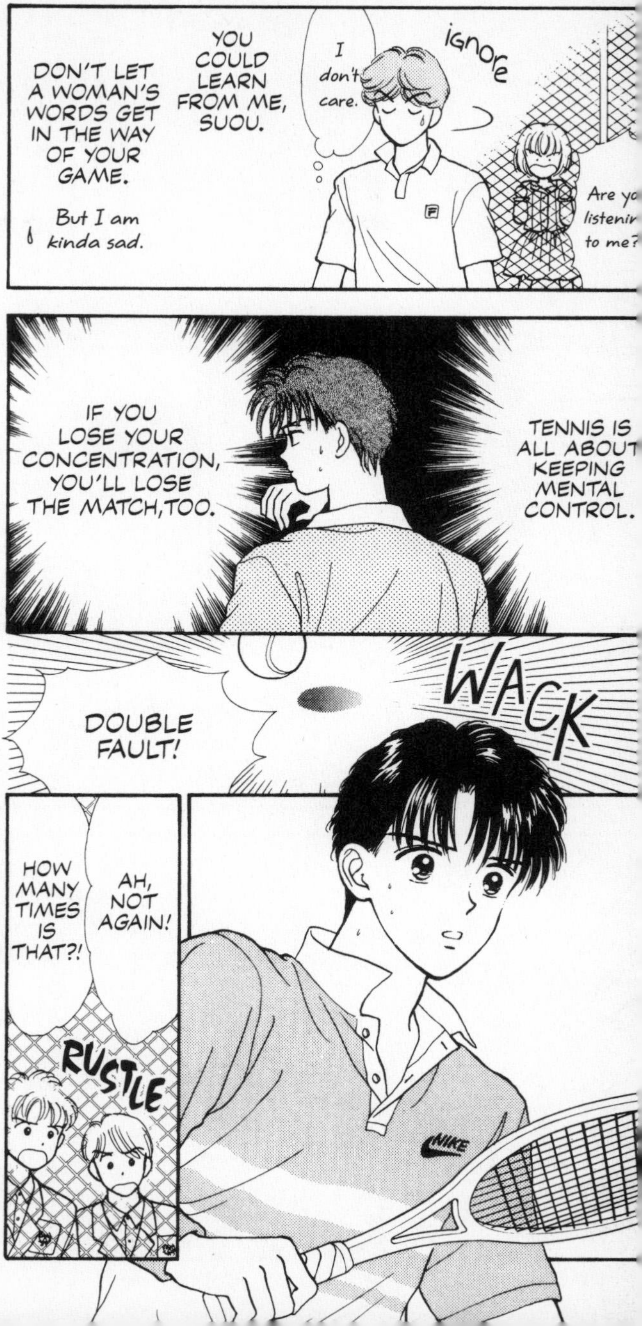
Are yo
listenir
to me?
ignore
I don't care.
YOU COULD LEARN FROM ME, SUOU.
DON'T LET A WOMAN'S WORDS GET IN THE WAY OF YOUR GAME.
But I am kinda sad.
TENNIS IS ALL ABOUT KEEPING MENTAL CONTROL.
IF YOU LOSE YOUR CONCENTRATION, YOU'LL LOSE THE MATCH,TOO.
WACK
DOUBLE FAULT!
NIKE
AH, NOT AGAIN!
HOW MANY TIMES IS THAT?!
RUSTLE

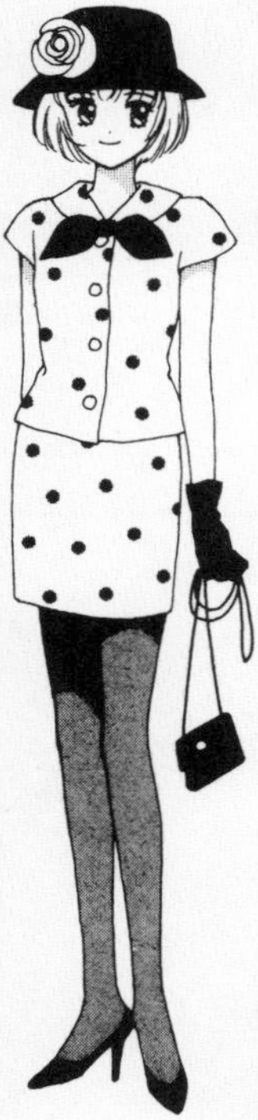

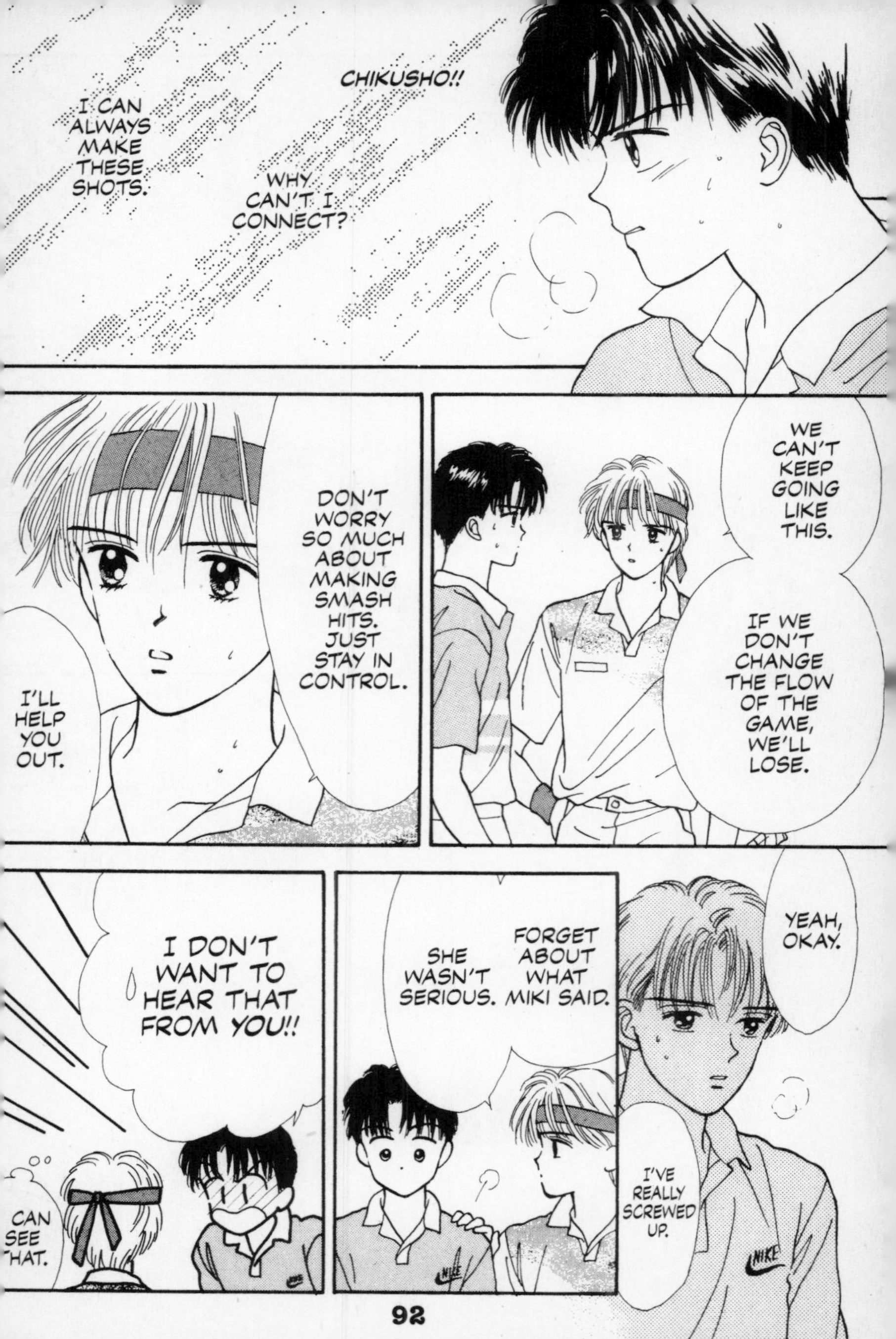
CHIKUSHO!!
WHY CAN'T I CONNECT?
I CAN ALWAYS MAKE THESE SHOTS.
WE CAN'T KEEP GOING LIKE THIS.
IF WE DON'T CHANGE THE FLOW OF THE GAME, WE'LL LOSE.
DON'T WORRY SO MUCH ABOUT MAKING SMASH HITS. JUST STAY IN CONTROL.
I'LL HELP YOU OUT.
YEAH, OKAY.
FORGET ABOUT WHAT MIKI SAID.
SHE WASN'T SERIOUS.
I'VE REALLY SCREWED UP.
I DON'T WANT TO HEAR THAT FROM YOU!!
CAN SEE THAT.

FREE TALK ③

When I first created the character Rokutanda, I didn't know what his hairstyle would look like, so I drew him like a paper doll with no hair. In my rough drafts, he's always bald. Here's what he looked like:

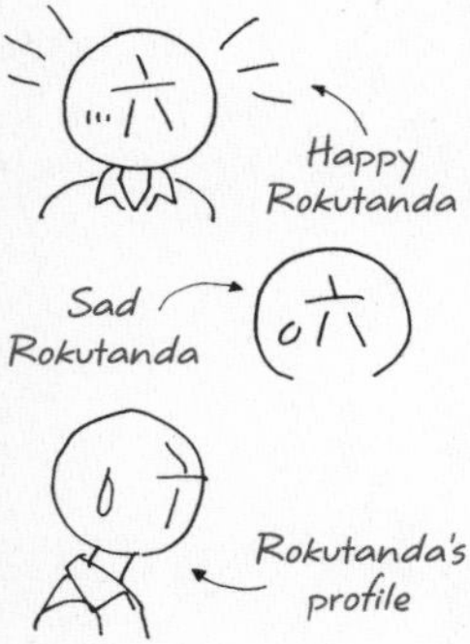

Happy Rokutanda
Sad Rokutanda
Rokutanda's profile

This way of drawing him really started to grow on me, so I wanted to draw him like this in the final version, too. But I didn't have the courage to do so. Even after I finalized his hairstyle and design, I still think of him as looking like a paper doll.

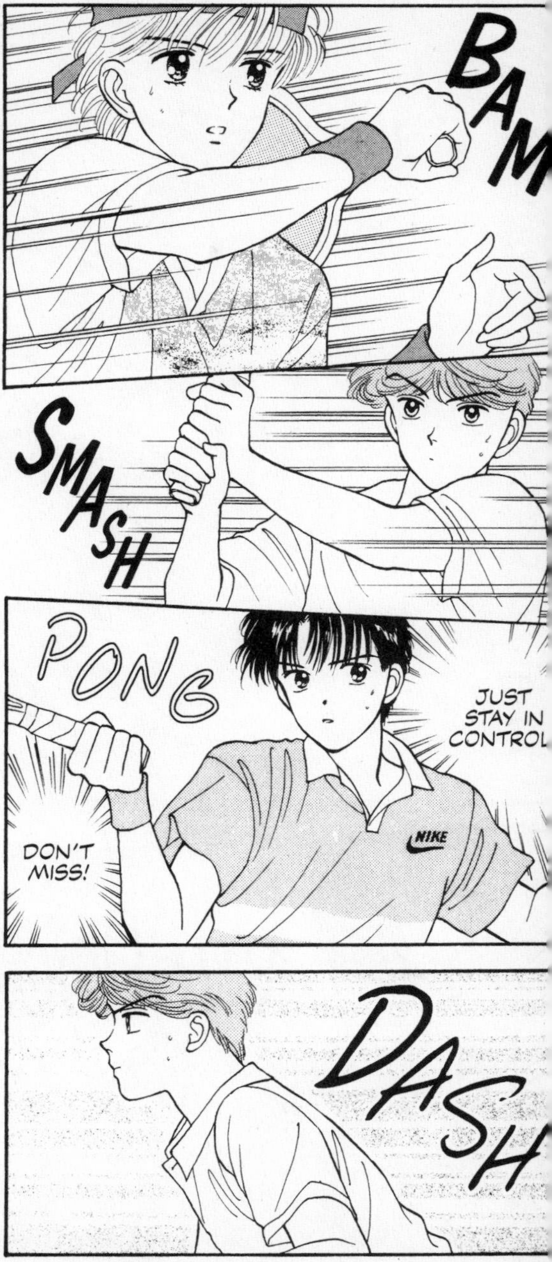

BAM
SMASH
JUST STAY IN CONTROL
PONG
DON'T MISS!
DASH

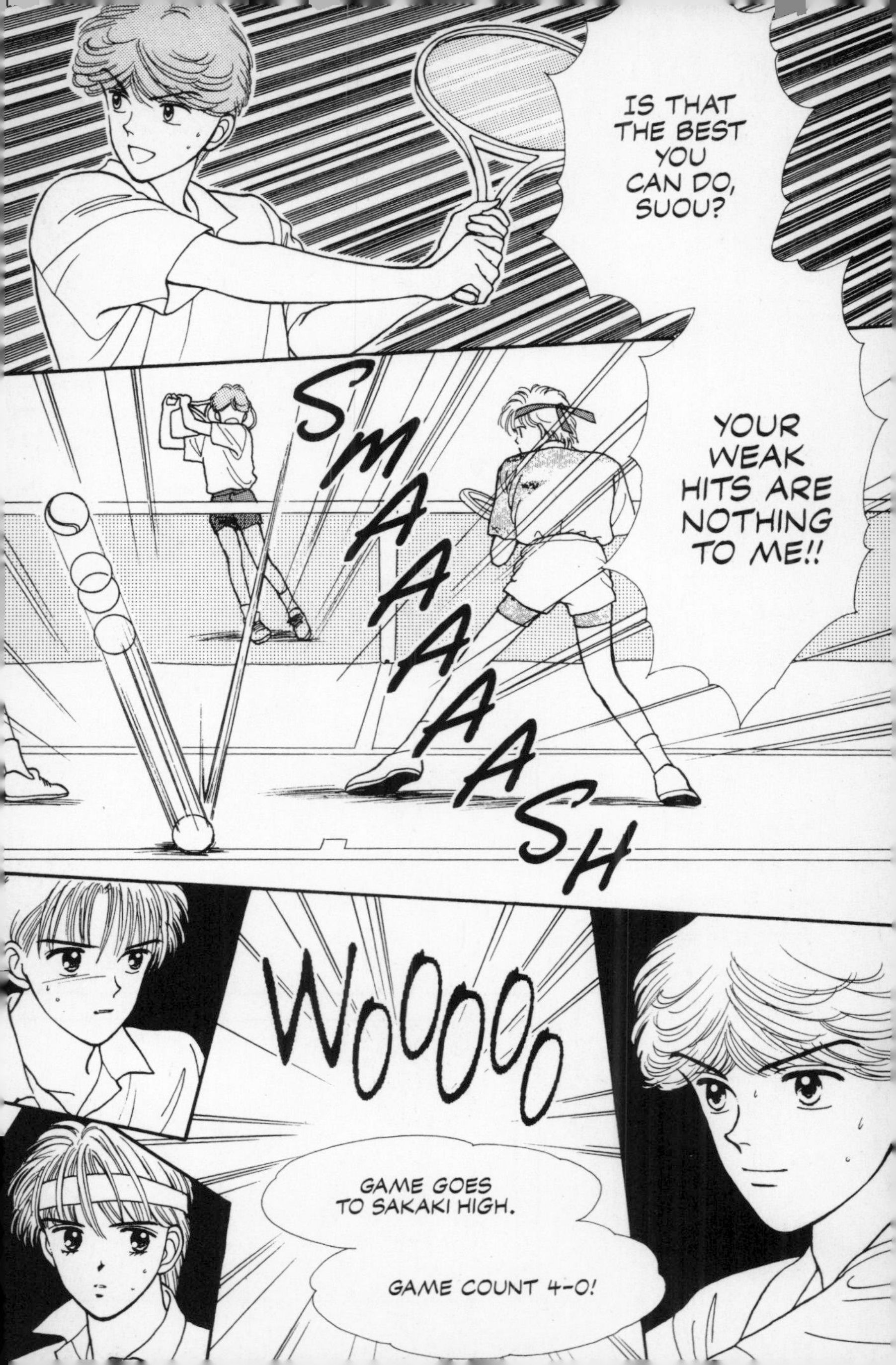
IS THAT THE BEST YOU CAN DO, SUOU?
YOUR WEAK HITS ARE NOTHING TO ME!!
SMAAAAASH
WOOOOO
GAME GOES TO SAKAKI HIGH.
GAME COUNT 4-0!

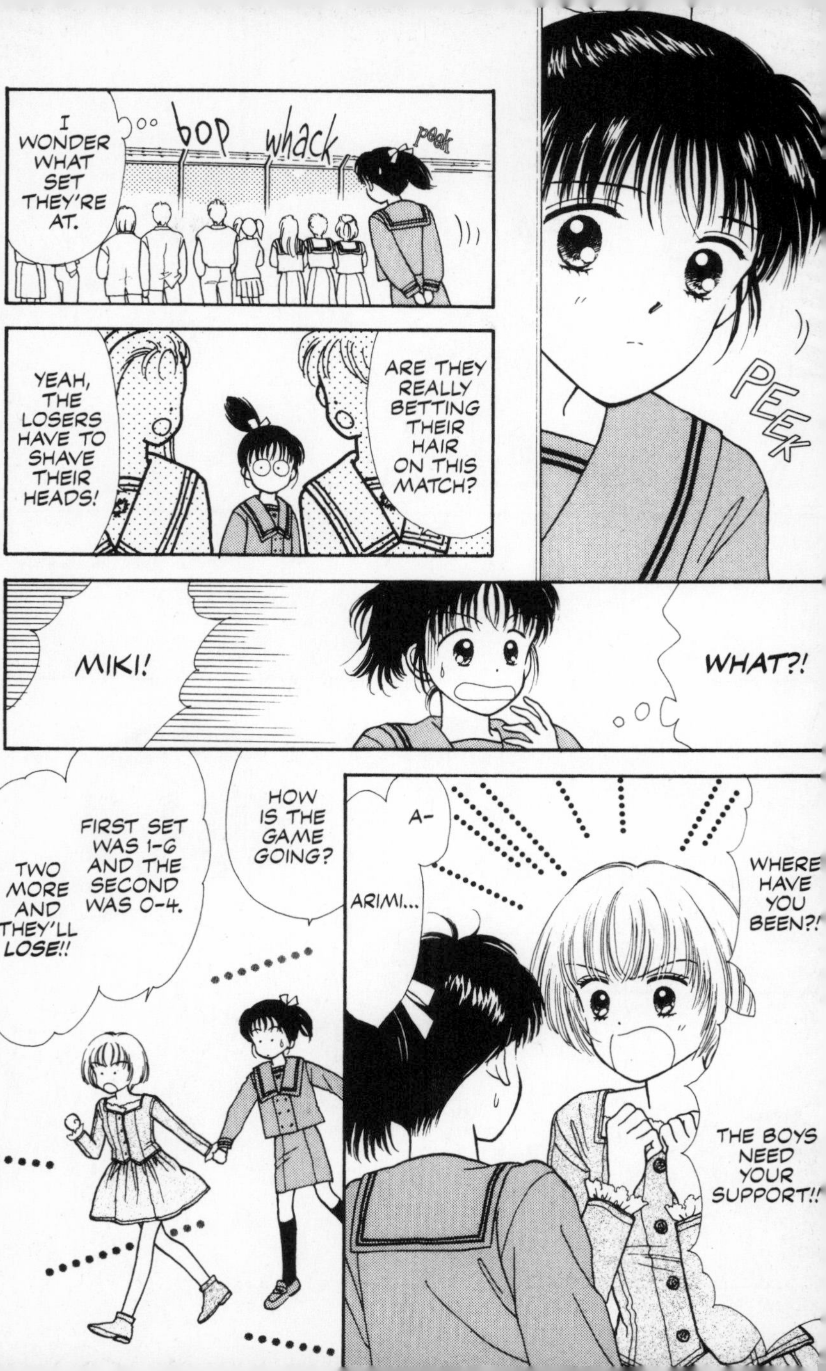
PEEK
I WONDER WHAT SET THEY'RE AT.
bop
whack
peek
ARE THEY REALLY BETTING THEIR HAIR ON THIS MATCH?
YEAH, THE LOSERS HAVE TO SHAVE THEIR HEADS!
WHAT?!
MIKI!
A-
ARIMI...
WHERE HAVE YOU BEEN?!
THE BOYS NEED YOUR SUPPORT!!
HOW IS THE GAME GOING?
FIRST SET WAS 1-6 AND THE SECOND WAS 0-4.
TWO MORE AND THEY'LL LOSE!!

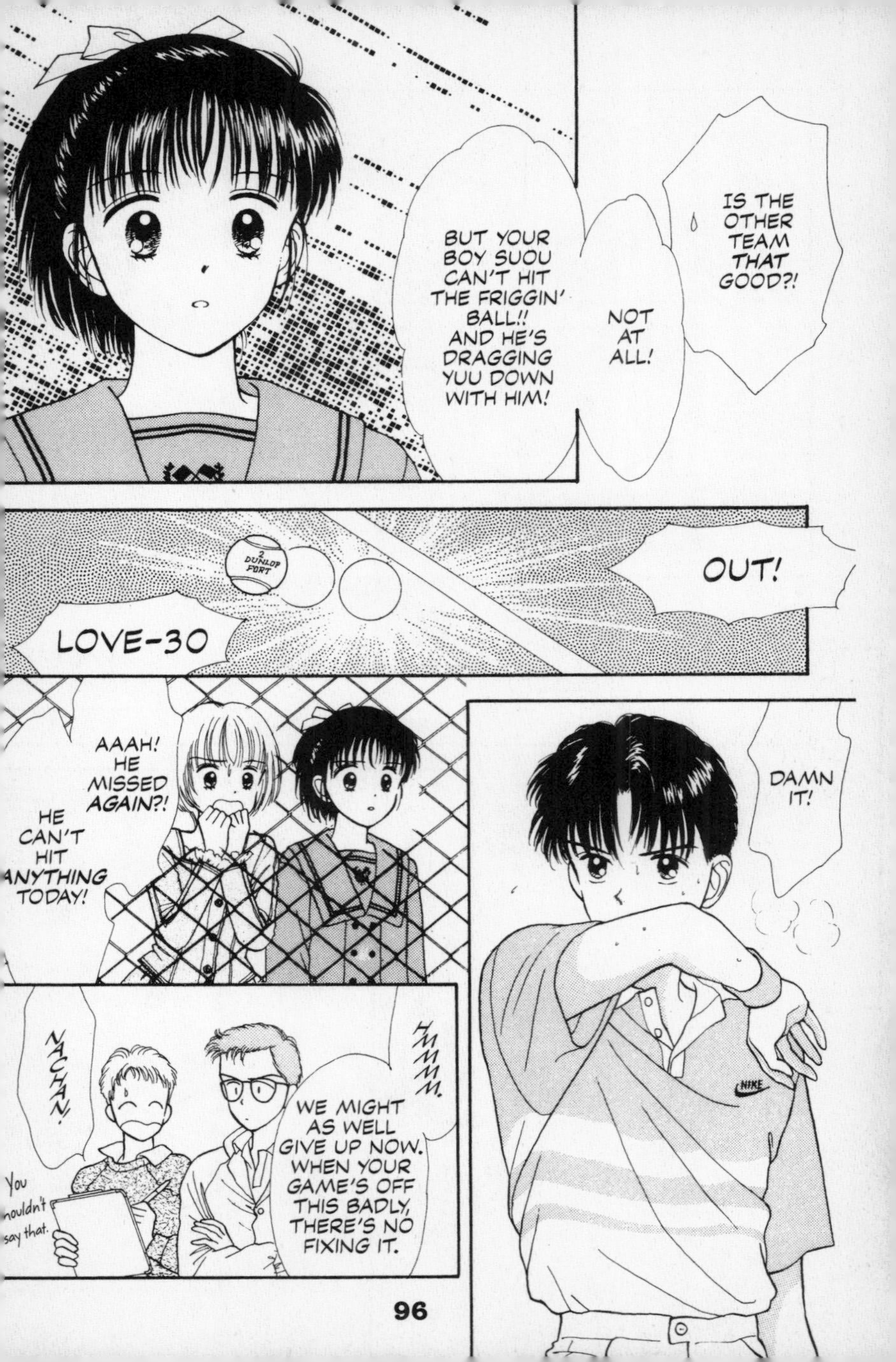

IS THE OTHER TEAM THAT GOOD?!
NOT AT ALL!
BUT YOUR BOY SUOU CAN'T HIT THE FRIGGIN' BALL!! AND HE'S DRAGGING YUU DOWN WITH HIM!
OUT!
LOVE-30
DAMN IT!
AAAH! HE MISSED AGAIN?!
HE CAN'T HIT ANYTHING TODAY!
HMMMM.
WE MIGHT AS WELL GIVE UP NOW. WHEN YOUR GAME'S OFF THIS BADLY, THERE'S NO FIXING IT.
NACHAN!
You nouldn't say that.

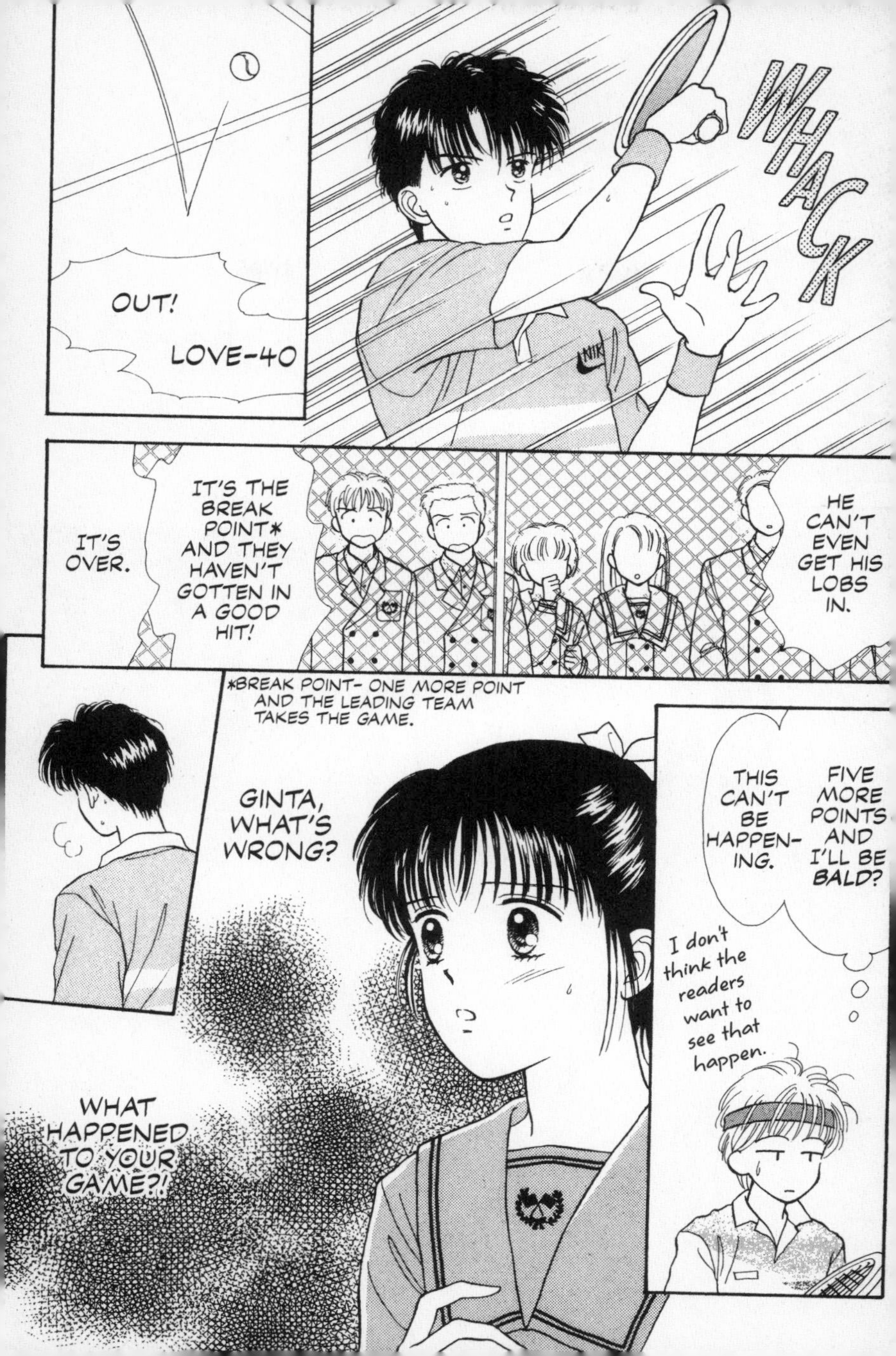
WHACK
OUT!
LOVE-40
HE CAN'T EVEN GET HIS LOBS IN.
IT'S THE BREAK POINT* AND THEY HAVEN'T GOTTEN IN A GOOD HIT!
IT'S OVER.
*BREAK POINT- ONE MORE POINT AND THE LEADING TEAM TAKES THE GAME.
FIVE MORE POINTS AND I'LL BE BALD?
THIS CAN'T BE HAPPENING.
I don't think the readers want to see that happen.
GINTA, WHAT'S WRONG?
WHAT HAPPENED TO YOUR GAME?!

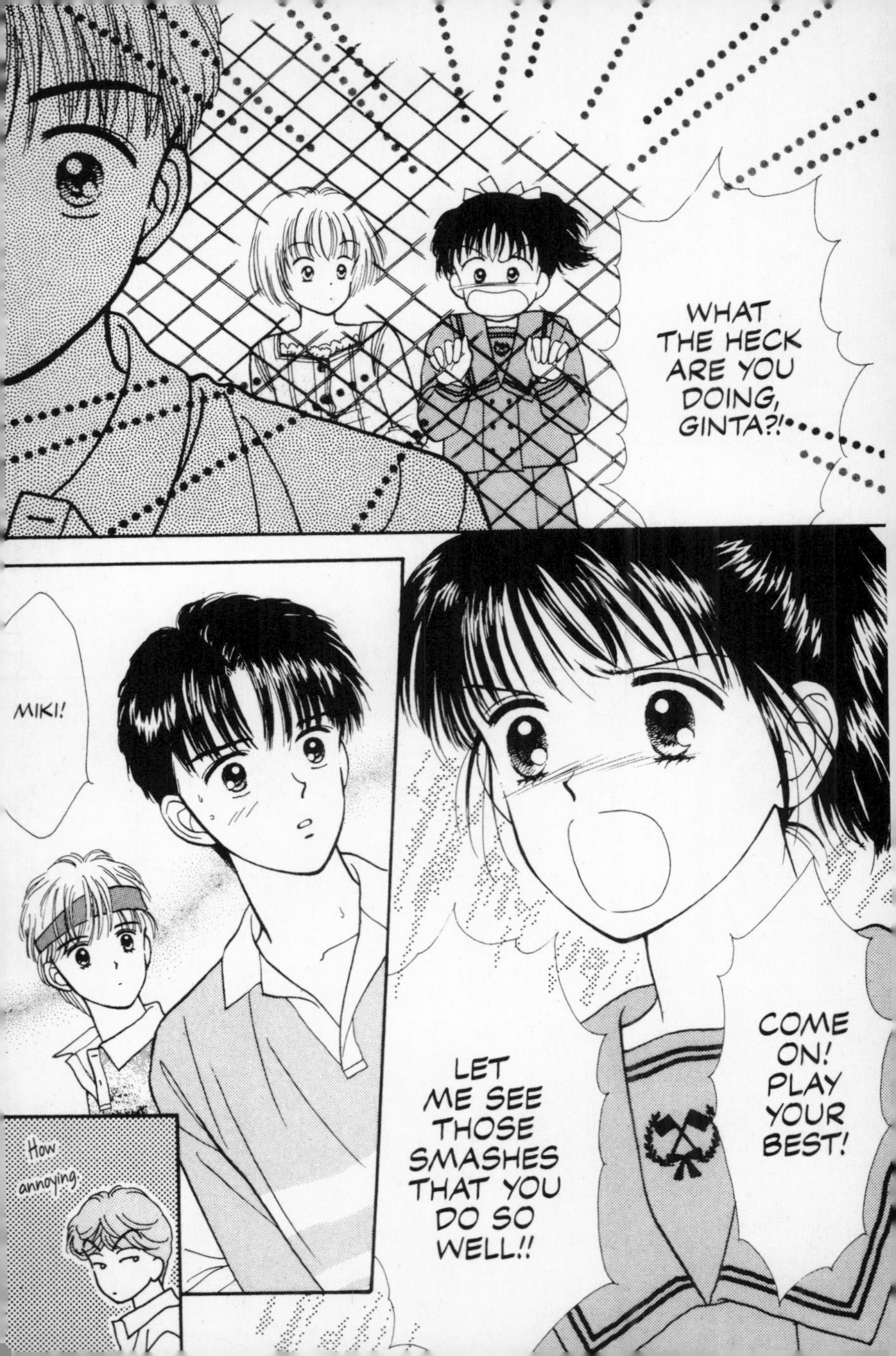
WHAT THE HECK ARE YOU DOING, GINTA?!
COME ON! PLAY YOUR BEST!
LET ME SEE THOSE SMASHES THAT YOU DO SO WELL!!
MIKI!
How annoying.

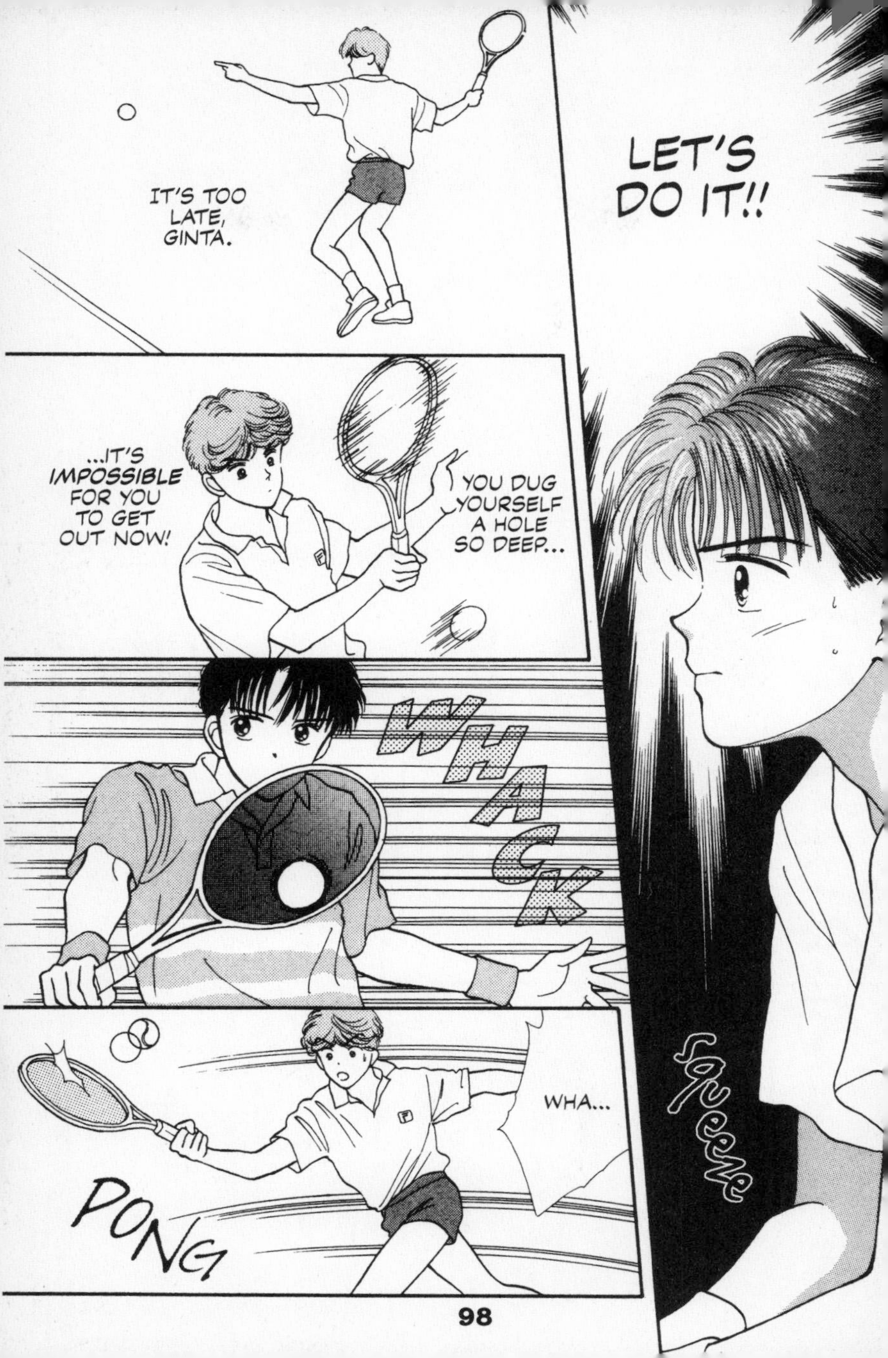
LET'S DO IT!!
SQUEEZE
IT'S TOO LATE, GINTA.
YOU DUG YOURSELF A HOLE SO DEEP...
...IT'S IMPOSSIBLE FOR YOU TO GET OUT NOW!
WHACK
WHA...
PONG

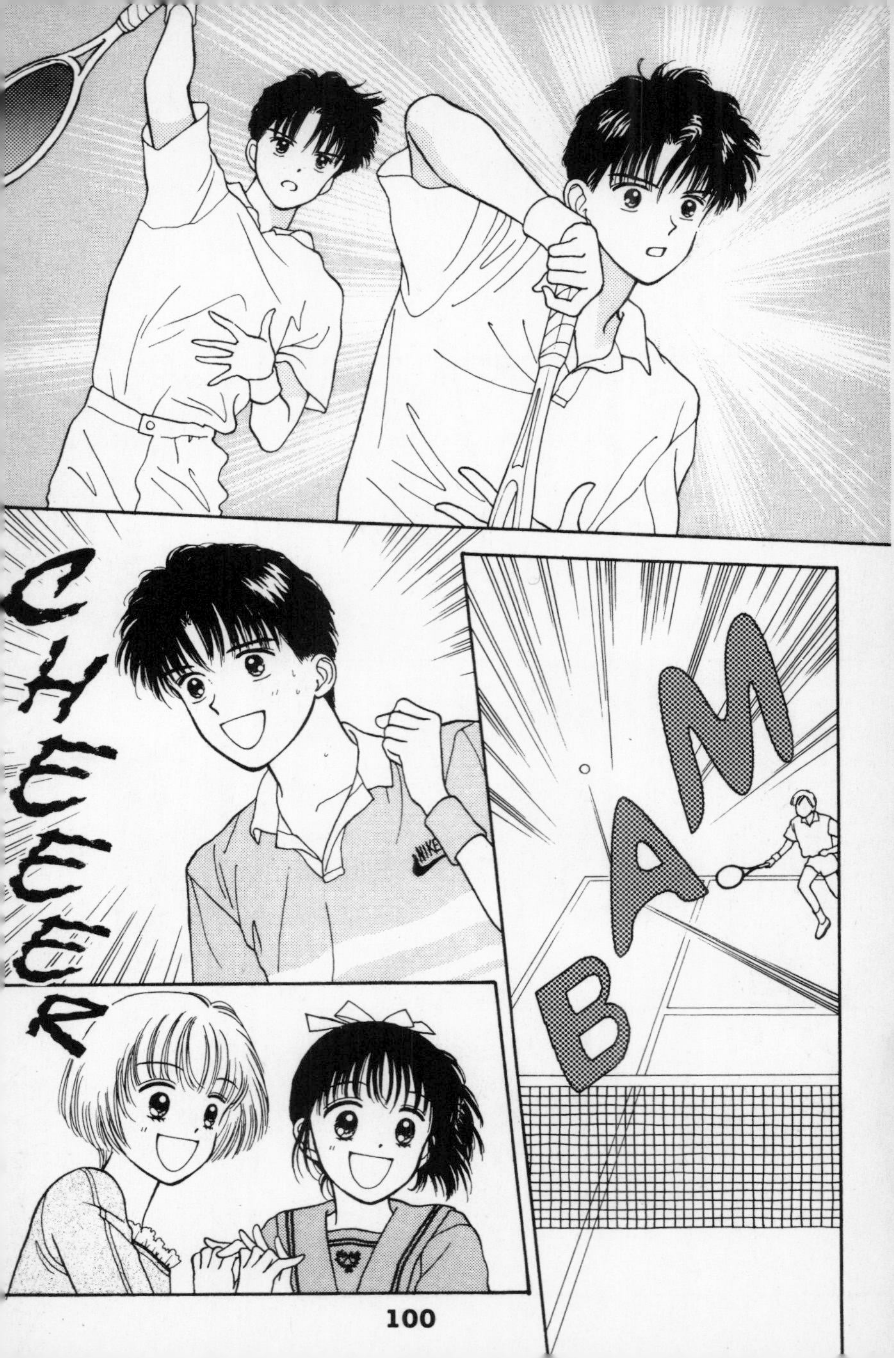
BAM
CHEER

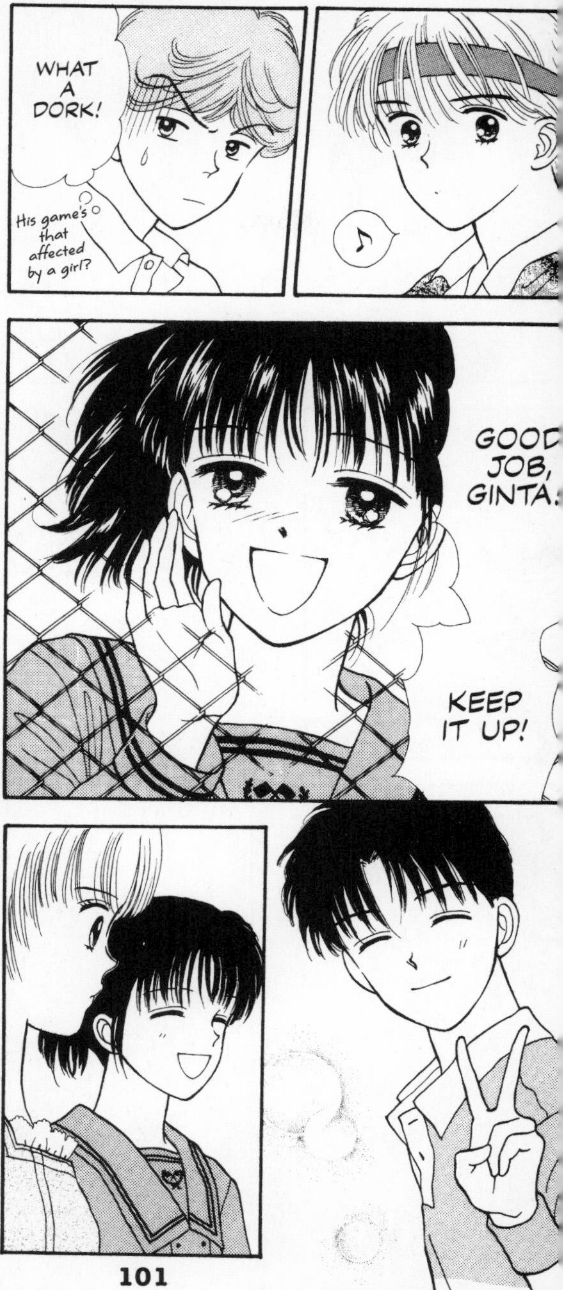
♪
WHAT A DORK!
His game's that affected by a girl?
GOOD JOB, GINTA!
KEEP IT UP!

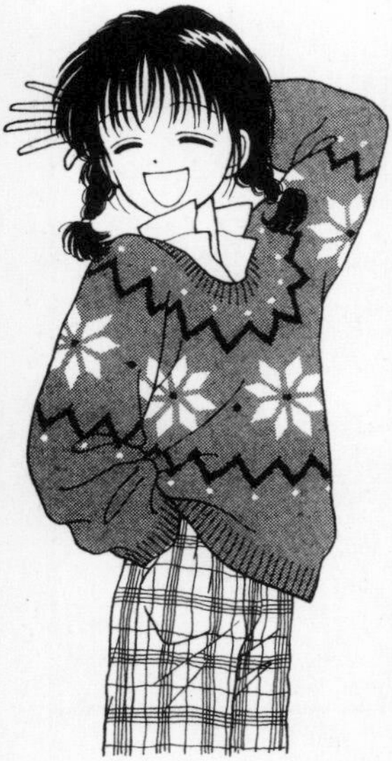

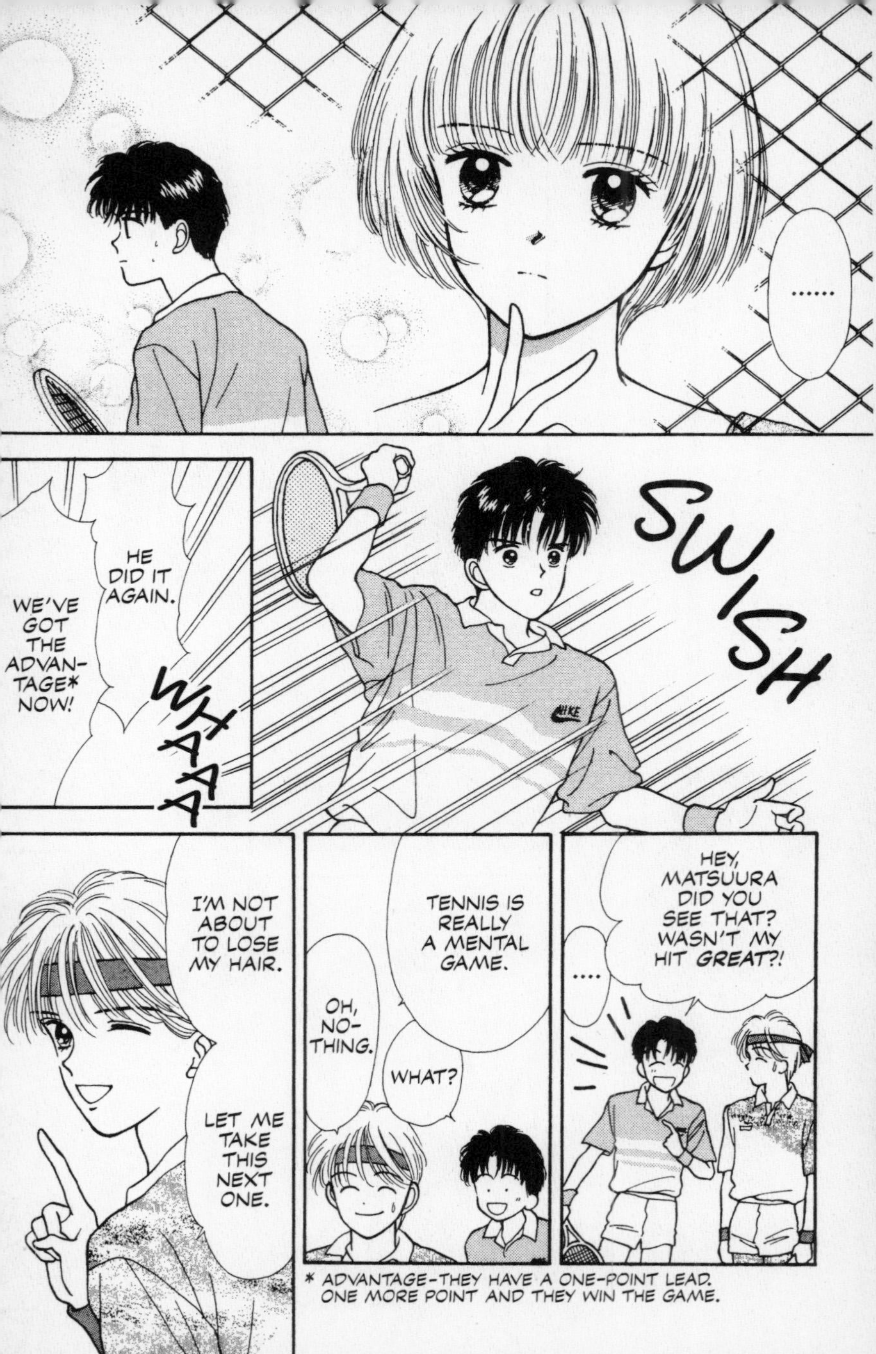
......
SWISH
HE DID IT AGAIN.
WE'VE GOT THE ADVANTAGE* NOW!
WHAAA
HEY, MATSUURA DID YOU SEE THAT? WASN'T MY HIT *GREAT*?!
....
TENNIS IS REALLY A MENTAL GAME.
WHAT?
OH, NO-THING.
I'M NOT ABOUT TO LOSE MY HAIR.
LET ME TAKE THIS NEXT ONE.

* ADVANTAGE-THEY HAVE A ONE-POINT LEAD. ONE MORE POINT AND THEY WIN THE GAME.

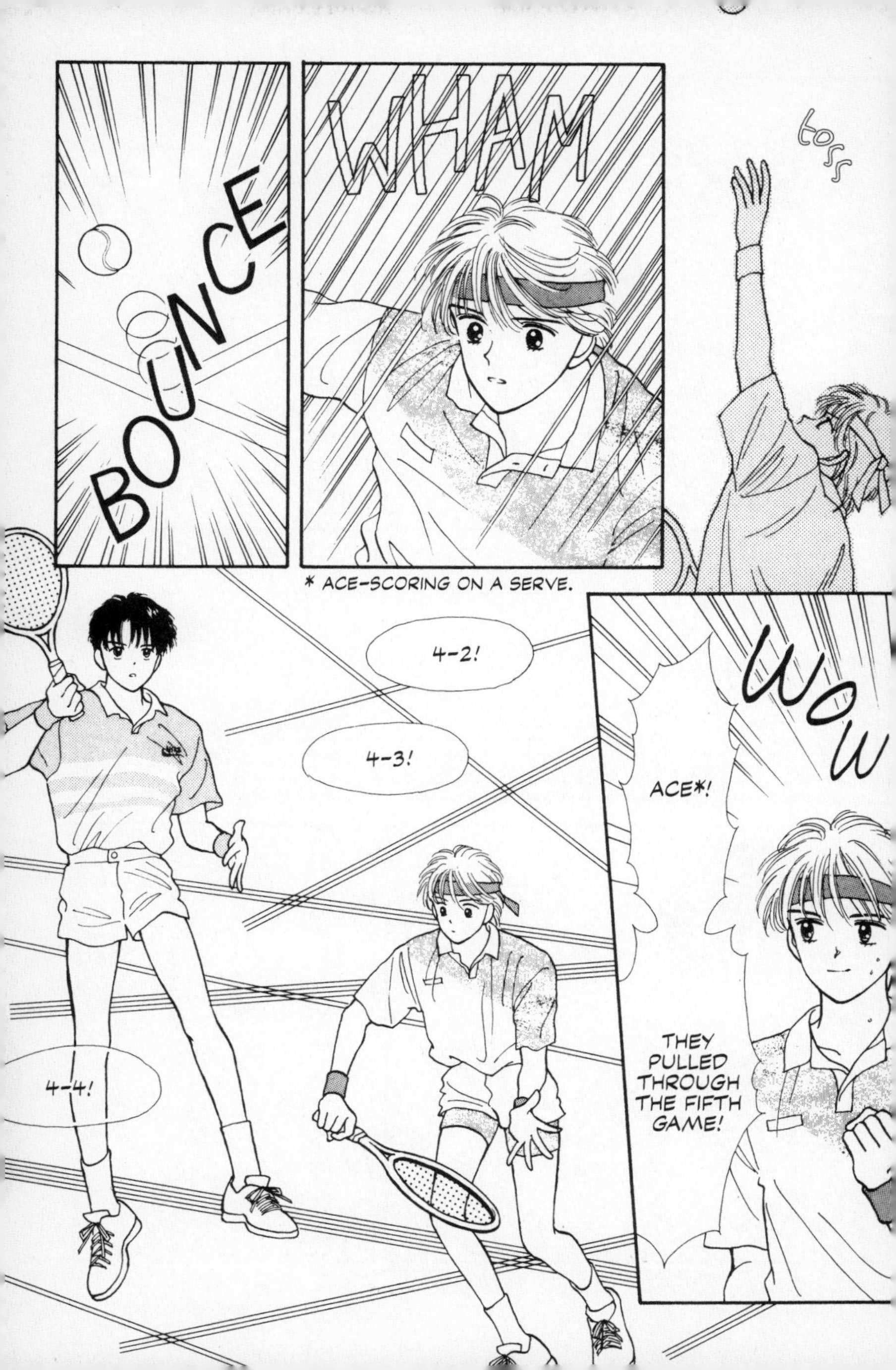
toss
WHAM
BOUNCE
WOW
ACE*!
THEY PULLED THROUGH THE FIFTH GAME!
4-2!
4-3!
4-4!
* ACE-SCORING ON A SERVE.

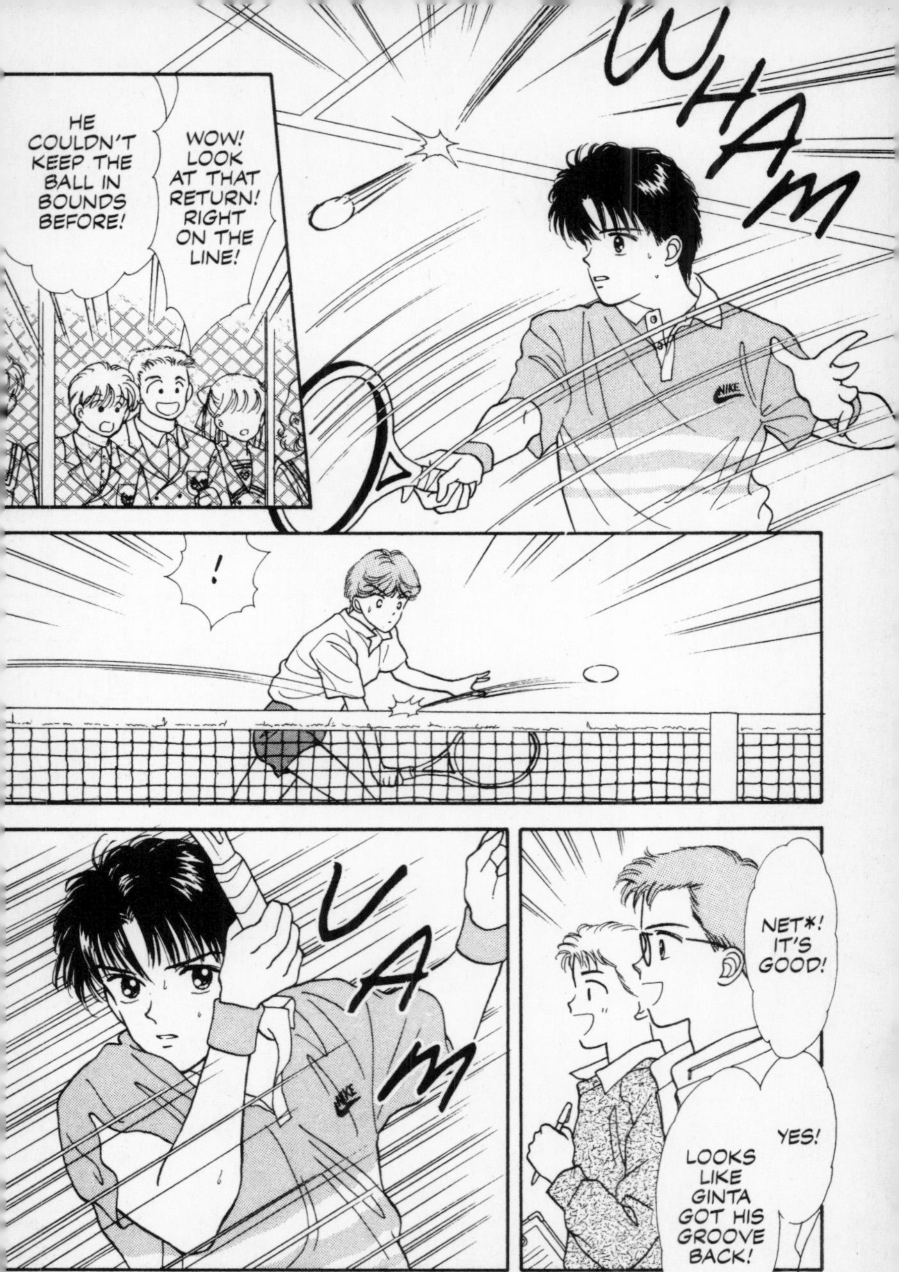
WHAM
WOW! LOOK AT THAT RETURN! RIGHT ON THE LINE!
HE COULDN'T KEEP THE BALL IN BOUNDS BEFORE!
!
NET*! IT'S GOOD!
YES!
LOOKS LIKE GINTA GOT HIS GROOVE BACK!
VAM

* WHEN THE BALL HITS THE NET BUT GOES INTO THE RIGHT SIDE OF THE COURT, IT'S CONSIDERED A LEGAL PLAY, EXCEPT ON SERVES.

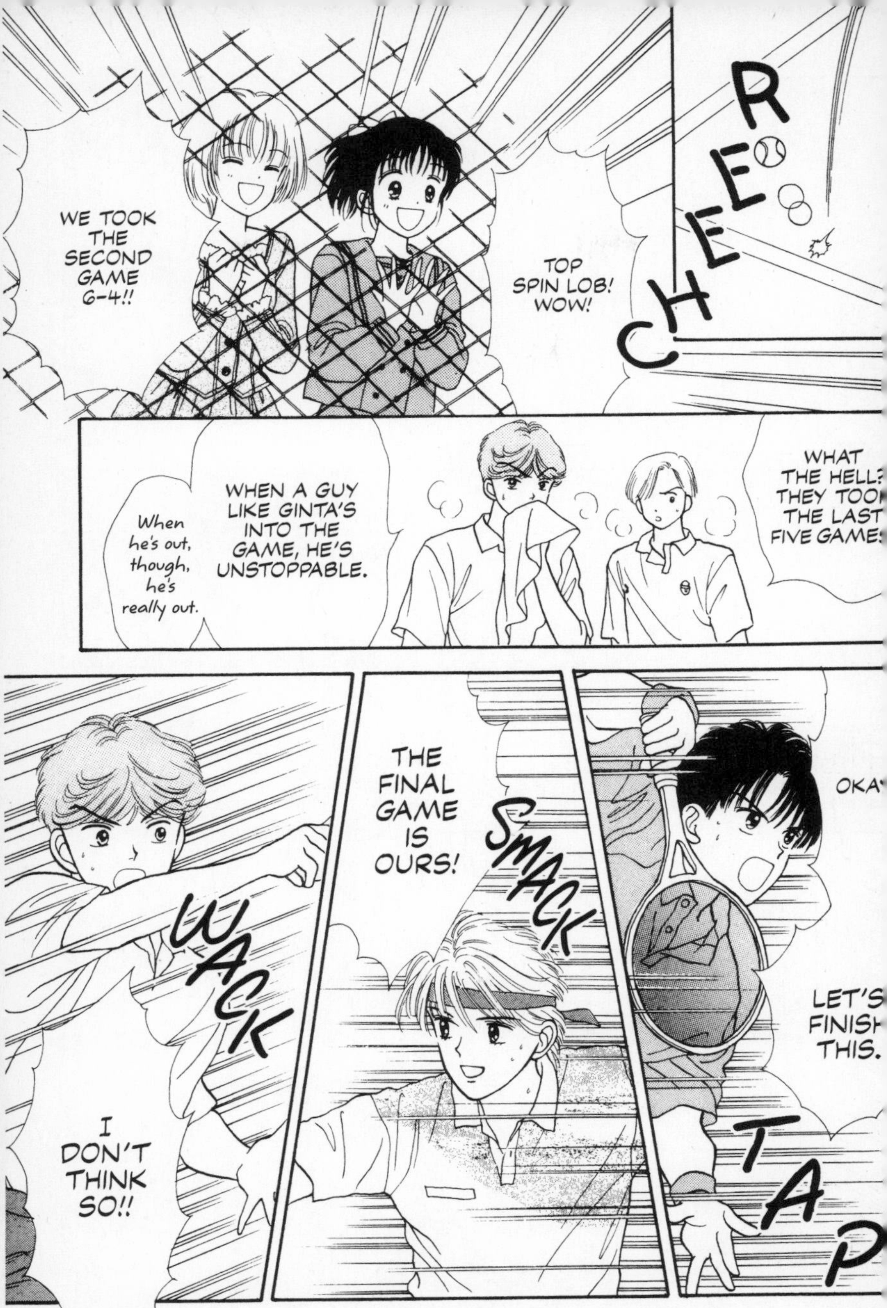

CHEER
TOP SPIN LOB! WOW!
WE TOOK THE SECOND GAME 6-4!!
WHAT THE HELL? THEY TOOK THE LAST FIVE GAMES
WHEN A GUY LIKE GINTA'S INTO THE GAME, HE'S UNSTOPPABLE.
When he's out, though, he's really out.
OKA
LET'S FINISH THIS.
TAP
THE FINAL GAME IS OURS!
SMACK
WACK
I DON'T THINK SO!!

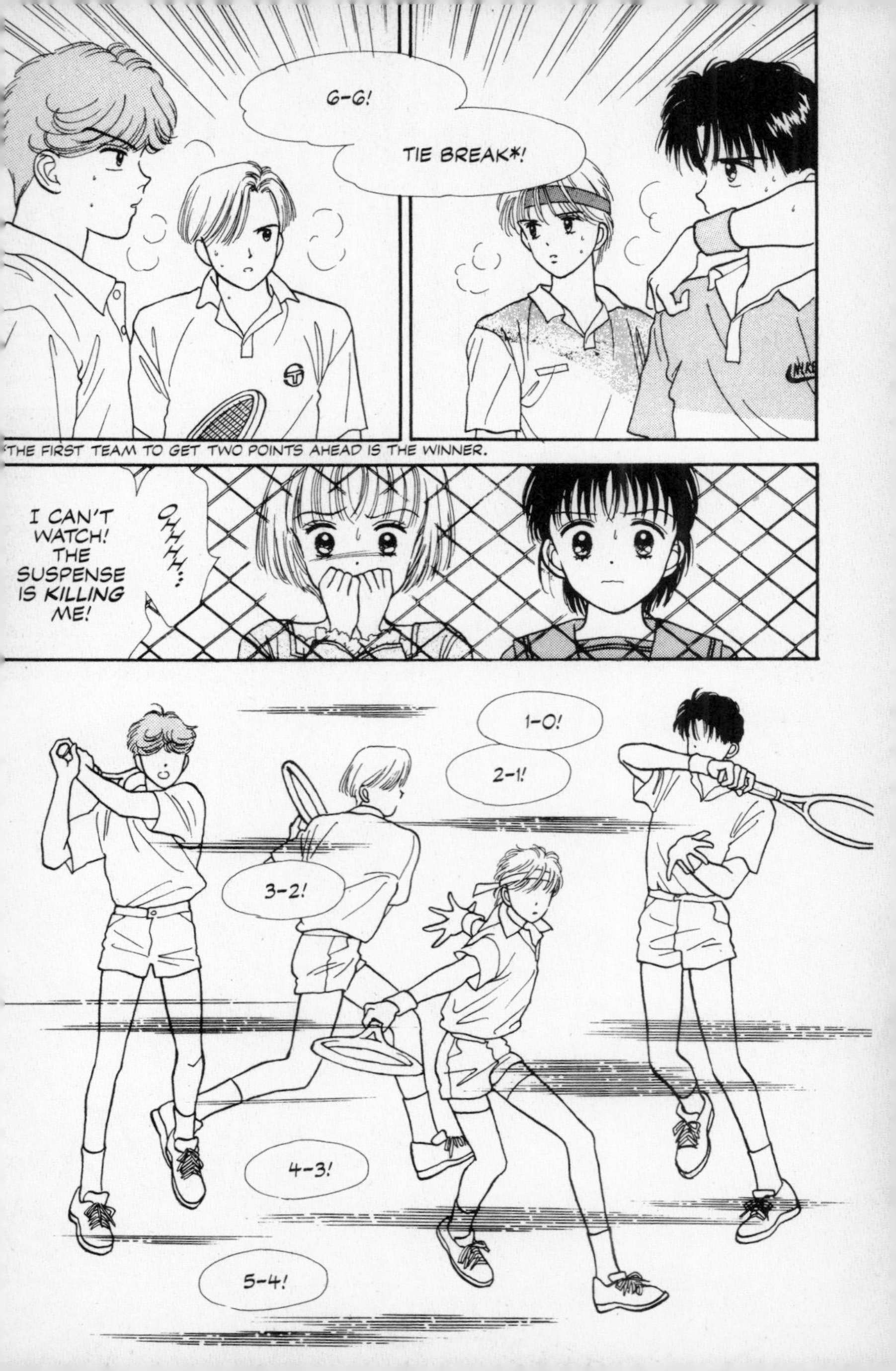
6-6!
TIE BREAK*!
I CAN'T WATCH! THE SUSPENSE IS KILLING ME!
OHHHH...
1-0!
2-1!
3-2!
4-3!
5-4!

*THE FIRST TEAM TO GET TWO POINTS AHEAD IS THE WINNER.

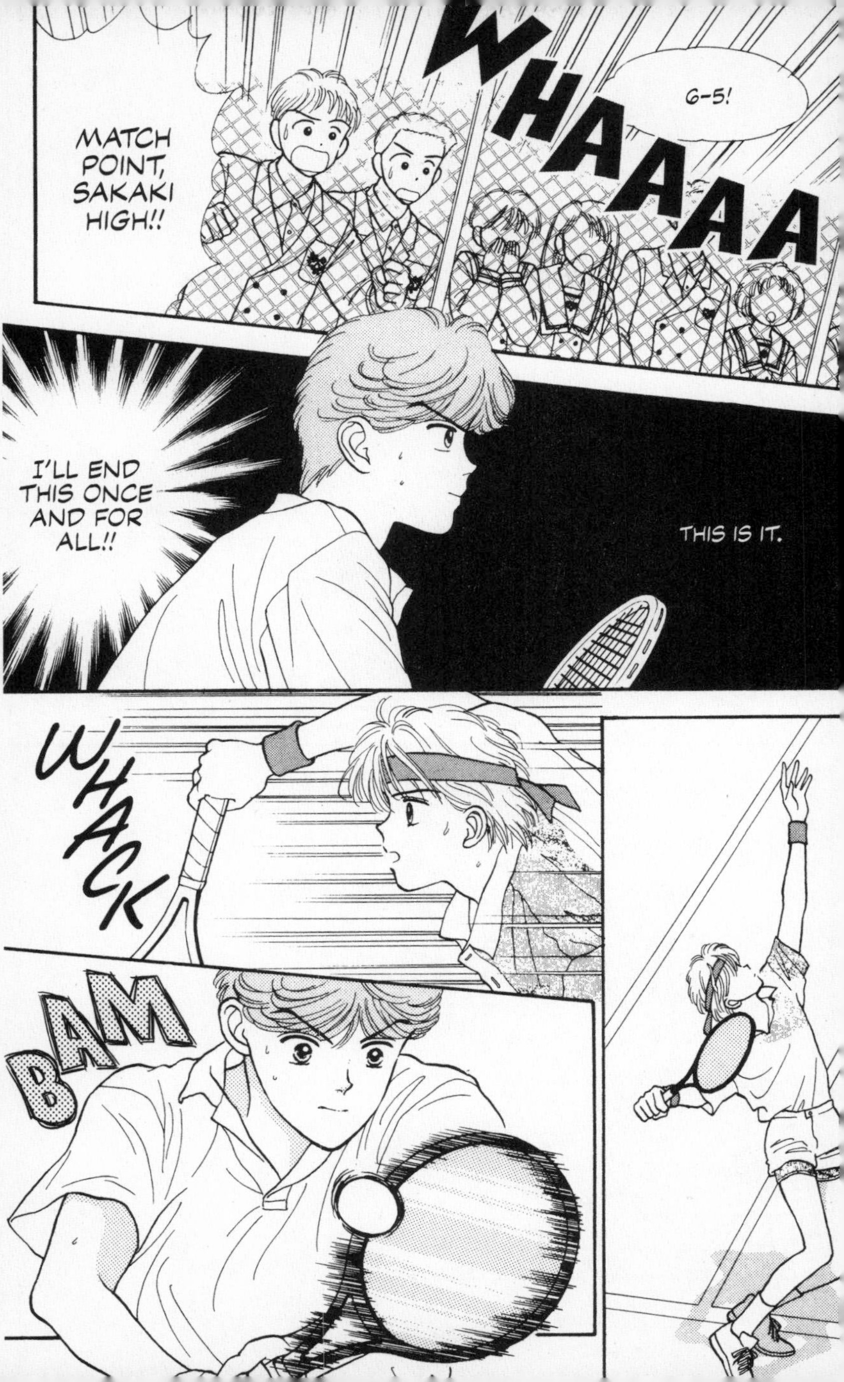
6-5!
WHAAAA
MATCH POINT, SAKAKI HIGH!!
THIS IS IT.
I'LL END THIS ONCE AND FOR ALL!!
WHACK
BAM

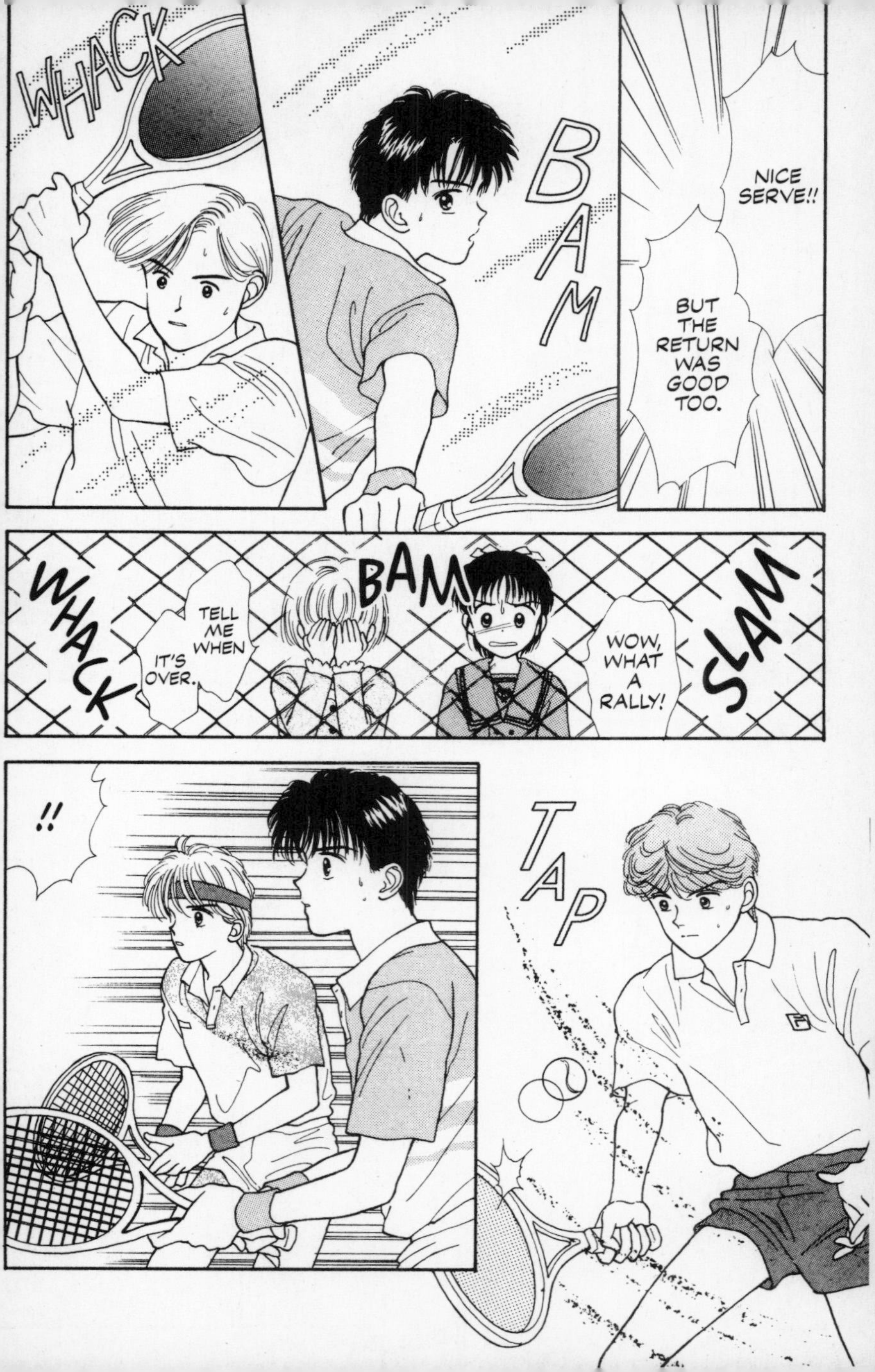
NICE SERVE!!
BUT THE RETURN WAS GOOD TOO.
BAM
WHACK
SLAM
WOW, WHAT A RALLY!
BAM
TELL ME WHEN IT'S OVER.
WHACK
TAP
!!

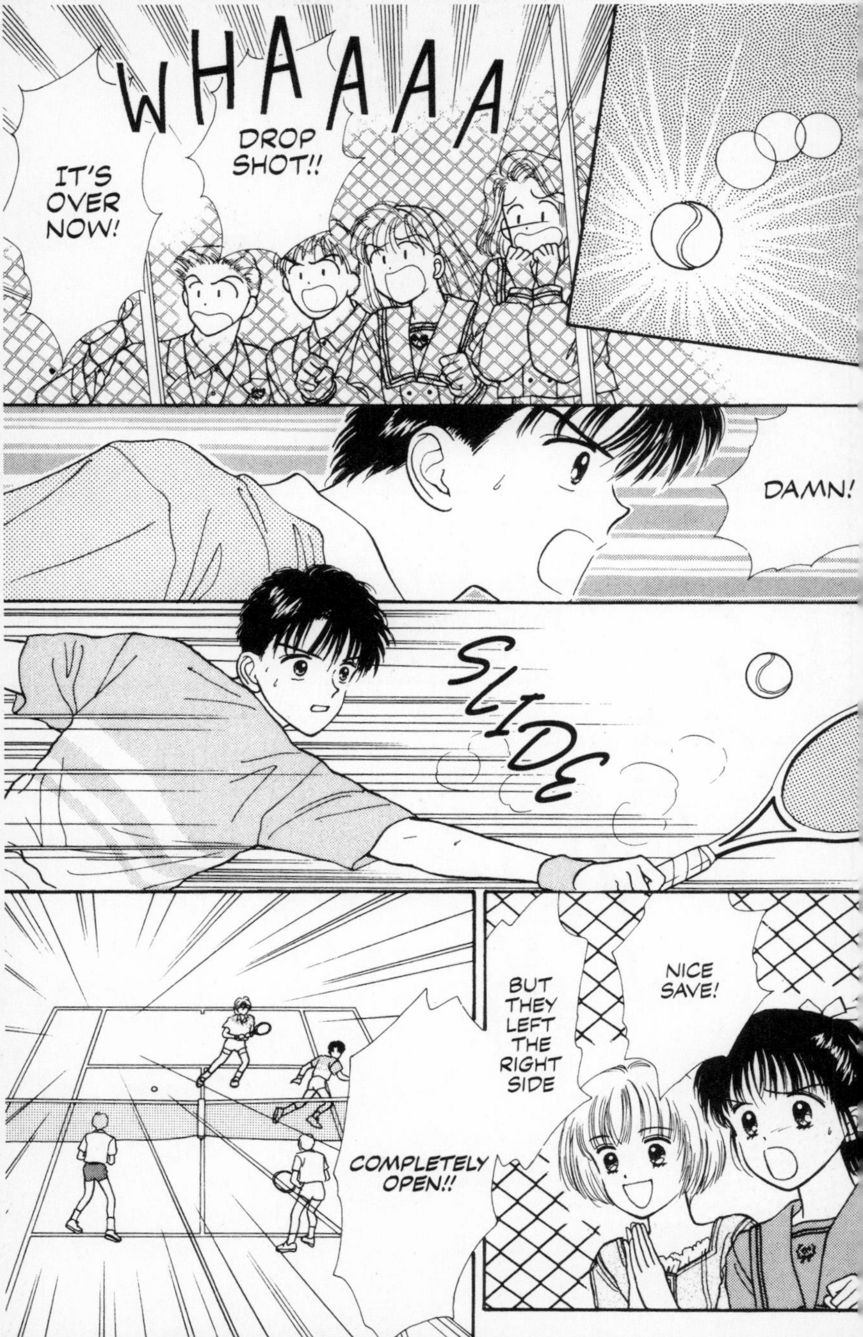
WHAAAAA
DROP SHOT!!
IT'S OVER NOW!
DAMN!
SLIDE
NICE SAVE!
BUT THEY LEFT THE RIGHT SIDE
COMPLETELY OPEN!!

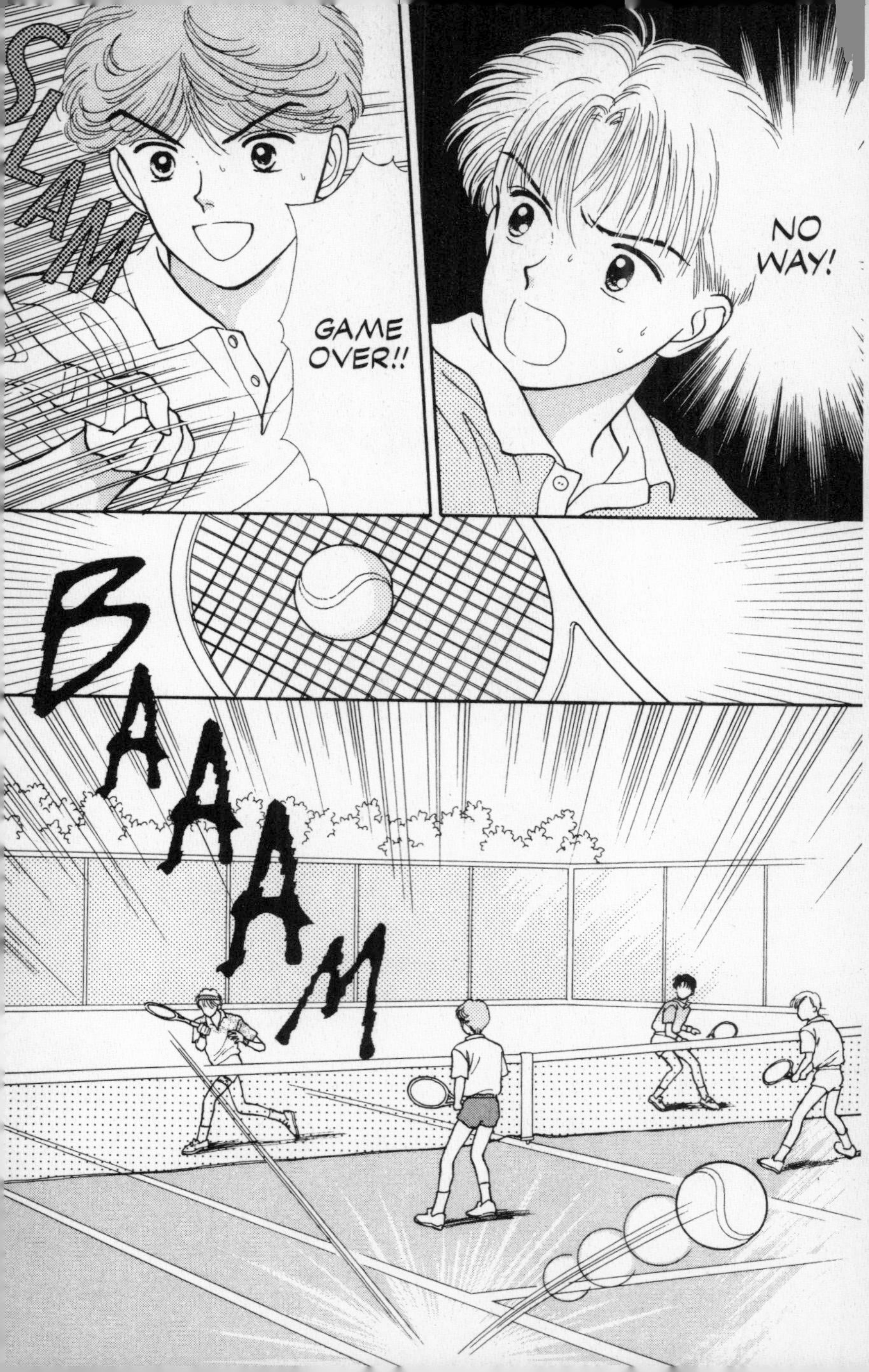
NO WAY!
SLAM
GAME OVER!!
BAAAM

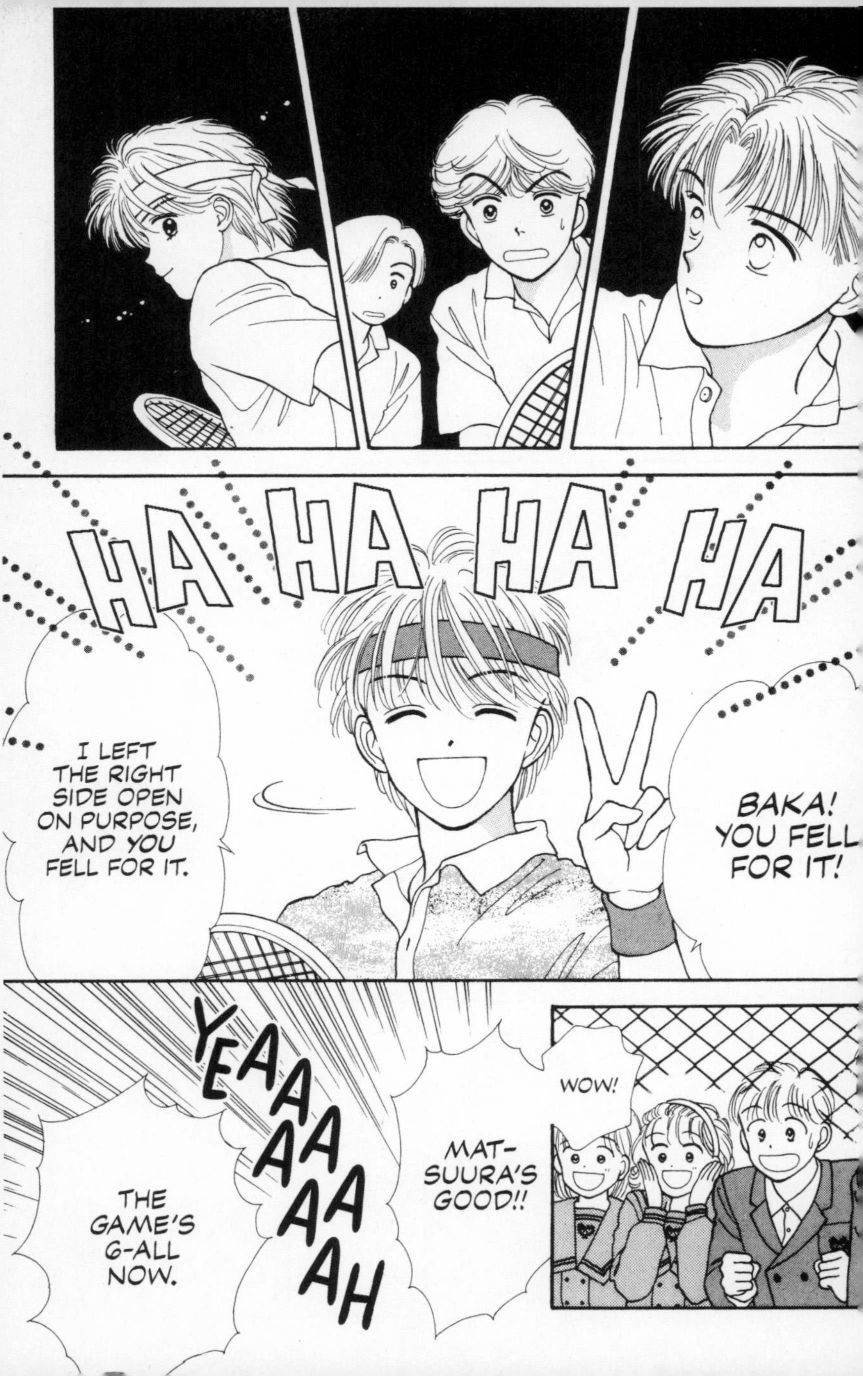
HA HA HA HA
BAKA! YOU FELL FOR IT!
I LEFT THE RIGHT SIDE OPEN ON PURPOSE, AND YOU FELL FOR IT.
WOW!
MAT-SUURA'S GOOD!!
YEAAAAAAAAH
THE GAME'S 6-ALL NOW.

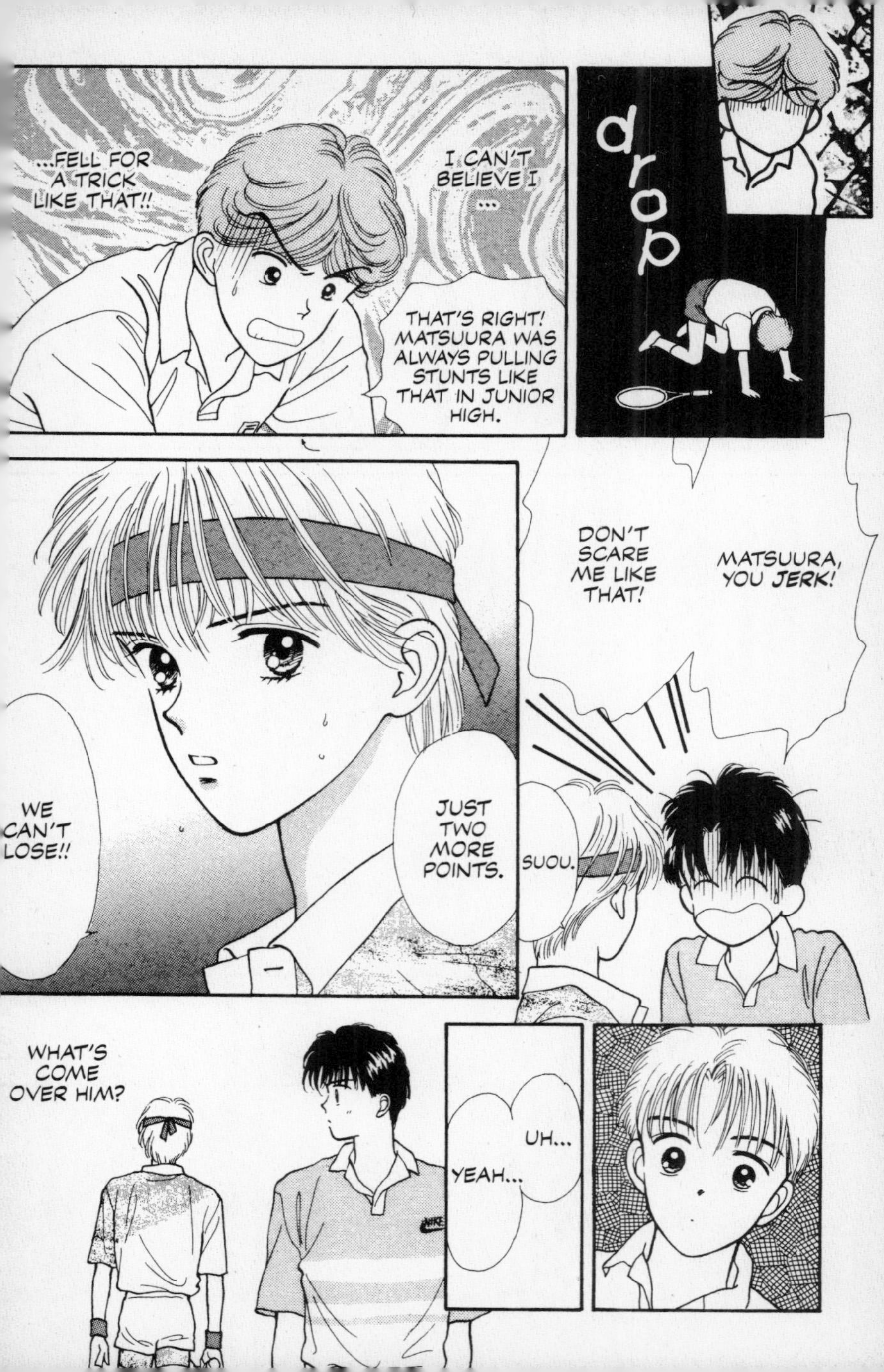
drop
I CAN'T BELIEVE I ...
...FELL FOR A TRICK LIKE THAT!!
THAT'S RIGHT! MATSUURA WAS ALWAYS PULLING STUNTS LIKE THAT IN JUNIOR HIGH.
MATSUURA, YOU JERK!
DON'T SCARE ME LIKE THAT!
SUOU.
JUST TWO MORE POINTS.
WE CAN'T LOSE!!
UH...
YEAH...
WHAT'S COME OVER HIM?

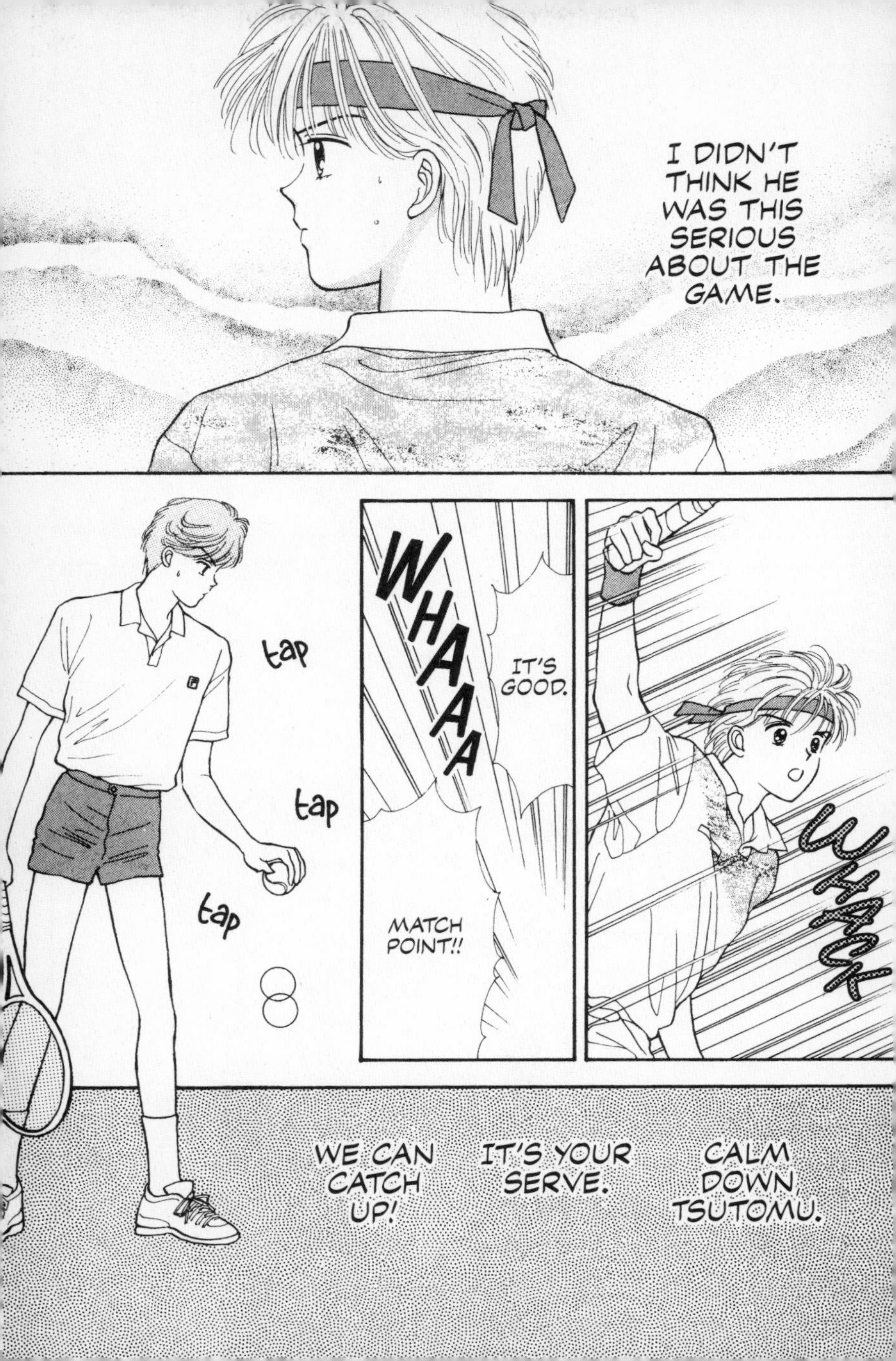
I DIDN'T THINK HE WAS THIS SERIOUS ABOUT THE GAME.
WHACK
WHAAAA
IT'S GOOD.
MATCH POINT!!
tap
tap
tap
CALM DOWN, TSUTOMU.
IT'S YOUR SERVE.
WE CAN CATCH UP!

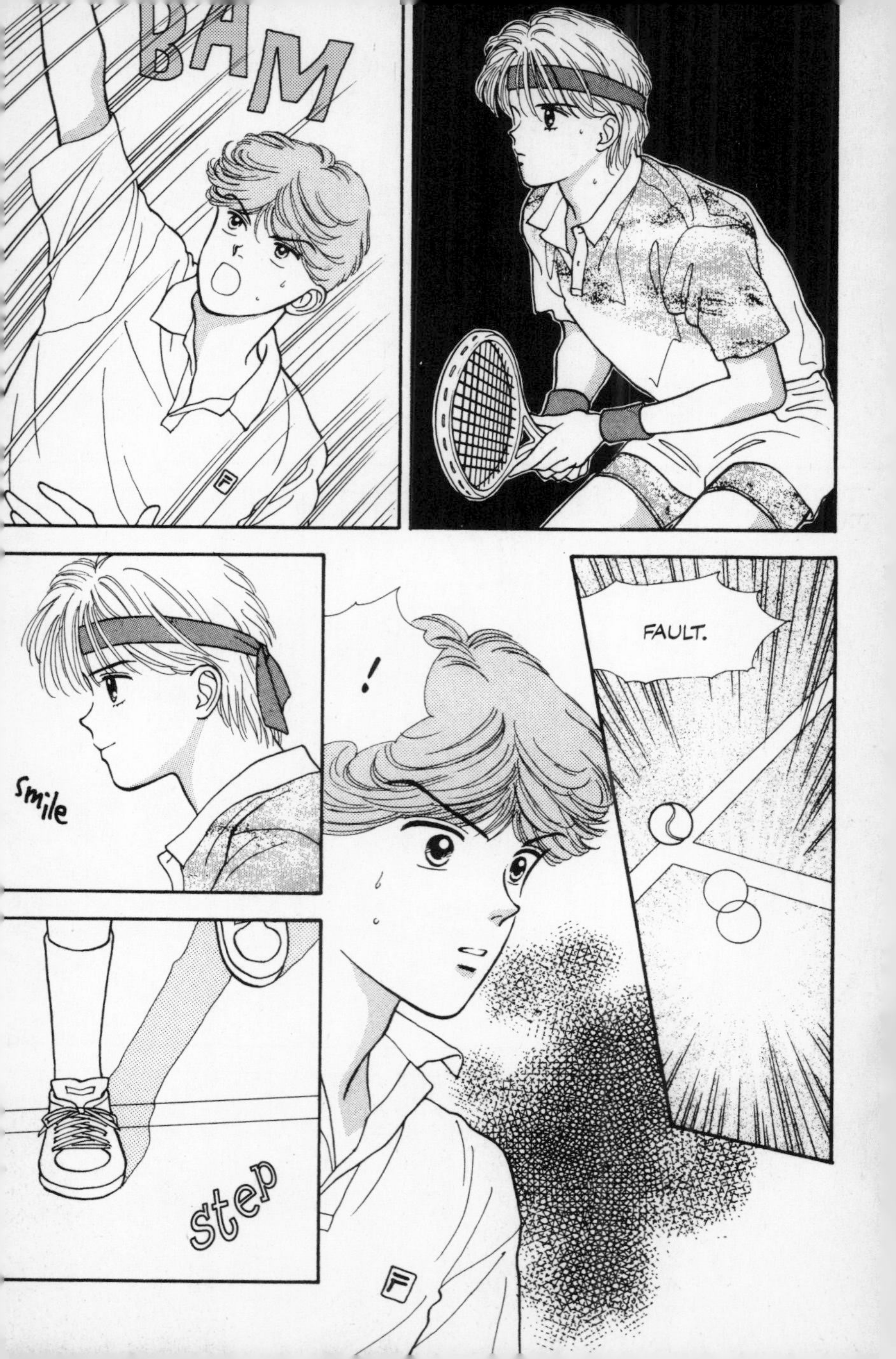
BAM
FAULT.
!
smile
step

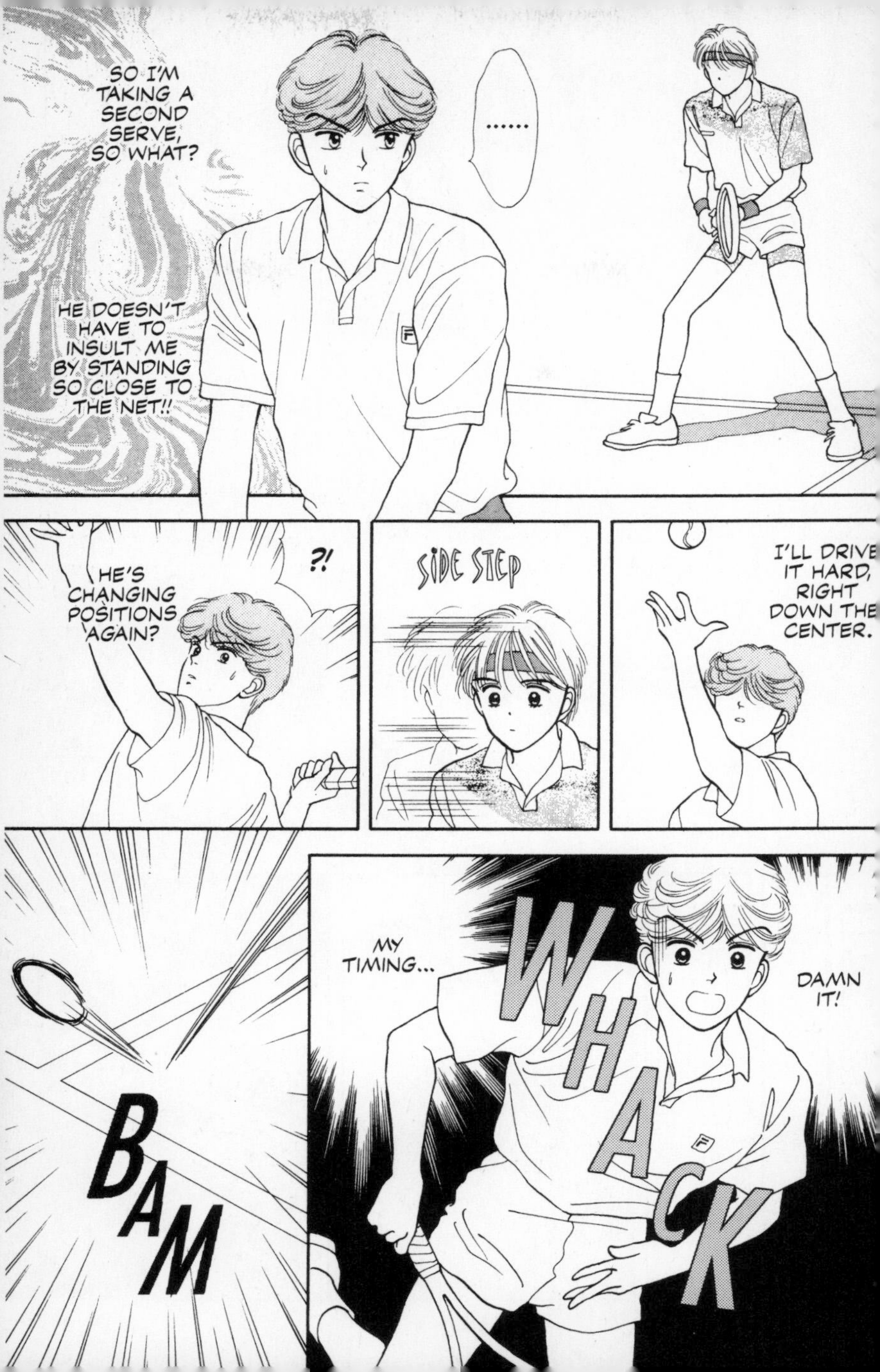
......
SO I'M TAKING A SECOND SERVE, SO WHAT?
HE DOESN'T HAVE TO INSULT ME BY STANDING SO CLOSE TO THE NET!!
I'LL DRIVE IT HARD, RIGHT DOWN THE CENTER.
SIDE STEP
?!
HE'S CHANGING POSITIONS AGAIN?
DAMN IT!
WHACK
MY TIMING...
BAM

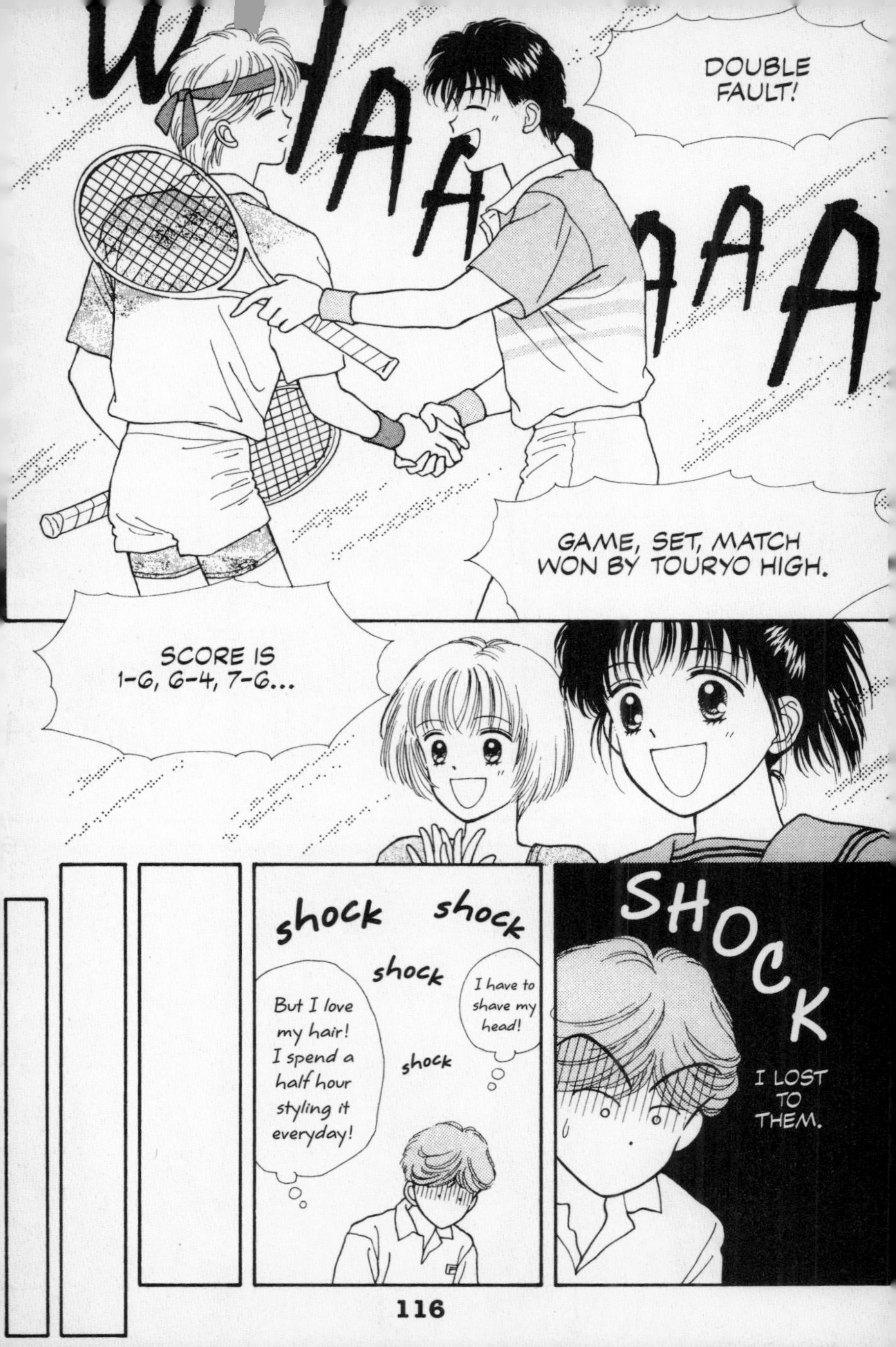
WHAAAAAAA
DOUBLE FAULT!
GAME, SET, MATCH WON BY TOURYO HIGH.
SCORE IS 1-6, 6-4, 7-6...
SHOCK
I LOST TO THEM.
shock
shock
shock
I have to shave my head!
But I love my hair! I spend a half hour styling it everyday!
shock

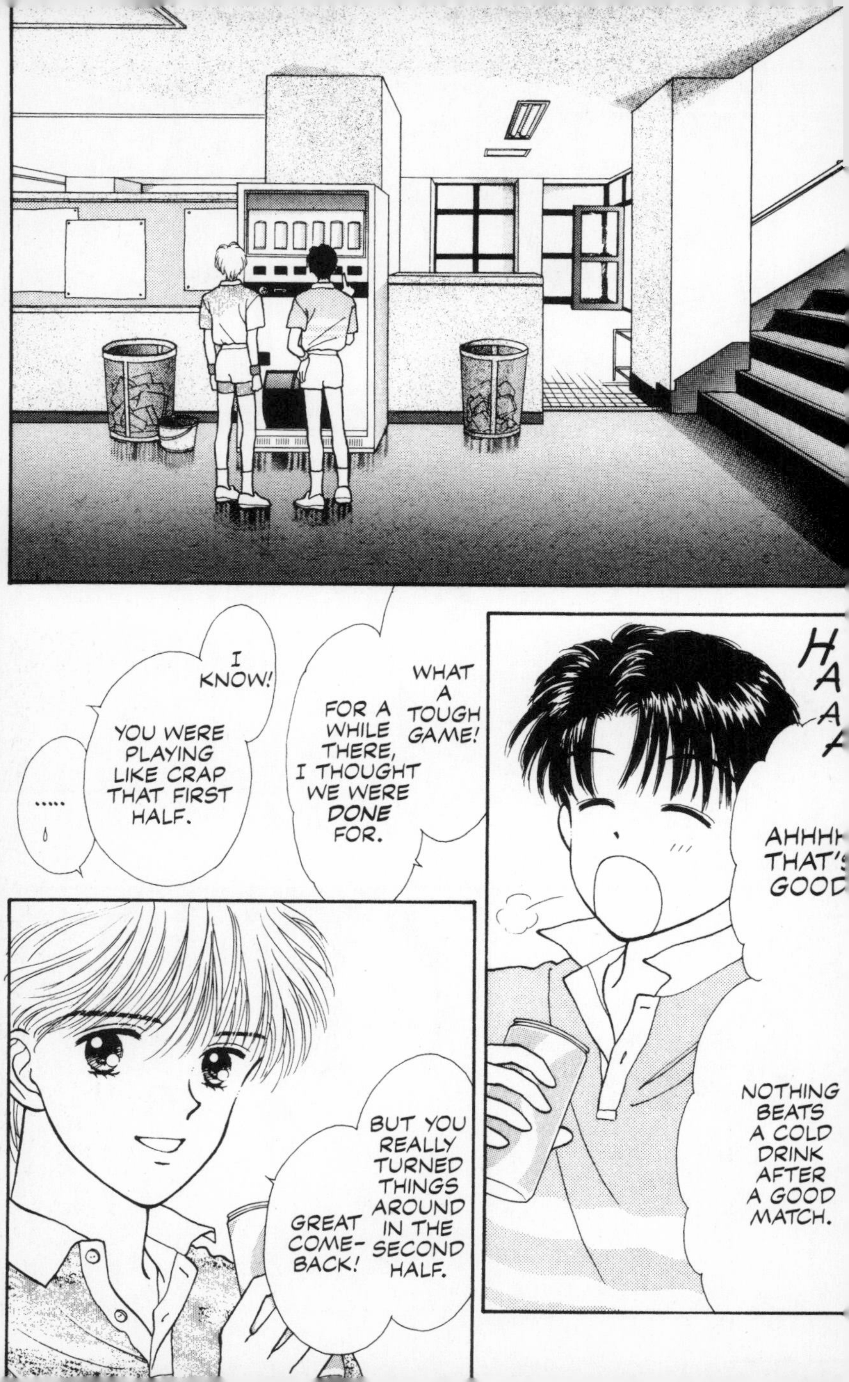
HAA
AHHH THAT'S GOOD
NOTHING BEATS A COLD DRINK AFTER A GOOD MATCH.
WHAT A TOUGH GAME!
FOR A WHILE THERE, I THOUGHT WE WERE *DONE* FOR.
I KNOW!
YOU WERE PLAYING LIKE CRAP THAT FIRST HALF.
.....
BUT YOU REALLY TURNED THINGS AROUND IN THE SECOND HALF.
GREAT COME-BACK!

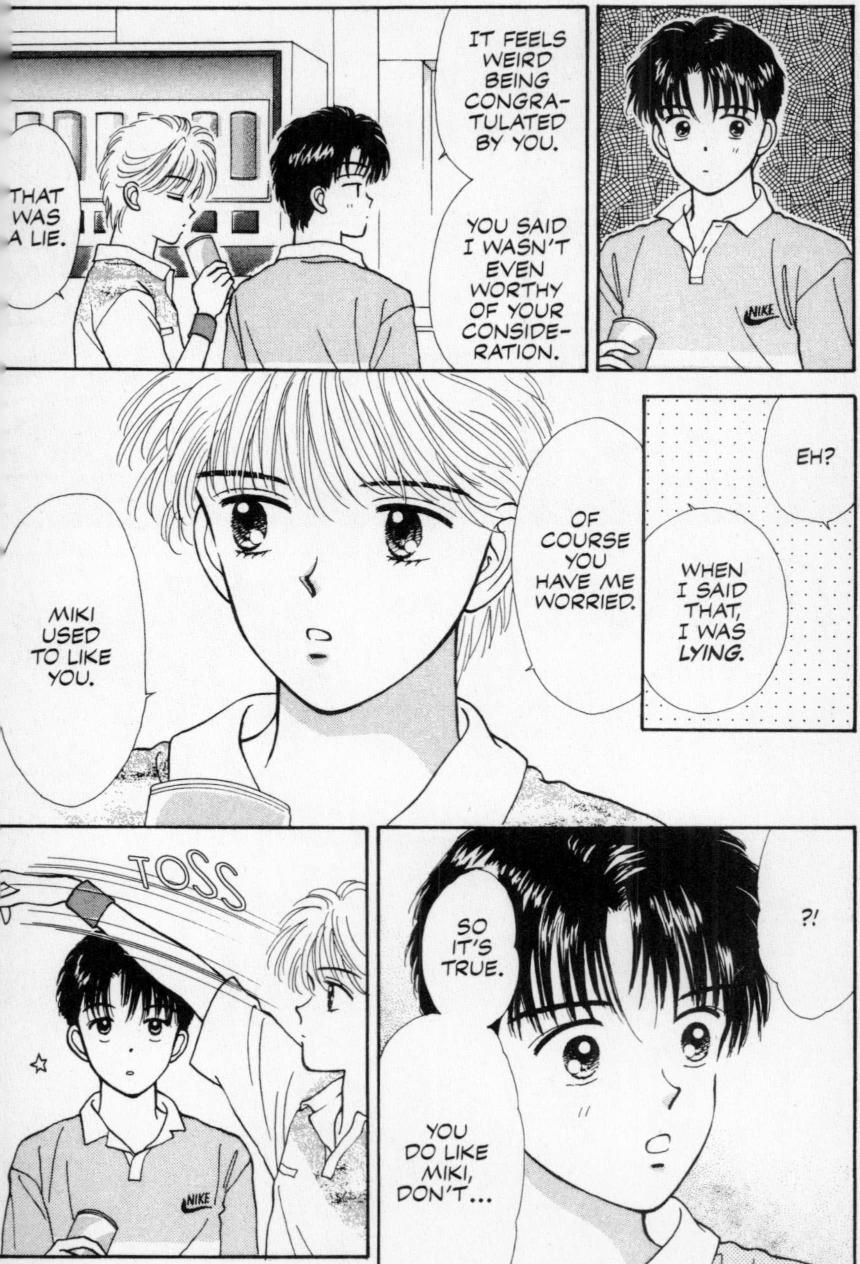
IT FEELS WEIRD BEING CONGRA-TULATED BY YOU.
YOU SAID I WASN'T EVEN WORTHY OF YOUR CONSIDE-RATION.
THAT WAS A LIE.
EH?
WHEN I SAID THAT, I WAS LYING.
OF COURSE YOU HAVE ME WORRIED.
MIKI USED TO LIKE YOU.
?!
SO IT'S TRUE.
YOU DO LIKE MIKI, DON'T...
TOSS

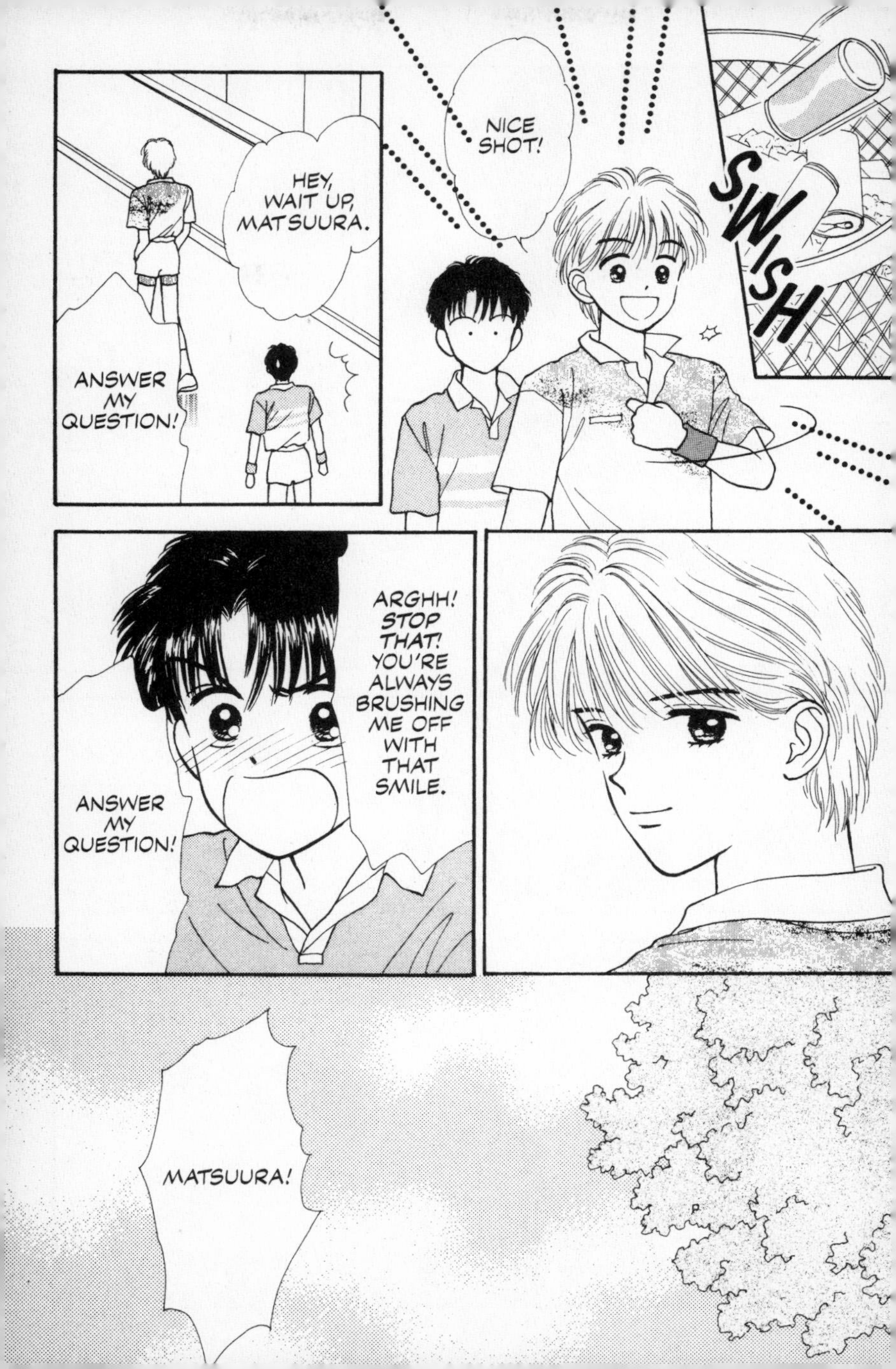
SWISH
NICE SHOT!
HEY, WAIT UP, MATSUURA.
ANSWER MY QUESTION!
ARGHH! STOP THAT! YOU'RE ALWAYS BRUSHING ME OFF WITH THAT SMILE.
ANSWER MY QUESTION!
MATSUURA!

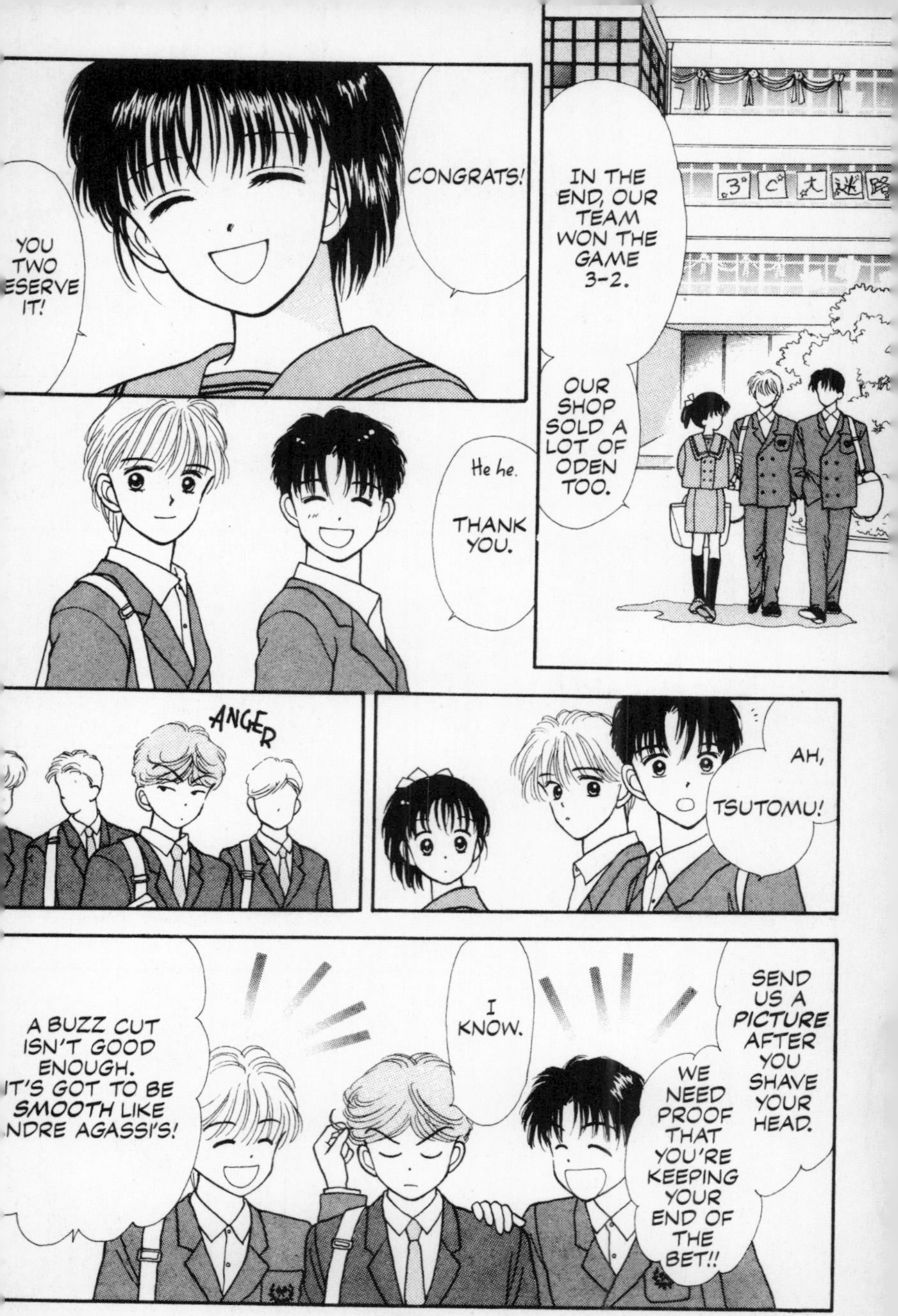
IN THE END, OUR TEAM WON THE GAME 3-2.
OUR SHOP SOLD A LOT OF ODEN TOO.
CONGRATS!
YOU TWO ESERVE IT!
He he.
THANK YOU.
AH, TSUTOMU!
ANGER
SEND US A PICTURE AFTER YOU SHAVE YOUR HEAD.
WE NEED PROOF THAT YOU'RE KEEPING YOUR END OF THE BET!!
I KNOW.
A BUZZ CUT ISN'T GOOD ENOUGH. IT'S GOT TO BE SMOOTH LIKE NDRE AGASSI'S!

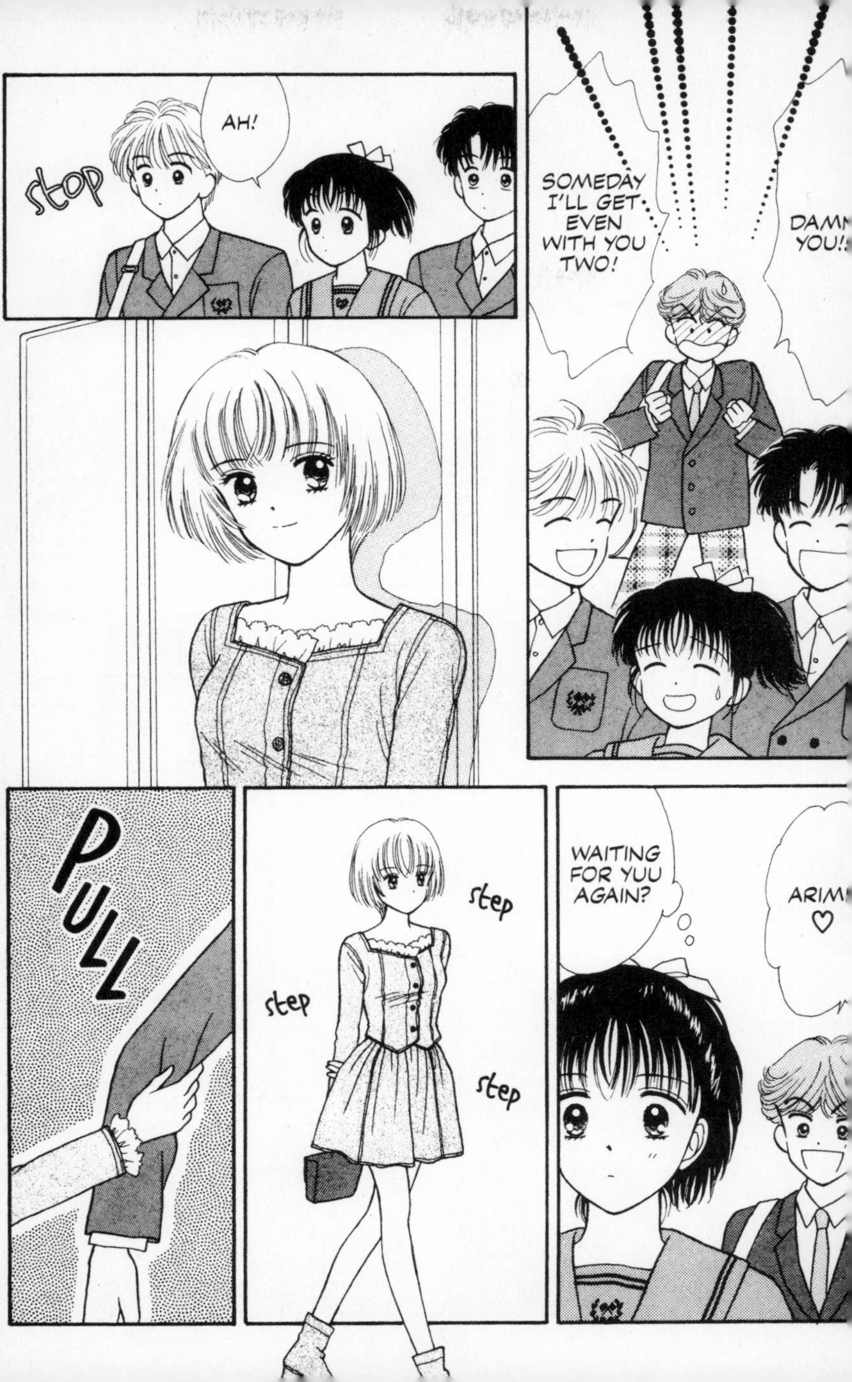
DAMN YOU!!
SOMEDAY I'LL GET EVEN WITH YOU TWO!
AH!
stop
ARIM ♡
WAITING FOR YUU AGAIN?
step
step
step
PULL

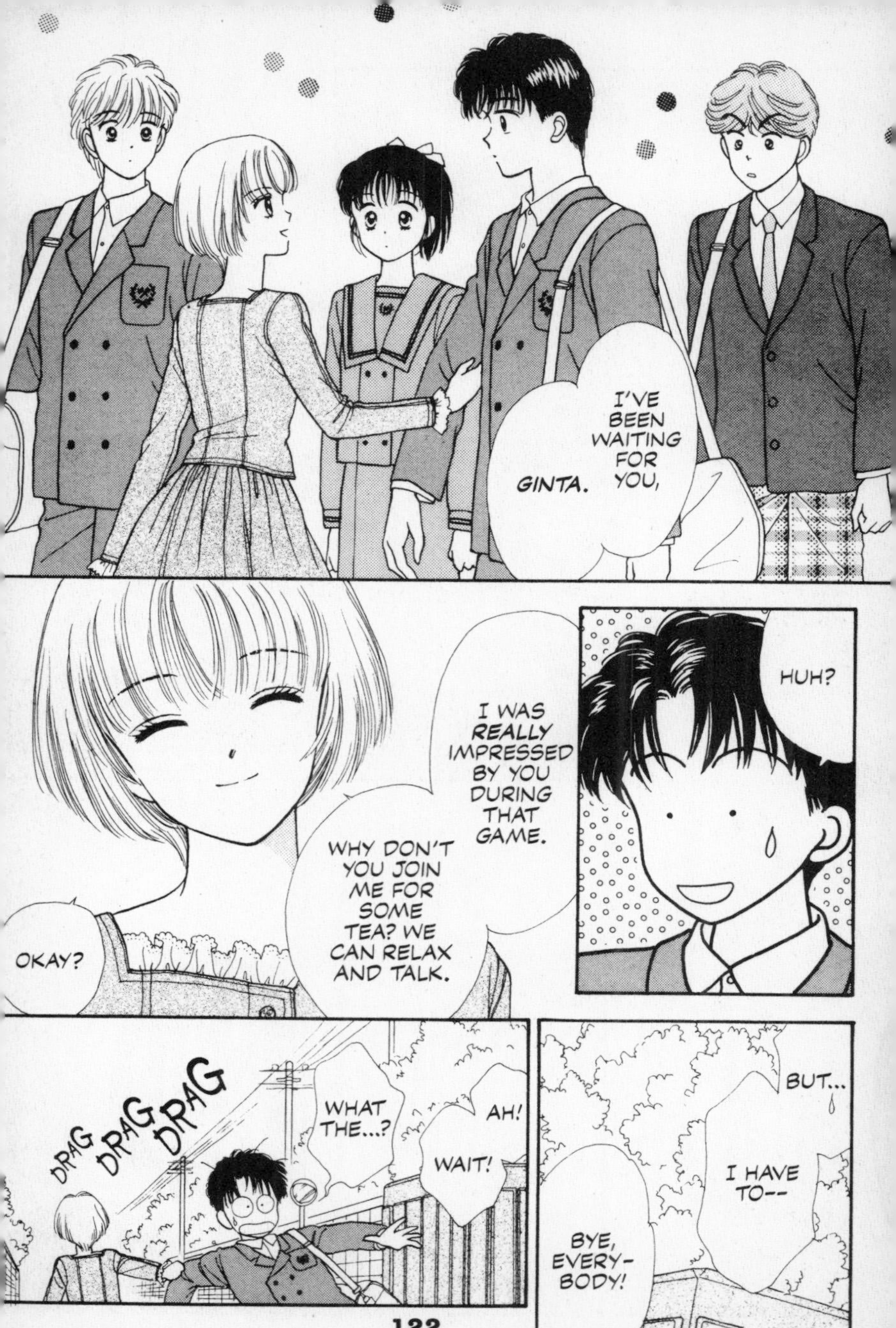
I'VE BEEN WAITING FOR YOU, GINTA.
HUH?
I WAS REALLY IMPRESSED BY YOU DURING THAT GAME.
WHY DON'T YOU JOIN ME FOR SOME TEA? WE CAN RELAX AND TALK.
OKAY?
BUT...
I HAVE TO--
BYE, EVERYBODY!
DRAG DRAG DRAG
WHAT THE...?
AH!
WAIT!

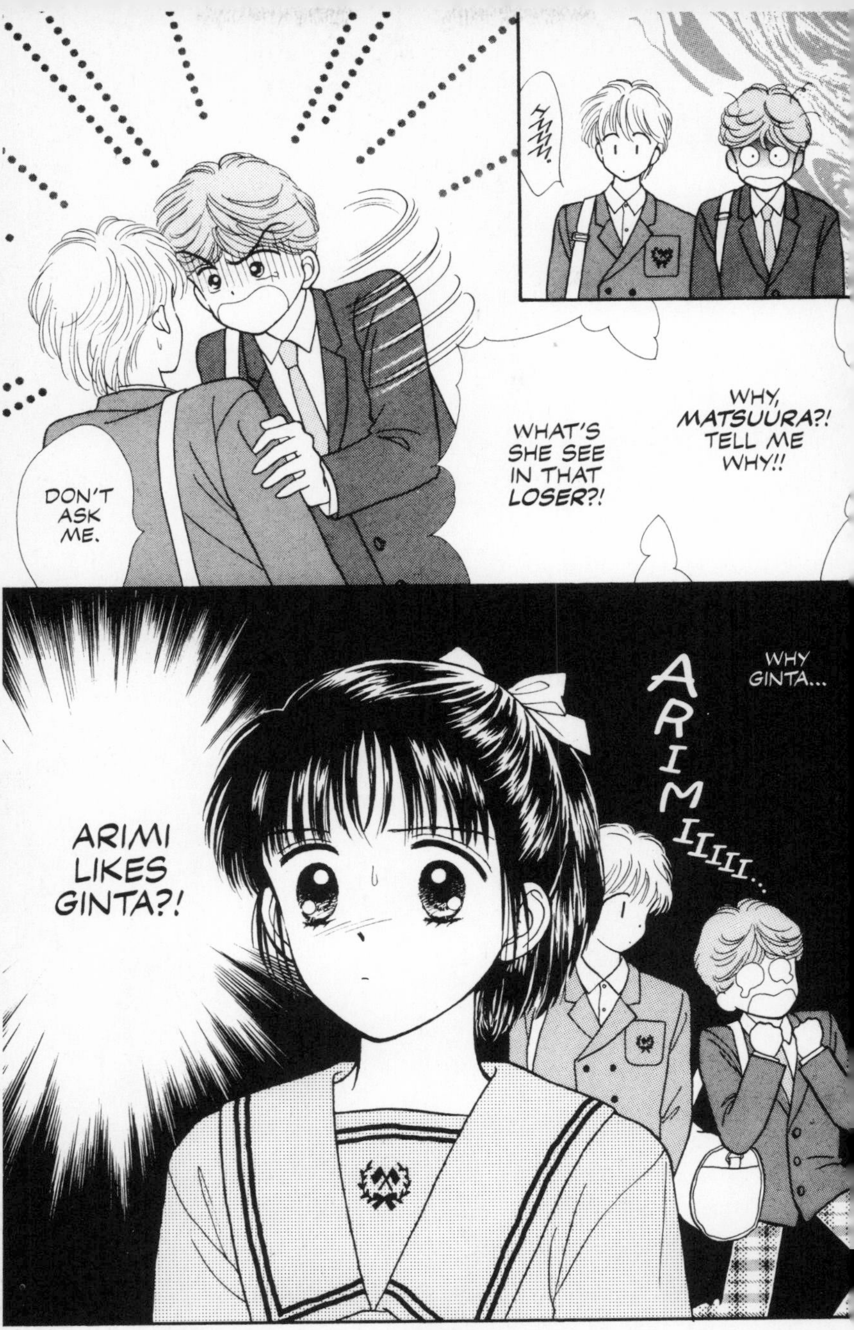
HMMM.
WHY, MATSUURA?! TELL ME WHY!!
WHAT'S SHE SEE IN THAT LOSER?!
DON'T ASK ME.
WHY GINTA...
ARIMIIIIII...
ARIMI LIKES GINTA?!

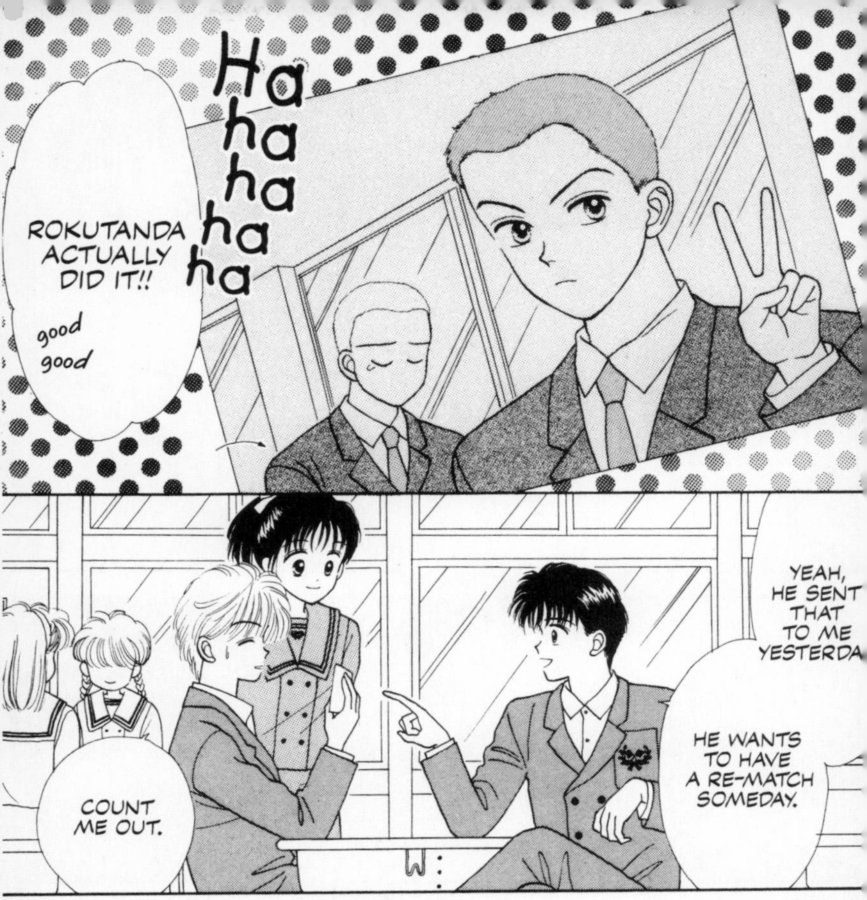
Hahahahahaha
ROKUTANDA ACTUALLY DID IT!!
good good
YEAH, HE SENT THAT TO ME YESTERDA
HE WANTS TO HAVE A RE-MATCH SOMEDAY.
COUNT ME OUT.

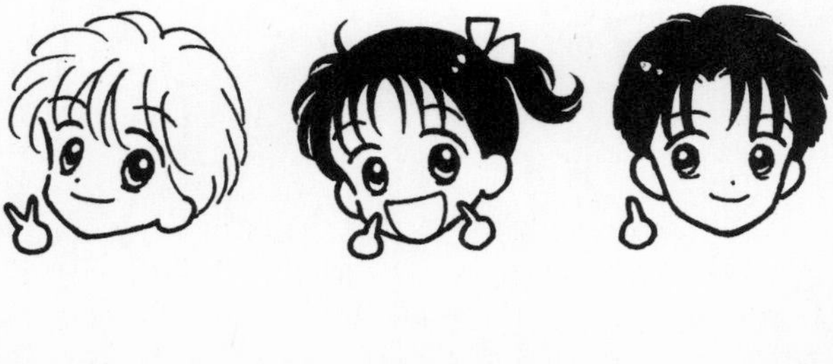

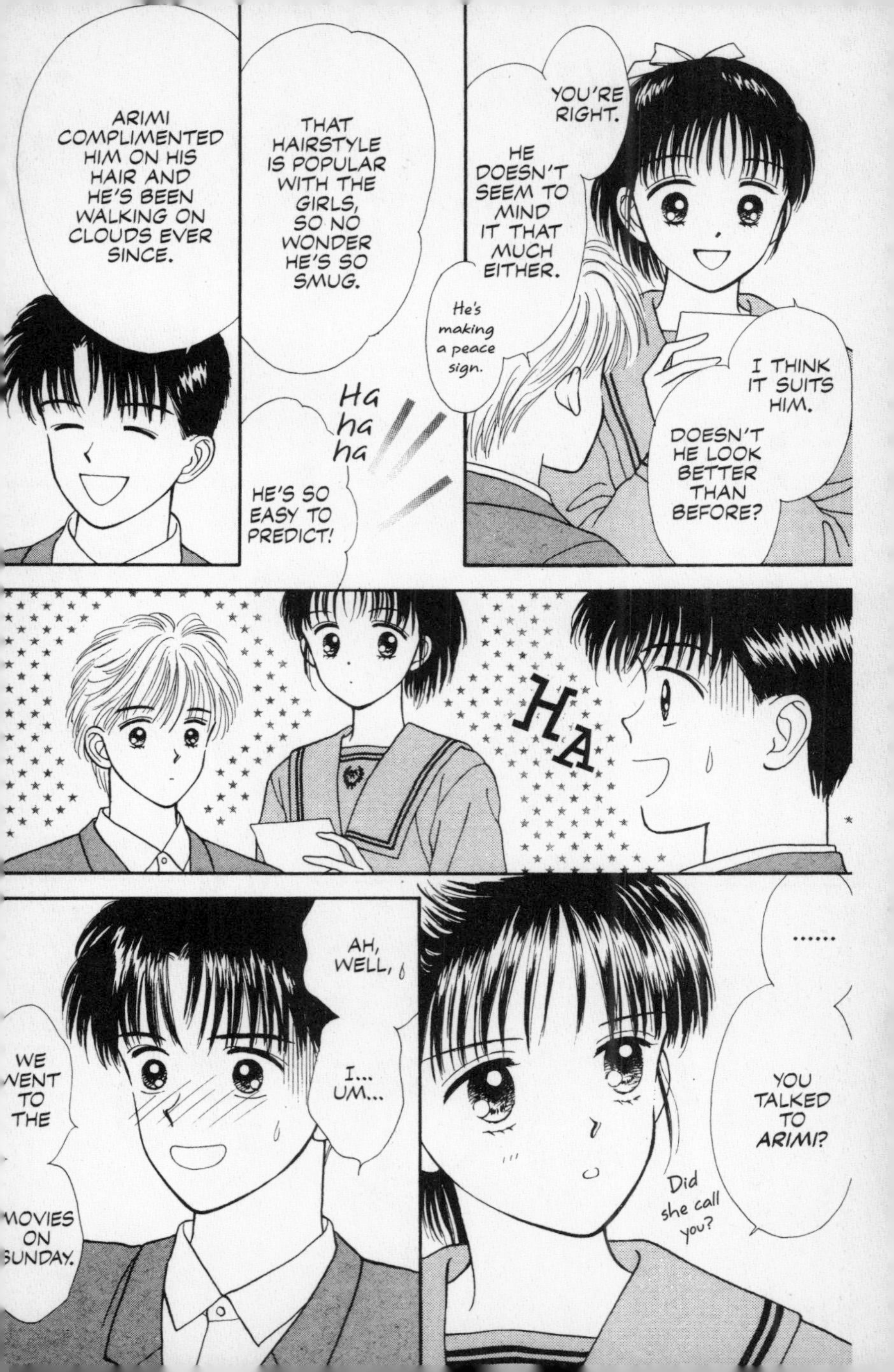
YOU'RE RIGHT.
HE DOESN'T SEEM TO MIND IT THAT MUCH EITHER.
He's making a peace sign.
I THINK IT SUITS HIM.
DOESN'T HE LOOK BETTER THAN BEFORE?
THAT HAIRSTYLE IS POPULAR WITH THE GIRLS, SO NO WONDER HE'S SO SMUG.
Ha ha ha
HE'S SO EASY TO PREDICT!
ARIMI COMPLIMENTED HIM ON HIS HAIR AND HE'S BEEN WALKING ON CLOUDS EVER SINCE.
HA HA
......
YOU TALKED TO ARIMI?
Did she call you?
AH, WELL,
I... UM...
WE WENT TO THE MOVIES ON SUNDAY.

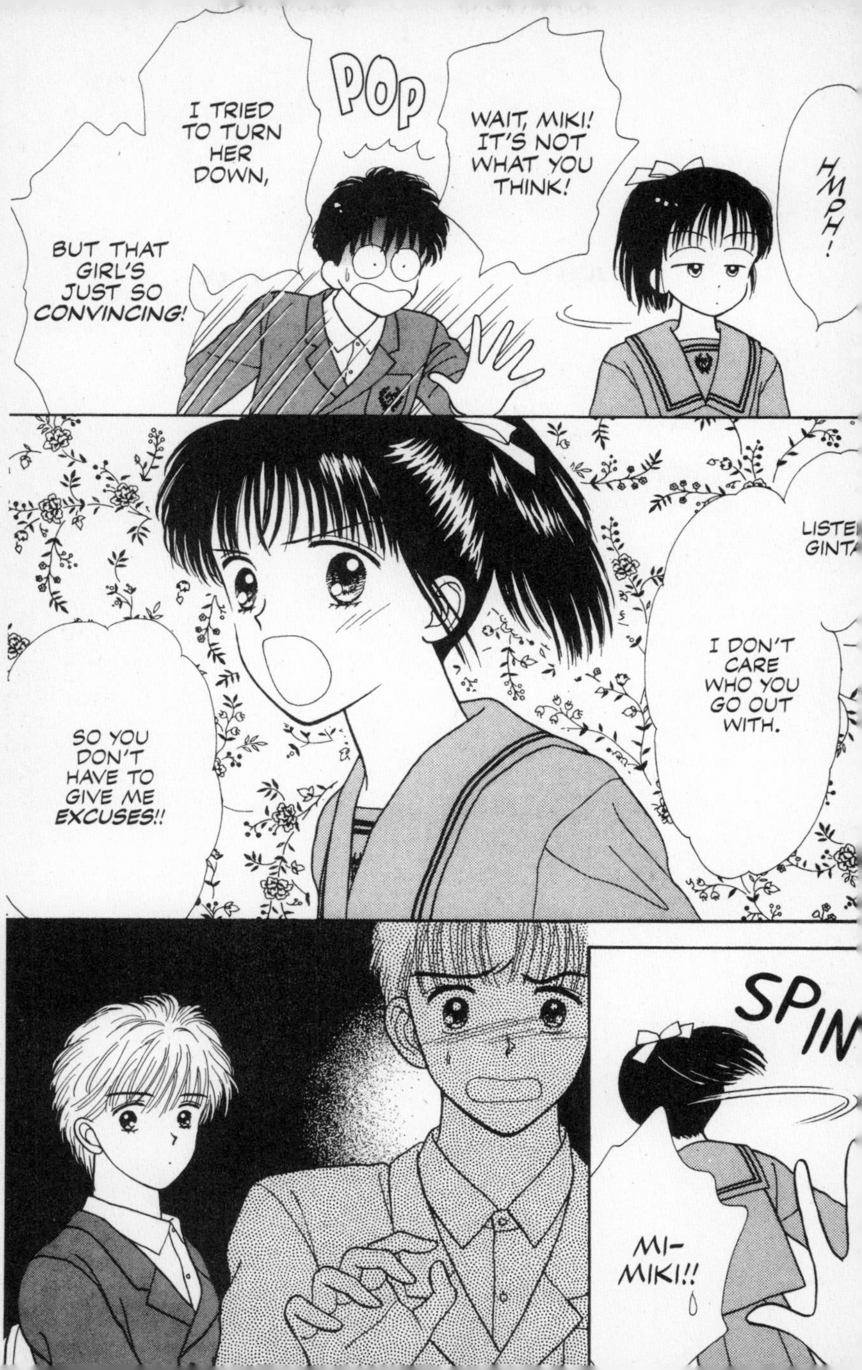
HMPH!
WAIT, MIKI! IT'S NOT WHAT YOU THINK!
POP
I TRIED TO TURN HER DOWN,
BUT THAT GIRL'S JUST SO CONVINCING!
LISTE GINT
I DON'T CARE WHO YOU GO OUT WITH.
SO YOU DON'T HAVE TO GIVE ME EXCUSES!!
SPIN
MI-MIKI!!

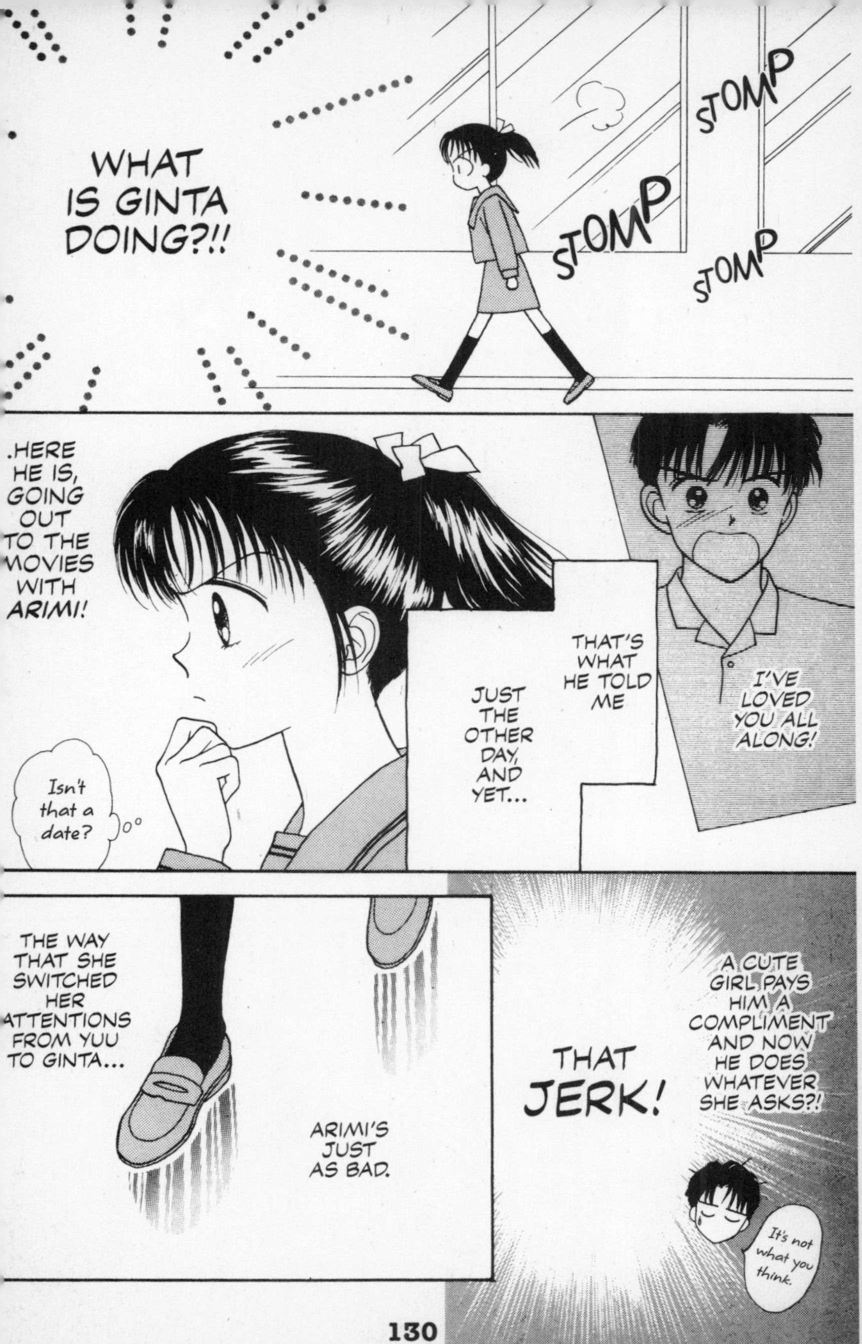
STOMP
STOMP
STOMP
WHAT IS GINTA DOING?!!
I'VE LOVED YOU ALL ALONG!
THAT'S WHAT HE TOLD ME
JUST THE OTHER DAY, AND YET...
HERE HE IS, GOING OUT TO THE MOVIES WITH ARIMI!
Isn't that a date?
A CUTE GIRL PAYS HIM A COMPLIMENT AND NOW HE DOES WHATEVER SHE ASKS?!
THAT JERK!
It's not what you think.
THE WAY THAT SHE SWITCHED HER ATTENTIONS FROM YUU TO GINTA...
ARIMI'S JUST AS BAD.

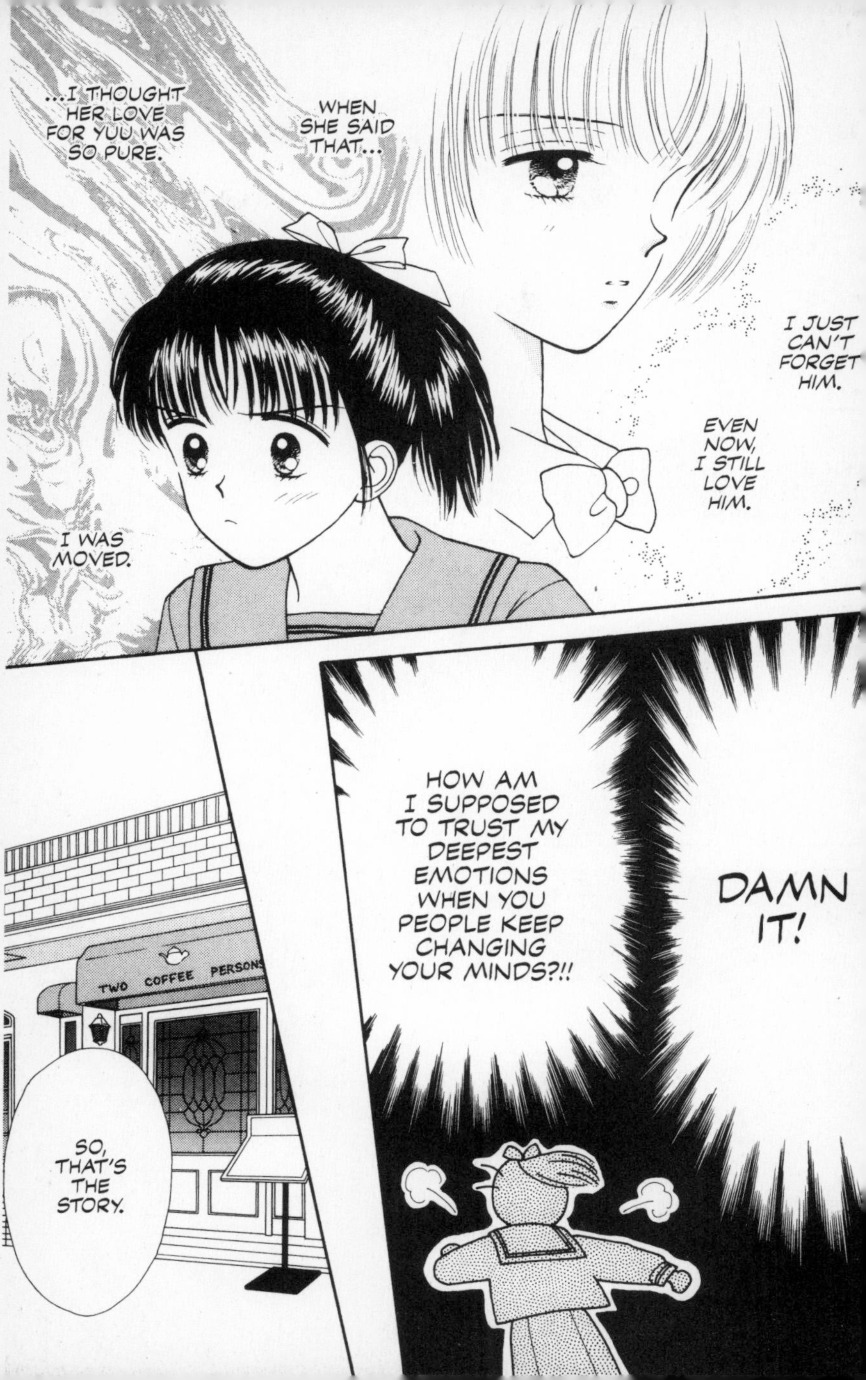
I JUST CAN'T FORGET HIM.
EVEN NOW, I STILL LOVE HIM.
WHEN SHE SAID THAT...
...I THOUGHT HER LOVE FOR YUU WAS SO PURE.
I WAS MOVED.
DAMN IT!
HOW AM I SUPPOSED TO TRUST MY DEEPEST EMOTIONS WHEN YOU PEOPLE KEEP CHANGING YOUR MINDS?!!
TWO COFFEE PERSONS
SO, THAT'S THE STORY.

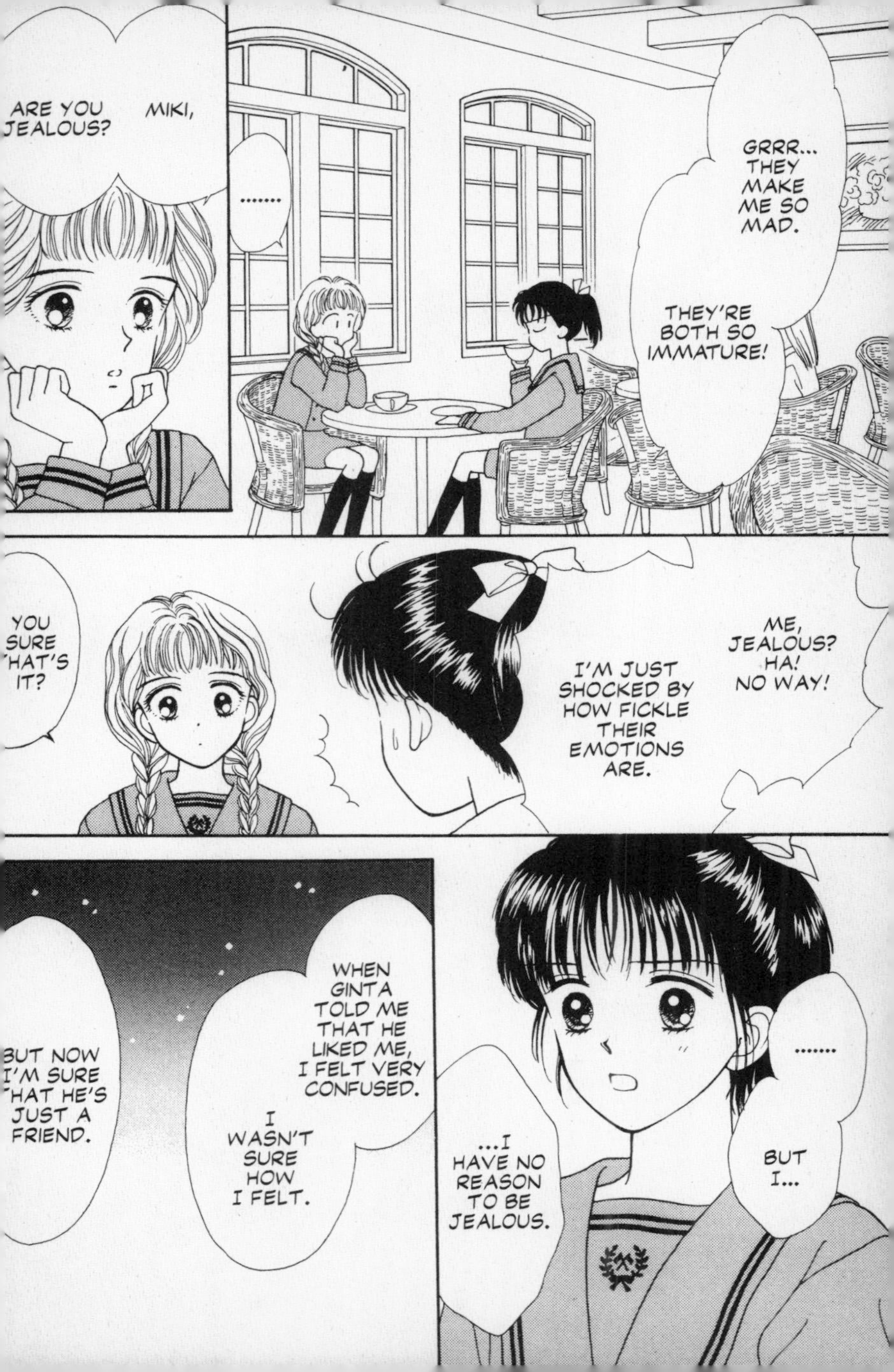
GRRR... THEY MAKE ME SO MAD.
THEY'RE BOTH SO IMMATURE!
....
MIKI,
ARE YOU JEALOUS?
ME, JEALOUS? HA! NO WAY!
I'M JUST SHOCKED BY HOW FICKLE THEIR EMOTIONS ARE.
YOU SURE HAT'S IT?
....
BUT I...
...I HAVE NO REASON TO BE JEALOUS.
WHEN GINTA TOLD ME THAT HE LIKED ME, I FELT VERY CONFUSED.
I WASN'T SURE HOW I FELT.
BUT NOW I'M SURE HAT HE'S JUST A FRIEND.

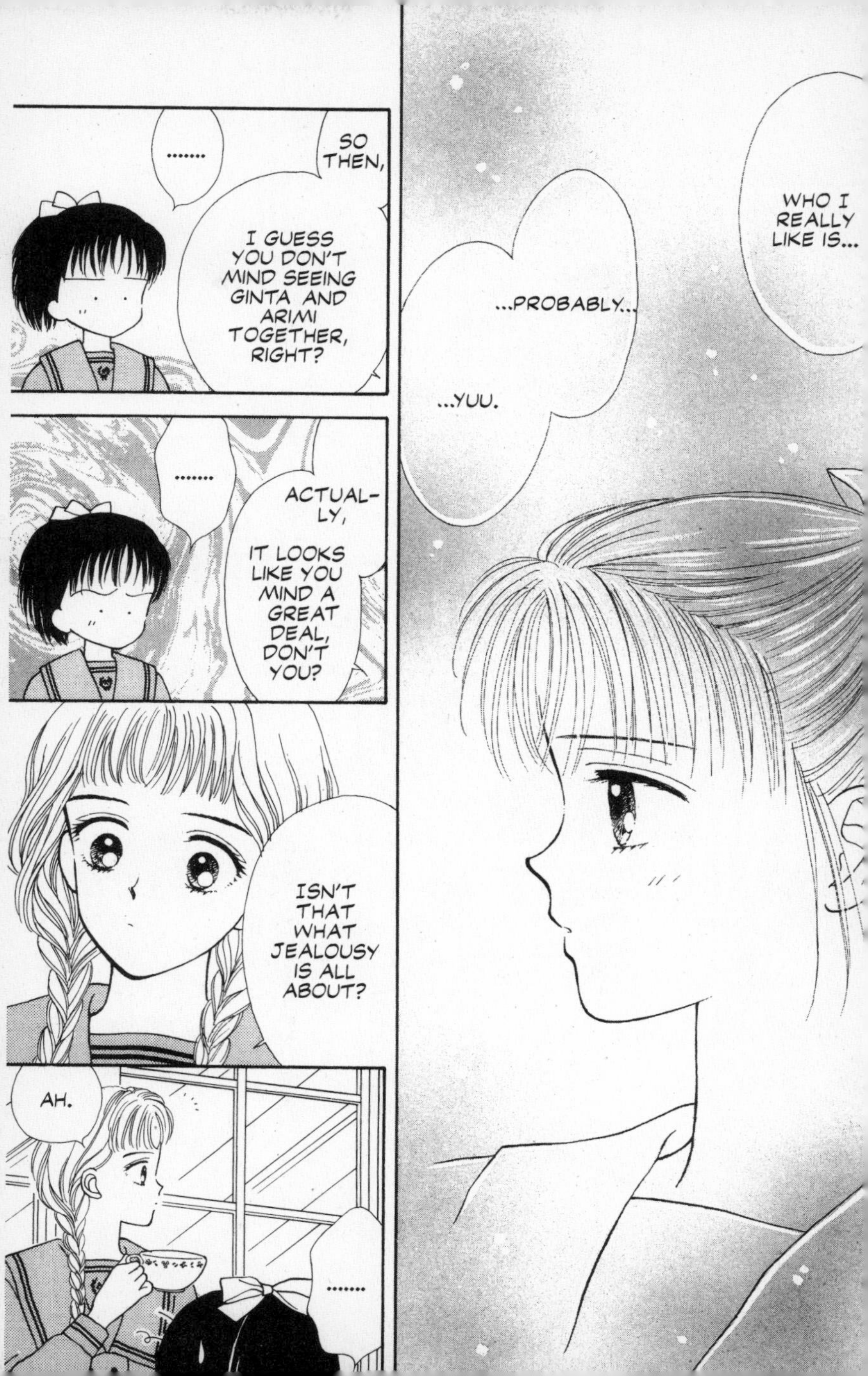
WHO I REALLY LIKE IS...
...PROBABLY...
...YUU.
SO THEN,
I GUESS YOU DON'T MIND SEEING GINTA AND ARIMI TOGETHER, RIGHT?
....
ACTUAL-LY,
IT LOOKS LIKE YOU MIND A GREAT DEAL, DON'T YOU?
....
ISN'T THAT WHAT JEALOUSY IS ALL ABOUT?
AH.
....

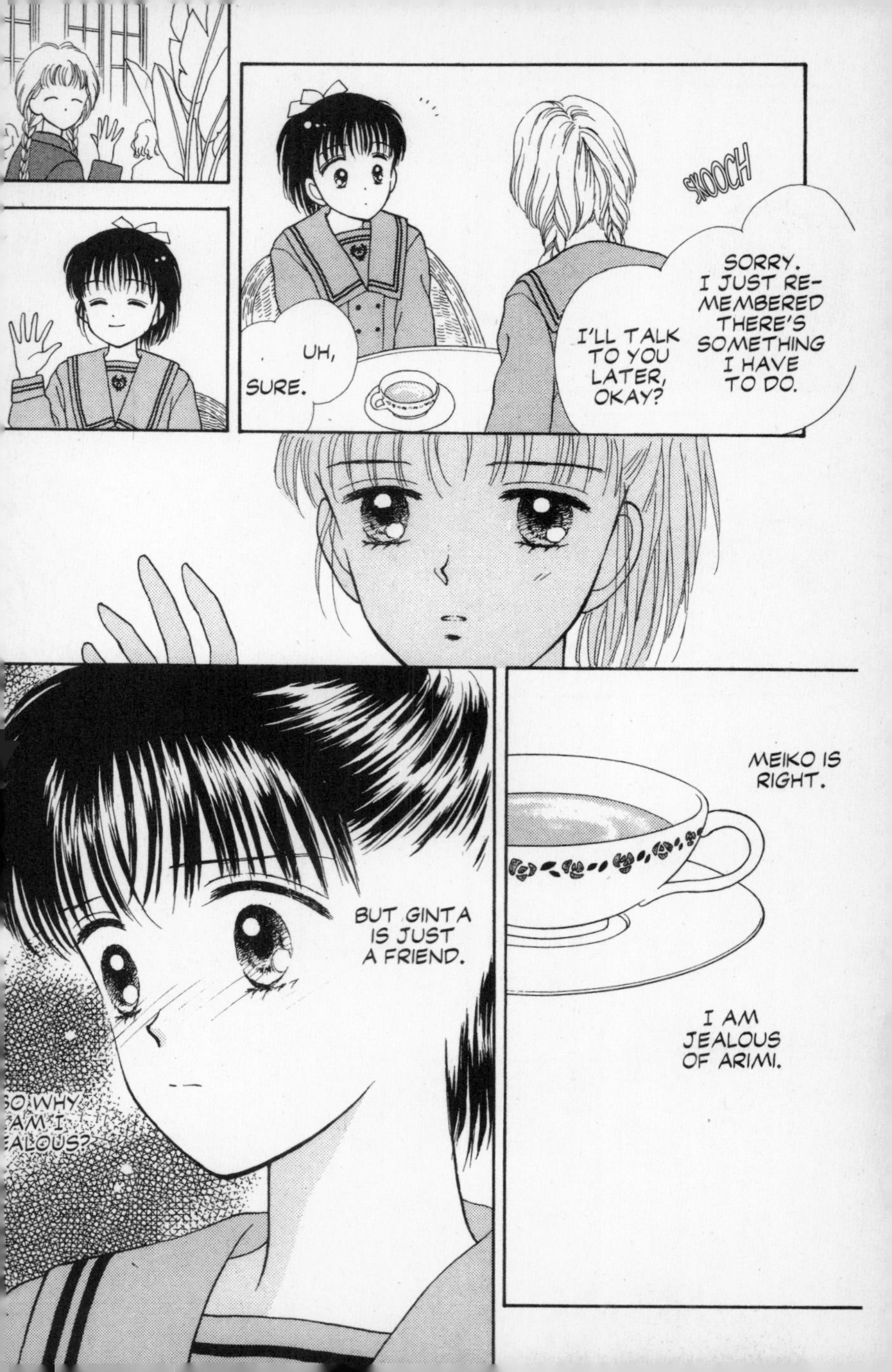
SKOOCH
SORRY. I JUST RE-MEMBERED THERE'S SOMETHING I HAVE TO DO.
I'LL TALK TO YOU LATER, OKAY?
UH, SURE.
MEIKO IS RIGHT.
I AM JEALOUS OF ARIMI.
BUT GINTA IS JUST A FRIEND.
SO WHY AM I EALOUS?

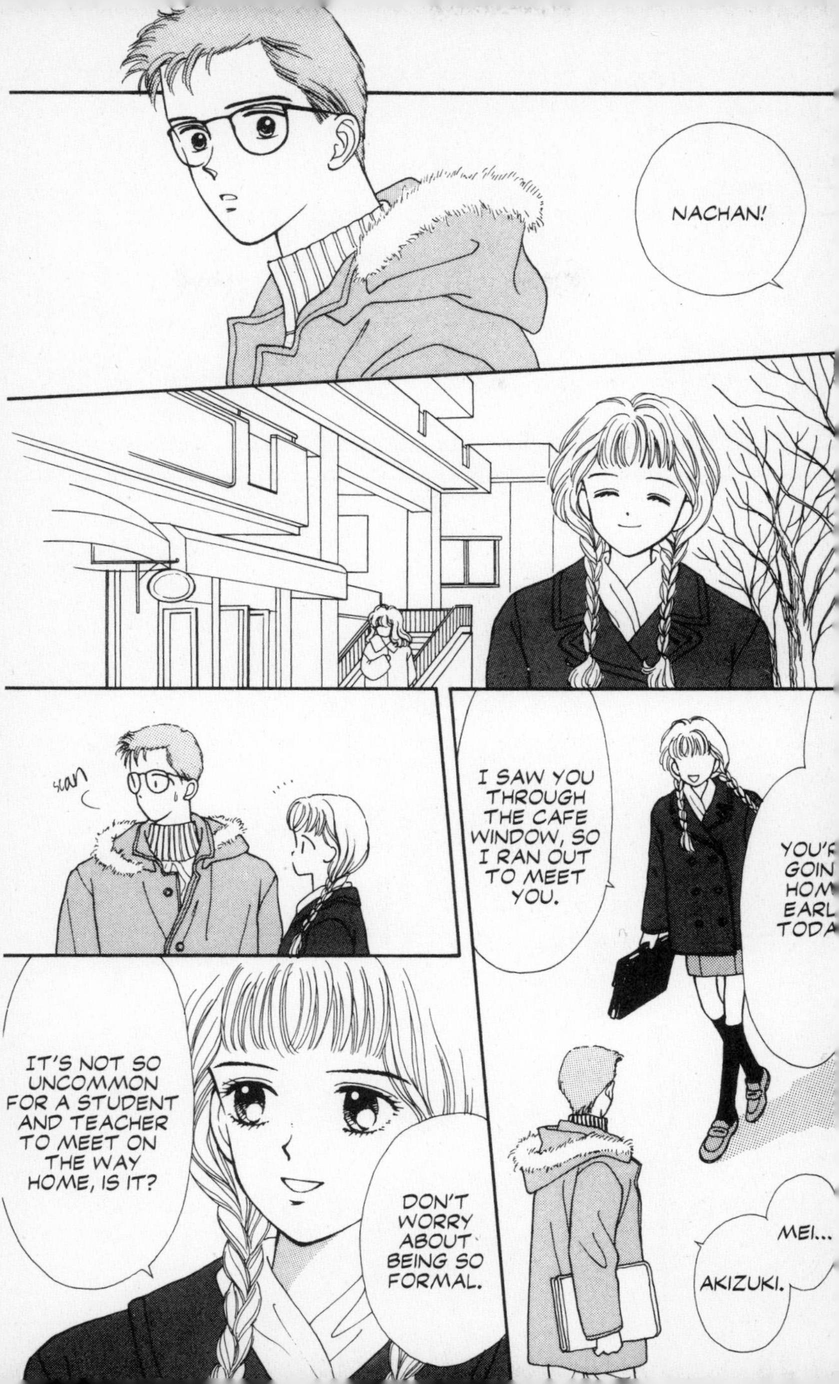
NACHAN!
YOU'R GOIN HOM EARL TODA
I SAW YOU THROUGH THE CAFE WINDOW, SO I RAN OUT TO MEET YOU.
MEI...
AKIZUKI.
scan
...
DON'T WORRY ABOUT BEING SO FORMAL.
IT'S NOT SO UNCOMMON FOR A STUDENT AND TEACHER TO MEET ON THE WAY HOME, IS IT?

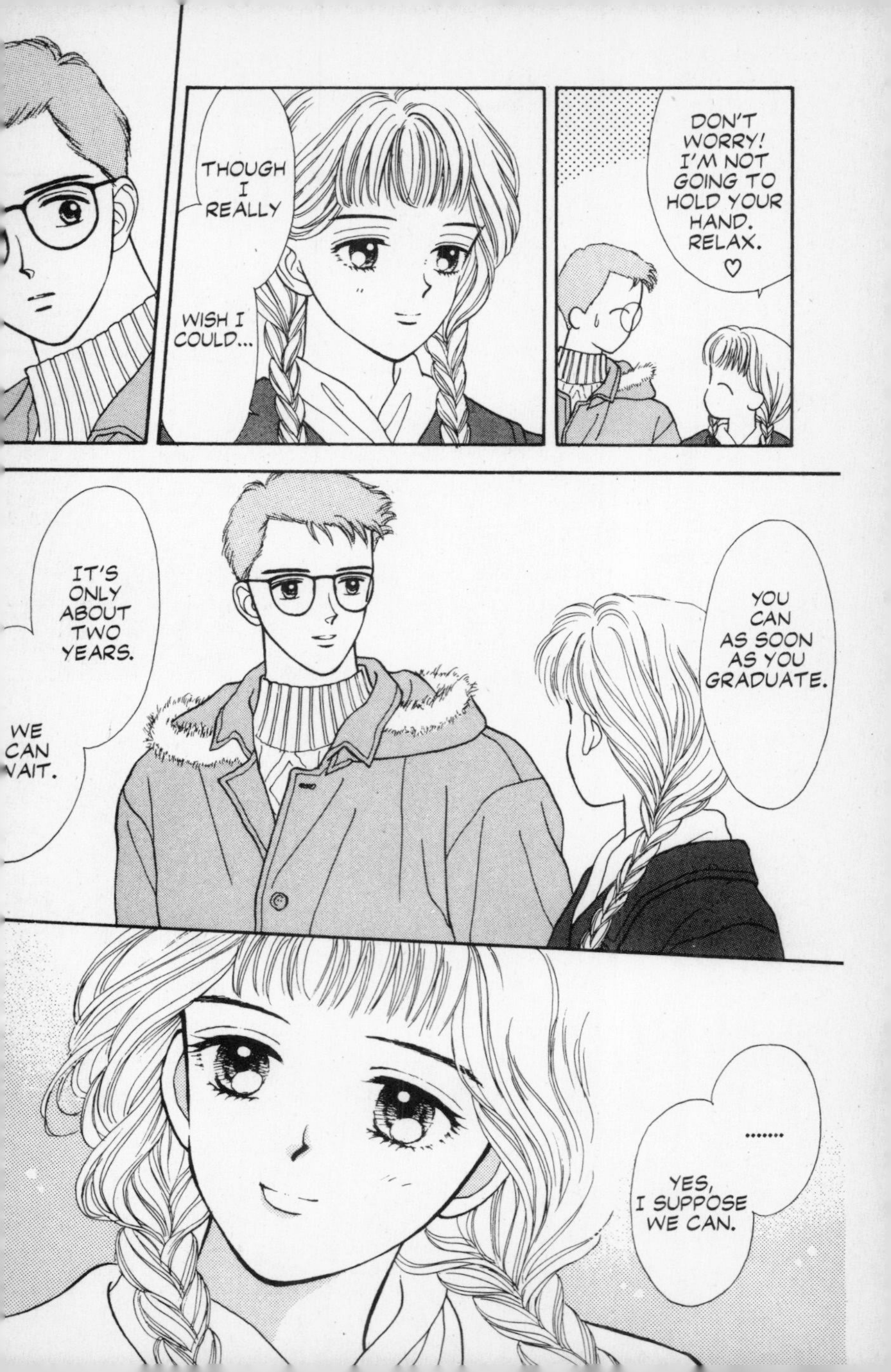
DON'T WORRY! I'M NOT GOING TO HOLD YOUR HAND. RELAX. ♡
THOUGH I REALLY
WISH I COULD...
YOU CAN AS SOON AS YOU GRADUATE.
IT'S ONLY ABOUT TWO YEARS.
WE CAN WAIT.
....
YES, I SUPPOSE WE CAN.

FREE TALK ④

Thank you everyone for the fan letters. Since I am so busy, I unfortunately can't reply to all your letters personally. But I will try to answer some of your questions now.

1 How do I become a good manga artist?

That's a tougher question than you might think.

If there's an easy way to become a good manga artist, I'd love to hear it! What I recommend doing is observing people and objects and then drawing them in your own style. Don't draw from your memories or imagination at first, but by observation and copying. If you practice enough, eventually you'll get good!

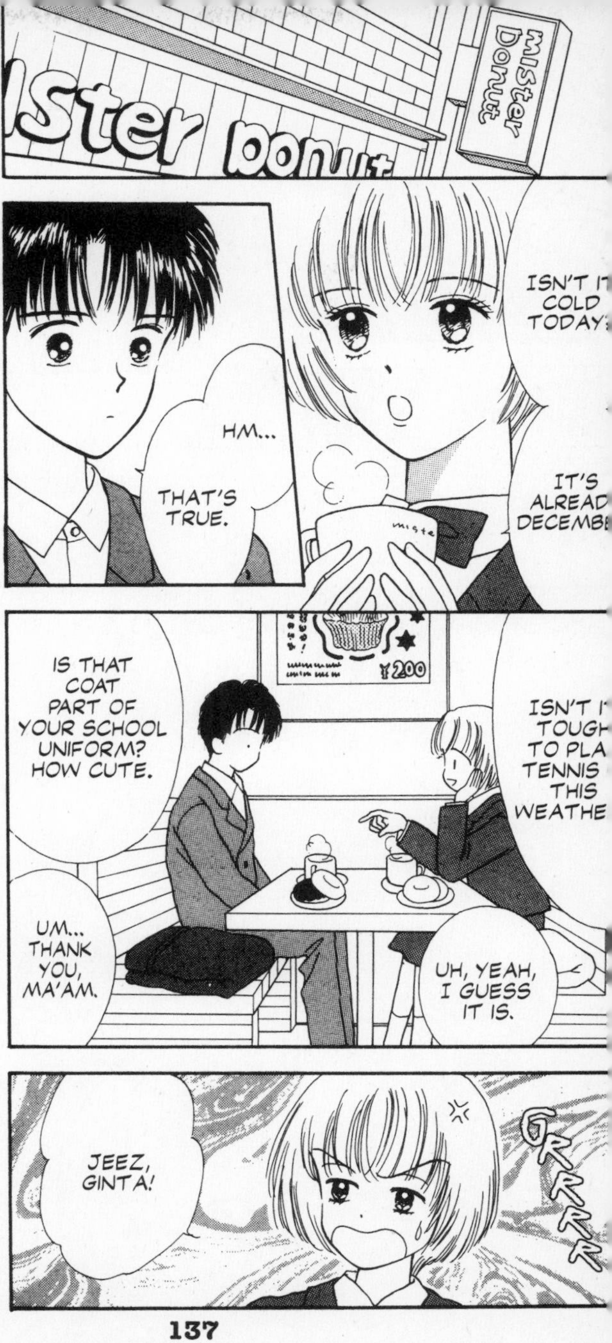

mister Donut
ister DONUT
ISN'T IT COLD TODAY?
IT'S ALREAD DECEMBE
HM...
THAT'S TRUE.
ISN'T I TOUGH TO PLA TENNIS THIS WEATHE
UH, YEAH, I GUESS IT IS.
¥200
IS THAT COAT PART OF YOUR SCHOOL UNIFORM? HOW CUTE.
UM... THANK YOU, MA'AM.
GRRRR
JEEZ, GINTA!

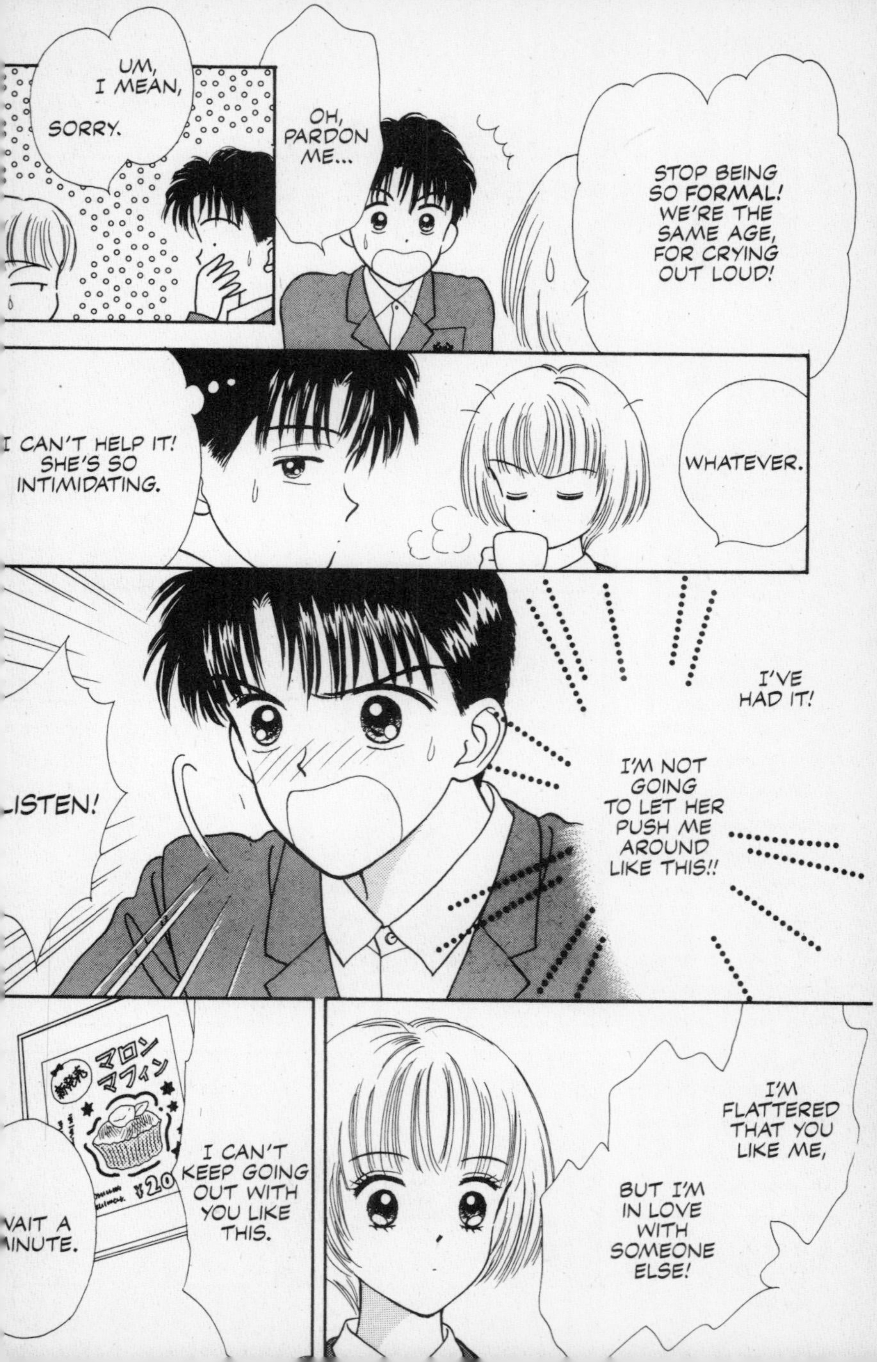
STOP BEING SO FORMAL! WE'RE THE SAME AGE, FOR CRYING OUT LOUD!
OH, PARDON ME...
UM, I MEAN, SORRY.
WHATEVER.
I CAN'T HELP IT! SHE'S SO INTIMIDATING.
I'VE HAD IT!
I'M NOT GOING TO LET HER PUSH ME AROUND LIKE THIS!!
LISTEN!
I'M FLATTERED THAT YOU LIKE ME,
BUT I'M IN LOVE WITH SOMEONE ELSE!
I CAN'T KEEP GOING OUT WITH YOU LIKE THIS.
マロン マフィン
AIT A INUTE.

FREE TALK ⑤

[2] Why do some of the characters call each other by their last names?

In Japan, students address their classmates by their last names until they get to know each other well. Being on a first-name basis with someone carries a lot more significance than it does in America.

[3] What's the big deal with the characters shaving their heads?

In feudal Japan, cutting ones' hair was a sign of humility and was taken very seriously. Monks shaved their heads, while samurai prized their long topknots. Back then, a woman cutting her hair short was considered scandalous.
A modern version of this tradition that's especially common with girls is cutting your hair after a breakup. But today young people are increasingly disregarding old values such as these. Men with shaved heads and women with short hairstyles are quite common in modern Japan.

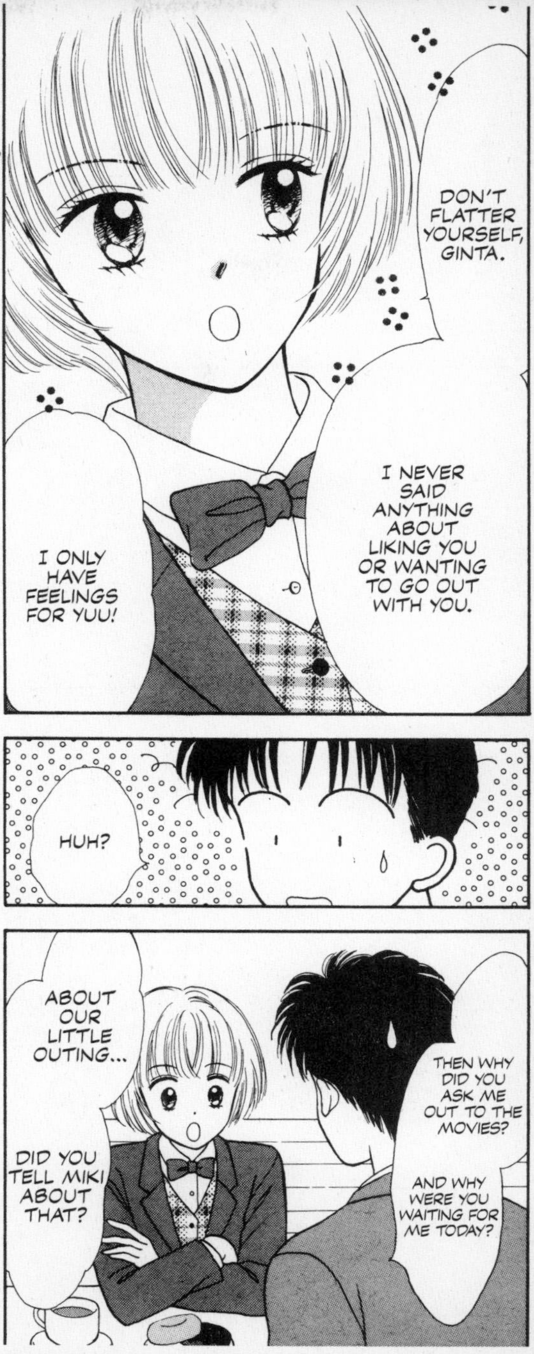
DON'T FLATTER YOURSELF, GINTA.
I NEVER SAID ANYTHING ABOUT LIKING YOU OR WANTING TO GO OUT WITH YOU.
I ONLY HAVE FEELINGS FOR YUU!
HUH?
THEN WHY DID YOU ASK ME OUT TO THE MOVIES?
AND WHY WERE YOU WAITING FOR ME TODAY?
ABOUT OUR LITTLE OUTING...
DID YOU TELL MIKI ABOUT THAT?

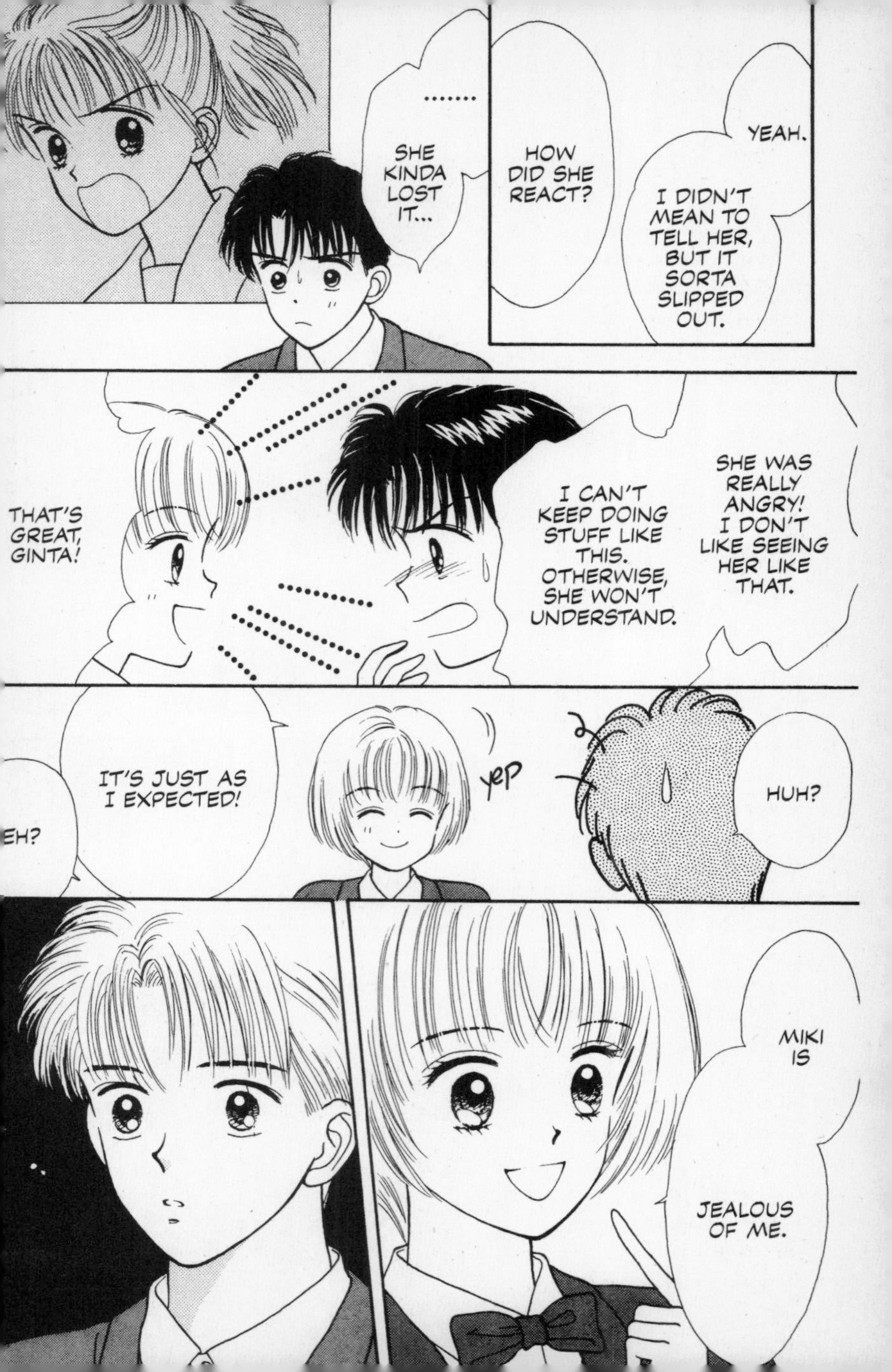

YEAH.
I DIDN'T MEAN TO TELL HER, BUT IT SORTA SLIPPED OUT.
HOW DID SHE REACT?
....
SHE KINDA LOST IT...
SHE WAS REALLY ANGRY! I DON'T LIKE SEEING HER LIKE THAT.
I CAN'T KEEP DOING STUFF LIKE THIS. OTHERWISE, SHE WON'T UNDERSTAND.
THAT'S GREAT, GINTA!
HUH?
YEP
IT'S JUST AS I EXPECTED!
EH?
MIKI IS
JEALOUS OF ME.

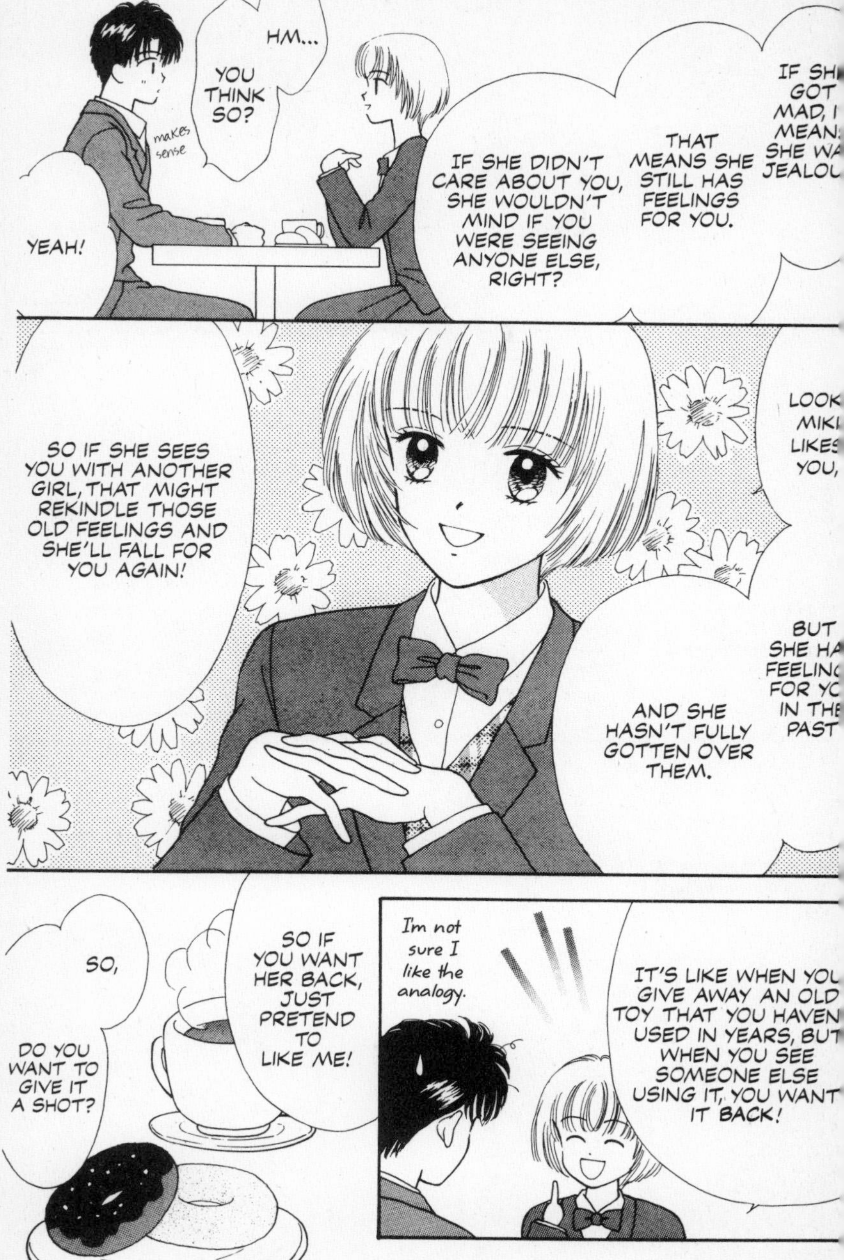
IF SH GOT MAD, I MEANS SHE WA JEALOU
THAT MEANS SHE STILL HAS FEELINGS FOR YOU.
IF SHE DIDN'T CARE ABOUT YOU, SHE WOULDN'T MIND IF YOU WERE SEEING ANYONE ELSE, RIGHT?
HM...
YOU THINK SO?
makes sense
YEAH!
LOOK MIKI LIKES YOU,
BUT SHE HA FEELING FOR YO IN THE PAST
AND SHE HASN'T FULLY GOTTEN OVER THEM.
SO IF SHE SEES YOU WITH ANOTHER GIRL, THAT MIGHT REKINDLE THOSE OLD FEELINGS AND SHE'LL FALL FOR YOU AGAIN!
IT'S LIKE WHEN YOU GIVE AWAY AN OLD TOY THAT YOU HAVEN USED IN YEARS, BUT WHEN YOU SEE SOMEONE ELSE USING IT, YOU WANT IT BACK!
I'm not sure I like the analogy.
SO IF YOU WANT HER BACK, JUST PRETEND TO LIKE ME!
SO,
DO YOU WANT TO GIVE IT A SHOT?

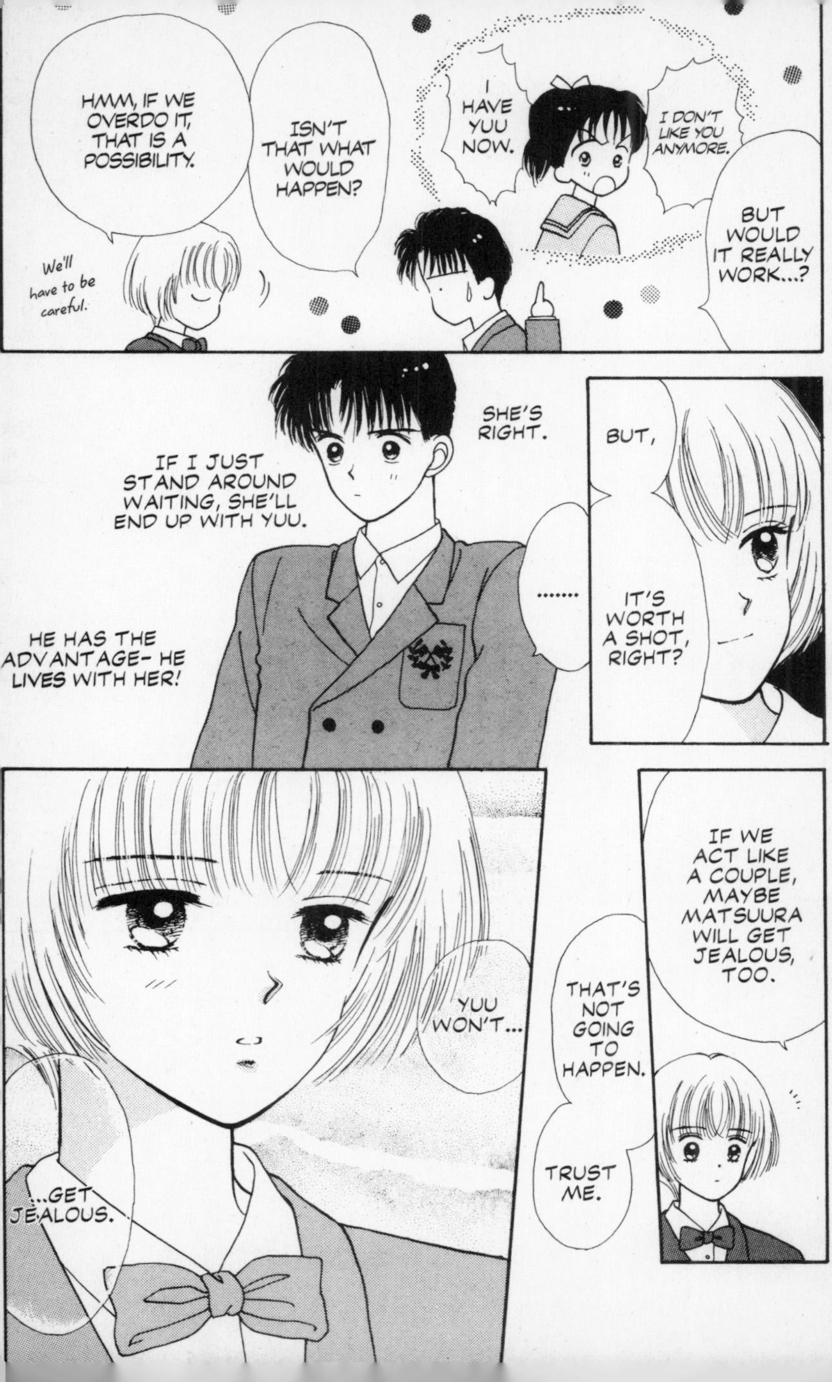
BUT WOULD IT REALLY WORK...?
I DON'T LIKE YOU ANYMORE.
I HAVE YUU NOW.
ISN'T THAT WHAT WOULD HAPPEN?
HMM, IF WE OVERDO IT, THAT IS A POSSIBILITY.
We'll have to be careful.
BUT,
IT'S WORTH A SHOT, RIGHT?
......
SHE'S RIGHT.
IF I JUST STAND AROUND WAITING, SHE'LL END UP WITH YUU.
HE HAS THE ADVANTAGE- HE LIVES WITH HER!
IF WE ACT LIKE A COUPLE, MAYBE MATSUURA WILL GET JEALOUS, TOO.
THAT'S NOT GOING TO HAPPEN.
TRUST ME.
YUU WON'T...
...GET JEALOUS.

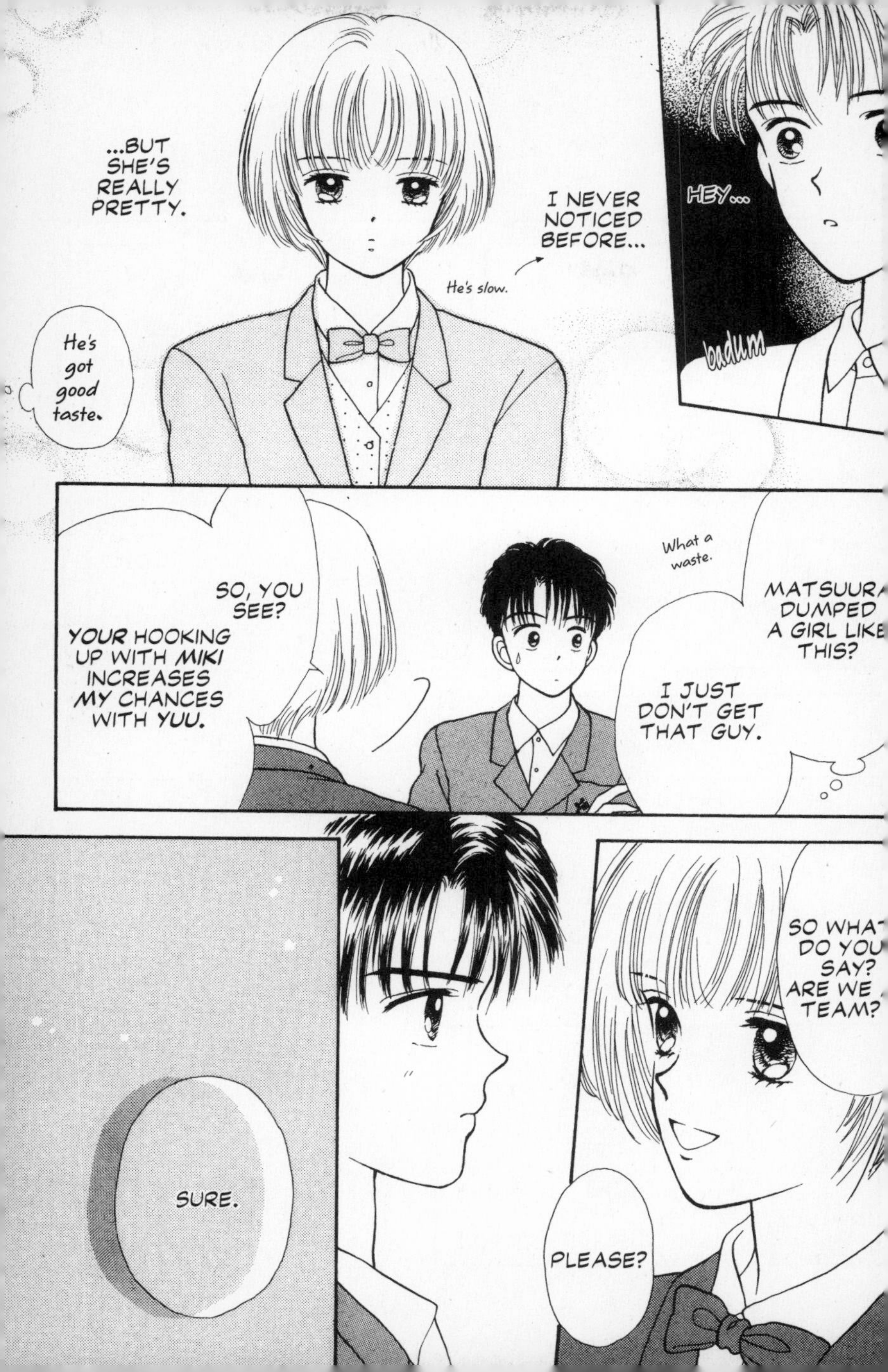
HEY...
badum
I NEVER NOTICED BEFORE...
He's slow.
...BUT SHE'S REALLY PRETTY.
He's got good taste.
What a waste.
MATSUURA DUMPED A GIRL LIKE THIS?
I JUST DON'T GET THAT GUY.
SO, YOU SEE? YOUR HOOKING UP WITH MIKI INCREASES MY CHANCES WITH YUU.
SO WHAT DO YOU SAY? ARE WE TEAM?
PLEASE?
SURE.

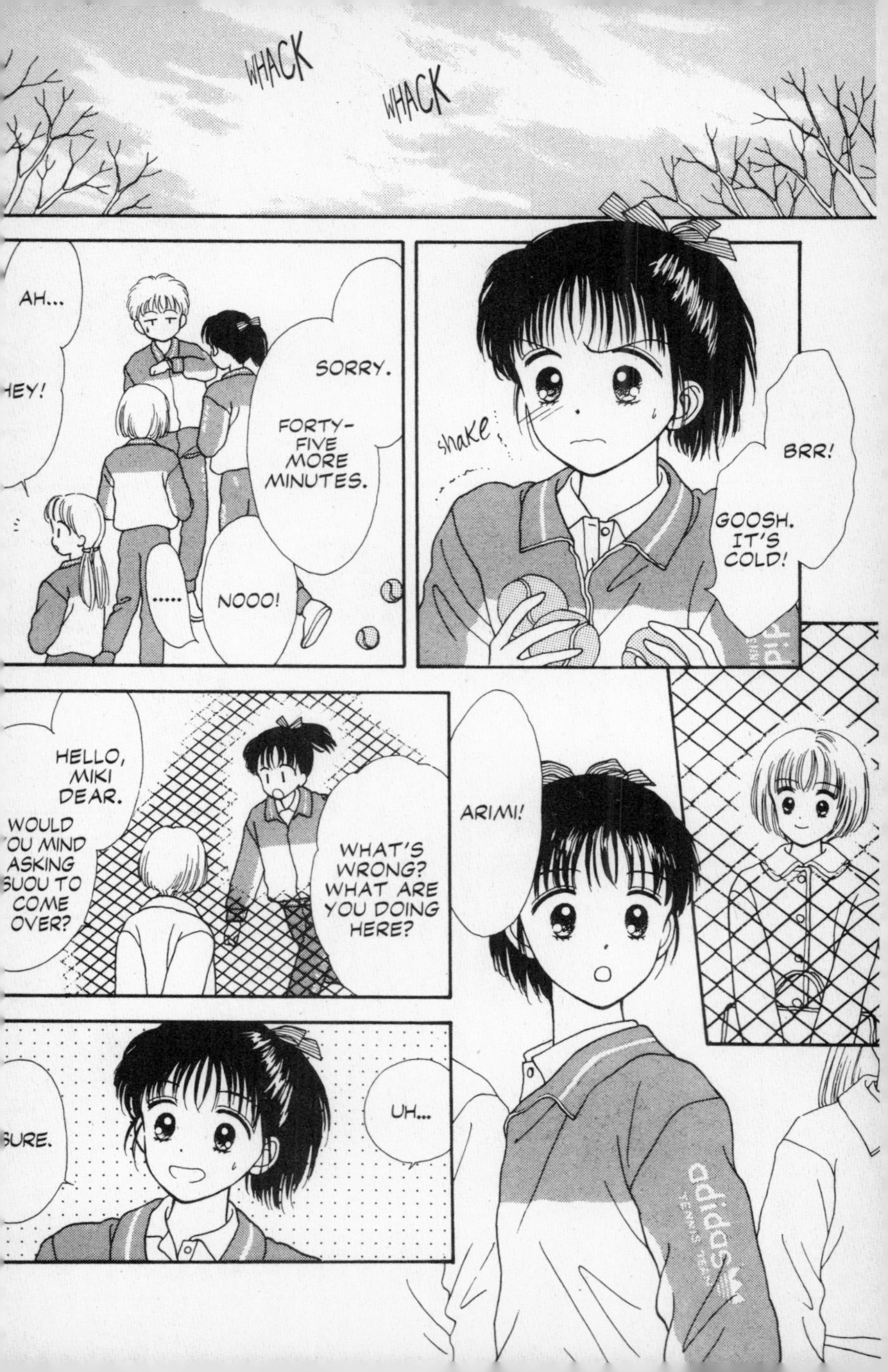
WHACK
WHACK
BRR!
GOOSH. IT'S COLD!
shake
SORRY.
FORTY-FIVE MORE MINUTES.
NOOO!
......
AH...
HEY!
ARIMI!
WHAT'S WRONG? WHAT ARE YOU DOING HERE?
HELLO, MIKI DEAR.
WOULD OU MIND ASKING SUOU TO COME OVER?
UH...
SURE.

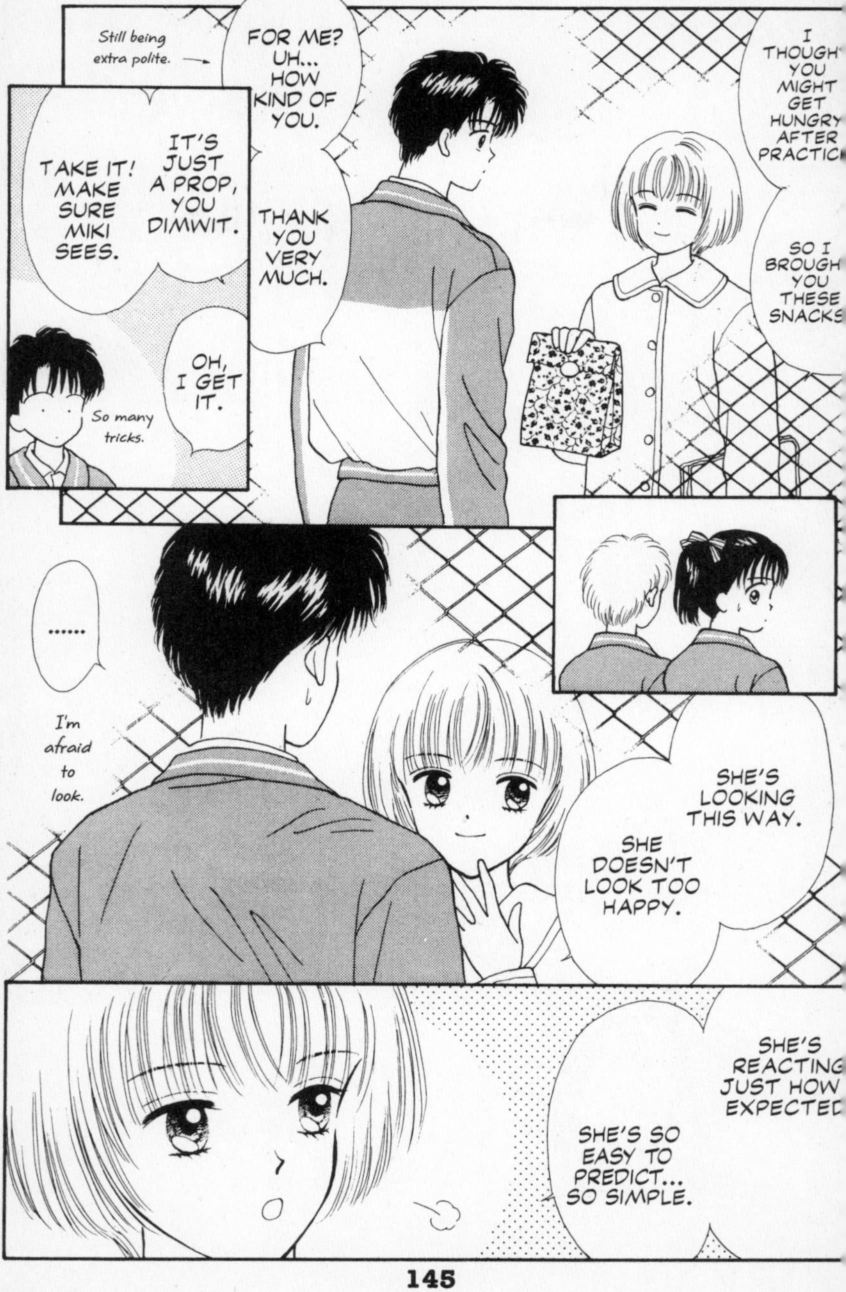
I THOUGHT YOU MIGHT GET HUNGRY AFTER PRACTIC
SO I BROUGH YOU THESE SNACKS
FOR ME? UH... HOW KIND OF YOU.
Still being extra polite.
THANK YOU VERY MUCH.
IT'S JUST A PROP, YOU DIMWIT.
TAKE IT! MAKE SURE MIKI SEES.
OH, I GET IT.
So many tricks.
SHE'S LOOKING THIS WAY.
SHE DOESN'T LOOK TOO HAPPY.
......
I'm afraid to look.
SHE'S REACTING JUST HOW EXPECTED
SHE'S SO EASY TO PREDICT... SO SIMPLE.

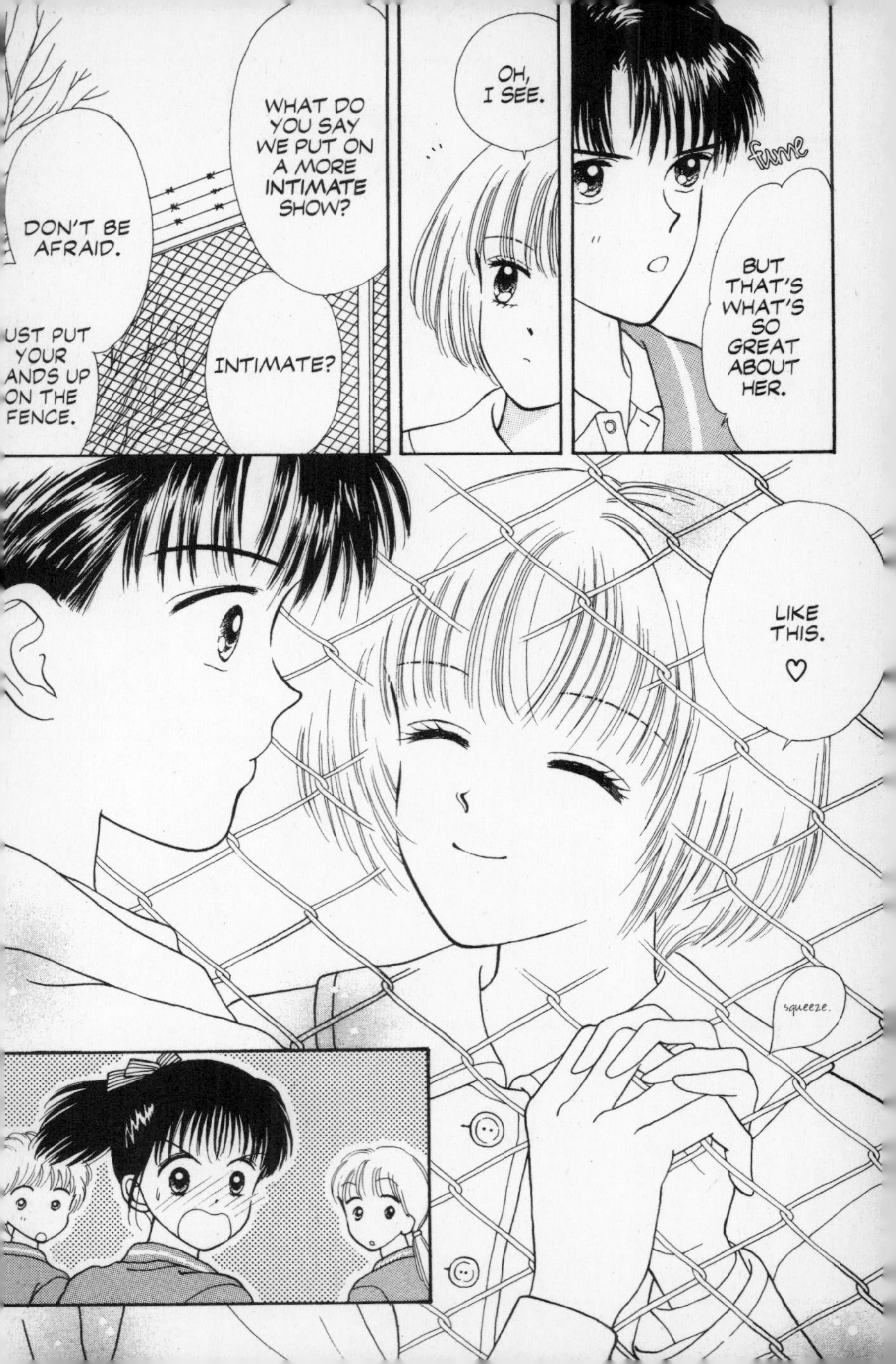
fume
BUT THAT'S WHAT'S SO GREAT ABOUT HER.
OH, I SEE.
WHAT DO YOU SAY WE PUT ON A MORE INTIMATE SHOW?
INTIMATE?
DON'T BE AFRAID.
UST PUT YOUR ANDS UP ON THE FENCE.
LIKE THIS. ♡
squeeze.

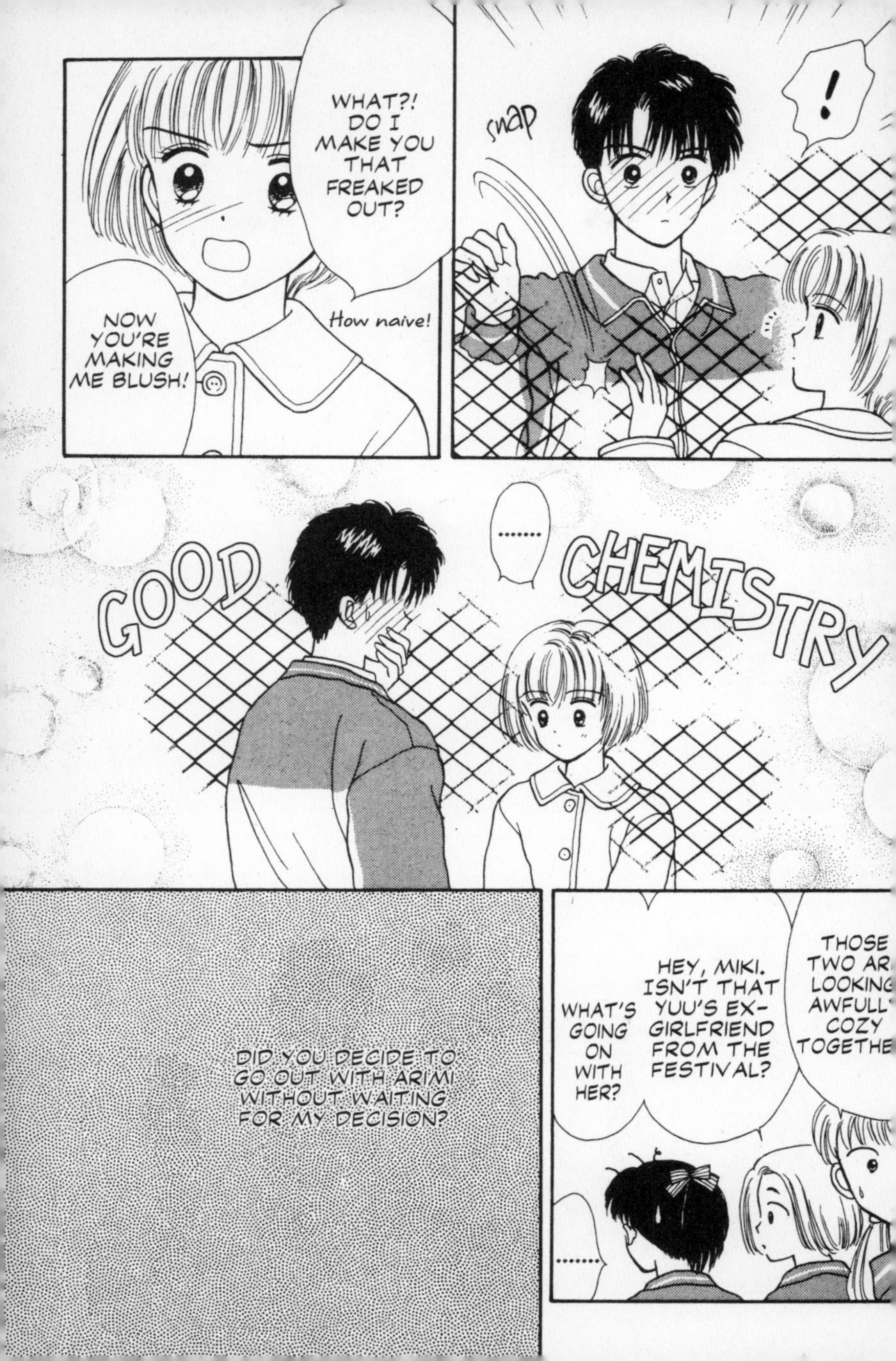
!
snap
WHAT?! DO I MAKE YOU THAT FREAKED OUT?
How naive!
NOW YOU'RE MAKING ME BLUSH!
....
GOOD CHEMISTRY
THOSE TWO AR LOOKING AWFULL COZY TOGETHE
HEY, MIKI. ISN'T THAT YUU'S EX-GIRLFRIEND FROM THE FESTIVAL?
WHAT'S GOING ON WITH HER?
....
DID YOU DECIDE TO GO OUT WITH ARIMI WITHOUT WAITING FOR MY DECISION?

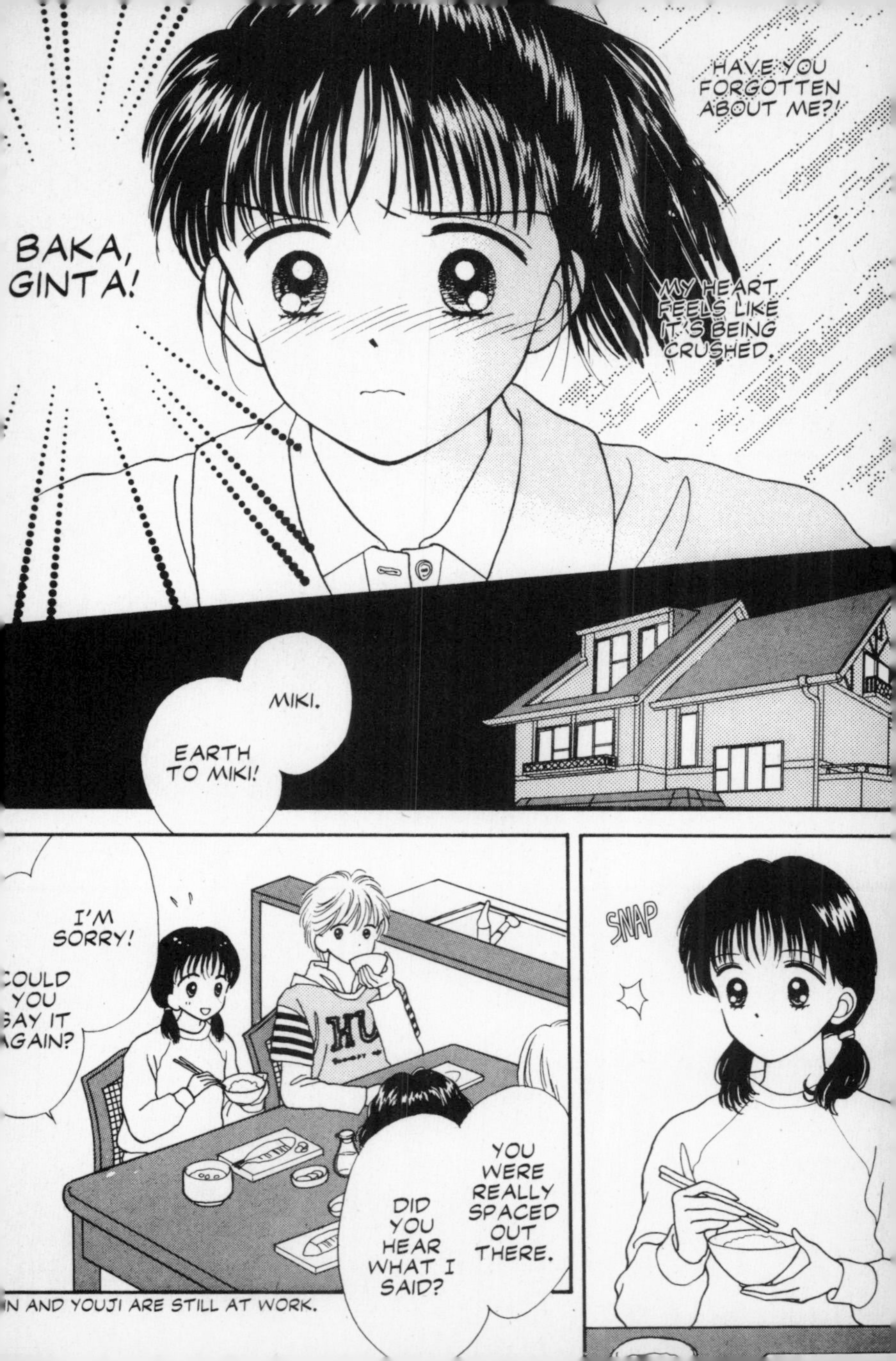
HAVE YOU FORGOTTEN ABOUT ME?!
MY HEART FEELS LIKE IT'S BEING CRUSHED.
BAKA, GINTA!
MIKI.
EARTH TO MIKI!
SNAP
YOU WERE REALLY SPACED OUT THERE.
DID YOU HEAR WHAT I SAID?
I'M SORRY!
COULD YOU SAY IT AGAIN?
N AND YOUJI ARE STILL AT WORK.

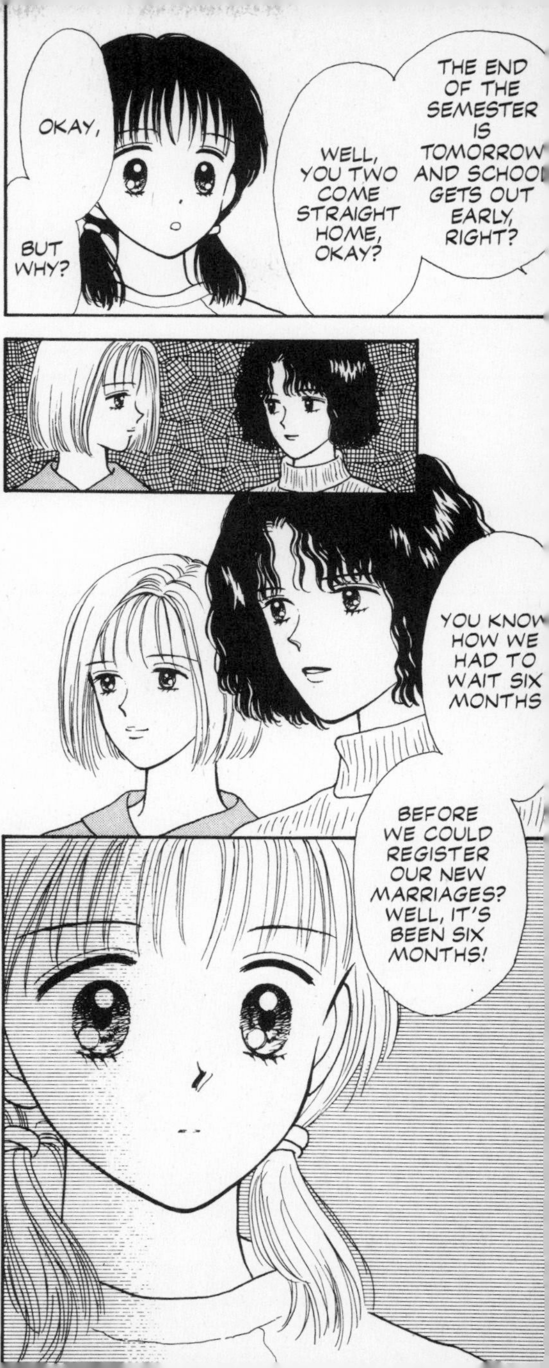
THE END OF THE SEMESTER IS TOMORROW AND SCHOOL GETS OUT EARLY, RIGHT?
WELL, YOU TWO COME STRAIGHT HOME, OKAY?
OKAY,
BUT WHY?
YOU KNOW HOW WE HAD TO WAIT SIX MONTHS
BEFORE WE COULD REGISTER OUR NEW MARRIAGES? WELL, IT'S BEEN SIX MONTHS!

FREE TALK ⑥

4 Why is manga art shaded with dots, patches, and stripes?

The shading effects in manga are the result of what's called screen tone. It's a kind of clear, sticky tape with a pattern printed on it that is cut to the shape of artwork and applied to the drawings. Screen tones can be just shades of gray achieved by different sizes and amounts of little black dots. They can also be complex patterns such as clouds, flowers, or newsprint. When Marmalade Boy was made, screen tones were all applied manually, but today, many manga artists (called manga-ka in Japan) use computers to achieve the same effects.

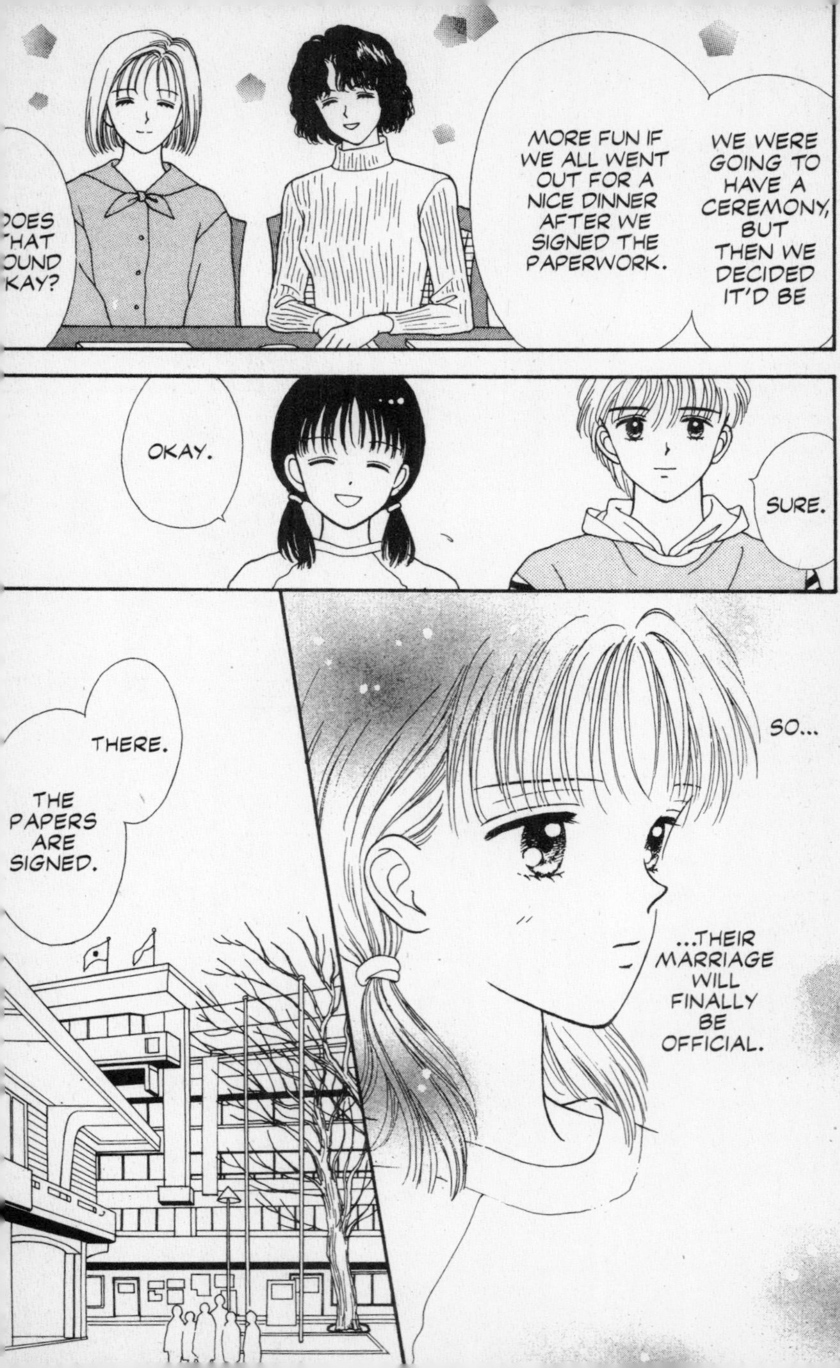
WE WERE GOING TO HAVE A CEREMONY, BUT THEN WE DECIDED IT'D BE MORE FUN IF WE ALL WENT OUT FOR A NICE DINNER AFTER WE SIGNED THE PAPERWORK.
DOES THAT OUND KAY?
SURE.
OKAY.
SO...
...THEIR MARRIAGE WILL FINALLY BE OFFICIAL.
THERE.
THE PAPERS ARE SIGNED.

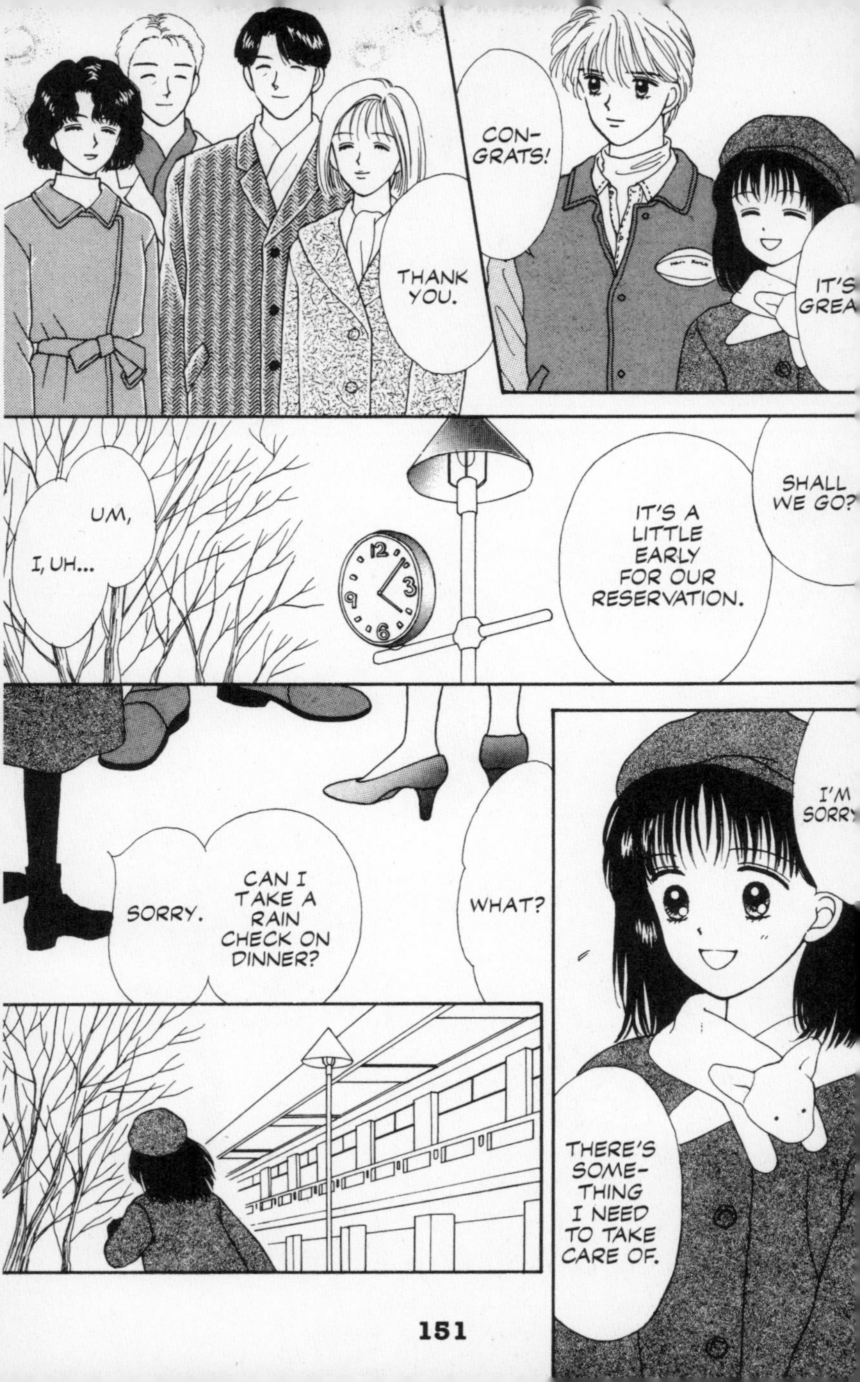
CON-GRATS!
IT'S GREA
THANK YOU.
SHALL WE GO?
IT'S A LITTLE EARLY FOR OUR RESERVATION.
UM,
I, UH...
I'M SORRY
THERE'S SOME-THING I NEED TO TAKE CARE OF.
WHAT?
SORRY.
CAN I TAKE A RAIN CHECK ON DINNER?

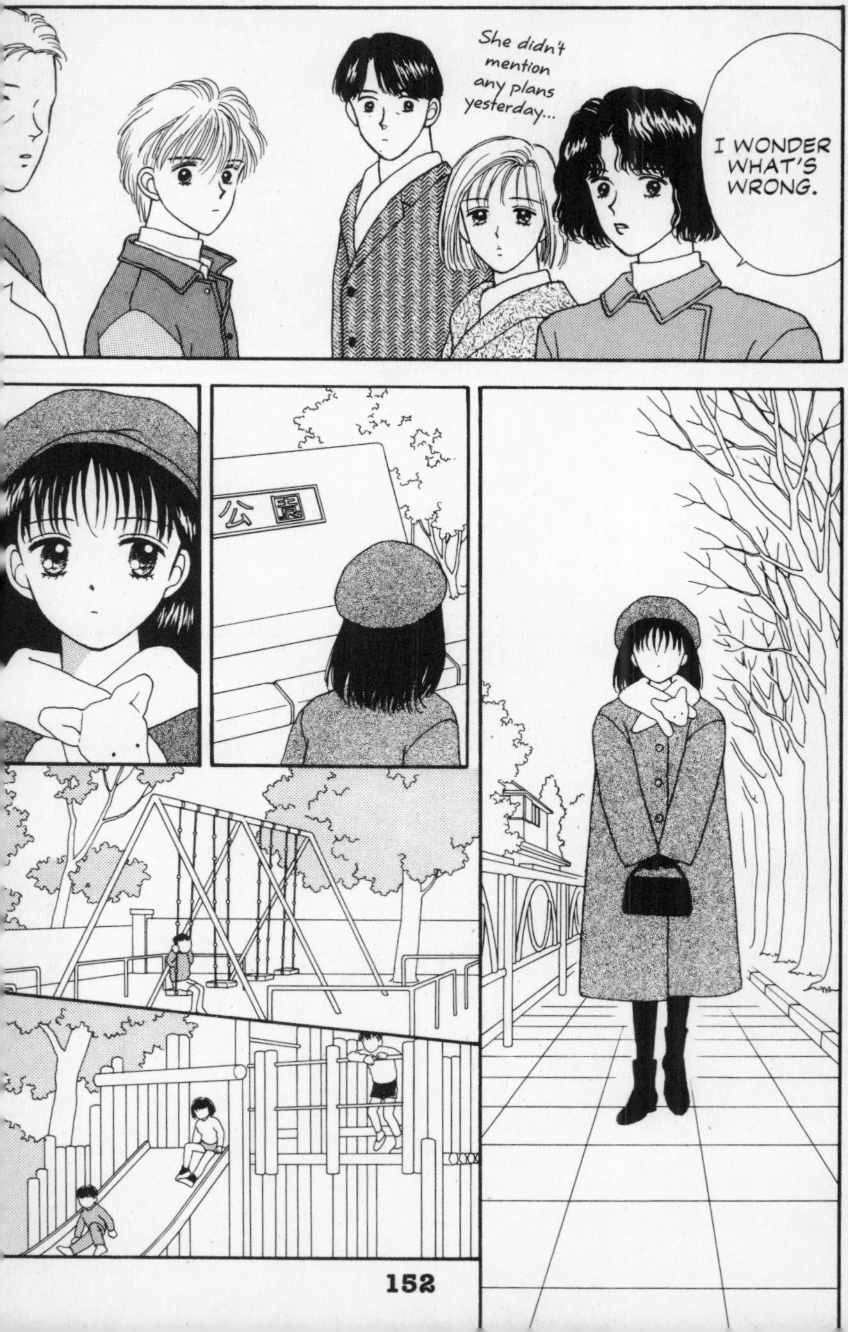
I WONDER WHAT'S WRONG.
She didn't mention any plans yesterday...
公園

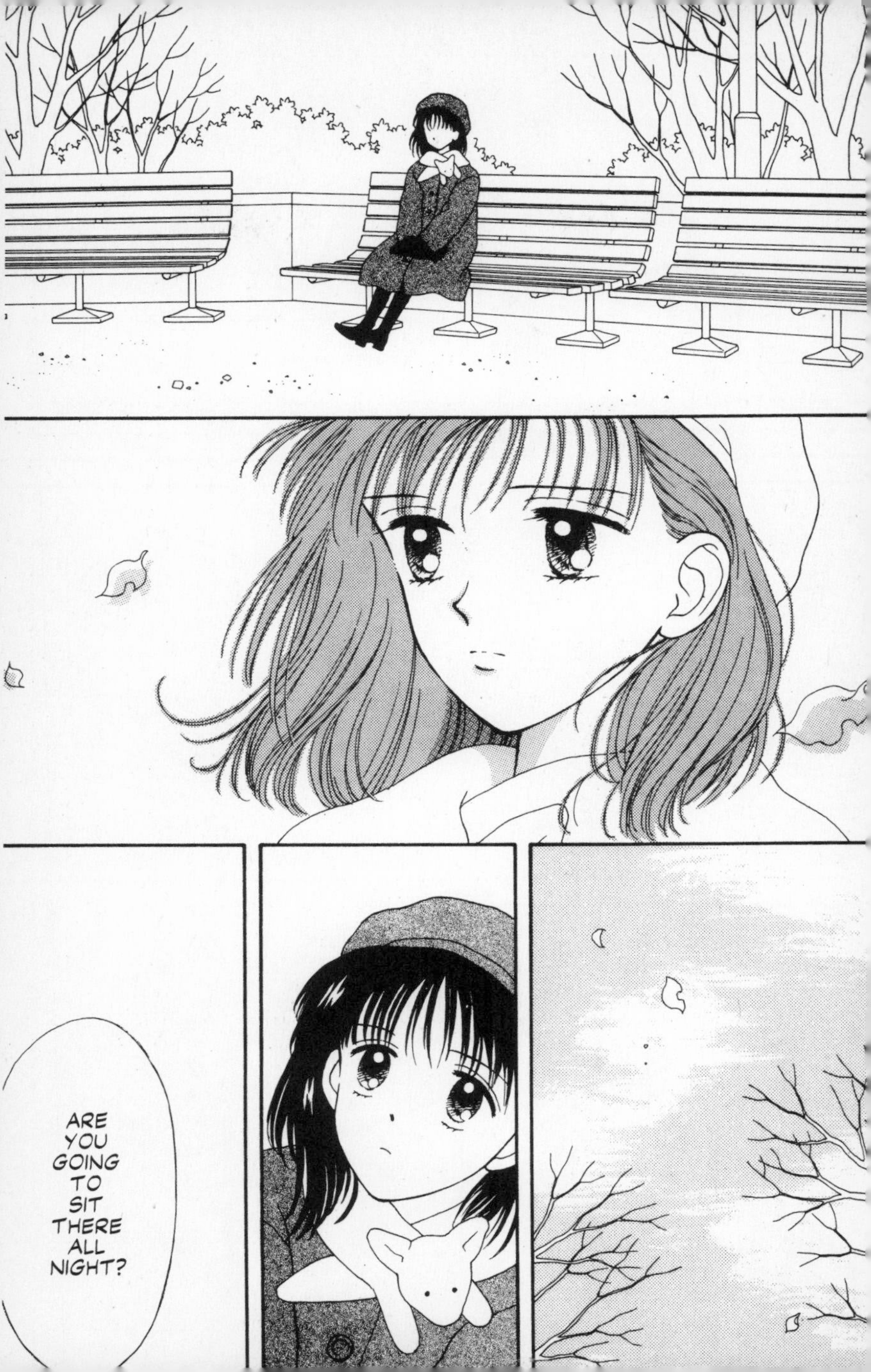
ARE YOU GOING TO SIT THERE ALL NIGHT?

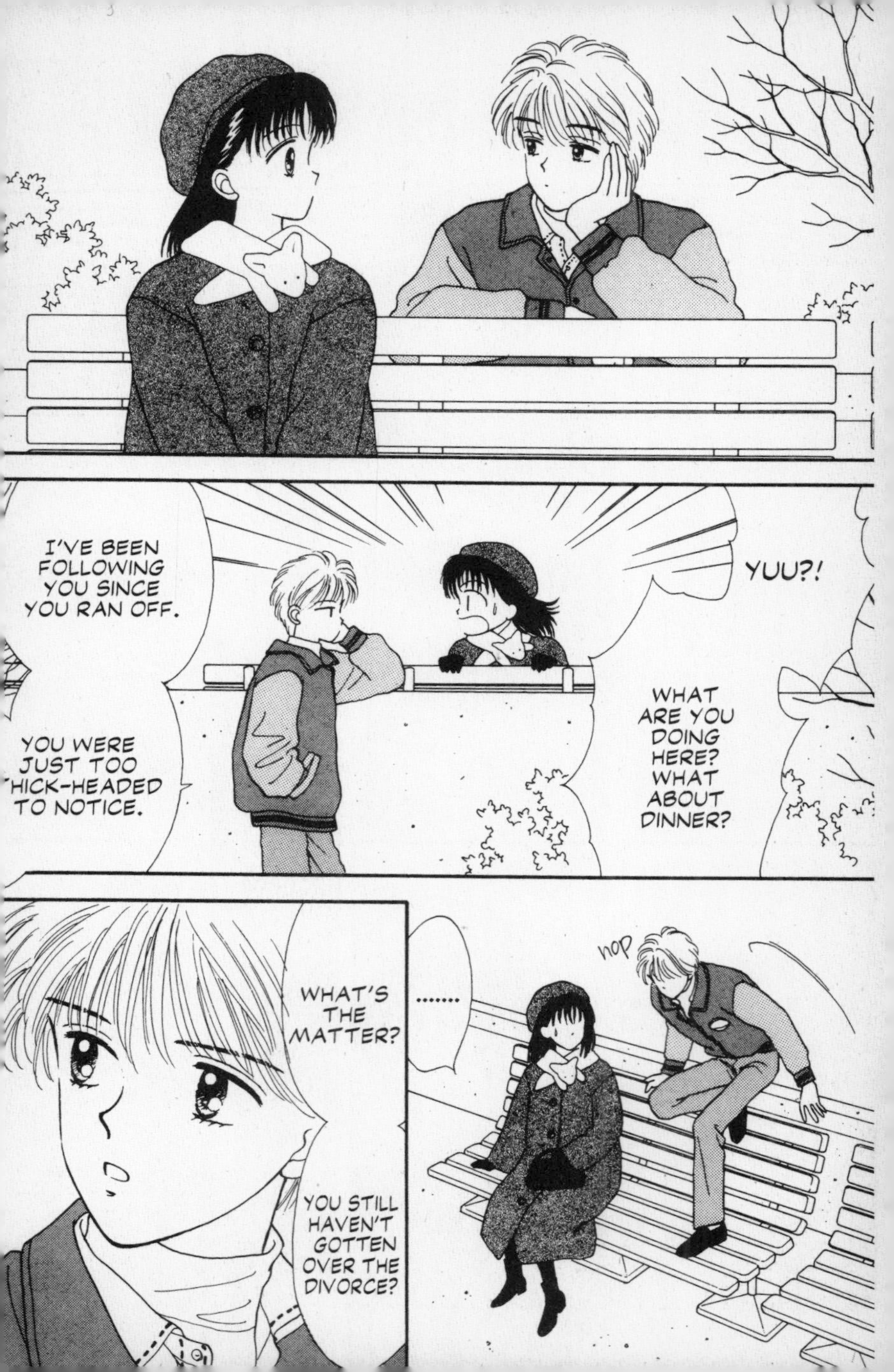
YUU?!
WHAT ARE YOU DOING HERE? WHAT ABOUT DINNER?
I'VE BEEN FOLLOWING YOU SINCE YOU RAN OFF.
YOU WERE JUST TOO THICK-HEADED TO NOTICE.
hop
....
WHAT'S THE MATTER?
YOU STILL HAVEN'T GOTTEN OVER THE DIVORCE?

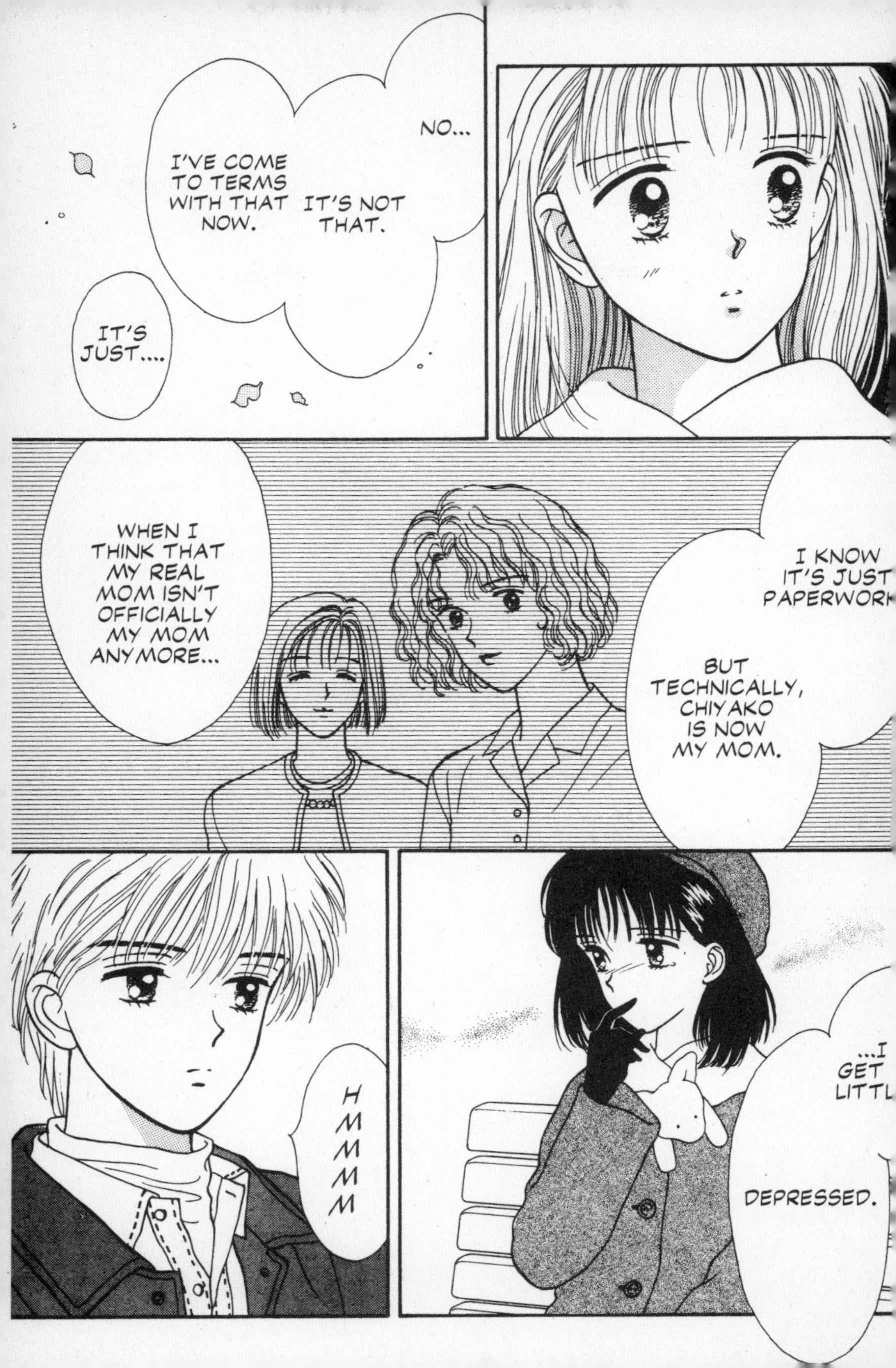
NO...
IT'S NOT THAT.
I'VE COME TO TERMS WITH THAT NOW.
IT'S JUST....
I KNOW IT'S JUST PAPERWOR
BUT TECHNICALLY, CHIYAKO IS NOW MY MOM.
WHEN I THINK THAT MY REAL MOM ISN'T OFFICIALLY MY MOM ANYMORE...
...I GET LITTL
DEPRESSED.
HMMMMM

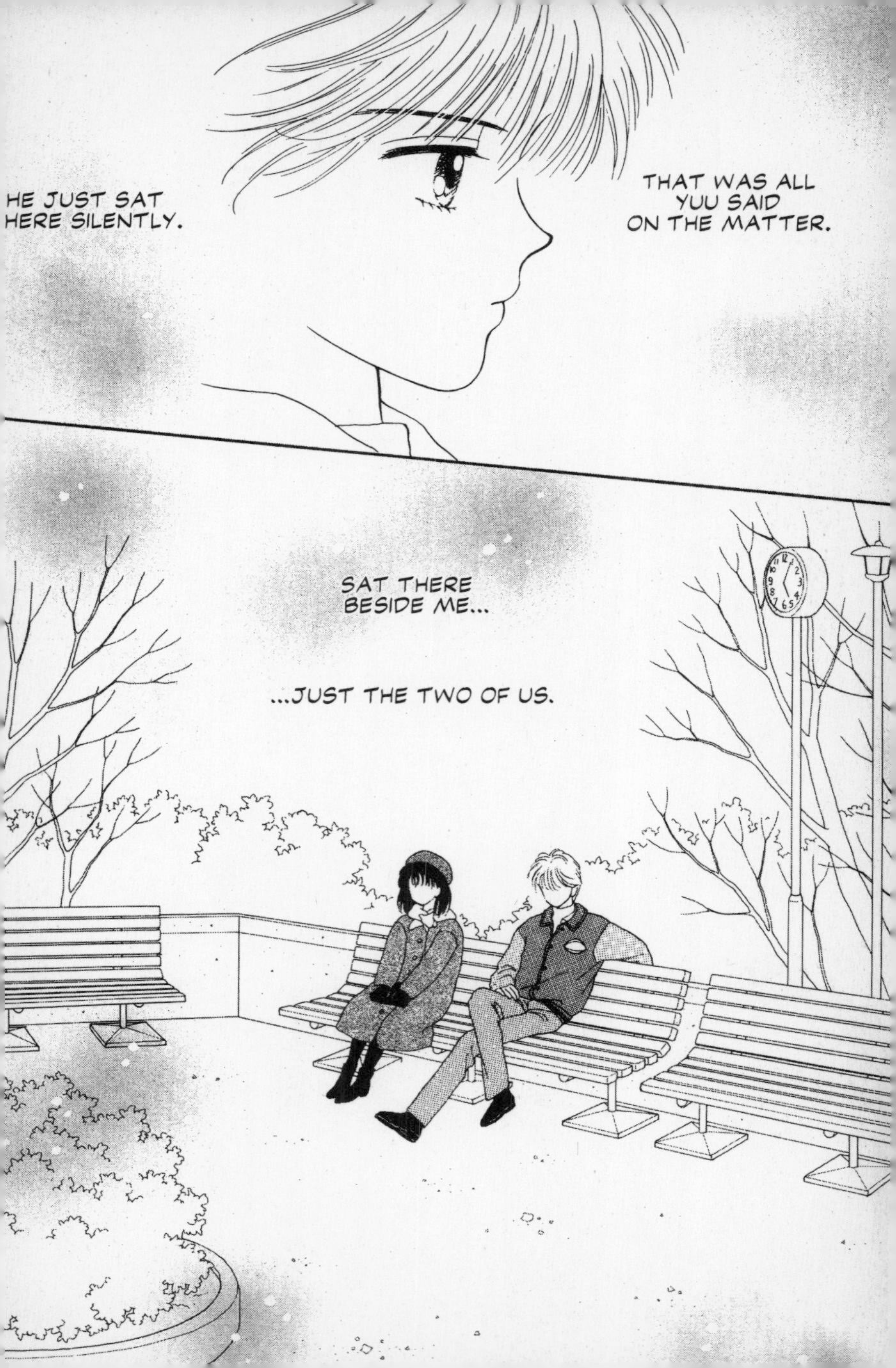

THAT WAS ALL YUU SAID ON THE MATTER.
HE JUST SAT HERE SILENTLY.
SAT THERE BESIDE ME...
...JUST THE TWO OF US.

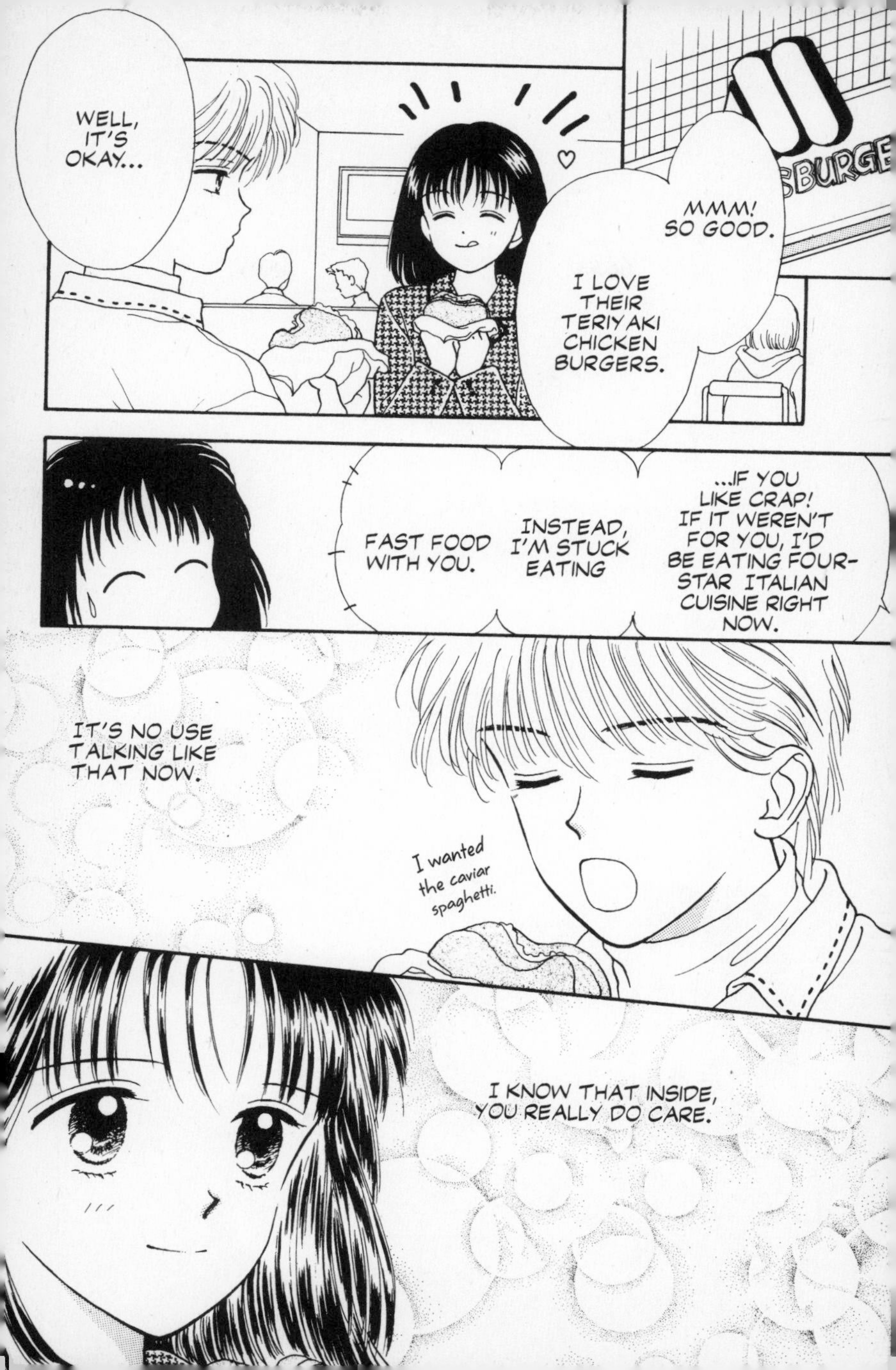
MMM! SO GOOD.
I LOVE THEIR TERIYAKI CHICKEN BURGERS.
WELL, IT'S OKAY...
...IF YOU LIKE CRAP! IF IT WEREN'T FOR YOU, I'D BE EATING FOUR-STAR ITALIAN CUISINE RIGHT NOW.
INSTEAD, I'M STUCK EATING
FAST FOOD WITH YOU.
IT'S NO USE TALKING LIKE THAT NOW.
I wanted the caviar spaghetti.
I KNOW THAT INSIDE, YOU REALLY DO CARE.

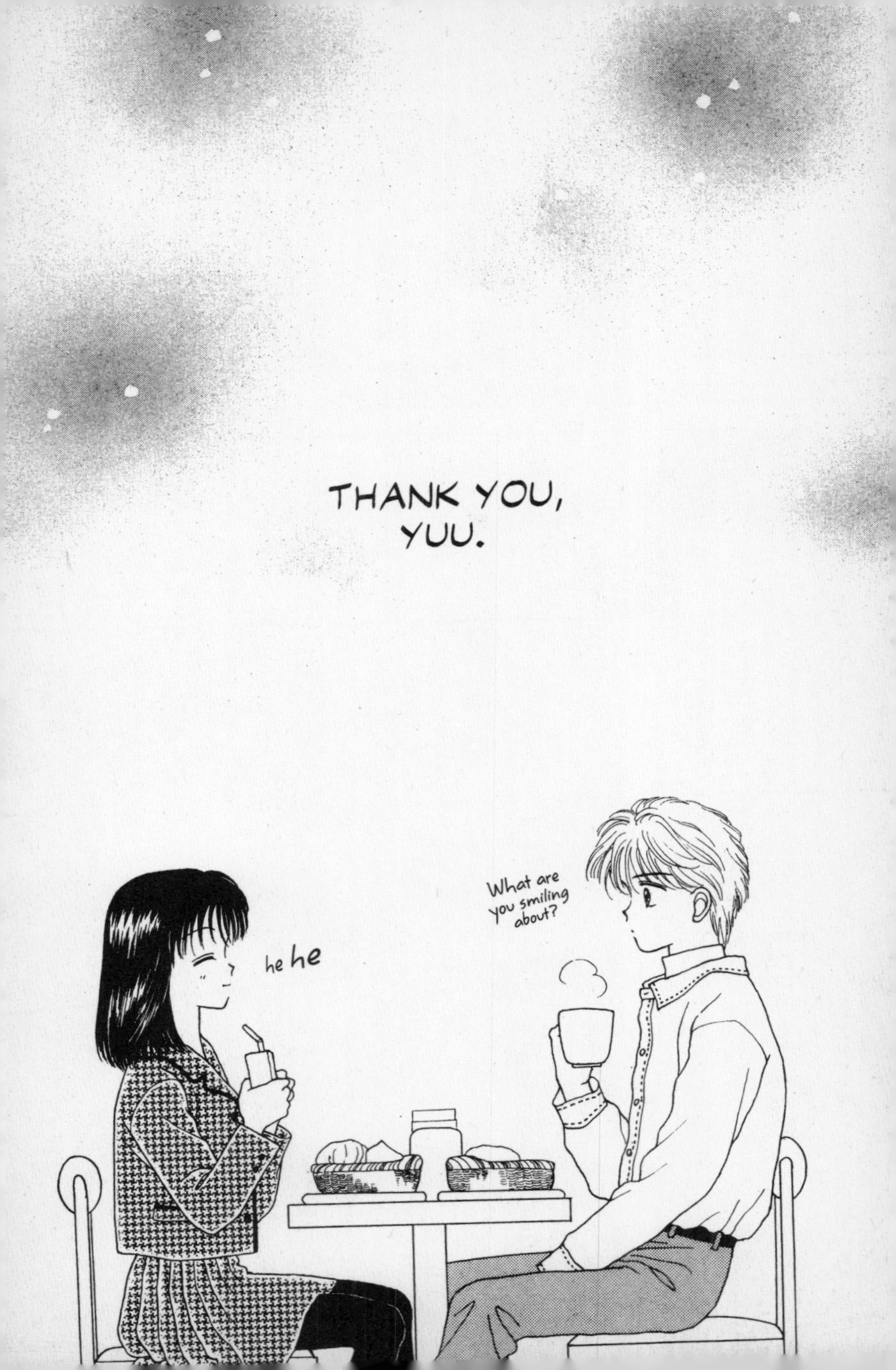
THANK YOU, YUU.
What are you smiling about?
he he

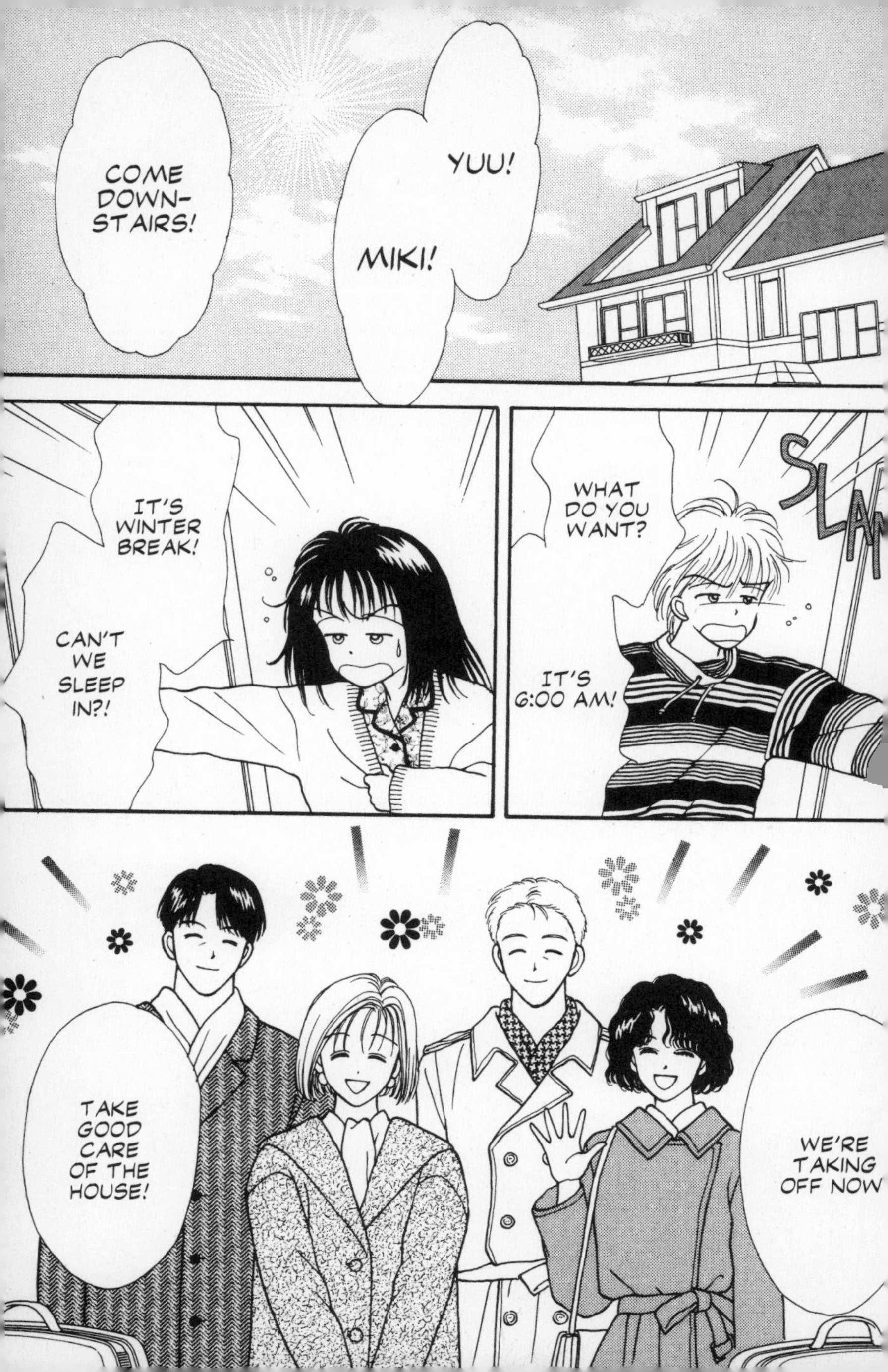
YUU!
MIKI!
COME DOWN-STAIRS!
SLA
WHAT DO YOU WANT?
IT'S 6:00 AM!
IT'S WINTER BREAK!
CAN'T WE SLEEP IN?!
WE'RE TAKING OFF NOW
TAKE GOOD CARE OF THE HOUSE!

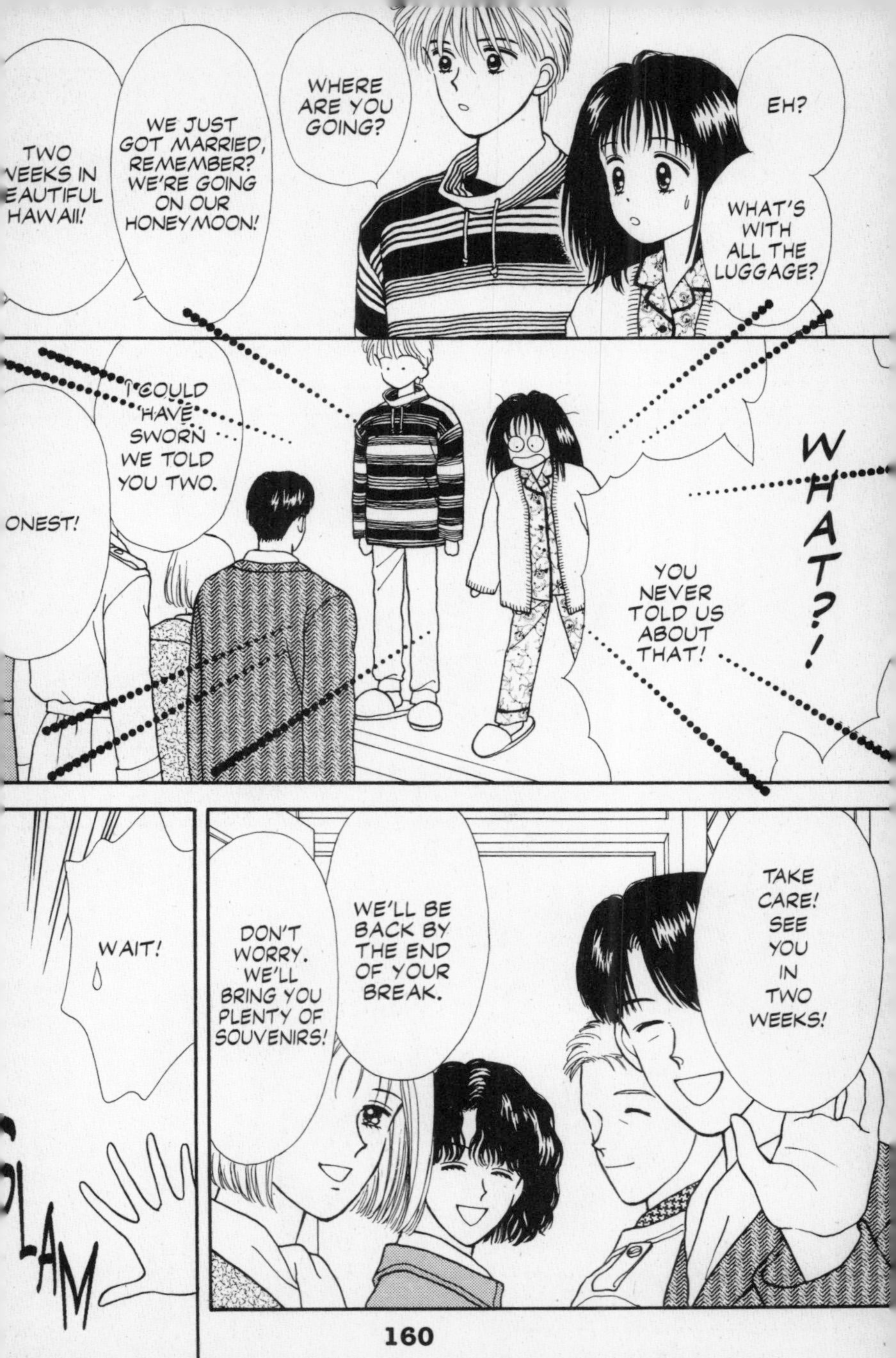
EH?
WHAT'S WITH ALL THE LUGGAGE?
WHERE ARE YOU GOING?
WE JUST GOT MARRIED, REMEMBER? WE'RE GOING ON OUR HONEYMOON!
TWO VEEKS IN EAUTIFUL HAWAII!
WHAT?!
YOU NEVER TOLD US ABOUT THAT!
I COULD HAVE SWORN WE TOLD YOU TWO.
ONEST!
TAKE CARE! SEE YOU IN TWO WEEKS!
WE'LL BE BACK BY THE END OF YOUR BREAK.
DON'T WORRY. WE'LL BRING YOU PLENTY OF SOUVENIRS!
WAIT!
SLAM

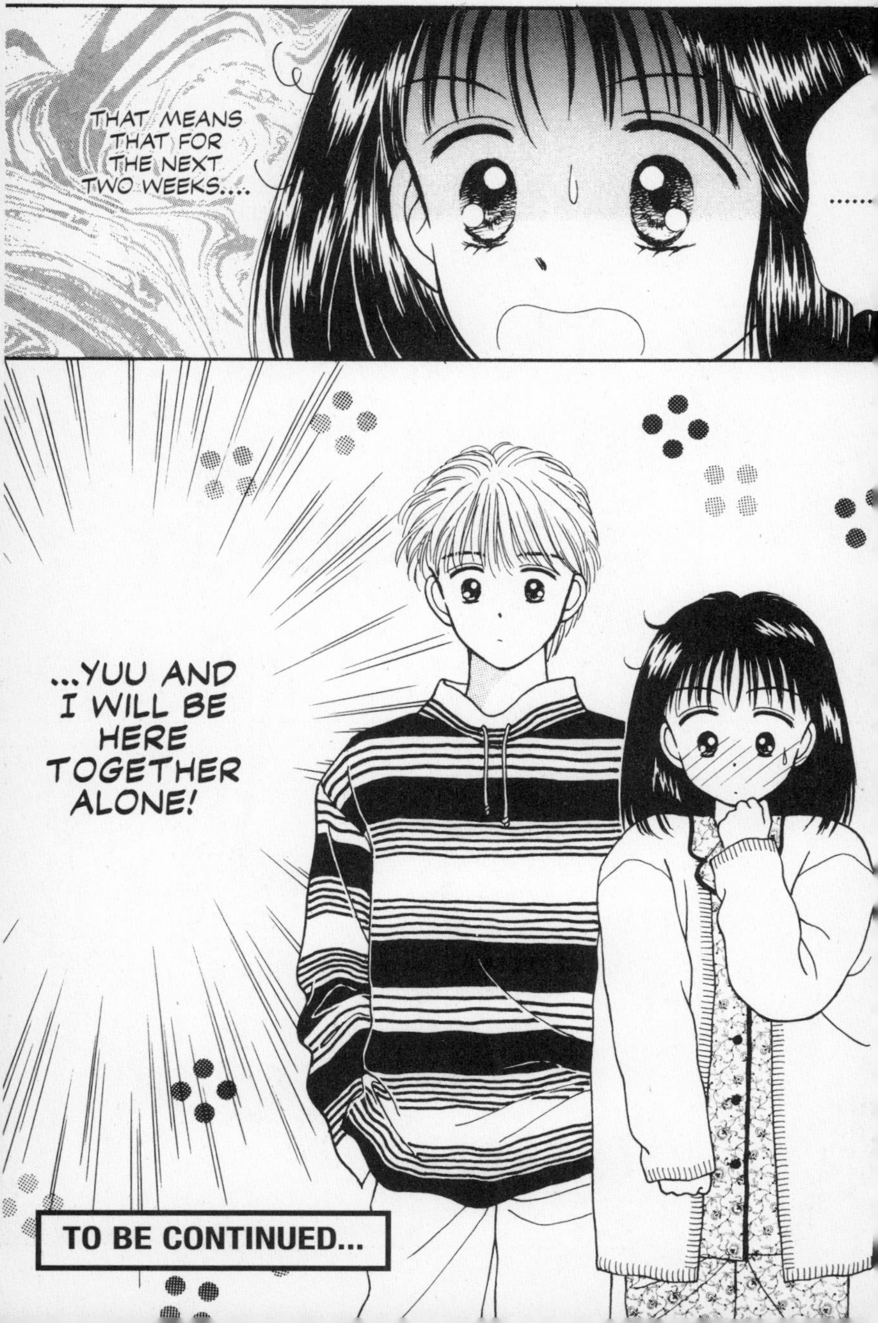
THAT MEANS THAT FOR THE NEXT TWO WEEKS....
......
...YUU AND I WILL BE HERE TOGETHER ALONE!
TO BE CONTINUED...

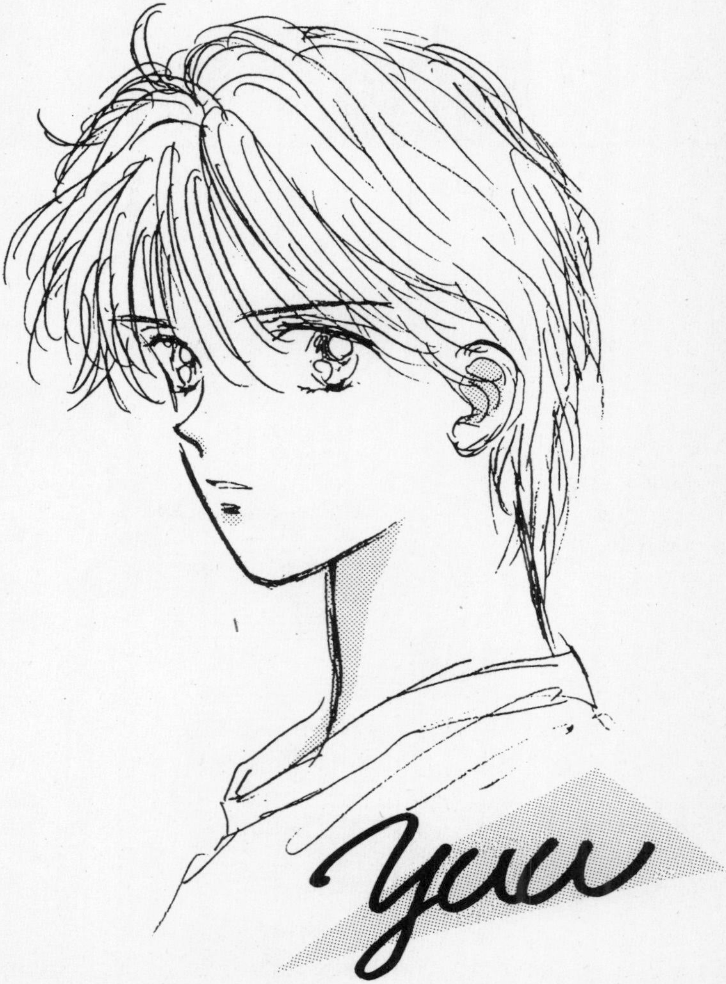
Yuu

FROM WATARU TO YOU II

HI, EVERY-ONE! WATARU YOSHIZUMI HERE.

YOU MIGHT HAVE NOTICED THERE WAS A LOT OF TENNIS IN THIS VOLUME.

MANY OF YOU PROBABLY DON'T KNOW THE RULES, SO I'LL DO MY BEST TO EXPLAIN THEM HERE.

I'M NOT USING A BOOK TO FIND THE RULES, BUT AM BASING THIS ON WHAT I REMEMBER. SO IF I OVERLOOK ANYTHING, PLEASE FORGIVE ME, 'KAY? ♡

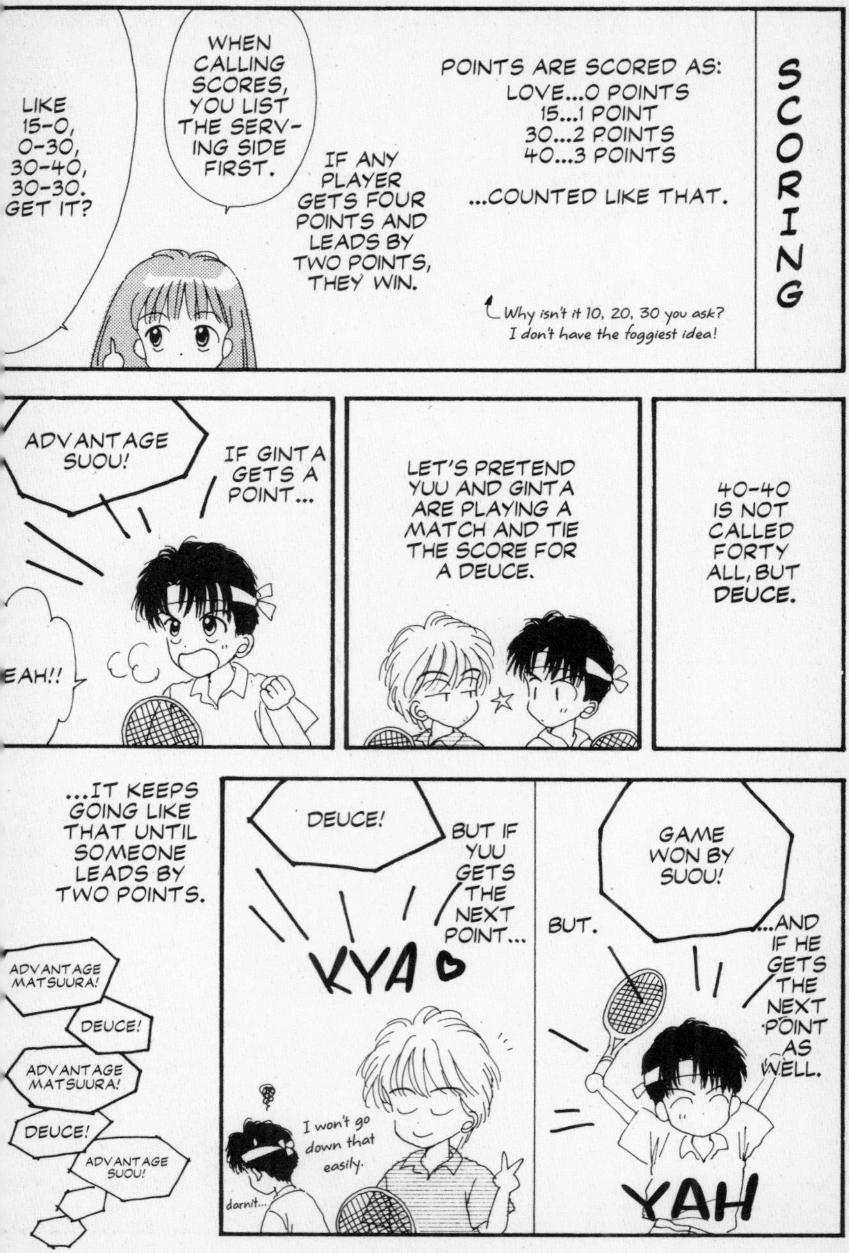
SCORING
POINTS ARE SCORED AS:
LOVE...0 POINTS
15...1 POINT
30...2 POINTS
40...3 POINTS
...COUNTED LIKE THAT.
Why isn't it 10, 20, 30 you ask? I don't have the foggiest idea!
IF ANY PLAYER GETS FOUR POINTS AND LEADS BY TWO POINTS, THEY WIN.
WHEN CALLING SCORES, YOU LIST THE SERVING SIDE FIRST.
LIKE 15-0, 0-30, 30-40, 30-30. GET IT?
40-40 IS NOT CALLED FORTY ALL, BUT DEUCE.
LET'S PRETEND YUU AND GINTA ARE PLAYING A MATCH AND TIE THE SCORE FOR A DEUCE.
IF GINTA GETS A POINT...
ADVANTAGE SUOU!
EAH!!
GAME WON BY SUOU!
...AND IF HE GETS THE NEXT POINT AS WELL.
BUT.
YAH
BUT IF YUU GETS THE NEXT POINT...
DEUCE!
KYA
I won't go down that easily.
darnit...
...IT KEEPS GOING LIKE THAT UNTIL SOMEONE LEADS BY TWO POINTS.
ADVANTAGE MATSUURA!
DEUCE!
ADVANTAGE MATSUURA!
DEUCE!
ADVANTAGE SUOU!

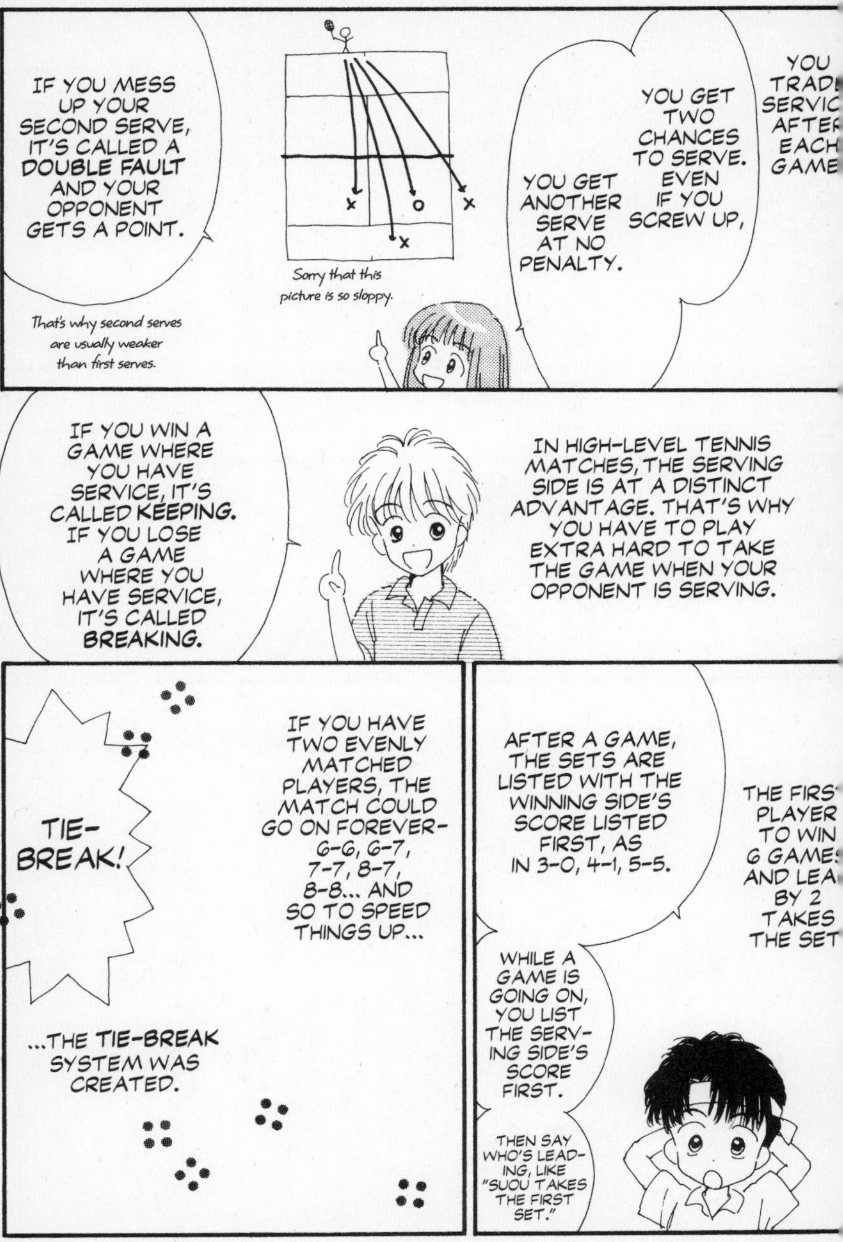
YOU TRAD SERVIC AFTE EACH GAME
YOU GET TWO CHANCES TO SERVE. EVEN IF YOU SCREW UP,
YOU GET ANOTHER SERVE AT NO PENALTY.
IF YOU MESS UP YOUR SECOND SERVE, IT'S CALLED A **DOUBLE FAULT** AND YOUR OPPONENT GETS A POINT.
Sorry that this picture is so sloppy.
That's why second serves are usually weaker than first serves.
IN HIGH-LEVEL TENNIS MATCHES, THE SERVING SIDE IS AT A DISTINCT ADVANTAGE. THAT'S WHY YOU HAVE TO PLAY EXTRA HARD TO TAKE THE GAME WHEN YOUR OPPONENT IS SERVING.
IF YOU WIN A GAME WHERE YOU HAVE SERVICE, IT'S CALLED **KEEPING.** IF YOU LOSE A GAME WHERE YOU HAVE SERVICE, IT'S CALLED **BREAKING.**
THE FIRS PLAYER TO WIN 6 GAME AND LEA BY 2 TAKES THE SET
AFTER A GAME, THE SETS ARE LISTED WITH THE WINNING SIDE'S SCORE LISTED FIRST, AS IN 3-0, 4-1, 5-5.
WHILE A GAME IS GOING ON, YOU LIST THE SERV-ING SIDE'S SCORE FIRST.
THEN SAY WHO'S LEAD-ING, LIKE "SUOU TAKES THE FIRST SET."
IF YOU HAVE TWO EVENLY MATCHED PLAYERS, THE MATCH COULD GO ON FOREVER- 6-6, 6-7, 7-7, 8-7, 8-8... AND SO TO SPEED THINGS UP...
TIE-BREAK!
...THE TIE-BREAK SYSTEM WAS CREATED.

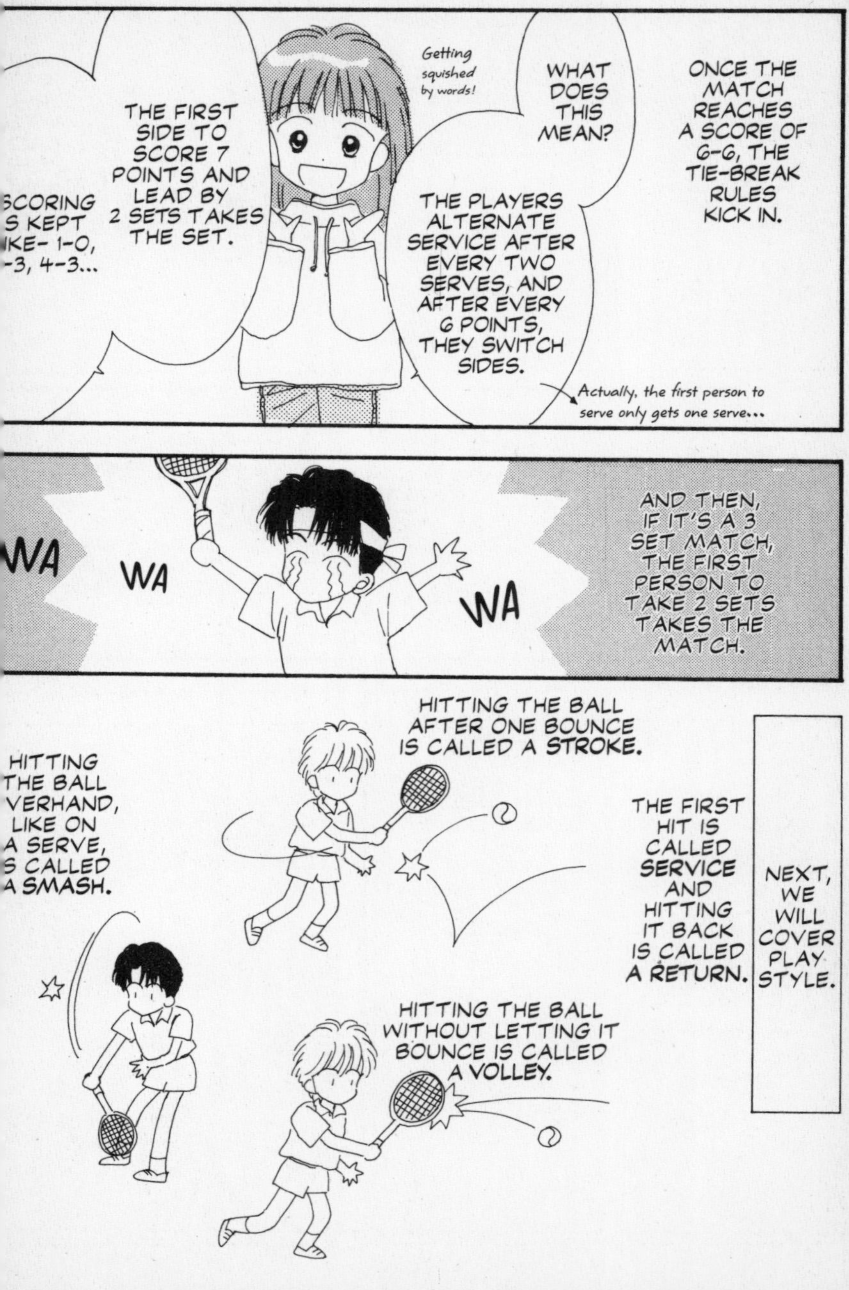

ONCE THE MATCH REACHES A SCORE OF 6-6, THE TIE-BREAK RULES KICK IN.
WHAT DOES THIS MEAN?
Getting squished by words!
THE PLAYERS ALTERNATE SERVICE AFTER EVERY TWO SERVES, AND AFTER EVERY 6 POINTS, THEY SWITCH SIDES.
Actually, the first person to serve only gets one serve...
THE FIRST SIDE TO SCORE 7 POINTS AND LEAD BY 2 SETS TAKES THE SET.
SCORING S KEPT IKE- 1-0, -3, 4-3...
AND THEN, IF IT'S A 3 SET MATCH, THE FIRST PERSON TO TAKE 2 SETS TAKES THE MATCH.
WA
WA
WA
NEXT, WE WILL COVER PLAY STYLE.
THE FIRST HIT IS CALLED SERVICE AND HITTING IT BACK IS CALLED A RETURN.
HITTING THE BALL AFTER ONE BOUNCE IS CALLED A STROKE.
HITTING THE BALL VERHAND, LIKE ON A SERVE, S CALLED A SMASH.
HITTING THE BALL WITHOUT LETTING IT BOUNCE IS CALLED A VOLLEY.

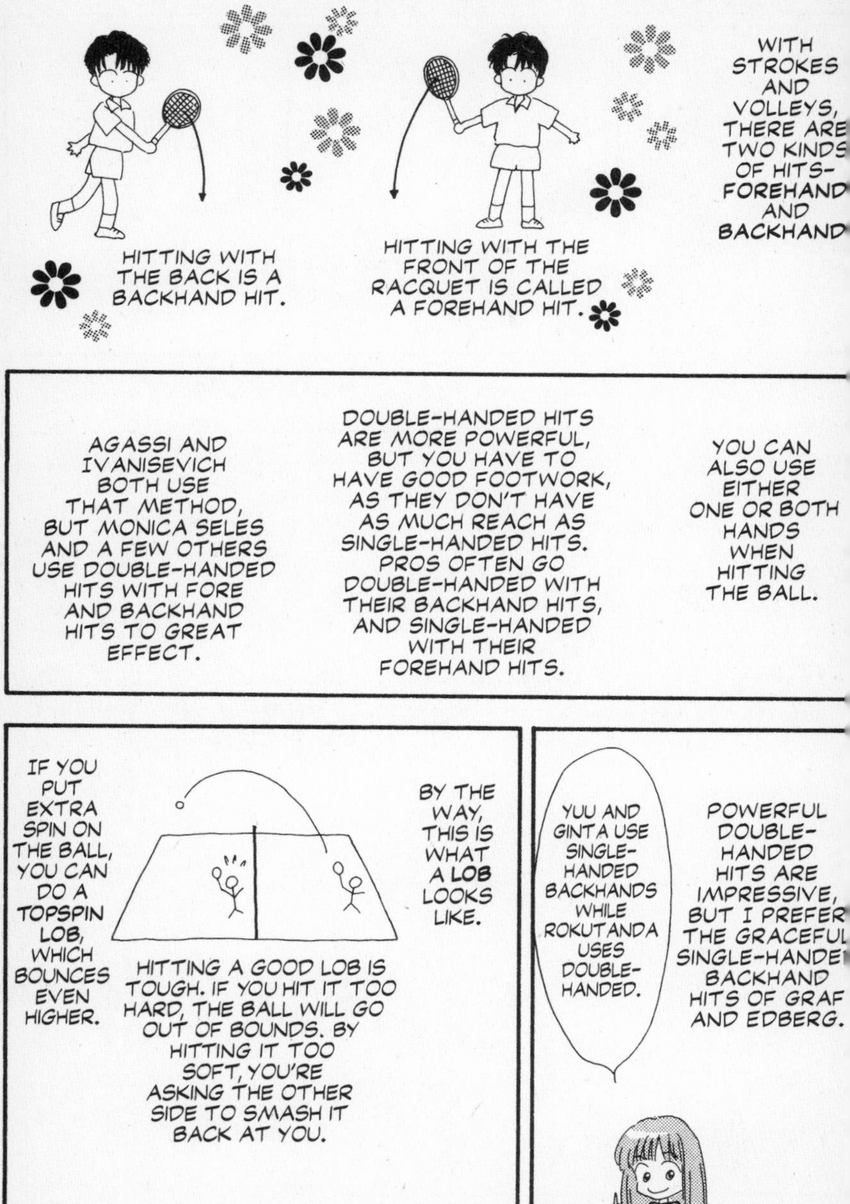
WITH STROKES AND VOLLEYS, THERE ARE TWO KINDS OF HITS- FOREHAND AND BACKHAND
HITTING WITH THE FRONT OF THE RACQUET IS CALLED A FOREHAND HIT.
HITTING WITH THE BACK IS A BACKHAND HIT.
YOU CAN ALSO USE EITHER ONE OR BOTH HANDS WHEN HITTING THE BALL.
DOUBLE-HANDED HITS ARE MORE POWERFUL, BUT YOU HAVE TO HAVE GOOD FOOTWORK, AS THEY DON'T HAVE AS MUCH REACH AS SINGLE-HANDED HITS. PROS OFTEN GO DOUBLE-HANDED WITH THEIR BACKHAND HITS, AND SINGLE-HANDED WITH THEIR FOREHAND HITS.
AGASSI AND IVANISEVICH BOTH USE THAT METHOD, BUT MONICA SELES AND A FEW OTHERS USE DOUBLE-HANDED HITS WITH FORE AND BACKHAND HITS TO GREAT EFFECT.
POWERFUL DOUBLE-HANDED HITS ARE IMPRESSIVE, BUT I PREFER THE GRACEFUL SINGLE-HANDE BACKHAND HITS OF GRAF AND EDBERG.
YUU AND GINTA USE SINGLE-HANDED BACKHANDS WHILE ROKUTANDA USES DOUBLE-HANDED.
BY THE WAY, THIS IS WHAT A LOB LOOKS LIKE.
HITTING A GOOD LOB IS TOUGH. IF YOU HIT IT TOO HARD, THE BALL WILL GO OUT OF BOUNDS. BY HITTING IT TOO SOFT, YOU'RE ASKING THE OTHER SIDE TO SMASH IT BACK AT YOU.
IF YOU PUT EXTRA SPIN ON THE BALL, YOU CAN DO A TOPSPIN LOB, WHICH BOUNCES EVEN HIGHER.

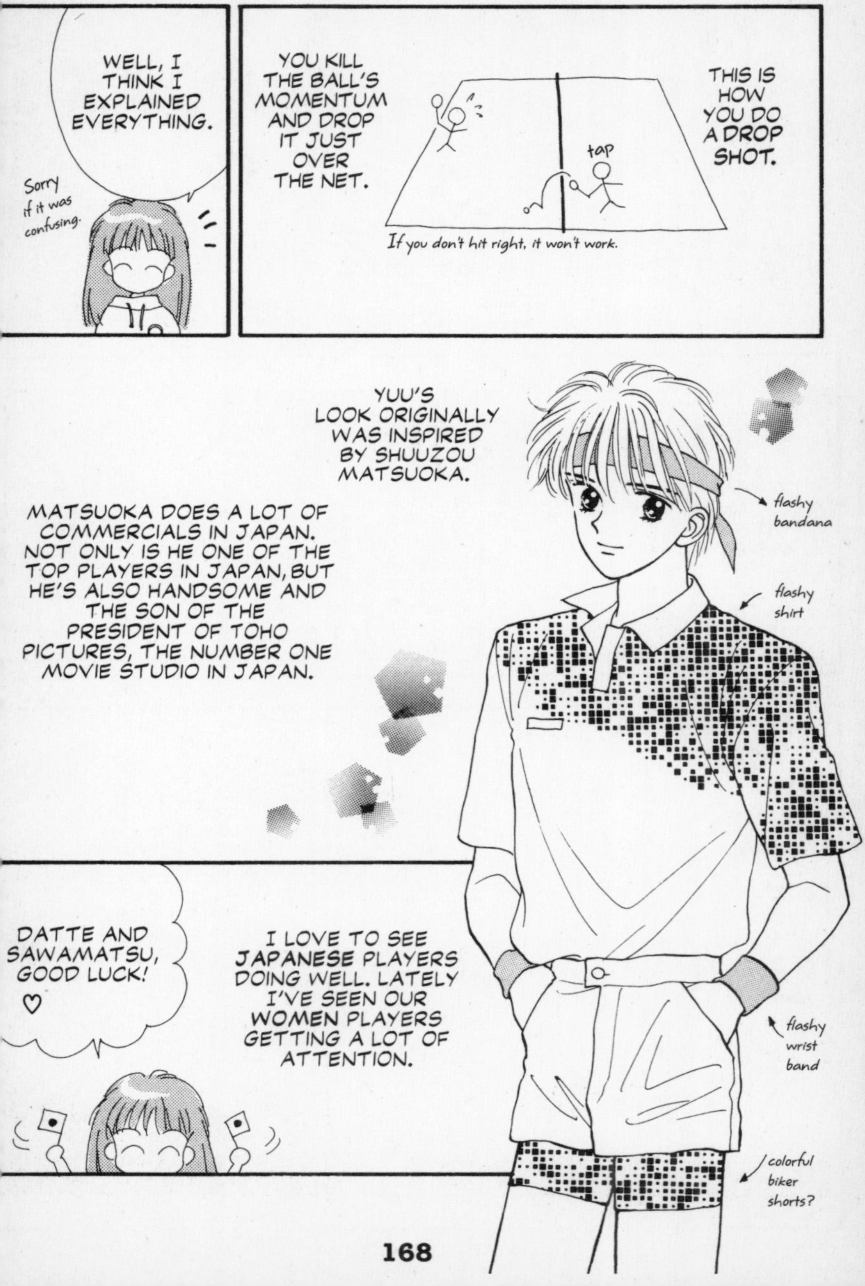
THIS IS HOW YOU DO A DROP SHOT.
YOU KILL THE BALL'S MOMENTUM AND DROP IT JUST OVER THE NET.
tap
If you don't hit right, it won't work.
WELL, I THINK I EXPLAINED EVERYTHING.
Sorry if it was confusing.
YUU'S LOOK ORIGINALLY WAS INSPIRED BY SHUUZOU MATSUOKA.
flashy bandana
flashy shirt
flashy wrist band
colorful biker shorts?
MATSUOKA DOES A LOT OF COMMERCIALS IN JAPAN. NOT ONLY IS HE ONE OF THE TOP PLAYERS IN JAPAN, BUT HE'S ALSO HANDSOME AND THE SON OF THE PRESIDENT OF TOHO PICTURES, THE NUMBER ONE MOVIE STUDIO IN JAPAN.
I LOVE TO SEE JAPANESE PLAYERS DOING WELL. LATELY I'VE SEEN OUR WOMEN PLAYERS GETTING A LOT OF ATTENTION.
DATTE AND SAWAMATSU, GOOD LUCK! ♡

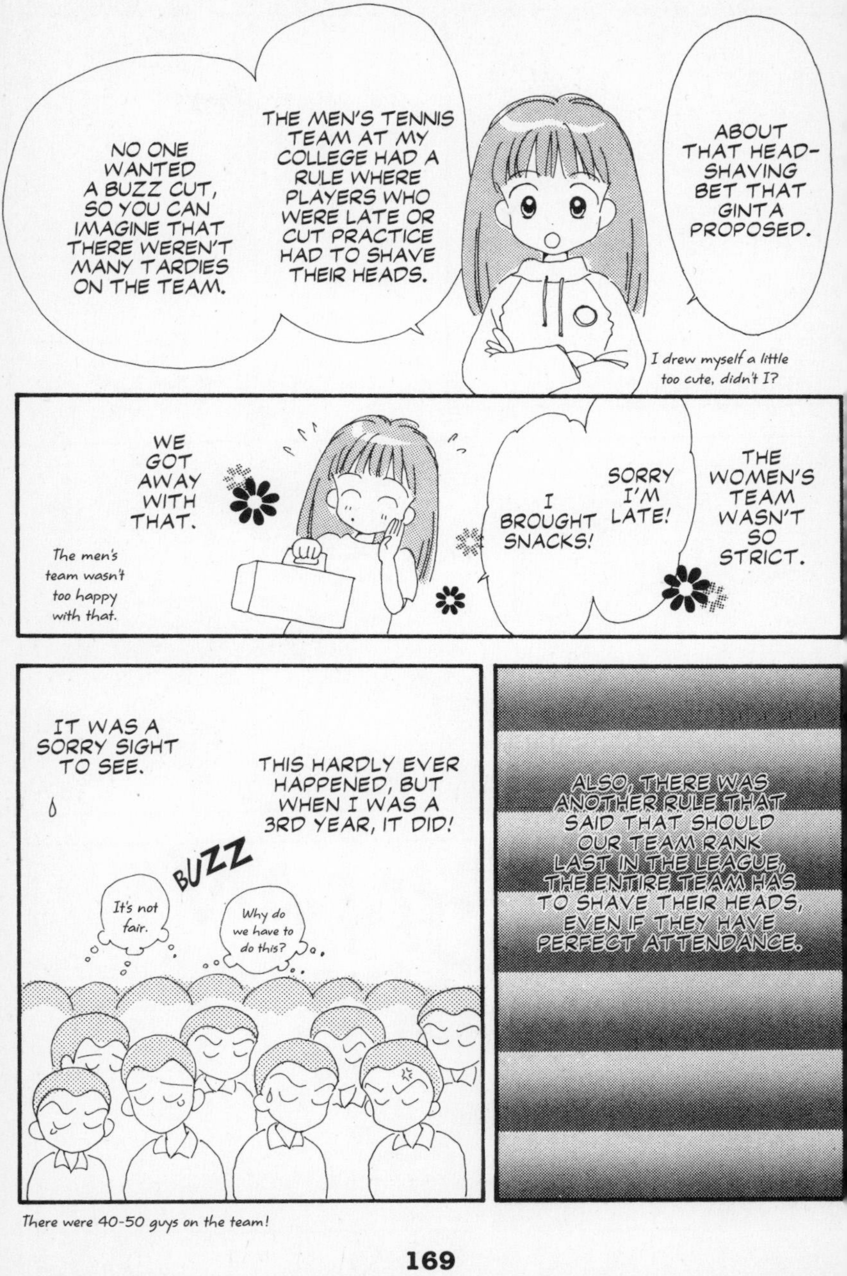
ABOUT THAT HEAD-SHAVING BET THAT GINTA PROPOSED.
THE MEN'S TENNIS TEAM AT MY COLLEGE HAD A RULE WHERE PLAYERS WHO WERE LATE OR CUT PRACTICE HAD TO SHAVE THEIR HEADS.
NO ONE WANTED A BUZZ CUT, SO YOU CAN IMAGINE THAT THERE WEREN'T MANY TARDIES ON THE TEAM.
I drew myself a little too cute, didn't I?
THE WOMEN'S TEAM WASN'T SO STRICT.
SORRY I'M LATE!
I BROUGHT SNACKS!
WE GOT AWAY WITH THAT.
The men's team wasn't too happy with that.
ALSO, THERE WAS ANOTHER RULE THAT SAID THAT SHOULD OUR TEAM RANK LAST IN THE LEAGUE, THE ENTIRE TEAM HAS TO SHAVE THEIR HEADS, EVEN IF THEY HAVE PERFECT ATTENDANCE.
THIS HARDLY EVER HAPPENED, BUT WHEN I WAS A 3RD YEAR, IT DID!
IT WAS A SORRY SIGHT TO SEE.
BUZZ
Why do we have to do this?
It's not fair.

There were 40-50 guys on the team!

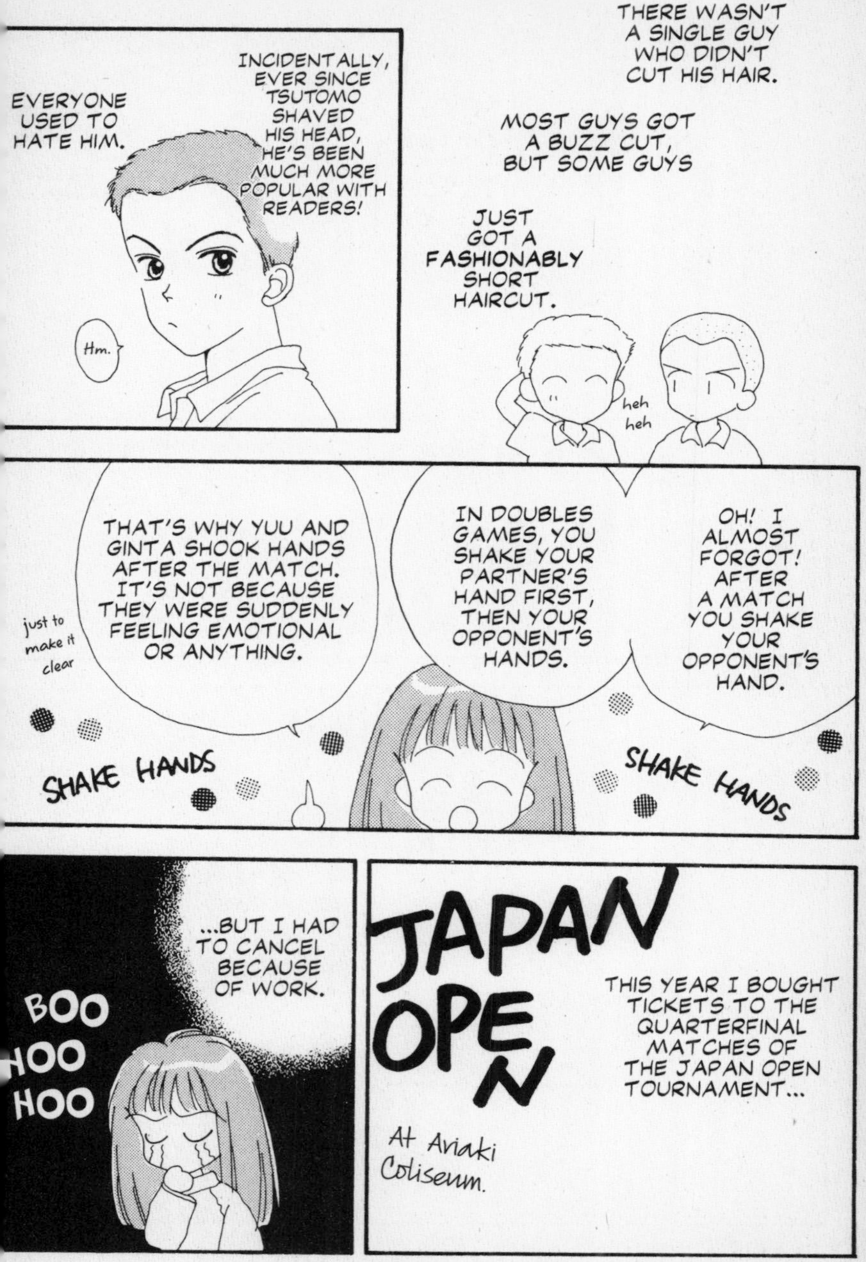

THERE WASN'T A SINGLE GUY WHO DIDN'T CUT HIS HAIR.
MOST GUYS GOT A BUZZ CUT, BUT SOME GUYS
JUST GOT A FASHIONABLY SHORT HAIRCUT.
heh heh
INCIDENTALLY, EVER SINCE TSUTOMO SHAVED HIS HEAD, HE'S BEEN MUCH MORE POPULAR WITH READERS!
EVERYONE USED TO HATE HIM.
Hm.
OH! I ALMOST FORGOT! AFTER A MATCH YOU SHAKE YOUR OPPONENT'S HAND.
IN DOUBLES GAMES, YOU SHAKE YOUR PARTNER'S HAND FIRST, THEN YOUR OPPONENT'S HANDS.
SHAKE HANDS
THAT'S WHY YUU AND GINTA SHOOK HANDS AFTER THE MATCH. IT'S NOT BECAUSE THEY WERE SUDDENLY FEELING EMOTIONAL OR ANYTHING.
just to make it clear
SHAKE HANDS
JAPAN OPEN
THIS YEAR I BOUGHT TICKETS TO THE QUARTERFINAL MATCHES OF THE JAPAN OPEN TOURNAMENT...
At Ariaki Coliseum.
...BUT I HAD TO CANCEL BECAUSE OF WORK.
BOO HOO HOO

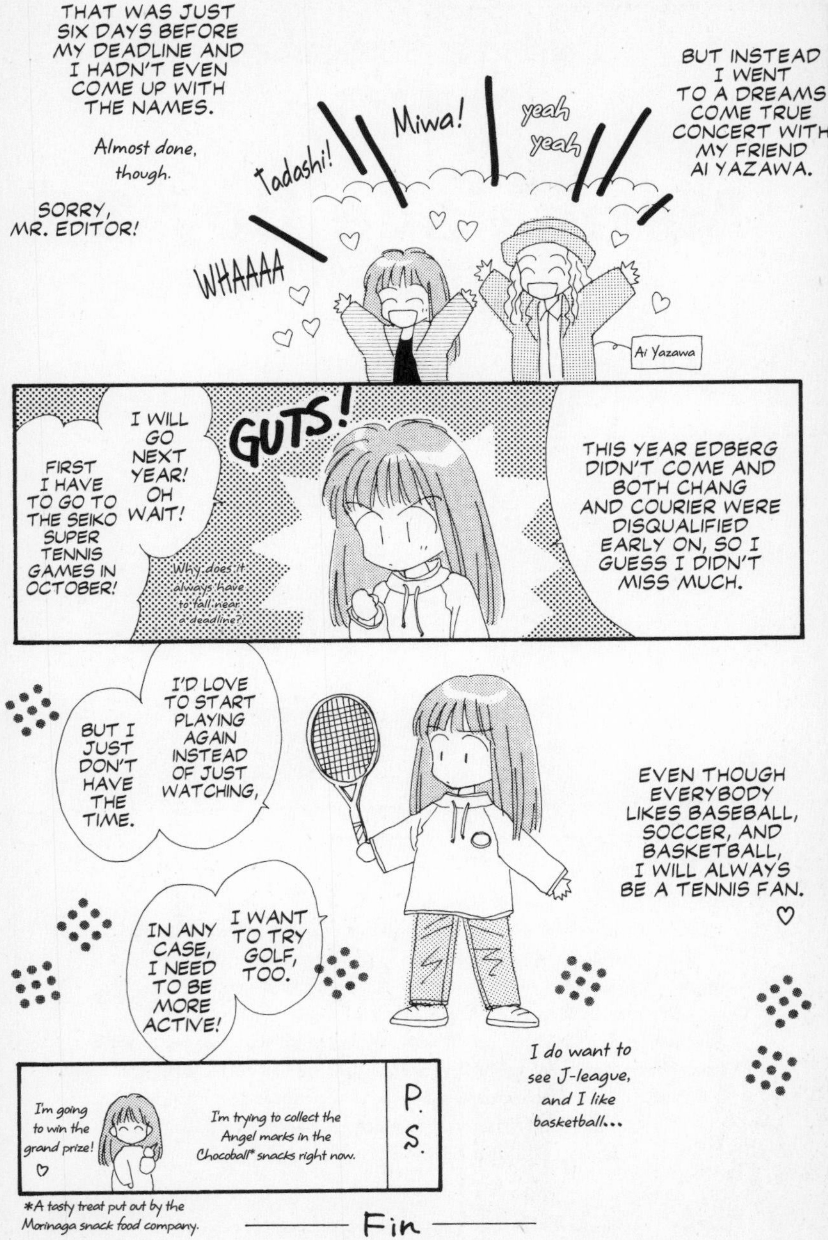
THAT WAS JUST SIX DAYS BEFORE MY DEADLINE AND I HADN'T EVEN COME UP WITH THE NAMES.
Almost done, though.
SORRY, MR. EDITOR!
BUT INSTEAD I WENT TO A DREAMS COME TRUE CONCERT WITH MY FRIEND AI YAZAWA.
yeah yeah
Miwa!
Tadashi!
WHAAAA
Ai Yazawa
THIS YEAR EDBERG DIDN'T COME AND BOTH CHANG AND COURIER WERE DISQUALIFIED EARLY ON, SO I GUESS I DIDN'T MISS MUCH.
GUTS!
I WILL GO NEXT YEAR! OH WAIT!
FIRST I HAVE TO GO TO THE SEIKO SUPER TENNIS GAMES IN OCTOBER!
Why does it always have to fall near a deadline?
EVEN THOUGH EVERYBODY LIKES BASEBALL, SOCCER, AND BASKETBALL, I WILL ALWAYS BE A TENNIS FAN. ♡
I do want to see J-league, and I like basketball...
I'D LOVE TO START PLAYING AGAIN INSTEAD OF JUST WATCHING,
BUT I JUST DON'T HAVE THE TIME.
I WANT TO TRY GOLF, TOO.
IN ANY CASE, I NEED TO BE MORE ACTIVE!
P.S.
I'm trying to collect the Angel marks in the Chocoball* snacks right now.
I'm going to win the grand prize! ♡

*A tasty treat put out by the Morinaga snack food company.

Fin

Coming in September
From TOKYOPOP...

Marmalade Boy 3

Three's definitely a crowd when Miki is caught in one agonizing
love triangle in the third volume of Marmalade Boy. With
major crushes on both Ginta and Yuu, she finds herself waging
an inner battle she knows she can never truly win. And
just when Miki's world can't get any more confusing, her best
friend suffers her own major love crisis and needs Miki's help-pronto!
Despite her whirlwind soap opera of romantic trauma, Miki
is determined to get the guy of her dreams...
if only she can figure out which one he is.

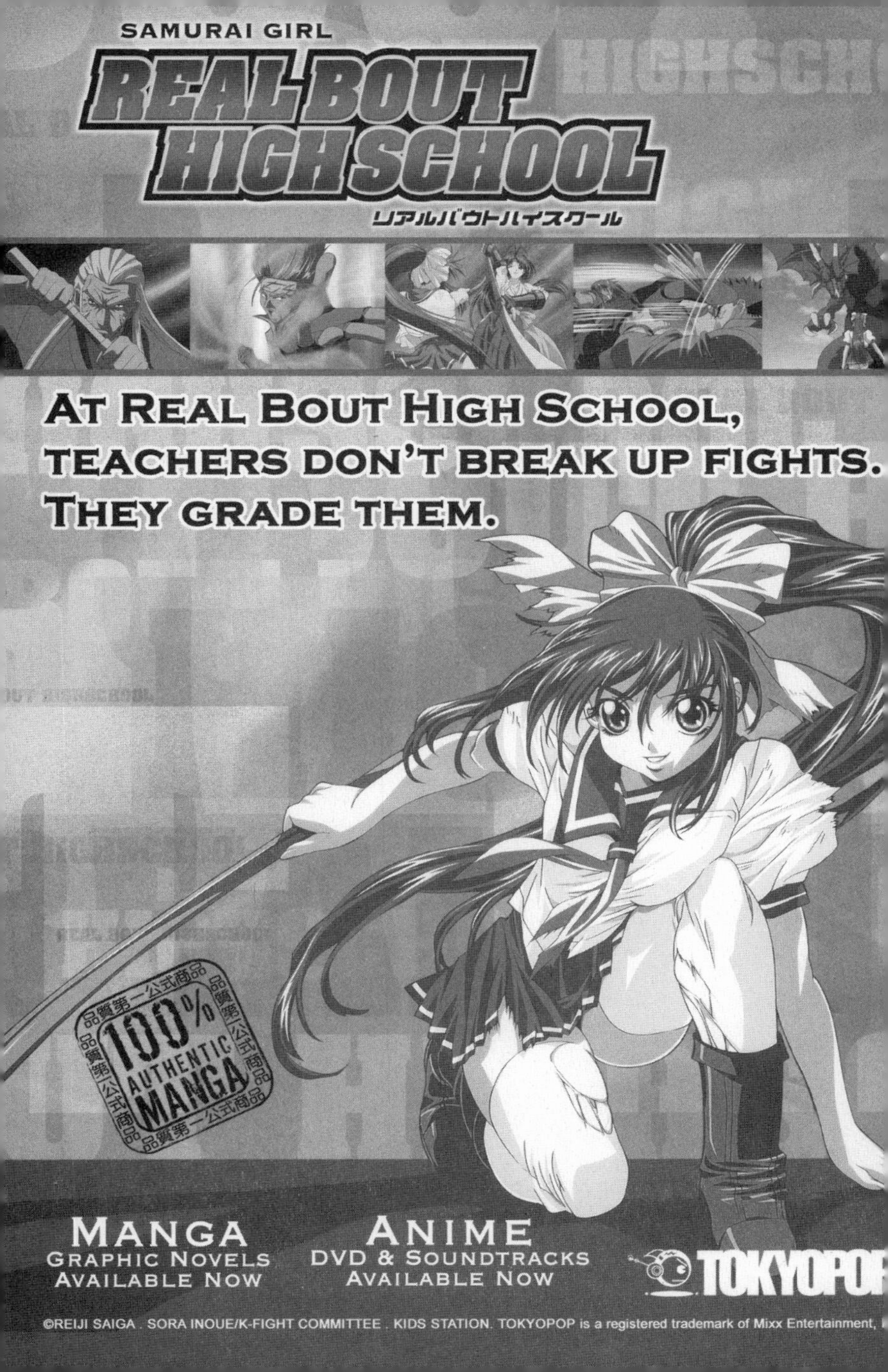

SAMURAI GIRL
REAL BOUT HIGH SCHOOL
リアルバウトハイスクール
AT REAL BOUT HIGH SCHOOL, TEACHERS DON'T BREAK UP FIGHTS. THEY GRADE THEM.
100% AUTHENTIC MANGA
品質第一公式商品
MANGA
GRAPHIC NOVELS
AVAILABLE NOW
ANIME
DVD & SOUNDTRACKS
AVAILABLE NOW
TOKYOPOP
©REIJI SAIGA . SORA INOUE/K-FIGHT COMMITTEE . KIDS STATION. TOKYOPOP is a registered trademark of Mixx Entertainment,

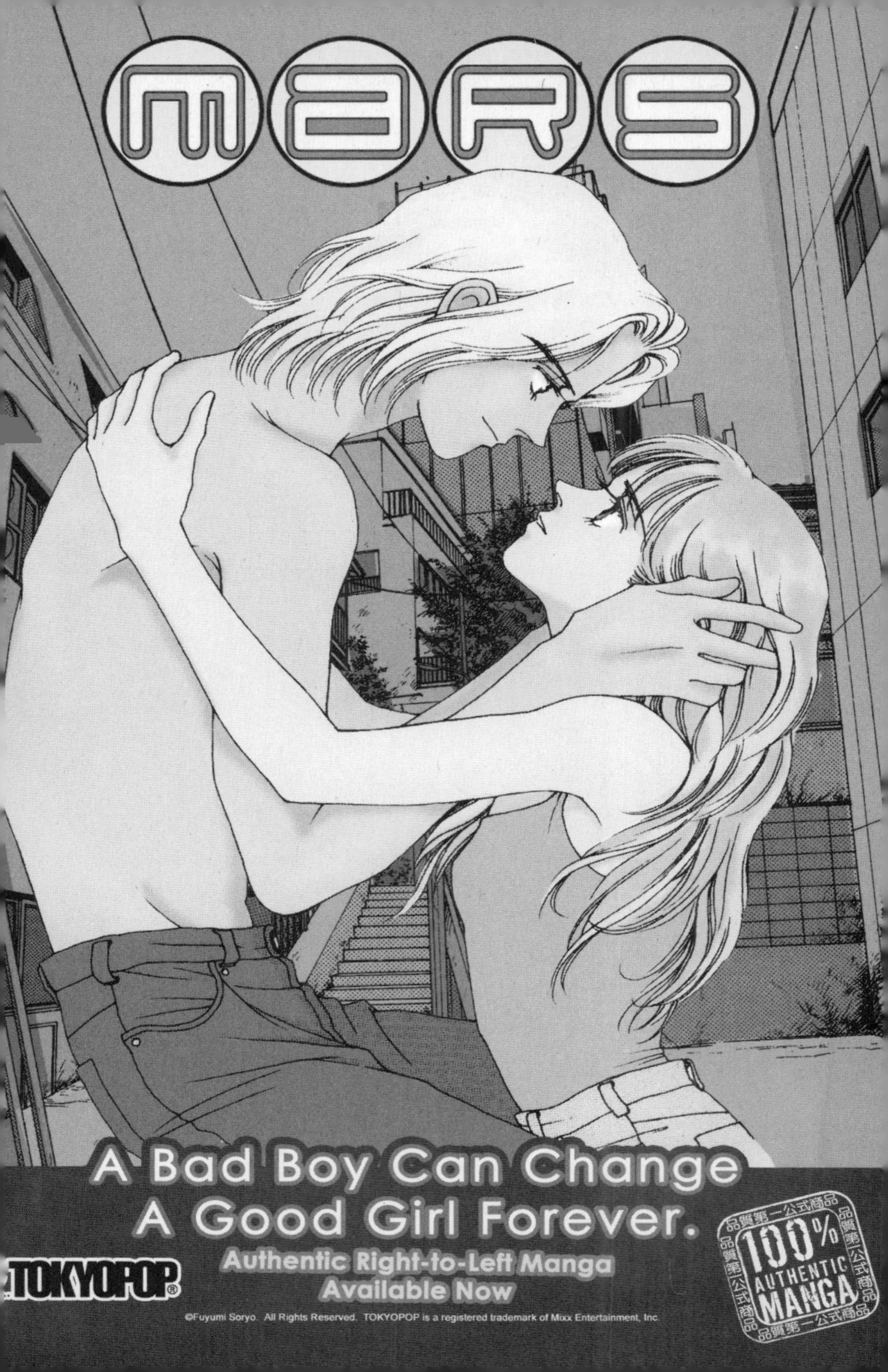
MARS
A Bad Boy Can Change
A Good Girl Forever.
Authentic Right-to-Left Manga
Available Now
TOKYOPOP®
©Fuyumi Soryo. All Rights Reserved. TOKYOPOP is a registered trademark of Mixx Entertainment, Inc.
100% AUTHENTIC MANGA
品質第一公式商品

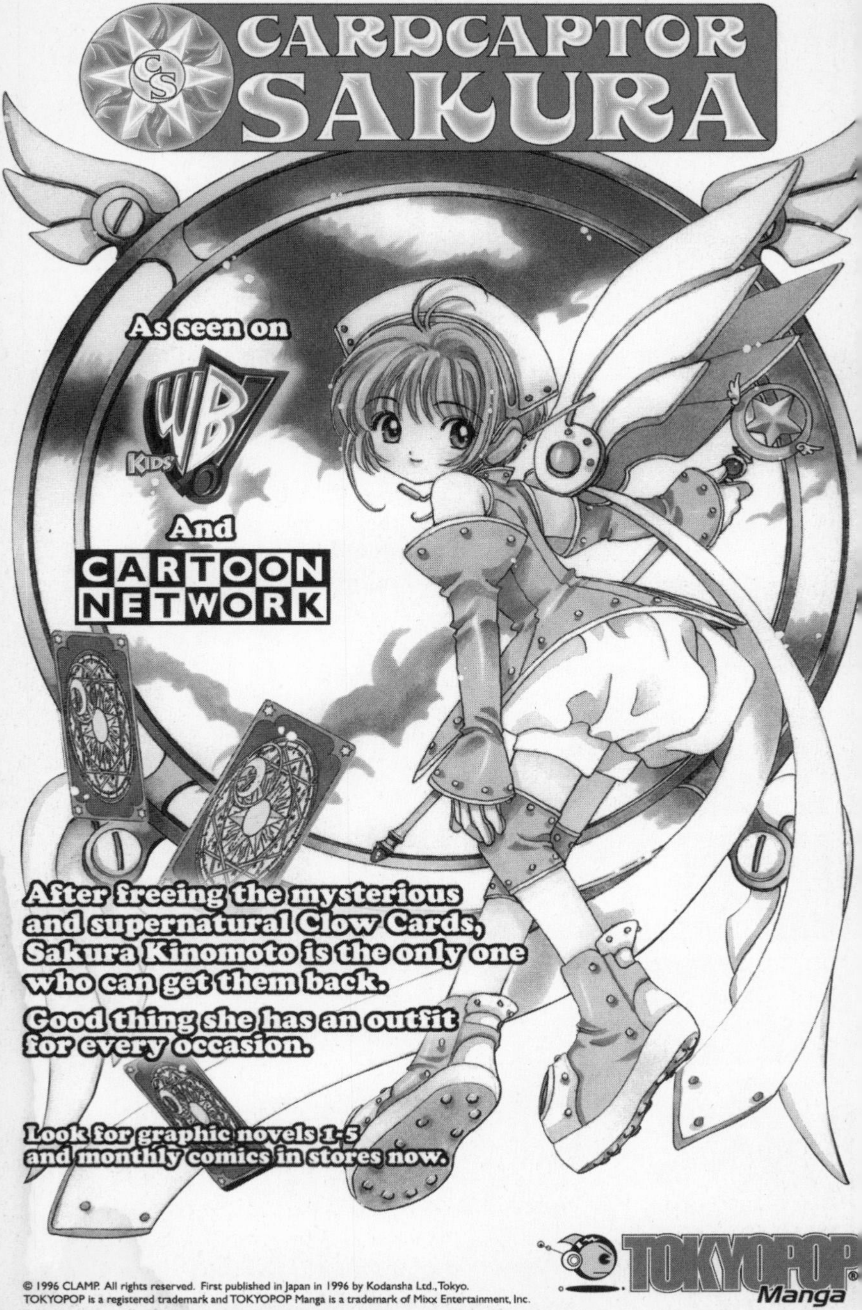

CARDCAPTOR SAKURA
As seen on
KIDS' WB
And
CARTOON NETWORK
After freeing the mysterious and supernatural Clow Cards, Sakura Kinomoto is the only one who can get them back.
Good thing she has an outfit for every occasion.
Look for graphic novels 1-5 and monthly comics in stores now.
TOKYOPOP® Manga

STOP!

This is the back of the book.
You wouldn't want to spoil a great ending!

This book is printed "manga-style," in the authentic Japanese right-to-left format. Since none of the artwork has been flipped or altered, readers get to experience the story just as the creator intended. You've been asking for it, so TOKYOPOP® delivered: authentic, hot-off-the-press, and far more fun!

DIRECTIONS

If this is your first time reading manga-style, here's a quick guide to help you understand how it works.

It's easy... just start in the top right panel and follow the numbers. Have fun, and look for more 100% authentic manga from TOKYOPOP®!